Volume 1
By Mario Kaneda

HAMBURG // LONDON // LOS ANGELES // TOKYO

Saving Life Volume 1
Created by Mario KANEDA

Translation - Alexis Kirsch
Script Editor - Jill Bentley
Copy Editors - Joseph Heller & Tim Leavey
Retouch and Lettering - Star Print Brokers
Production Artist - Rui Kyo
Graphic Designer - Marian Tavarro

Editor - Cindy Suzuki
Print Production Manager - Lucas Rivera
Managing Editor - Vy Nguyen
Senior Designer - Louis Csontos
Art Director - Al-Insan Lashley
Director of Sales and Manufacturing - Allyson De Simone
Associate Publisher - Marco F. Pavia
President and C.O.O. - John Parker
C.E.O. and Chief Creative Officer - Stu Levy

A **TOKYOPOP** Manga

TOKYOPOP Inc.
5900 Wilshire Blvd. Suite 2000
Los Angeles, CA 90036

E-mail: info@TOKYOPOP.com
Come visit us online at www.TOKYOPOP.com

ISBN: 978-1-4278-1422-7

First TOKYOPOP printing: November 2010
10 9 8 7 6 5 4 3 2 1
Printed in the USA

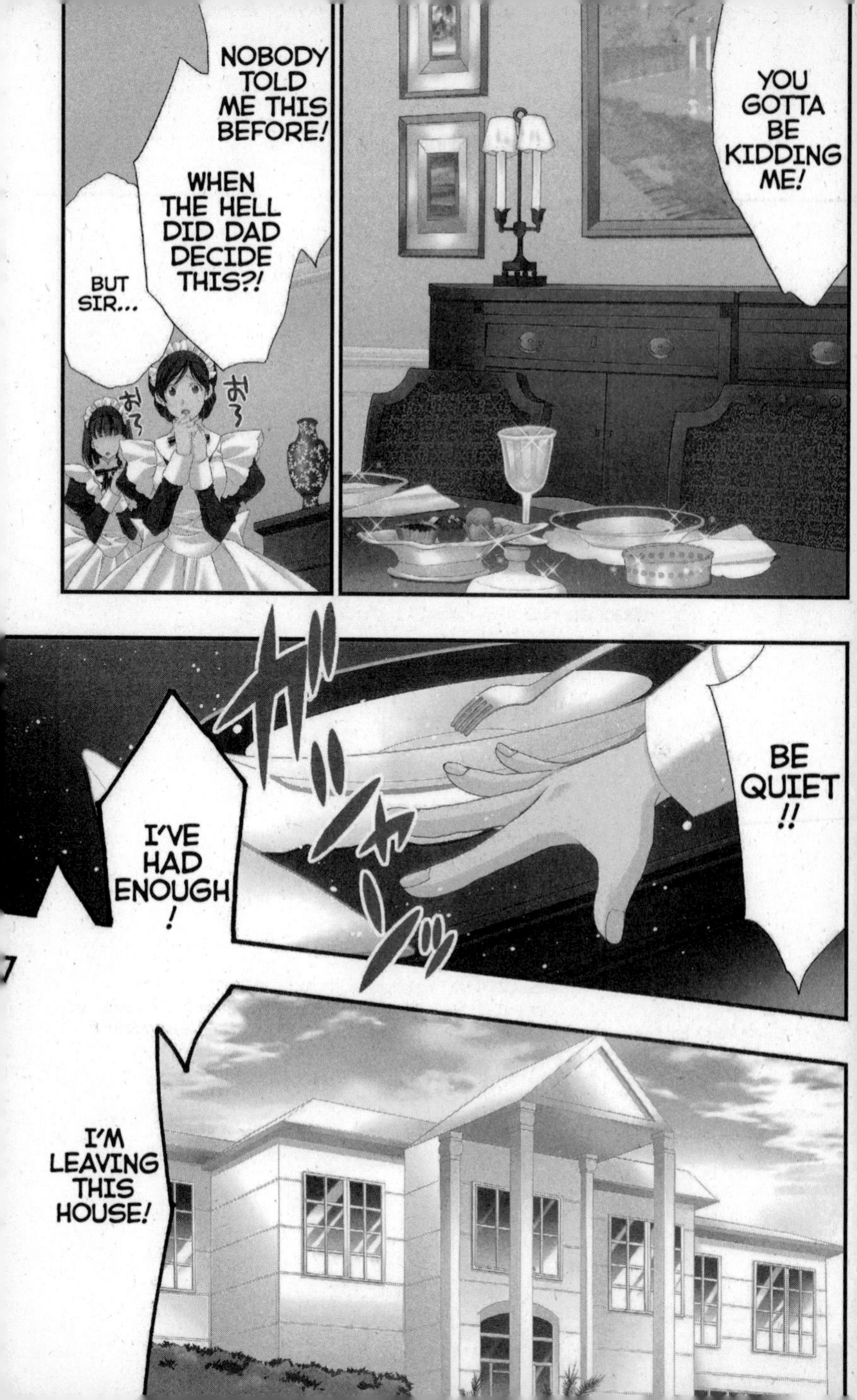
YOU GOTTA BE KIDDING ME!
NOBODY TOLD ME THIS BEFORE!
WHEN THE HELL DID DAD DECIDE THIS?!
BUT SIR...
おろ
おろ
BE QUIET!!
I'VE HAD ENOUGH!
I'M LEAVING THIS HOUSE!

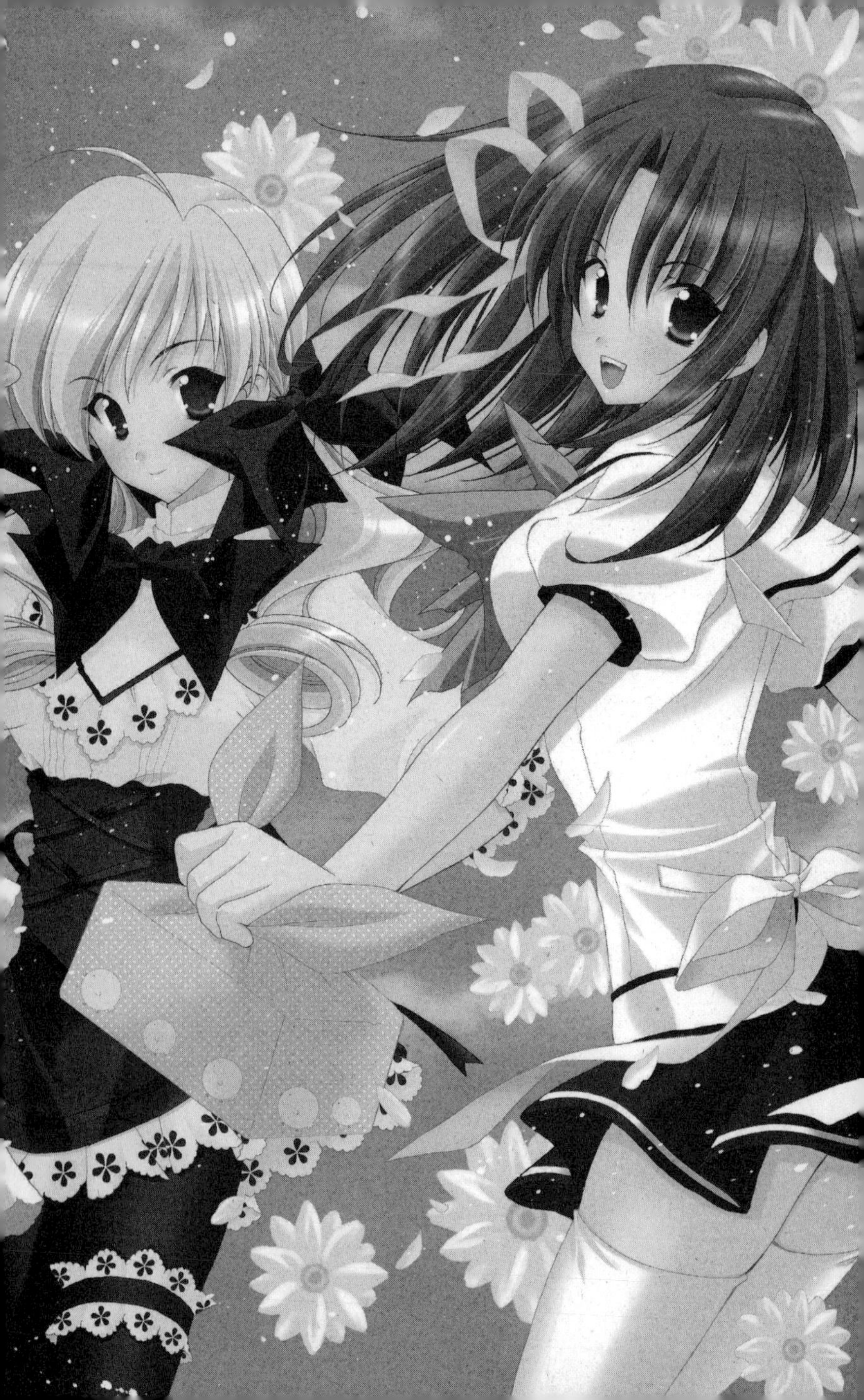

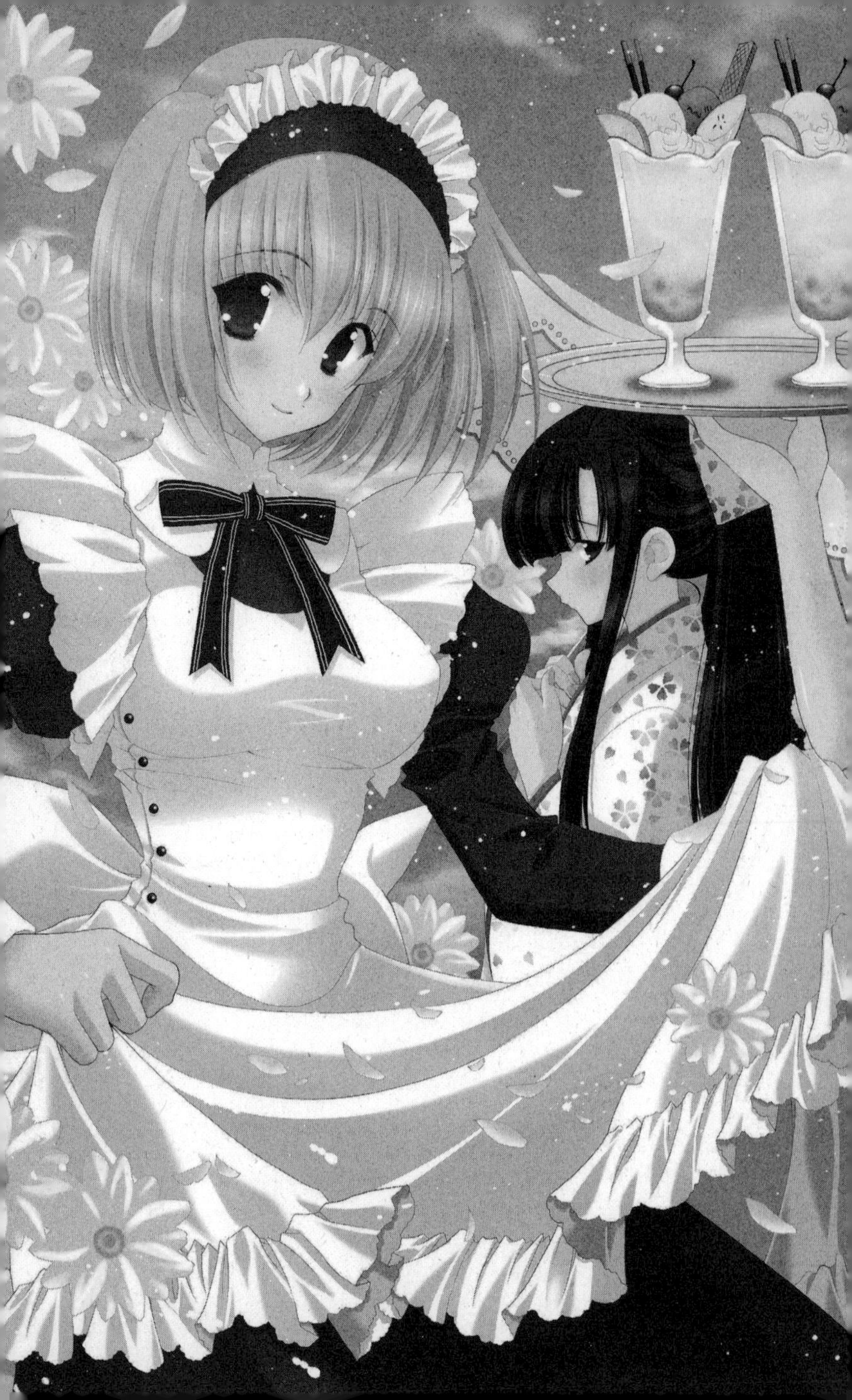

CONTENTS
SAVING LIFE 01 / MARIO KANEDA

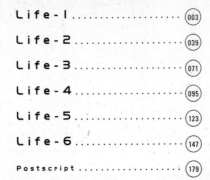

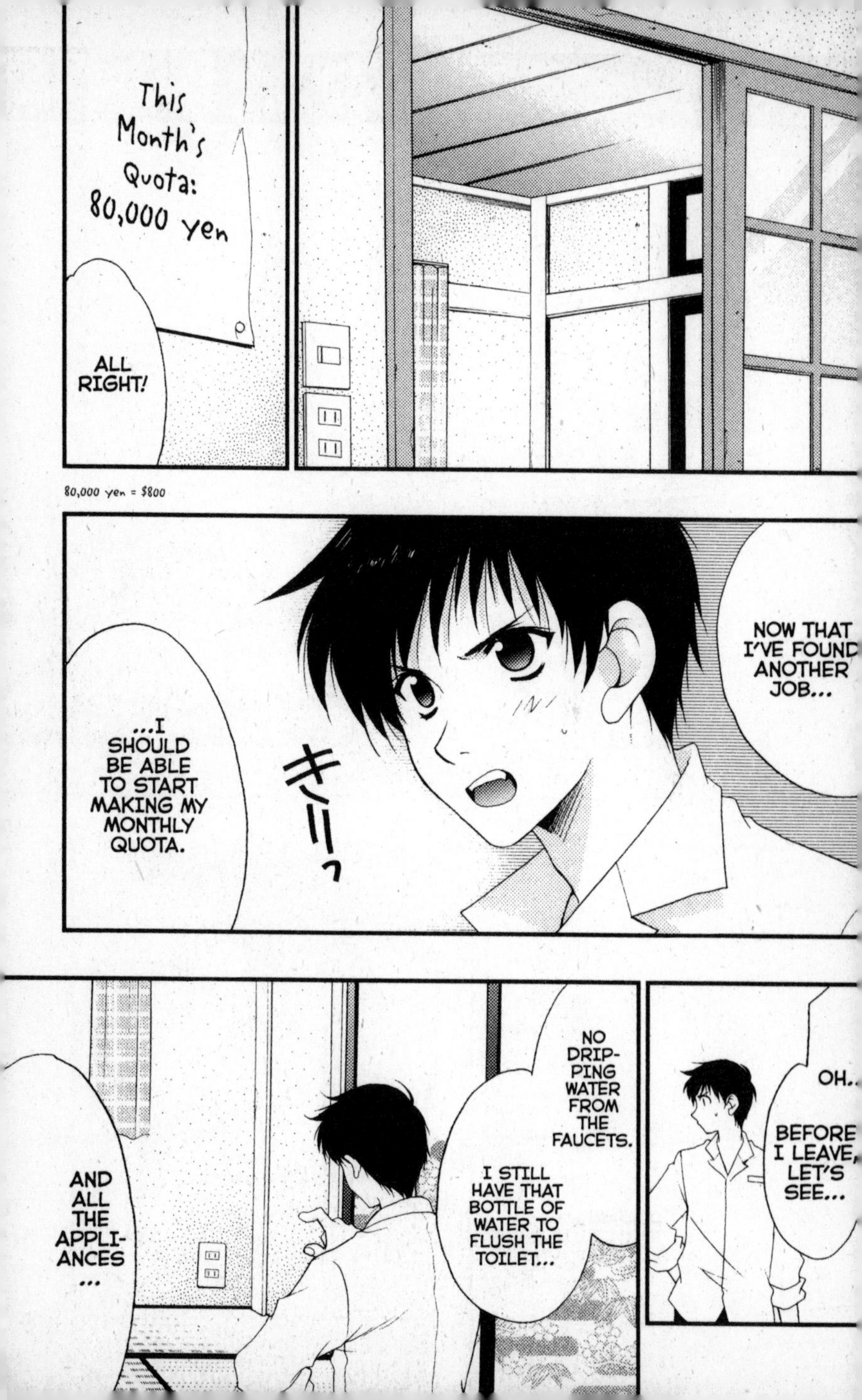
This Month's Quota: 80,000 yen
ALL RIGHT!
NOW THAT I'VE FOUND ANOTHER JOB...
...I SHOULD BE ABLE TO START MAKING MY MONTHLY QUOTA.
きりっ
OH...
BEFORE I LEAVE, LET'S SEE...
NO DRIPPING WATER FROM THE FAUCETS.
I STILL HAVE THAT BOTTLE OF WATER TO FLUSH THE TOILET...
AND ALL THE APPLIANCES...
80,000 yen = $800

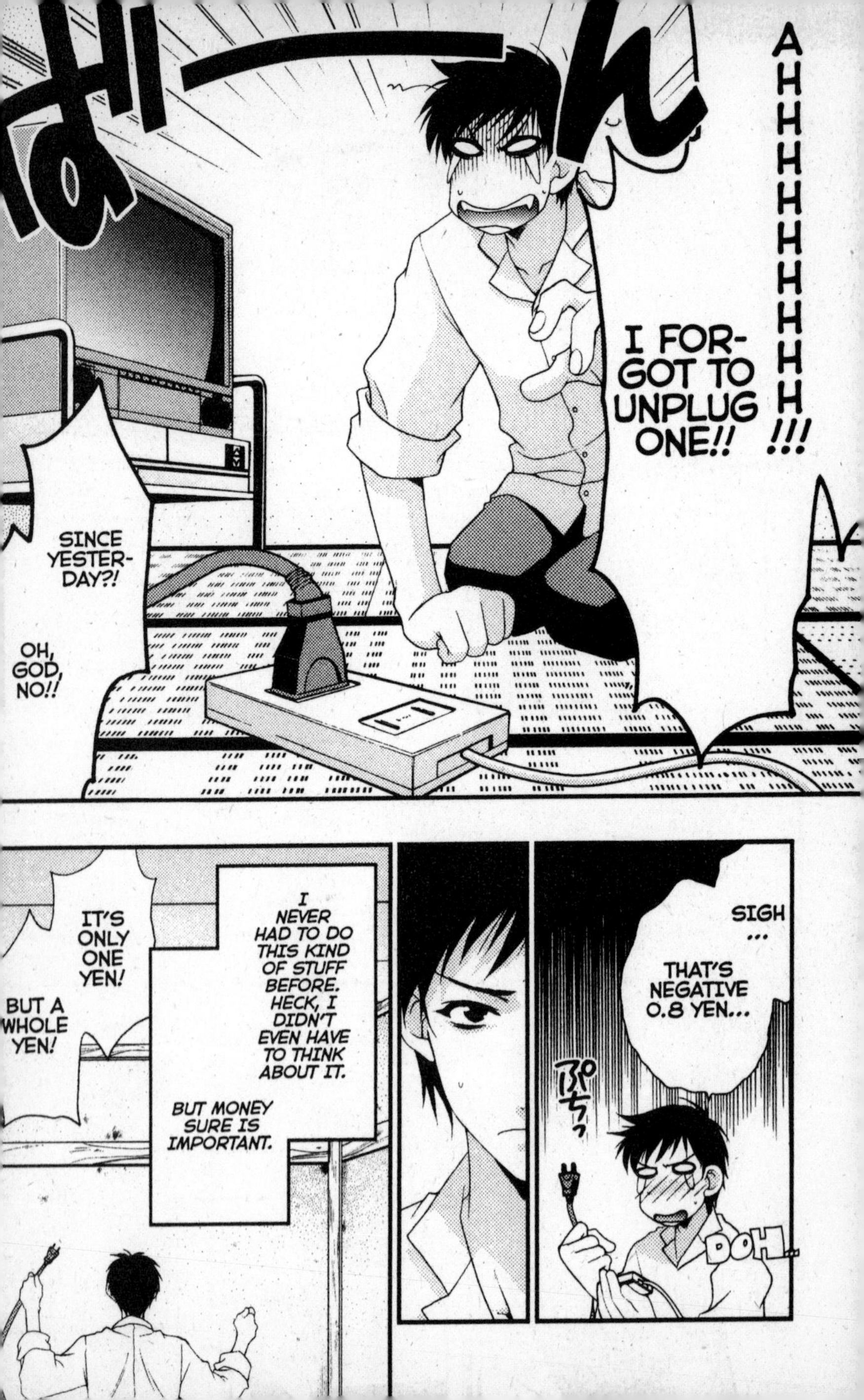
ばーん
AHHHHHHHHHH!!!
I FOR-GOT TO UNPLUG ONE!!
SINCE YESTER-DAY?!
OH, GOD, NO!!
SIGH ...
THAT'S NEGATIVE 0.8 YEN...
ぷちっ
DOH...
I NEVER HAD TO DO THIS KIND OF STUFF BEFORE. HECK, I DIDN'T EVEN HAVE TO THINK ABOUT IT.
BUT MONEY SURE IS IMPORTANT.
IT'S ONLY ONE YEN!
BUT A WHOLE YEN!

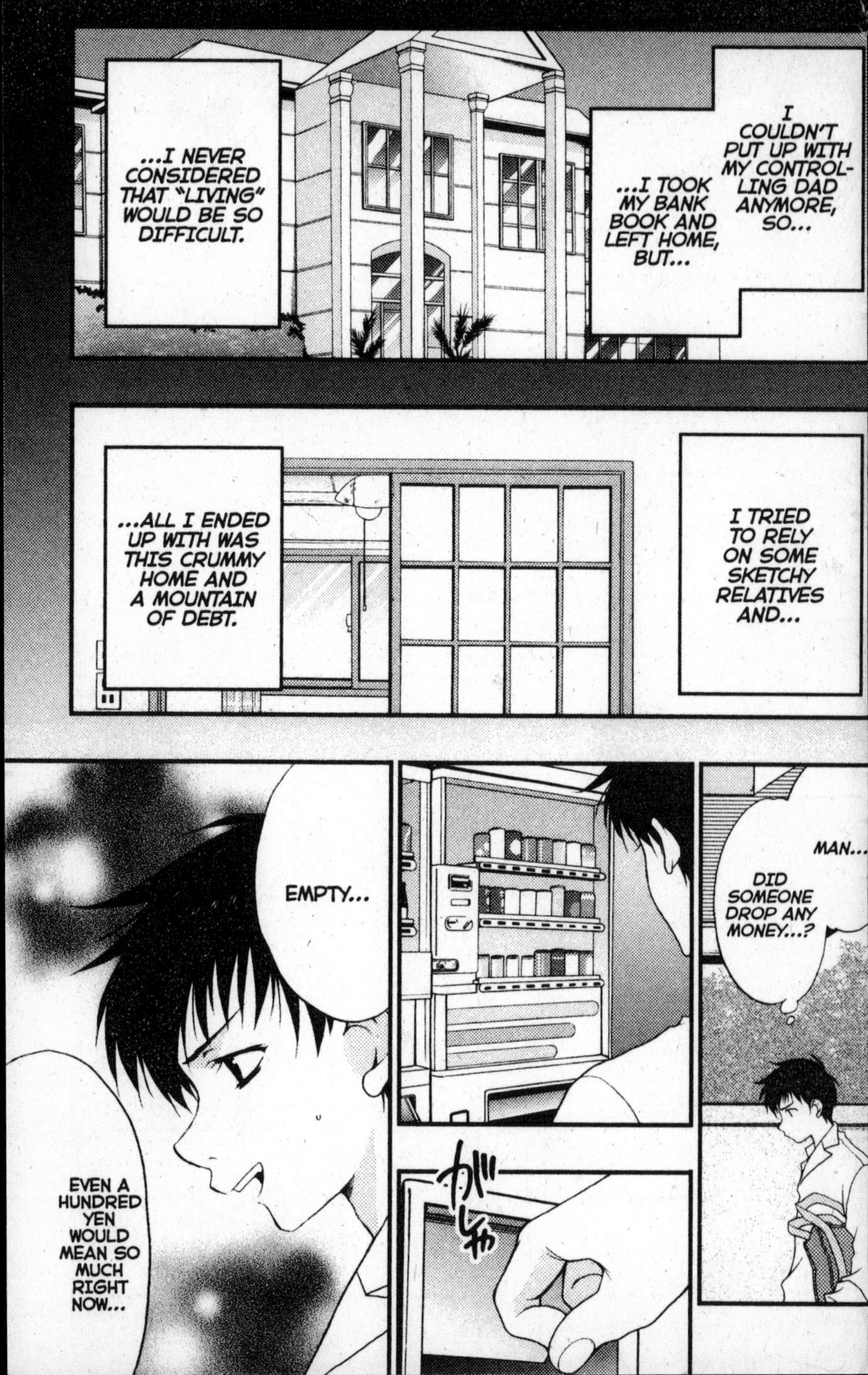
I COULDN'T PUT UP WITH MY CONTROL-LING DAD ANYMORE, SO...
...I TOOK MY BANK BOOK AND LEFT HOME, BUT...
...I NEVER CONSIDERED THAT "LIVING" WOULD BE SO DIFFICULT.
I TRIED TO RELY ON SOME SKETCHY RELATIVES AND...
...ALL I ENDED UP WITH WAS THIS CRUMMY HOME AND A MOUNTAIN OF DEBT.
MAN...
DID SOMEONE DROP ANY MONEY...?
EMPTY...
がしゃ
EVEN A HUNDRED YEN WOULD MEAN SO MUCH RIGHT NOW...

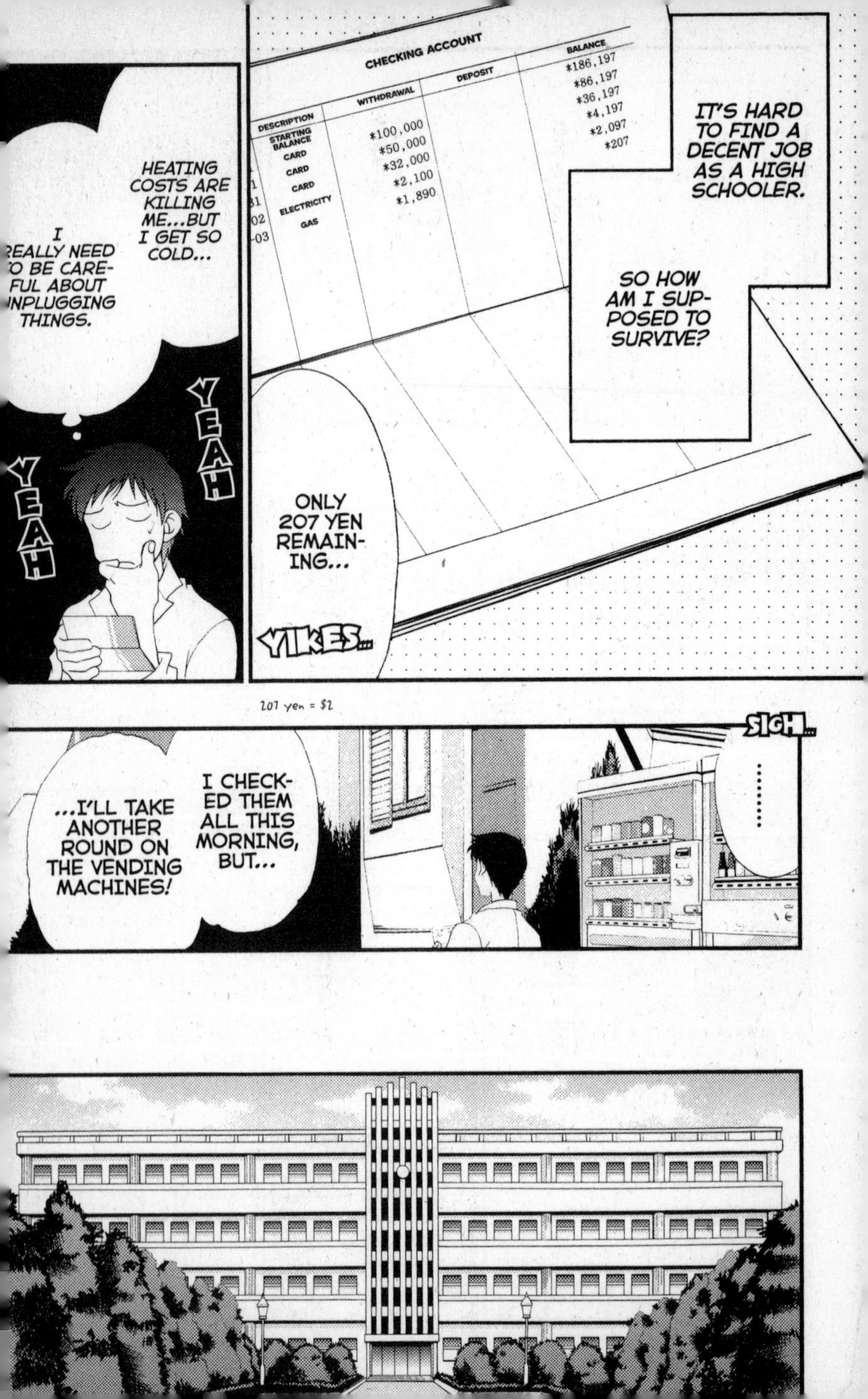
CHECKING ACCOUNT
DESCRIPTION
WITHDRAWAL
DEPOSIT
BALANCE
STARTING BALANCE *186,197
1 CARD *100,000 *86,197
1 CARD *50,000 *36,197
31 CARD *32,000 *4,197
02 ELECTRICITY *2,100 *2,097
-03 GAS *1,890 *207
IT'S HARD TO FIND A DECENT JOB AS A HIGH SCHOOLER.
SO HOW AM I SUPPOSED TO SURVIVE?
ONLY 207 YEN REMAINING...
YIKES...
HEATING COSTS ARE KILLING ME...BUT I GET SO COLD...
I EALLY NEED O BE CAREFUL ABOUT NPLUGGING THINGS.
YEAH
YEAH
207 yen = $2
SIGH...
......
I CHECKED THEM ALL THIS MORNING, BUT...
...I'LL TAKE ANOTHER ROUND ON THE VENDING MACHINES!

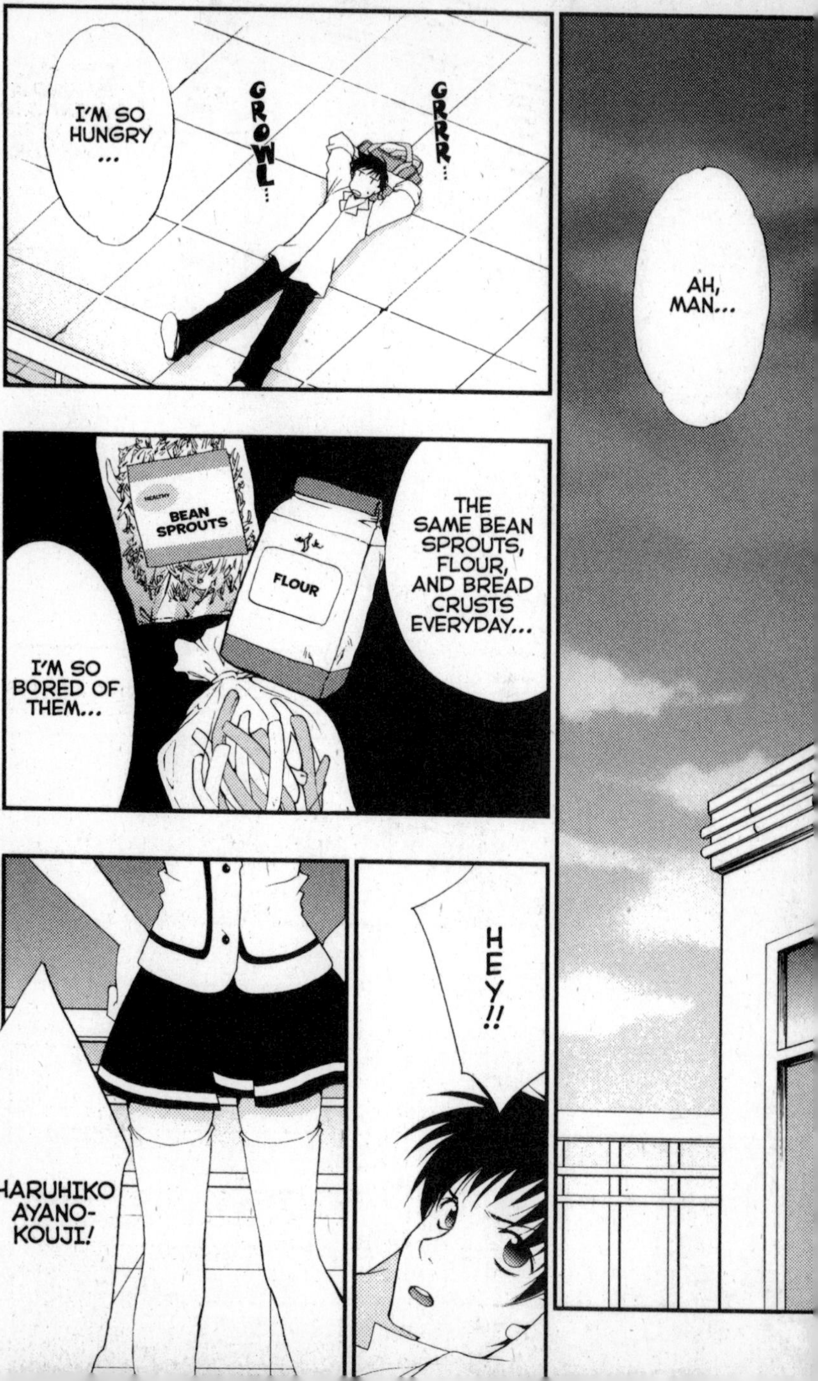
AH, MAN...
GRRR...
GROWL...
I'M SO HUNGRY ...
THE SAME BEAN SPROUTS, FLOUR, AND BREAD CRUSTS EVERYDAY...
HEALTHY
BEAN SPROUTS
FLOUR
I'M SO BORED OF THEM...
HEY!!
HARUHIKO AYANO-KOUJI!

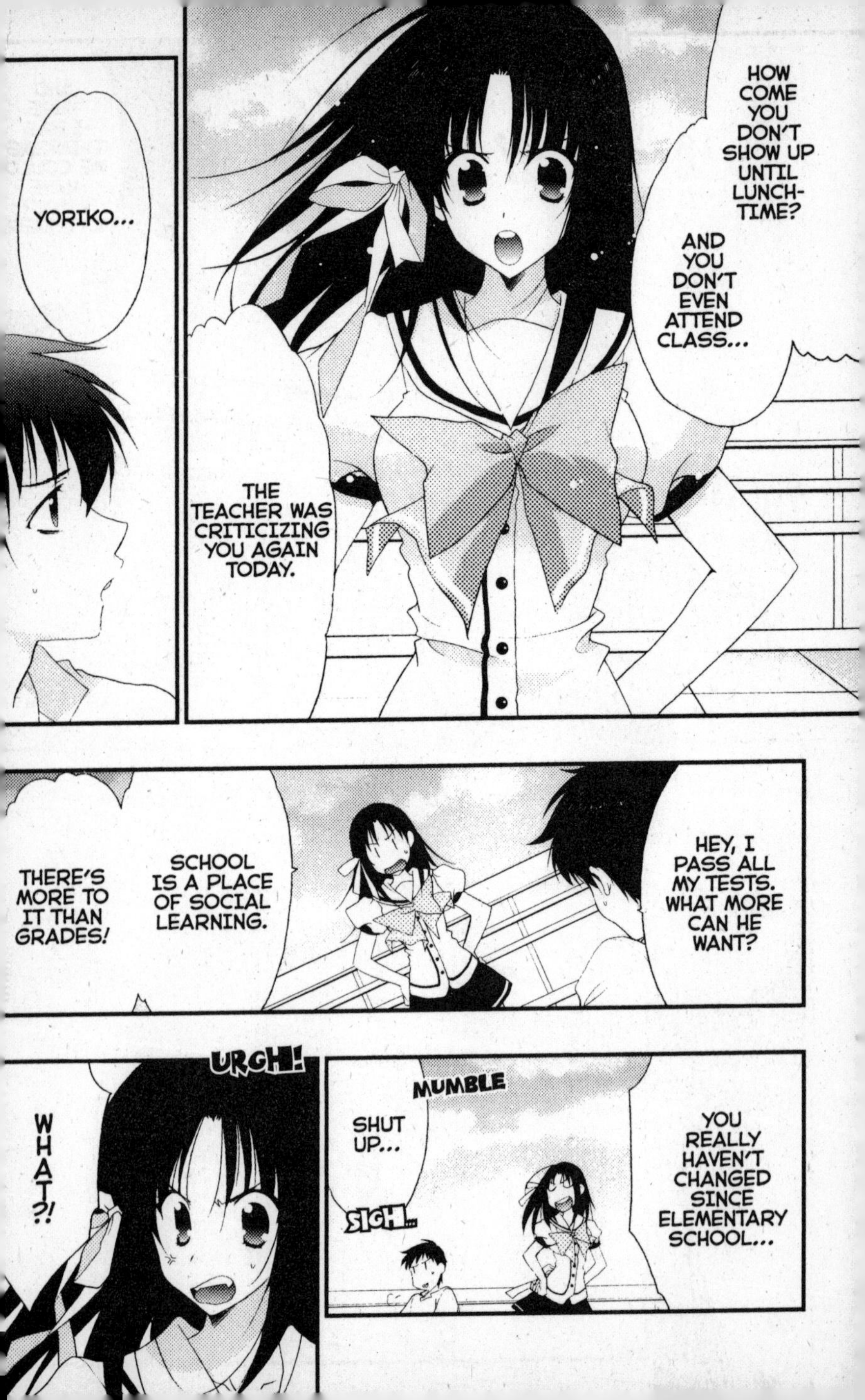
HOW COME YOU DON'T SHOW UP UNTIL LUNCH-TIME?
AND YOU DON'T EVEN ATTEND CLASS...
THE TEACHER WAS CRITICIZING YOU AGAIN TODAY.
YORIKO...
HEY, I PASS ALL MY TESTS. WHAT MORE CAN HE WANT?
SCHOOL IS A PLACE OF SOCIAL LEARNING.
THERE'S MORE TO IT THAN GRADES!
YOU REALLY HAVEN'T CHANGED SINCE ELEMENTARY SCHOOL...
MUMBLE
SHUT UP...
SIGH...
URGH!
WHAT?!

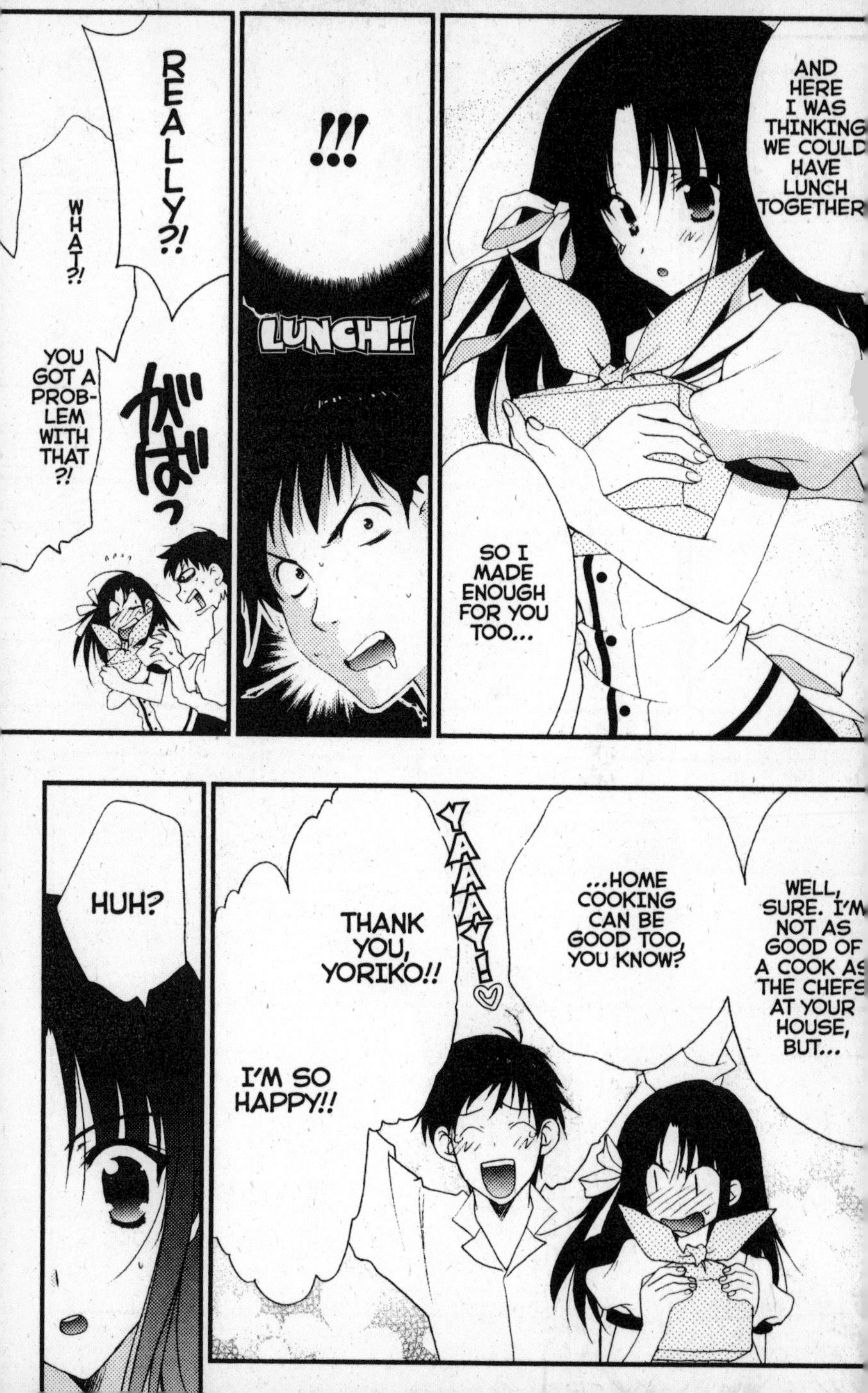
AND HERE I WAS THINKING WE COULD HAVE LUNCH TOGETHER
SO I MADE ENOUGH FOR YOU TOO...
!!!
LUNCH!!
REALLY?!
WHAT?!
がばっ
YOU GOT A PROB-LEM WITH THAT?!
WELL, SURE. I'M NOT AS GOOD OF A COOK AS THE CHEFS AT YOUR HOUSE, BUT...
...HOME COOKING CAN BE GOOD TOO, YOU KNOW?
YAAAAY!
THANK YOU, YORIKO!!
I'M SO HAPPY!!
HUH?

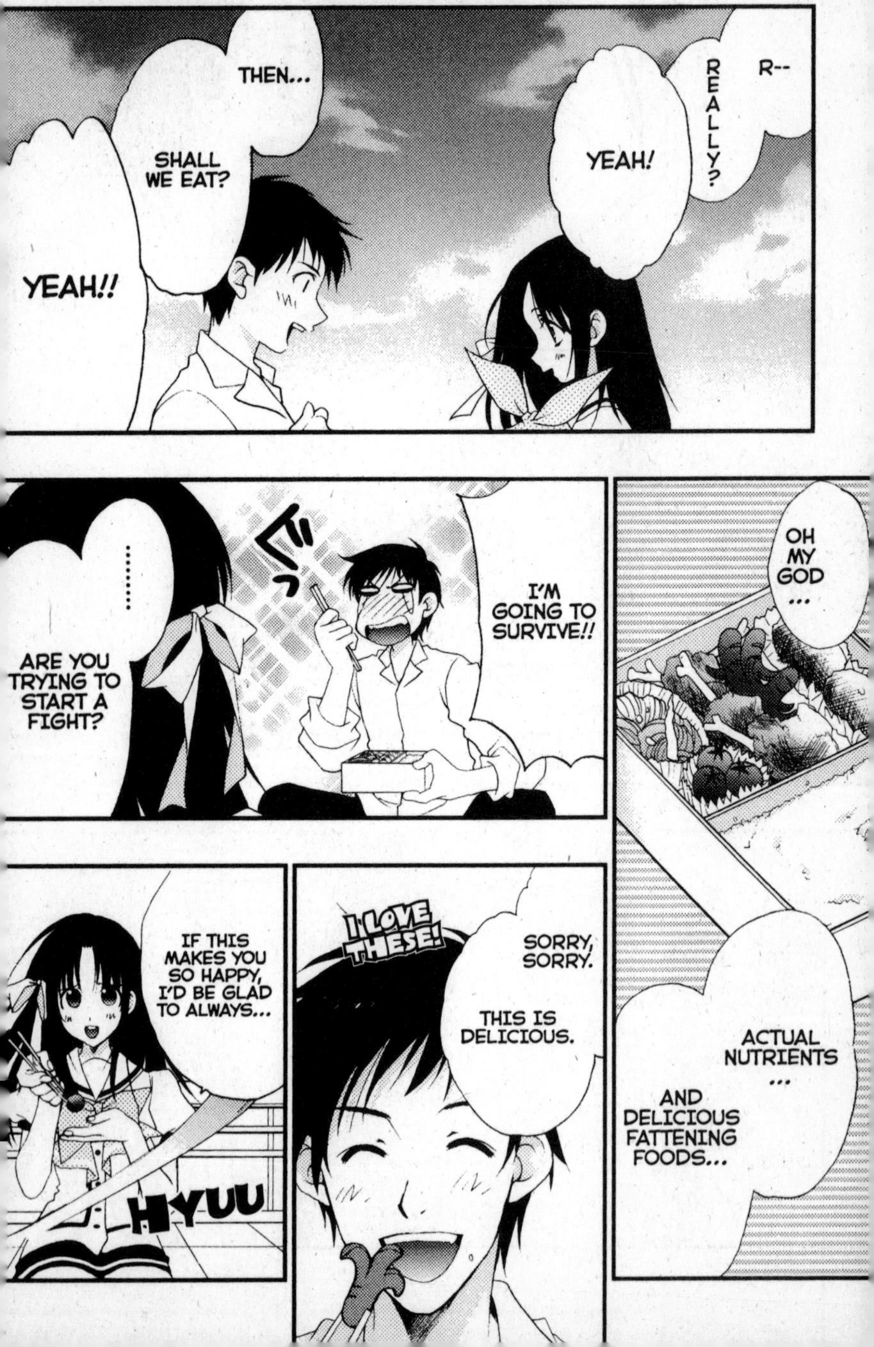
R-- REALLY?
YEAH!
THEN...
SHALL WE EAT?
YEAH!!
OH MY GOD ...
ACTUAL NUTRIENTS ...
AND DELICIOUS FATTENING FOODS...
I'M GOING TO SURVIVE!!
ぐっ
......
ARE YOU TRYING TO START A FIGHT?
I LOVE THESE!
SORRY, SORRY.
THIS IS DELICIOUS.
IF THIS MAKES YOU SO HAPPY, I'D BE GLAD TO ALWAYS...
HYUU

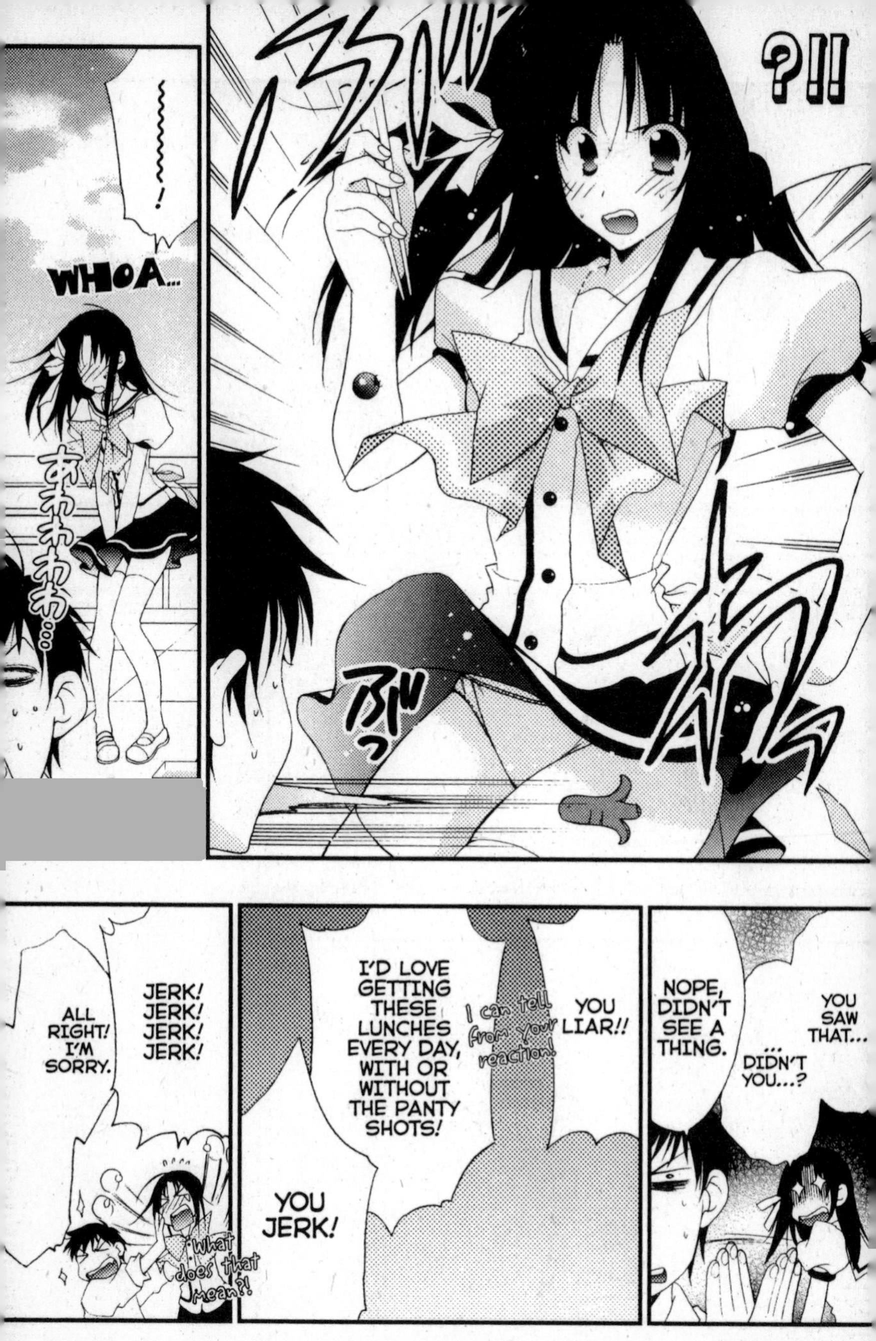
?!!
～～～～～!
WHOA...
あわわわわ…
YOU SAW THAT...
... DIDN'T YOU...?
NOPE, DIDN'T SEE A THING.
YOU LIAR!!
I can tell from your reaction!
I'D LOVE GETTING THESE LUNCHES EVERY DAY, WITH OR WITHOUT THE PANTY SHOTS!
YOU JERK!
JERK! JERK! JERK! JERK!
ALL RIGHT! I'M SORRY.
What does that mean?!

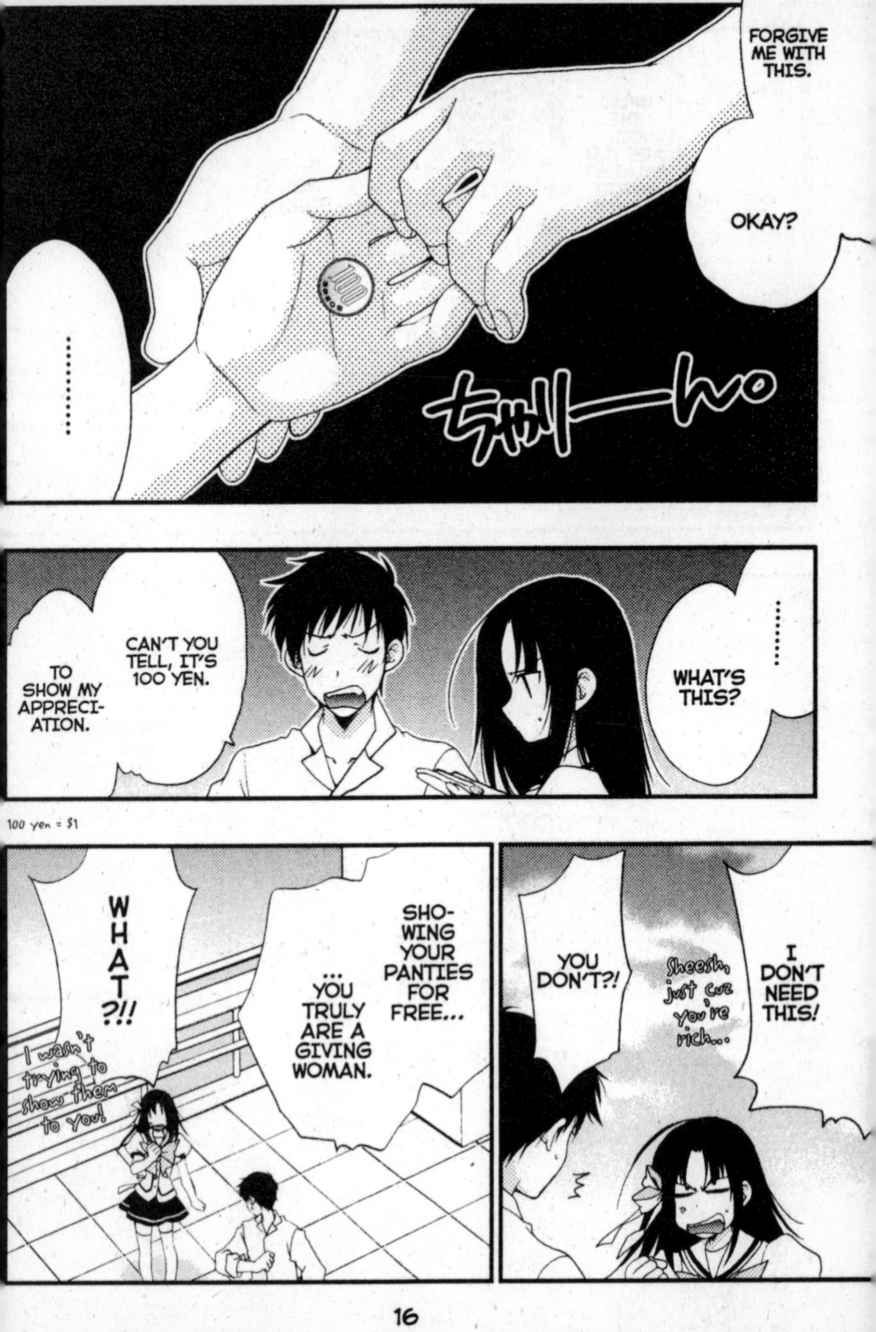
FORGIVE ME WITH THIS.
OKAY?
ちゃりーん
......
......
WHAT'S THIS?
CAN'T YOU TELL, IT'S 100 YEN.
TO SHOW MY APPRECIATION.
I DON'T NEED THIS!
Sheesh, just cuz you're rich...
YOU DON'T?!
SHOWING YOUR PANTIES FOR FREE...
...YOU TRULY ARE A GIVING WOMAN.
WHAT?!!
I wasn't trying to show them to you!

100 yen = $1

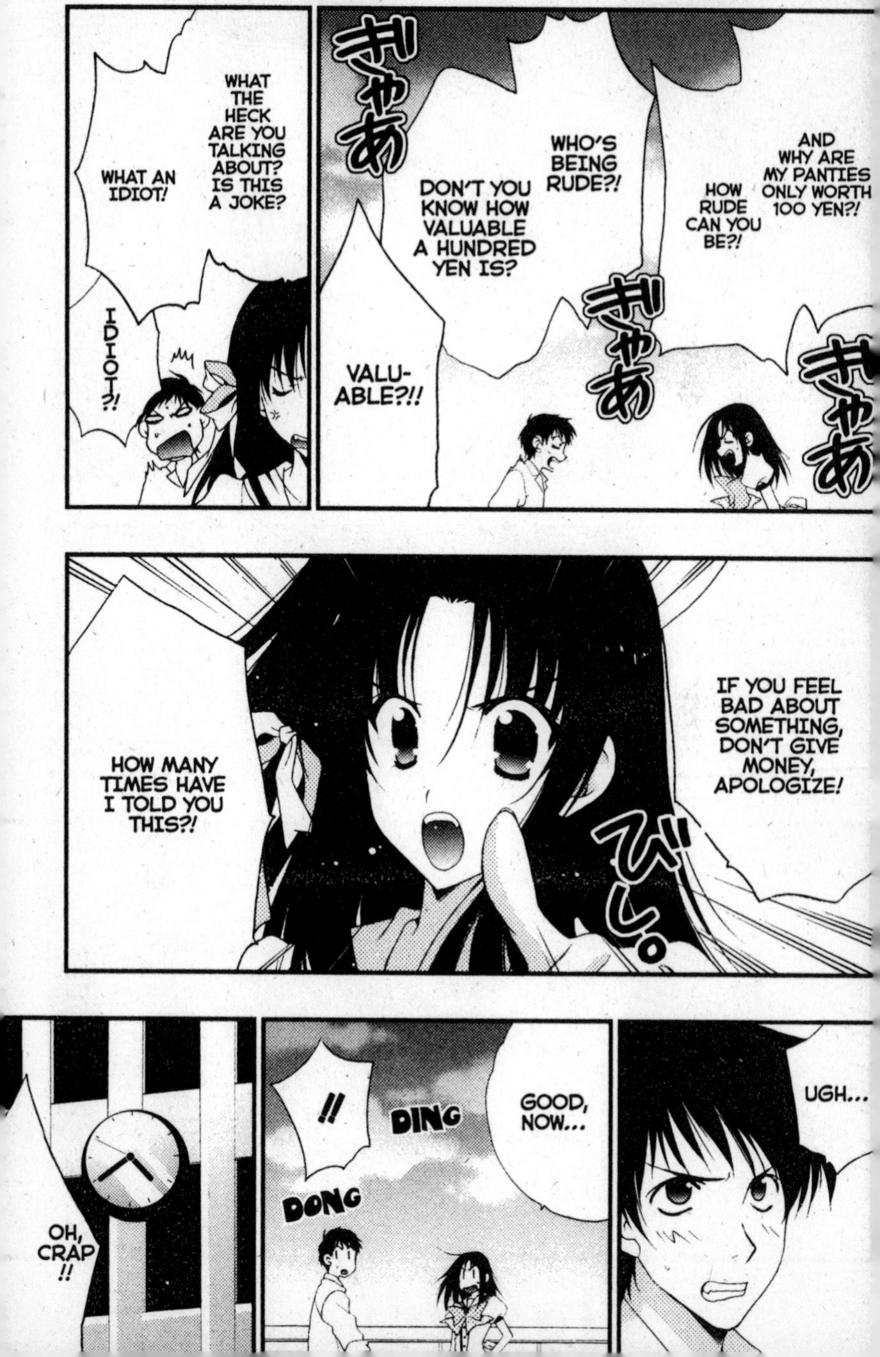
AND WHY ARE MY PANTIES ONLY WORTH 100 YEN?!
HOW RUDE CAN YOU BE?!
ぎゃあ
WHO'S BEING RUDE?!
DON'T YOU KNOW HOW VALUABLE A HUNDRED YEN IS?
ぎゃあ
VALU-ABLE?!!
ぎゃあ
WHAT THE HECK ARE YOU TALKING ABOUT? IS THIS A JOKE?
WHAT AN IDIOT!
IDIOT?!
IF YOU FEEL BAD ABOUT SOMETHING, DON'T GIVE MONEY, APOLOGIZE!
びし。
HOW MANY TIMES HAVE I TOLD YOU THIS?!
UGH...
GOOD, NOW...
!!
DING
DONG
OH, CRAP!!

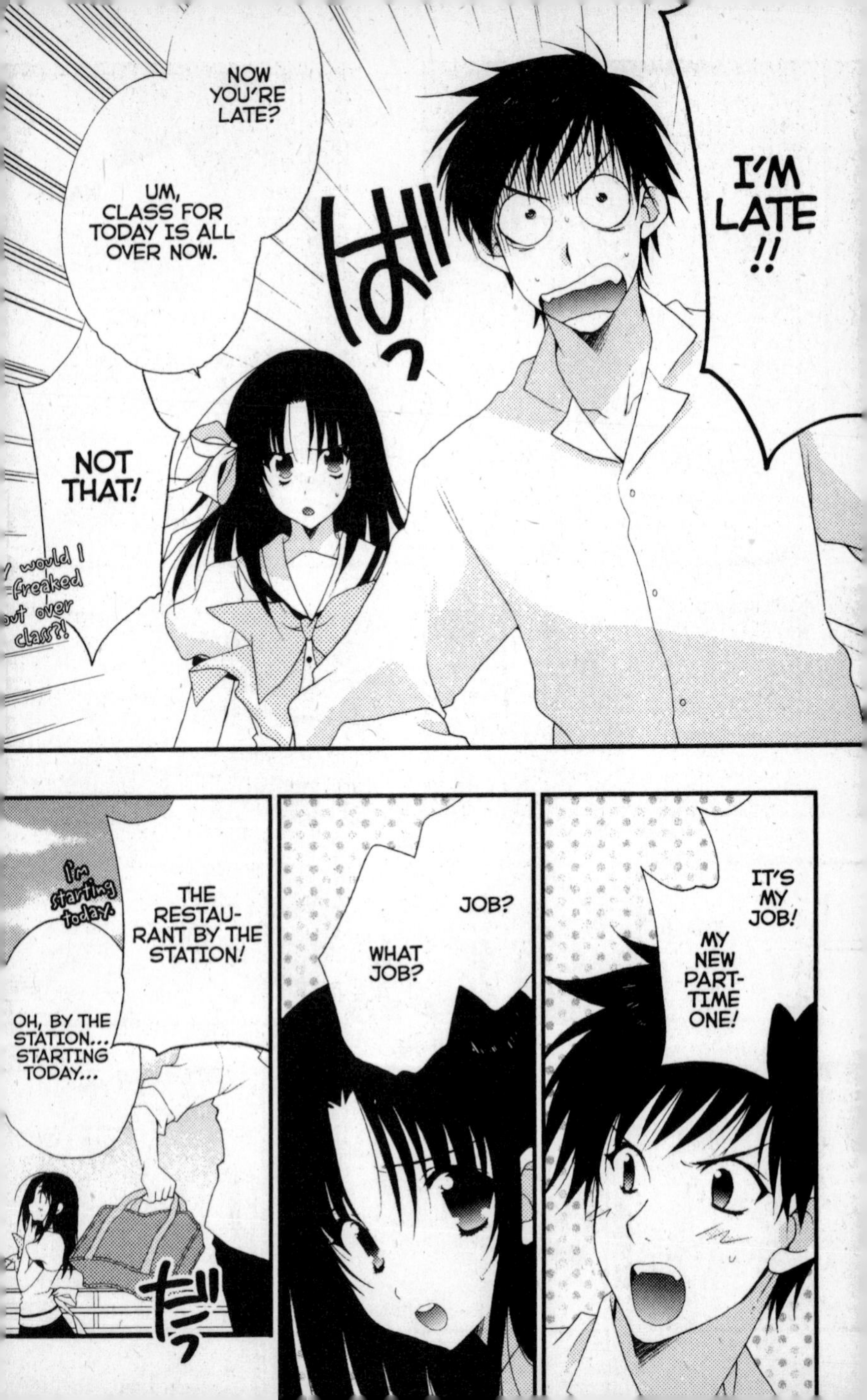
I'M LATE!!
はっ
NOW YOU'RE LATE?
UM, CLASS FOR TODAY IS ALL OVER NOW.
NOT THAT!
would I freaked out over class?!
IT'S MY JOB!
MY NEW PART-TIME ONE!
JOB?
WHAT JOB?
THE RESTAURANT BY THE STATION!
I'm starting today!
OH, BY THE STATION... STARTING TODAY...
だっ

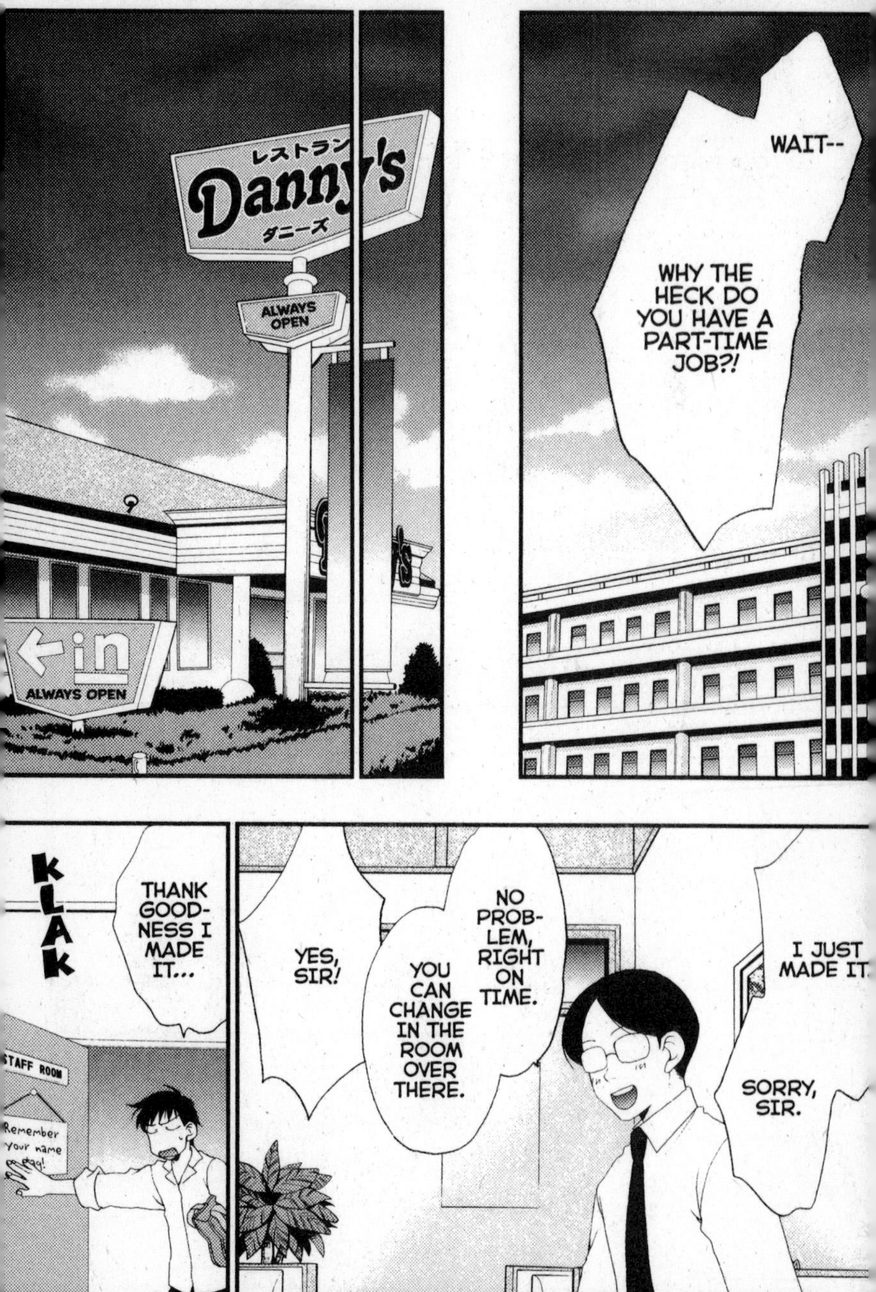
WAIT--
WHY THE HECK DO YOU HAVE A PART-TIME JOB?!
レストラン
Danny's
ダニーズ
ALWAYS OPEN
in
ALWAYS OPEN
I JUST MADE IT.
SORRY, SIR.
NO PROBLEM, RIGHT ON TIME.
YOU CAN CHANGE IN THE ROOM OVER THERE.
YES, SIR!
KLAK
THANK GOODNESS I MADE IT...
STAFF ROOM
Remember your name tag!

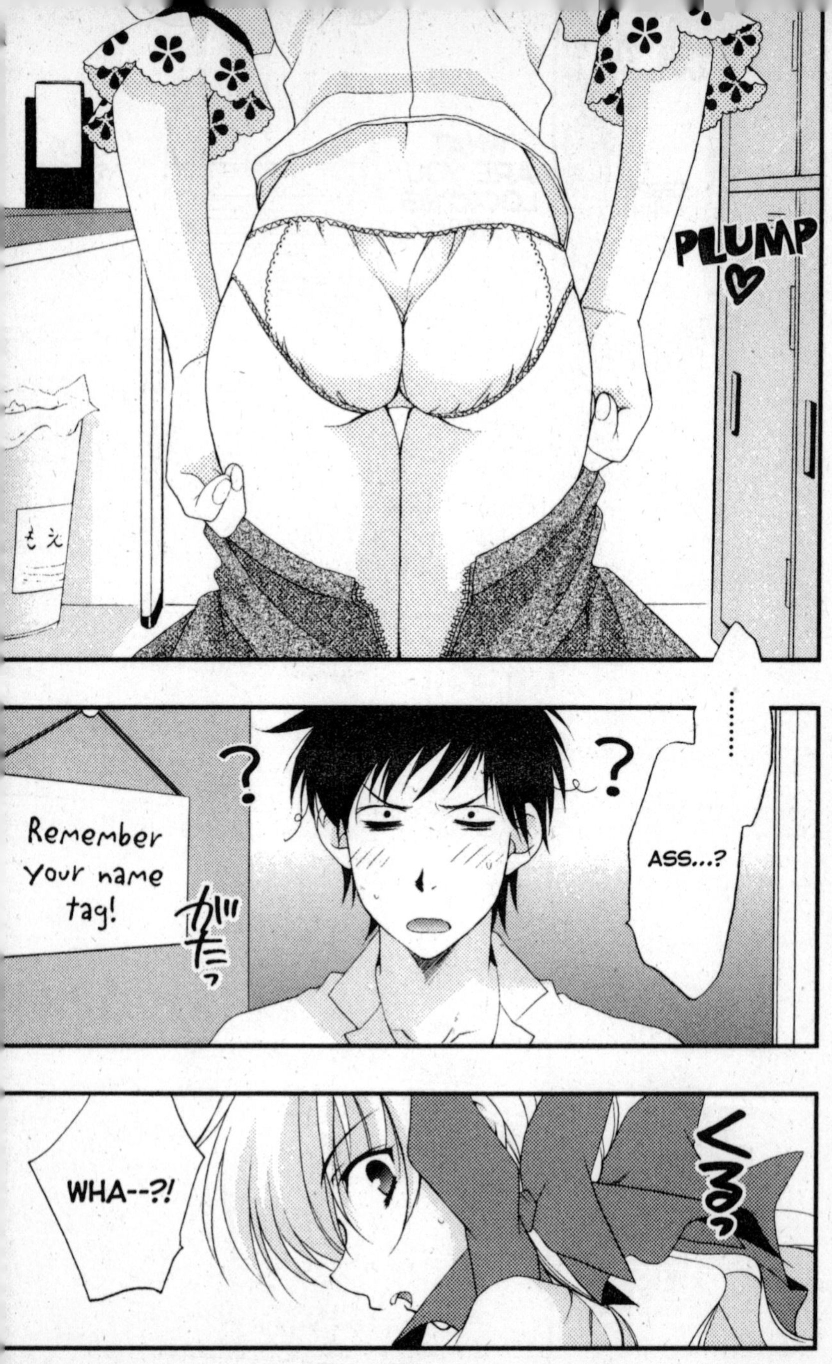
PLUMP ♥
......
ASS...?
? ?
Remember your name tag!
がたっ
くるっ
WHA--?!

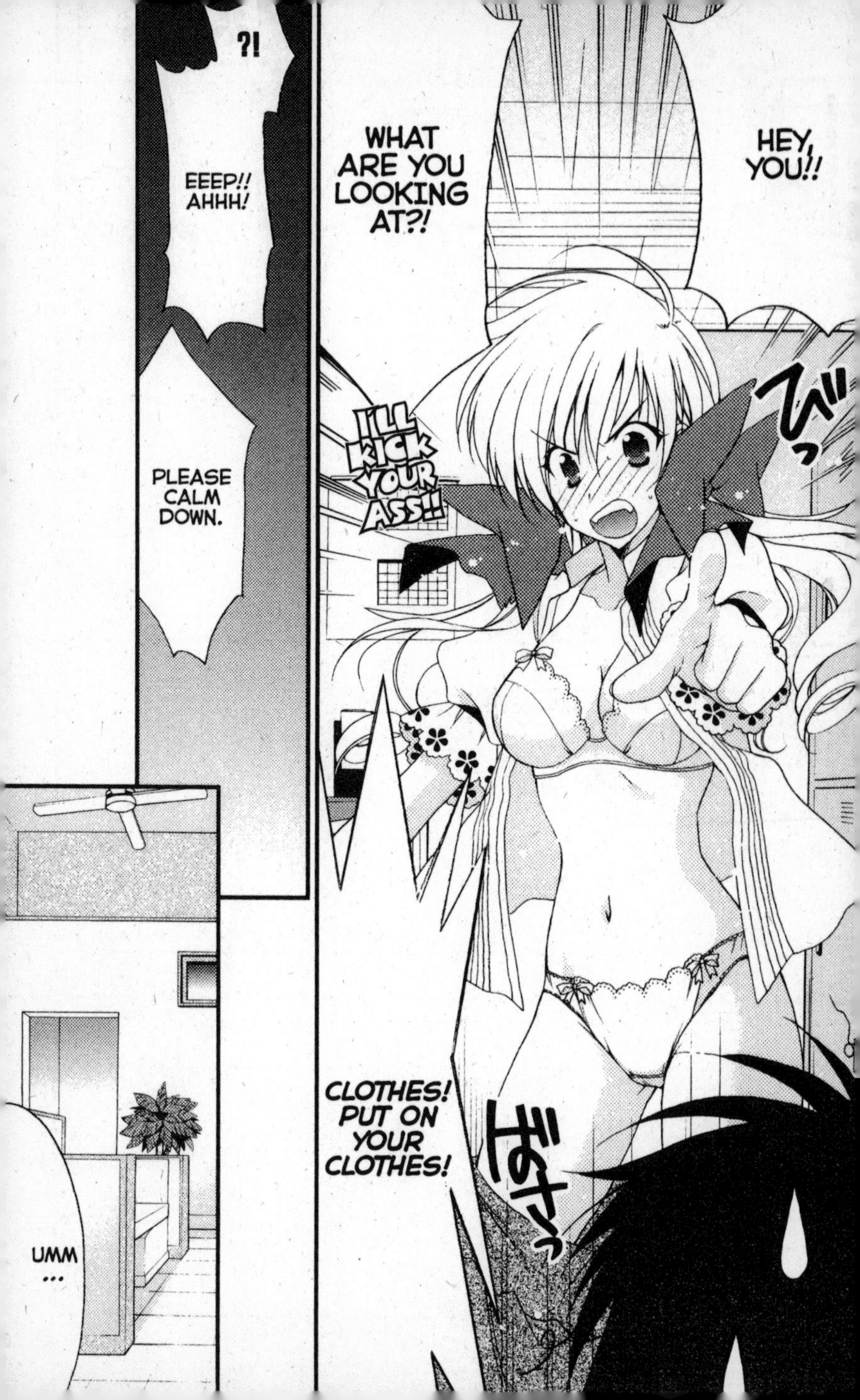
HEY, YOU!!
WHAT ARE YOU LOOKING AT?!
I'LL KICK YOUR ASS!!
CLOTHES! PUT ON YOUR CLOTHES!
?!
EEEP!! AHHH!
PLEASE CALM DOWN.
UMM...

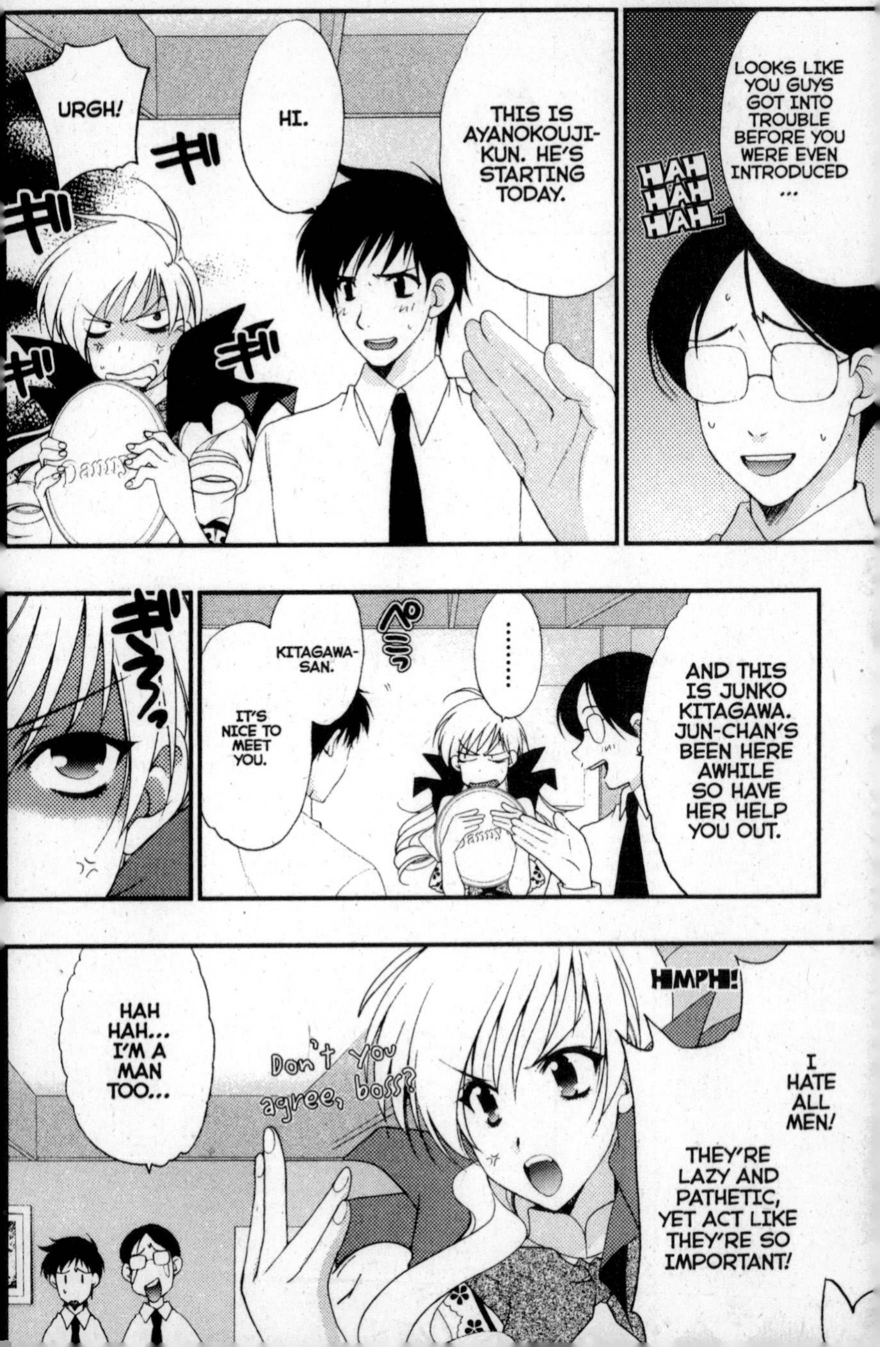
HAH HAH HAH...
LOOKS LIKE YOU GUYS GOT INTO TROUBLE BEFORE YOU WERE EVEN INTRODUCED ...
THIS IS AYANOKOUJI-KUN. HE'S STARTING TODAY.
HI.
URGH!
ギ
ギ
ギ
ギ
AND THIS IS JUNKO KITAGAWA. JUN-CHAN'S BEEN HERE AWHILE SO HAVE HER HELP YOU OUT.
....
ぺこっ
KITAGAWA-SAN.
IT'S NICE TO MEET YOU.
ぎろっ
HMPH!
I HATE ALL MEN!
THEY'RE LAZY AND PATHETIC, YET ACT LIKE THEY'RE SO IMPORTANT!
Don't you agree, boss?
HAH HAH... I'M A MAN TOO...

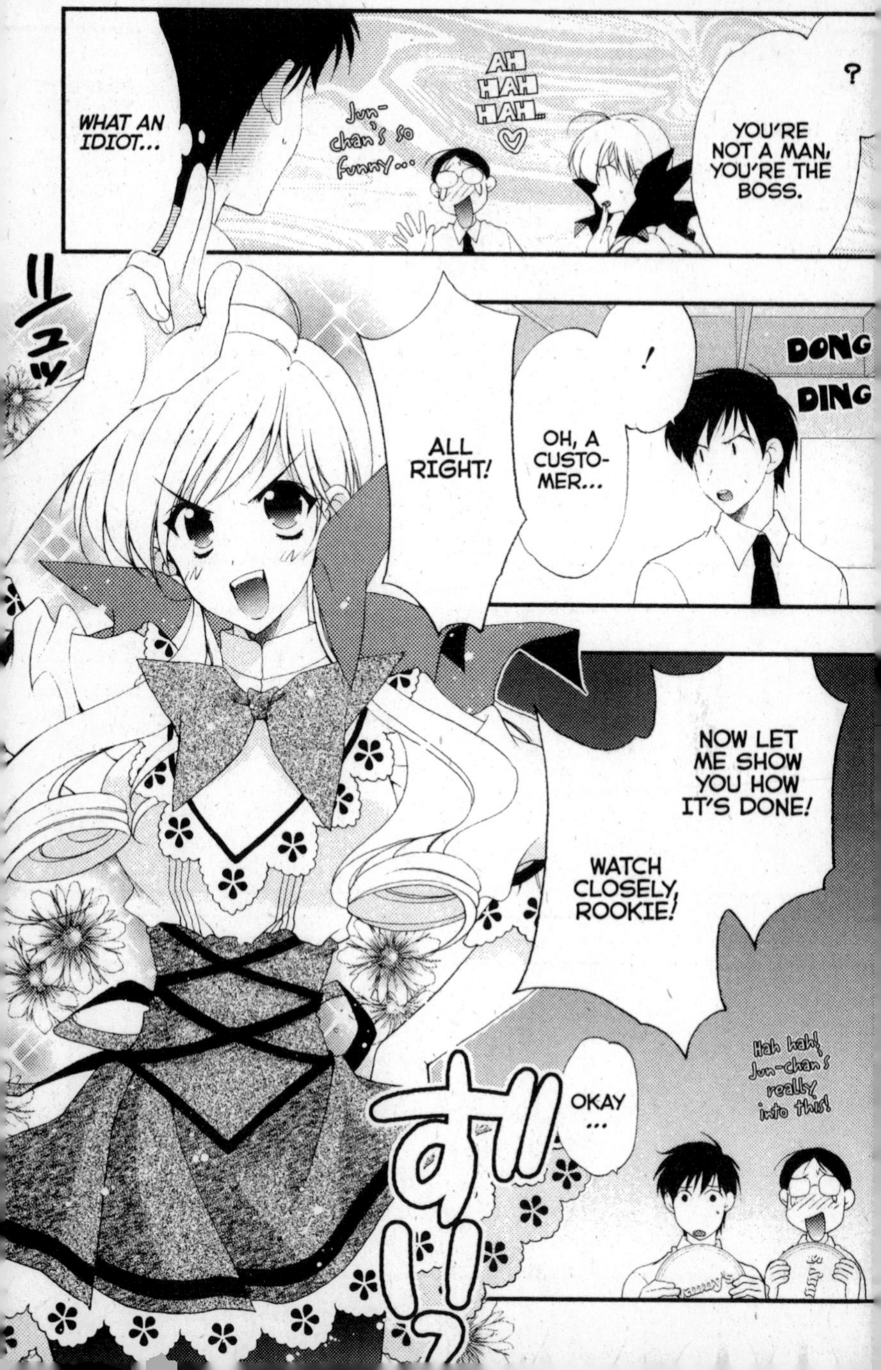
?
YOU'RE NOT A MAN, YOU'RE THE BOSS.
AH HAH HAH... ♡
Jun-chan's so funny...
WHAT AN IDIOT...
DONG
DING
!
OH, A CUSTO-MER...
ALL RIGHT!
NOW LET ME SHOW YOU HOW IT'S DONE!
WATCH CLOSELY, ROOKIE!
Hah hah! Jun-chan's really into this!
OKAY...

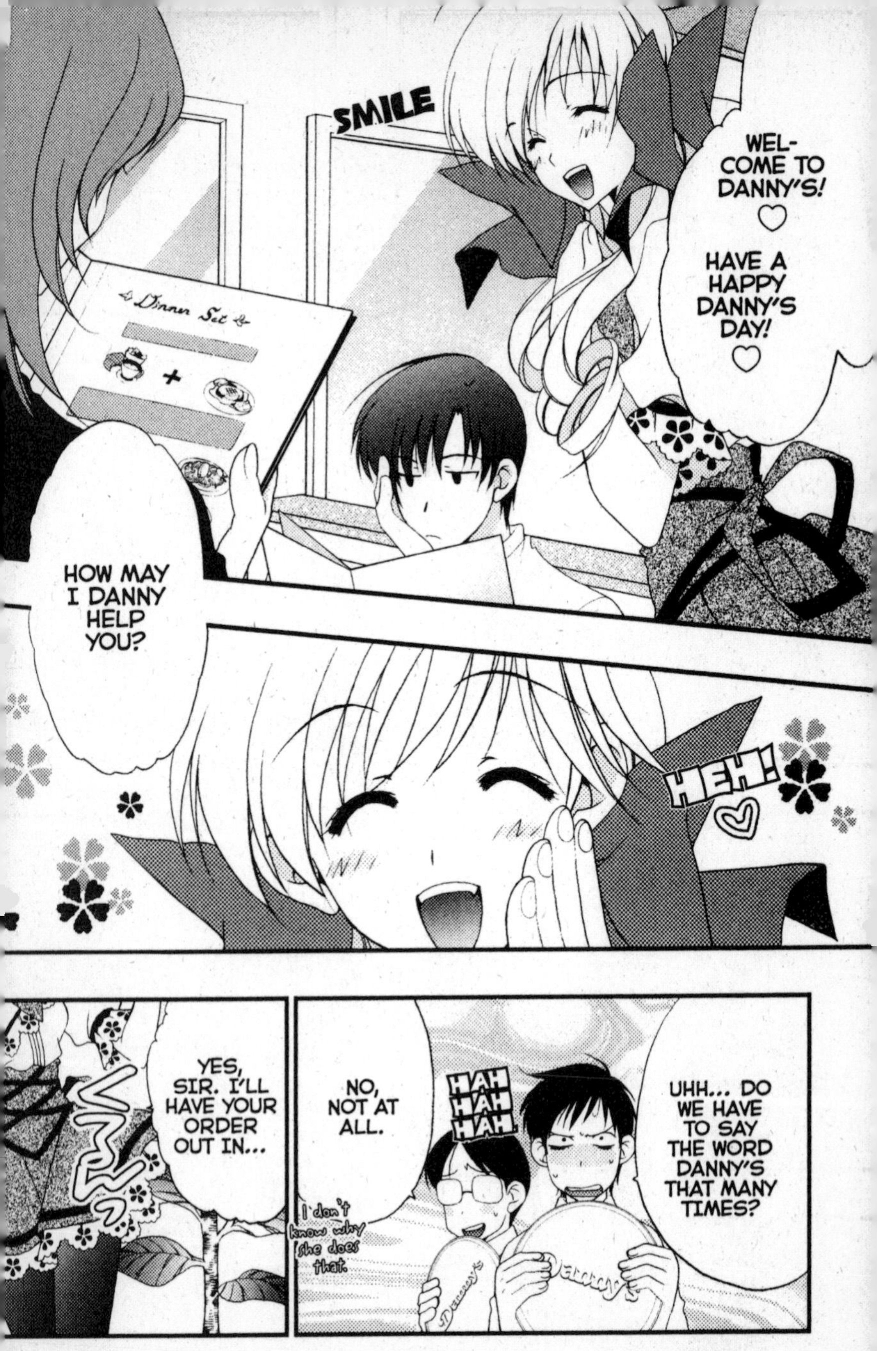
SMILE
WEL-COME TO DANNY'S! ♡
HAVE A HAPPY DANNY'S DAY! ♡
Dinner Set
HOW MAY I DANNY HELP YOU?
HEH! ♡
UHH... DO WE HAVE TO SAY THE WORD DANNY'S THAT MANY TIMES?
HAH HAH HAH.
NO, NOT AT ALL.
I don't know why she does that.
YES, SIR. I'LL HAVE YOUR ORDER OUT IN...

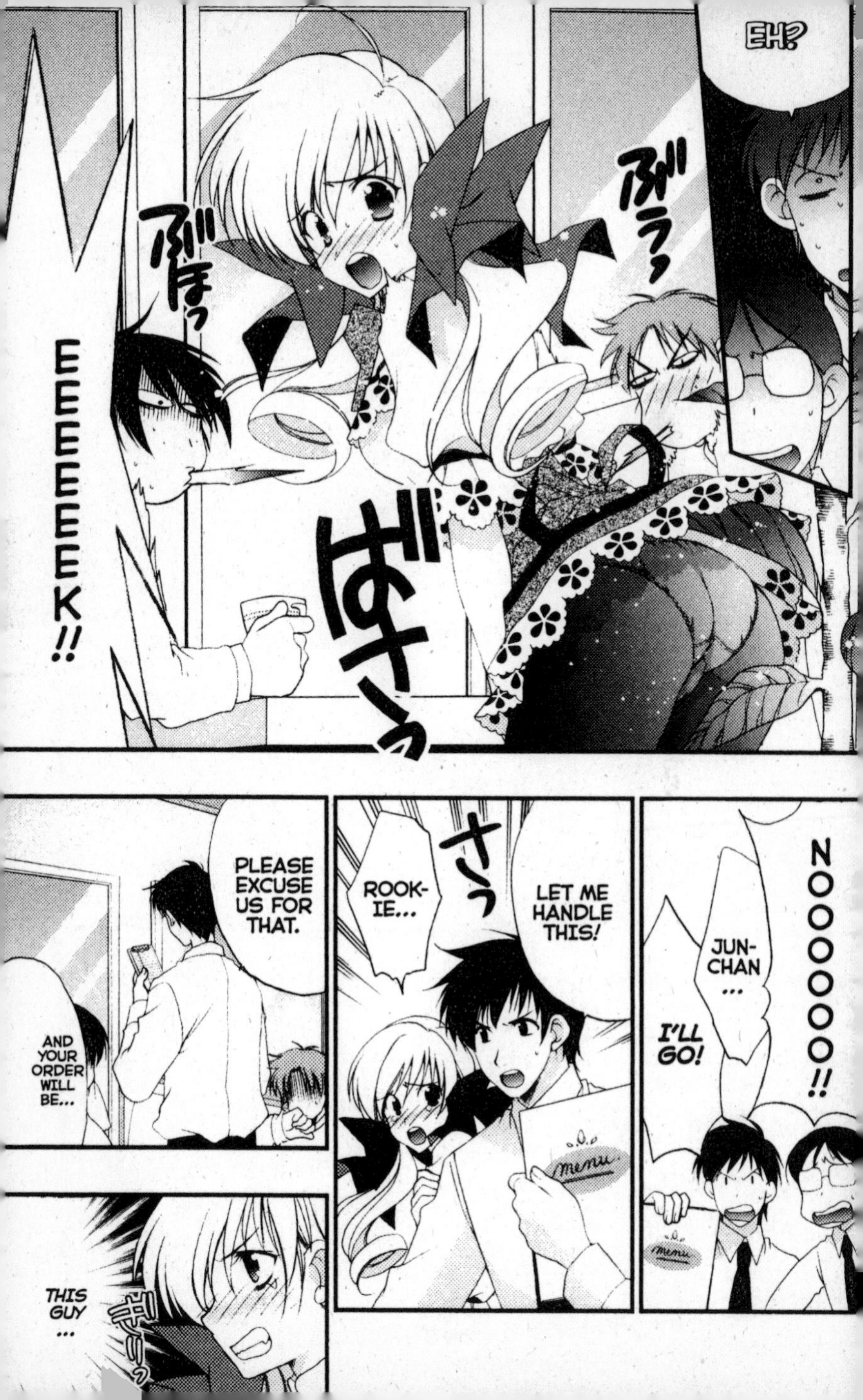
EH?
ぶフッ
ぶほっ
EEEEEEEEK!!
ぱさっ
NOOOOOO!!
JUN-CHAN... I'LL GO!
LET ME HANDLE THIS!
さっ
ROOK-IE...
menu
menu
PLEASE EXCUSE US FOR THAT.
AND YOUR ORDER WILL BE...
THIS GUY...
ギリッ

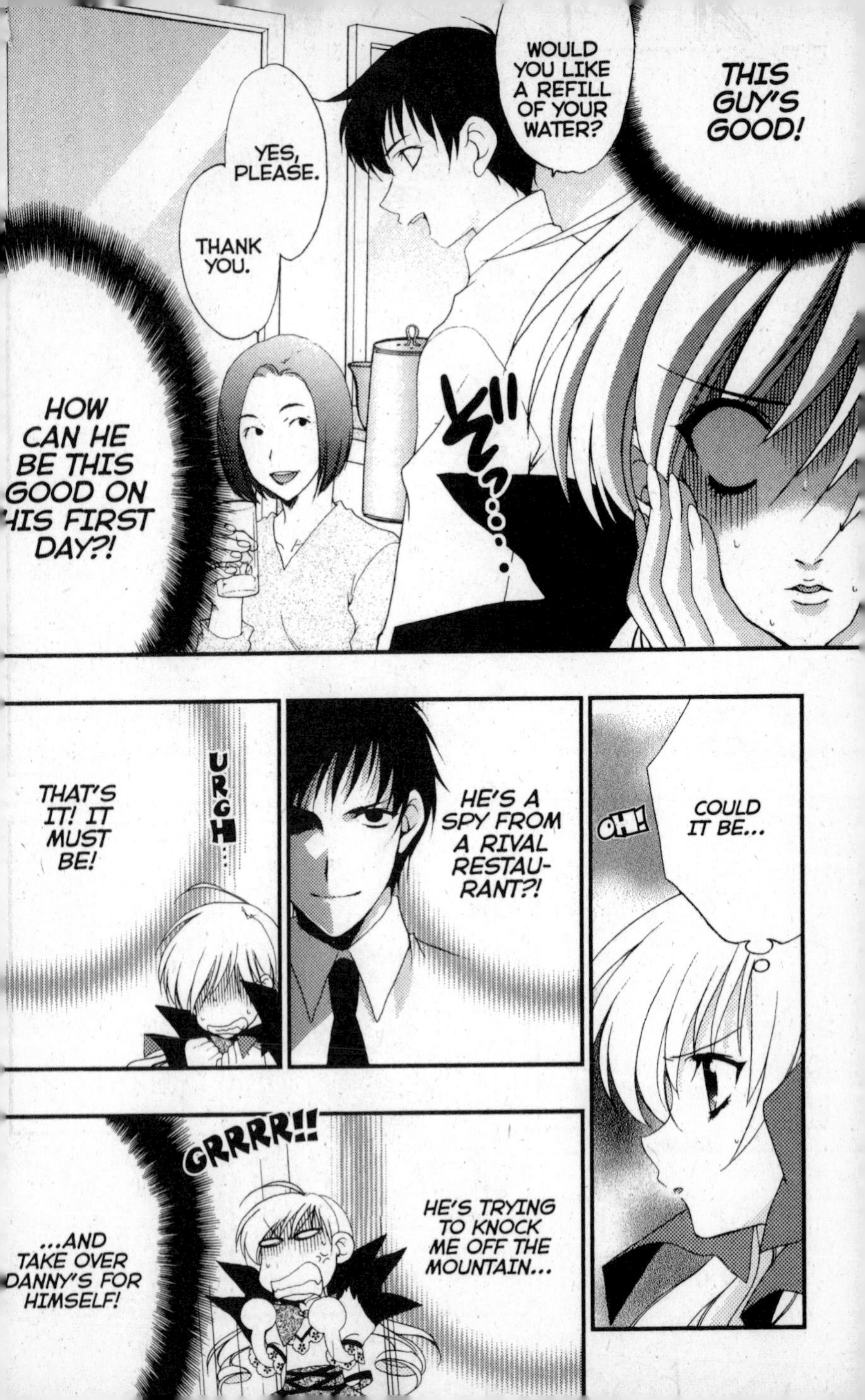
THIS GUY'S GOOD!
WOULD YOU LIKE A REFILL OF YOUR WATER?
YES, PLEASE.
THANK YOU.
HOW CAN HE BE THIS GOOD ON HIS FIRST DAY?!
OH!
COULD IT BE...
HE'S A SPY FROM A RIVAL RESTAU-RANT?!
URGH...
THAT'S IT! IT MUST BE!
HE'S TRYING TO KNOCK ME OFF THE MOUNTAIN...
GRRRR!!
...AND TAKE OVER DANNY'S FOR HIMSELF!

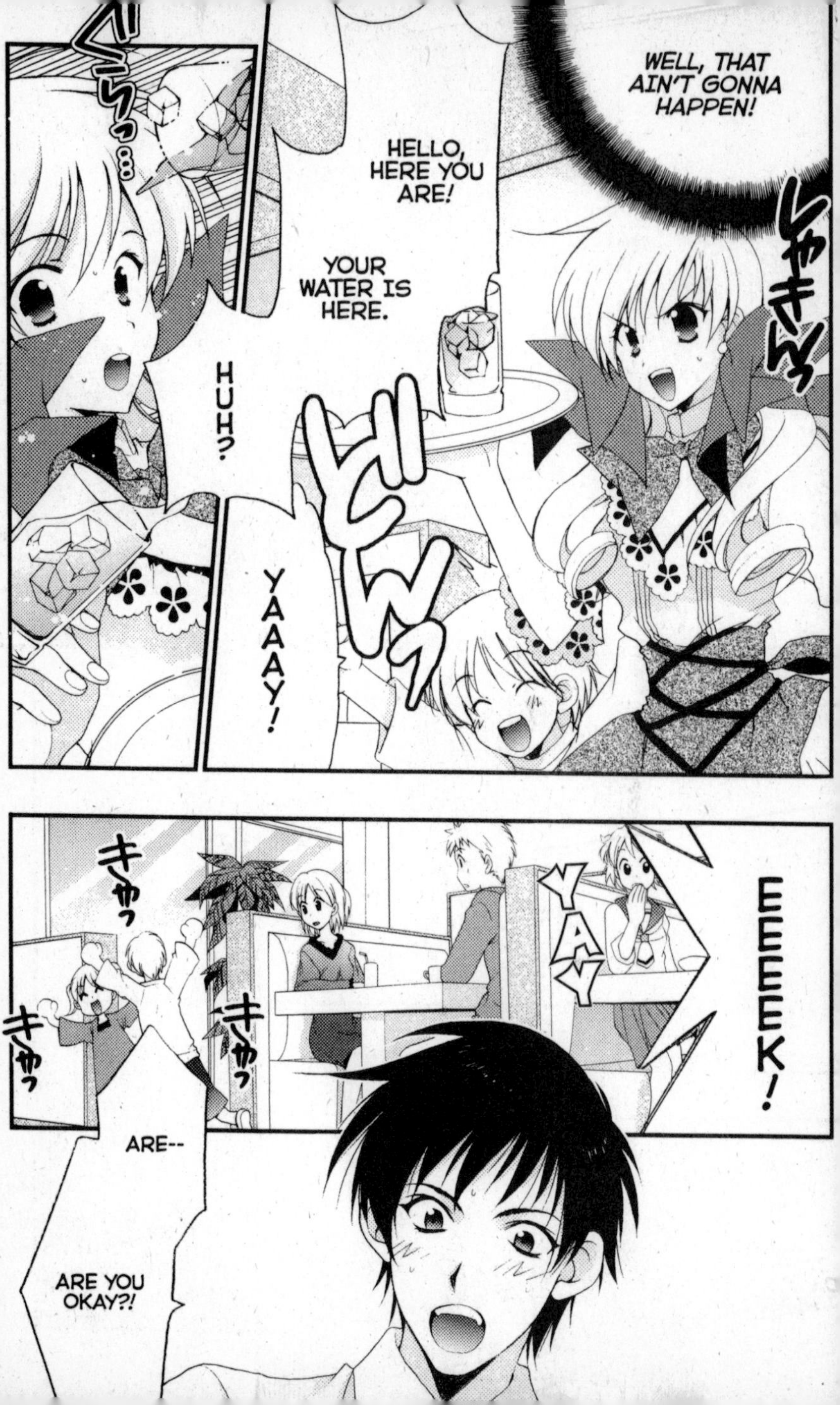
WELL, THAT AIN'T GONNA HAPPEN!
しゃきんっ
HELLO, HERE YOU ARE!
YOUR WATER IS HERE.
ぐらっ…
HUH?
どんっ
YAAAAY!
EEEEK!
YAY
きゃっ
きゃっ
きゃっ
ARE--
ARE YOU OKAY?!

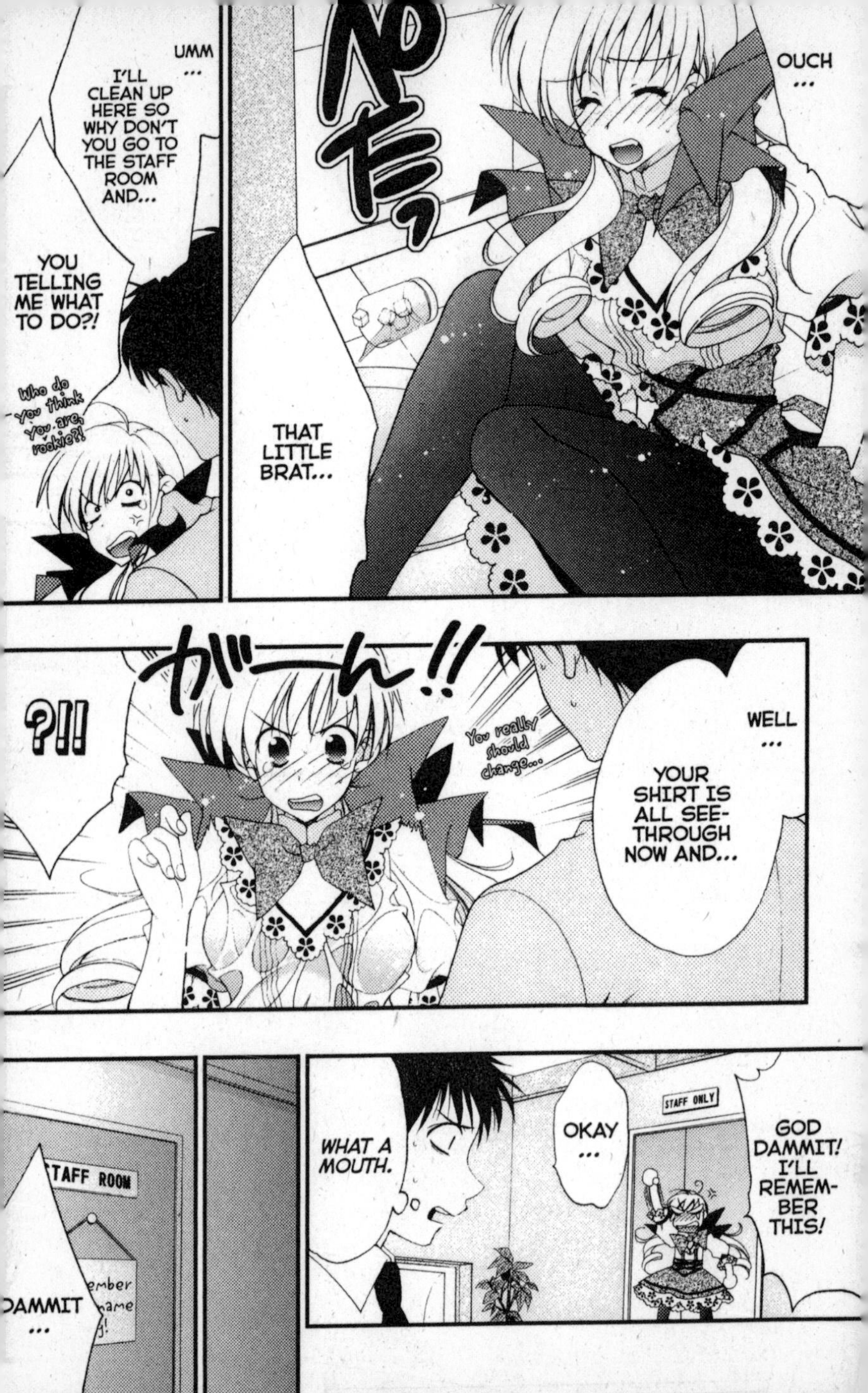
OUCH...
ぺたっ
THAT LITTLE BRAT...
UMM... I'LL CLEAN UP HERE SO WHY DON'T YOU GO TO THE STAFF ROOM AND...
YOU TELLING ME WHAT TO DO?!
Who do you think you are, rookie?!
WELL... YOUR SHIRT IS ALL SEE-THROUGH NOW AND...
You really should change...
がーん!!
?!!
GOD DAMMIT! I'LL REMEMBER THIS!
STAFF ONLY
OKAY...
WHAT A MOUTH.
STAFF ROOM
DAMMIT...

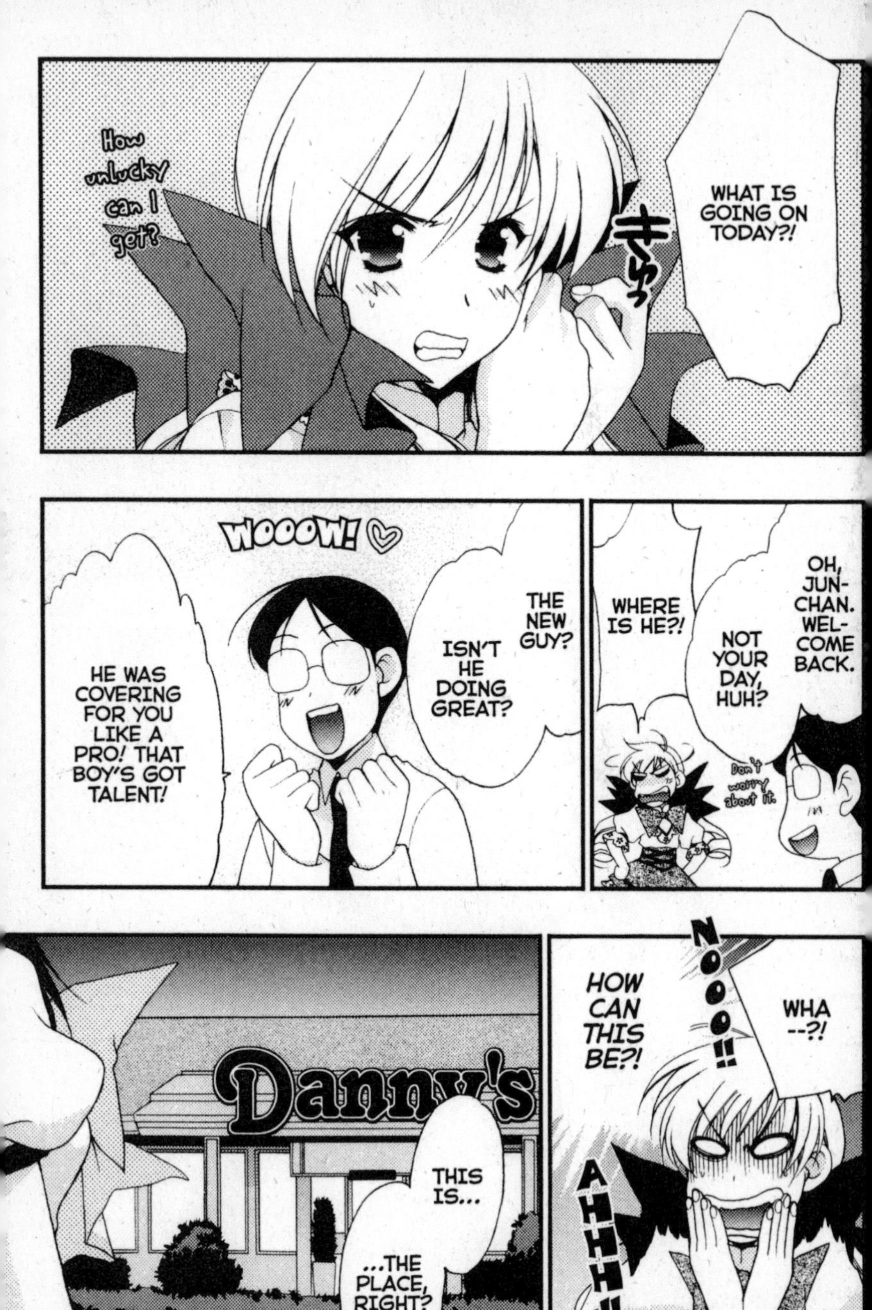
WHAT IS GOING ON TODAY?!
How unlucky can I get?
OH, JUN-CHAN. WELCOME BACK.
NOT YOUR DAY, HUH?
WHERE IS HE?!
Don't worry about it.
THE NEW GUY?
ISN'T HE DOING GREAT?
WOOOW! ♡
HE WAS COVERING FOR YOU LIKE A PRO! THAT BOY'S GOT TALENT!
WHA--?!
NOOOO!!
HOW CAN THIS BE?!
AHHHH!!
Danny's
THIS IS...
...THE PLACE, RIGHT?

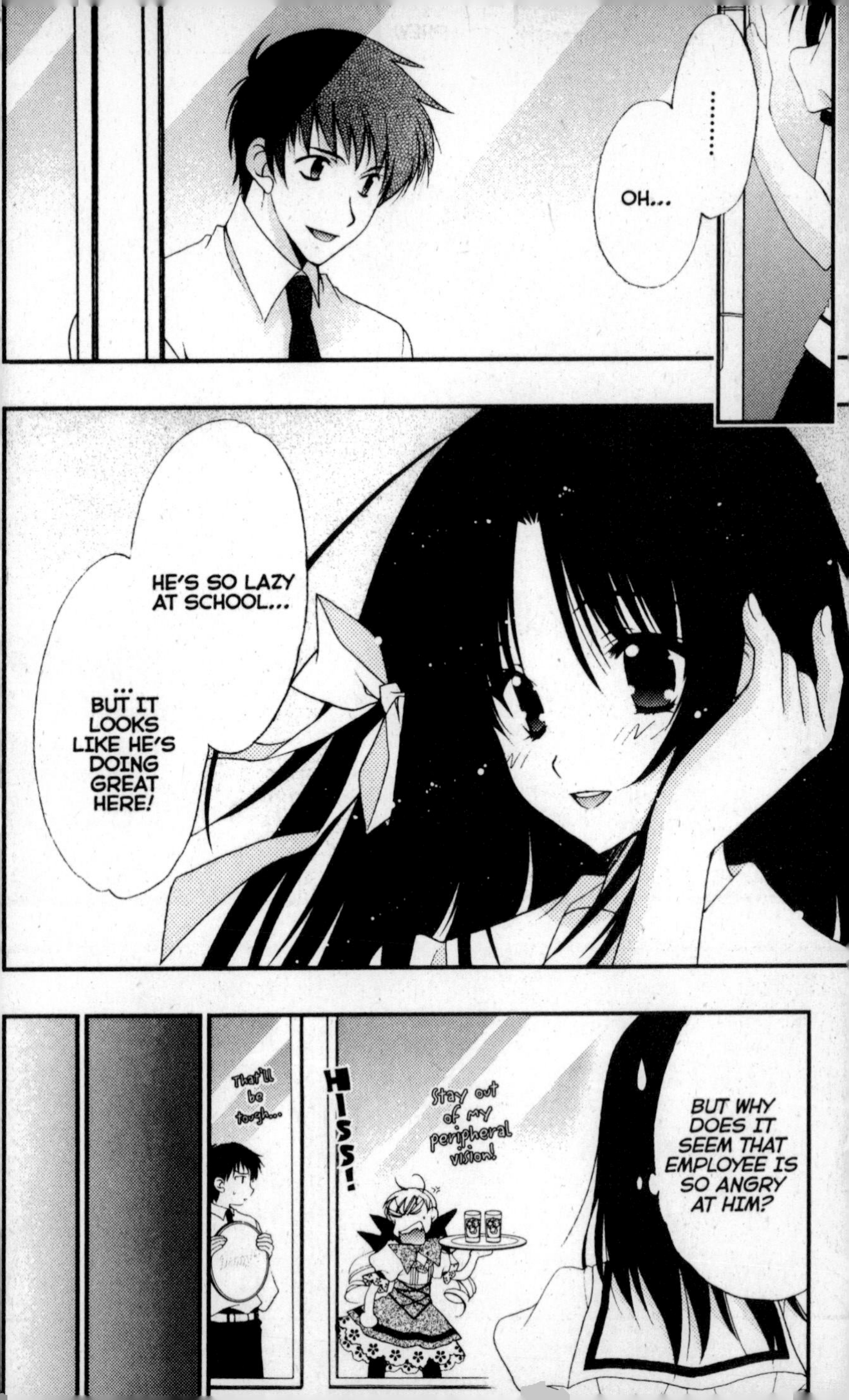
......
OH...
HE'S SO LAZY AT SCHOOL...
... BUT IT LOOKS LIKE HE'S DOING GREAT HERE!
BUT WHY DOES IT SEEM THAT EMPLOYEE IS SO ANGRY AT HIM?
Stay out of my peripheral vision!
HISS!
That'll be tough...

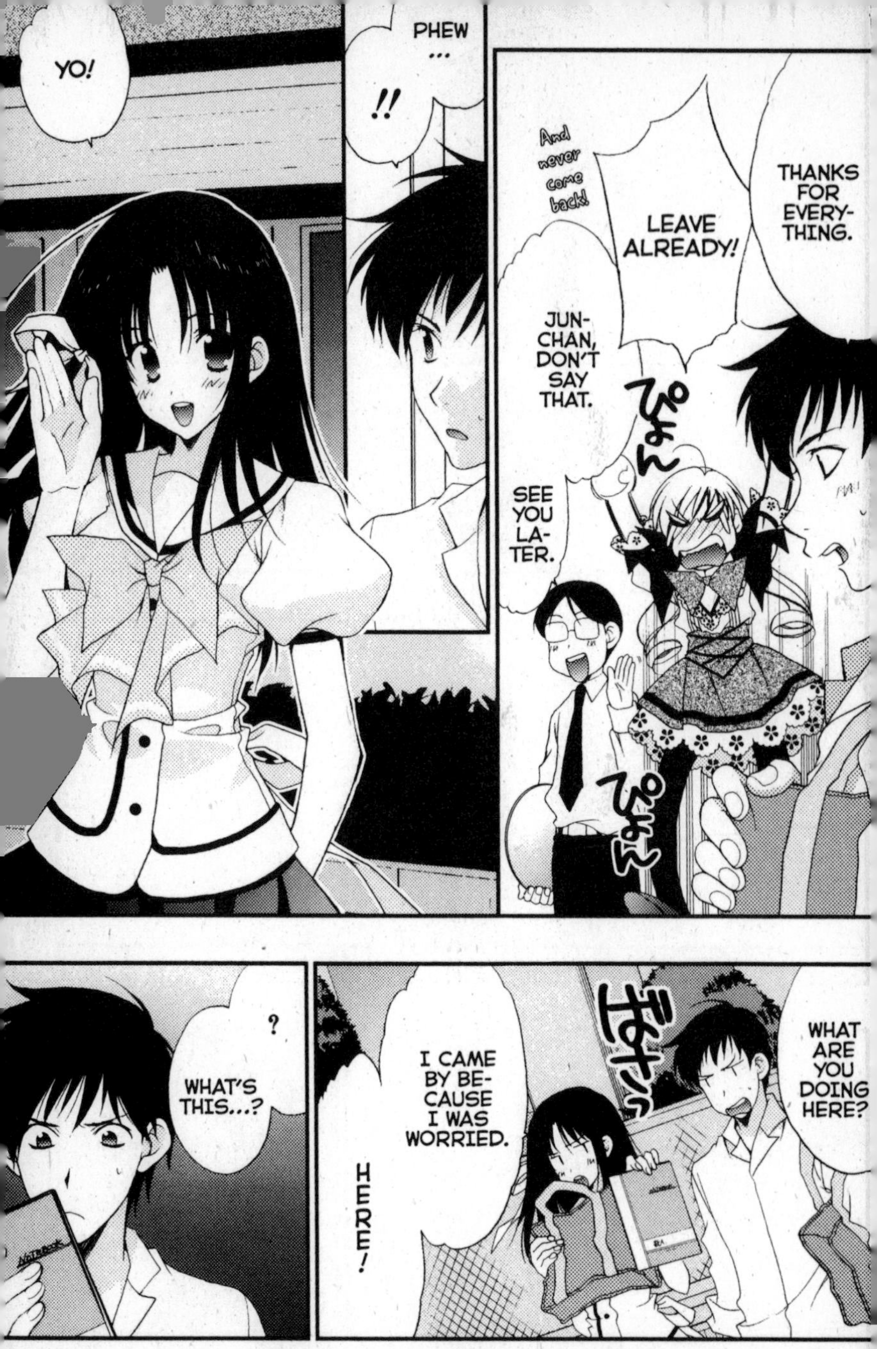
THANKS FOR EVERY-THING.
LEAVE ALREADY!
And never come back!
JUN-CHAN, DON'T SAY THAT.
ぴょん
SEE YOU LA-TER.
ぴょん
PHEW ...
!!
YO!
WHAT ARE YOU DOING HERE?
I CAME BY BE-CAUSE I WAS WORRIED.
HERE!
?
WHAT'S THIS...?
NOTEBOOK

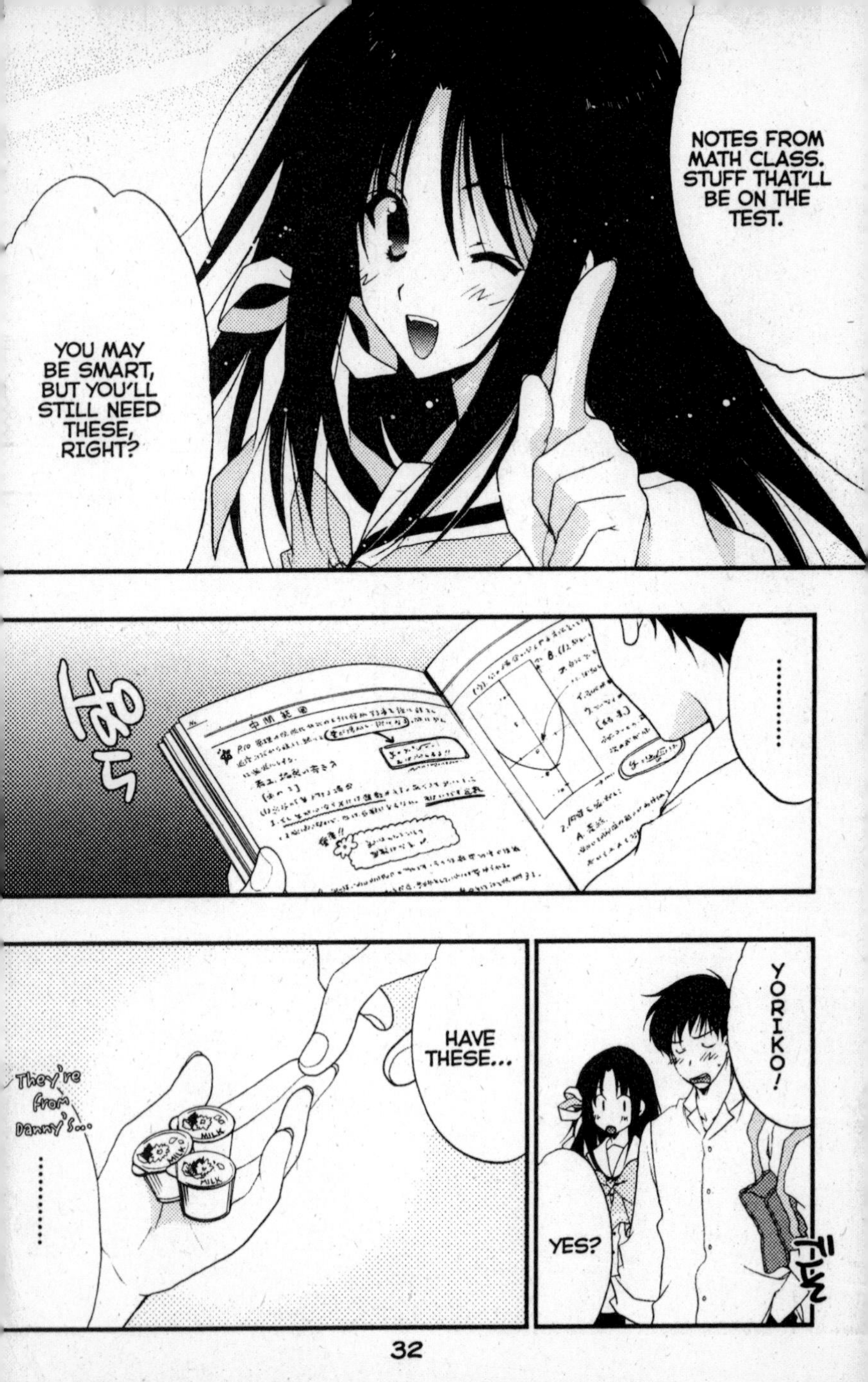
NOTES FROM MATH CLASS. STUFF THAT'LL BE ON THE TEST.
YOU MAY BE SMART, BUT YOU'LL STILL NEED THESE, RIGHT?
......
ぱら
YORIKO!
YES?
デーン
HAVE THESE...
They're from Danny's...
......
MILK
MILK
MILK

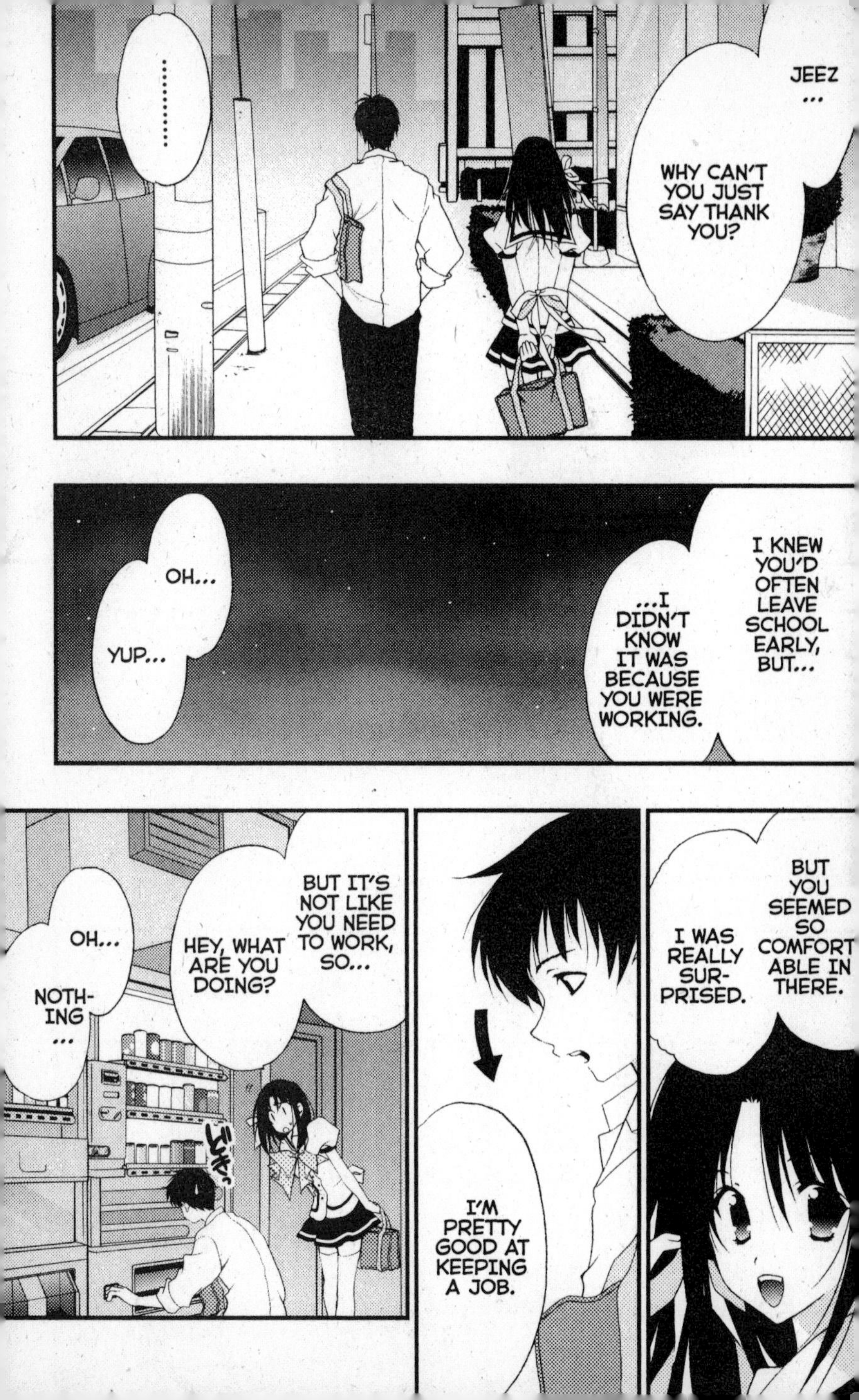
JEEZ...
WHY CAN'T YOU JUST SAY THANK YOU?
......
I KNEW YOU'D OFTEN LEAVE SCHOOL EARLY, BUT...
...I DIDN'T KNOW IT WAS BECAUSE YOU WERE WORKING.
OH...
YUP...
BUT YOU SEEMED SO COMFORT ABLE IN THERE.
I WAS REALLY SUR- PRISED.
I'M PRETTY GOOD AT KEEPING A JOB.
BUT IT'S NOT LIKE YOU NEED TO WORK, SO...
HEY, WHAT ARE YOU DOING?
OH...
NOTH- ING...

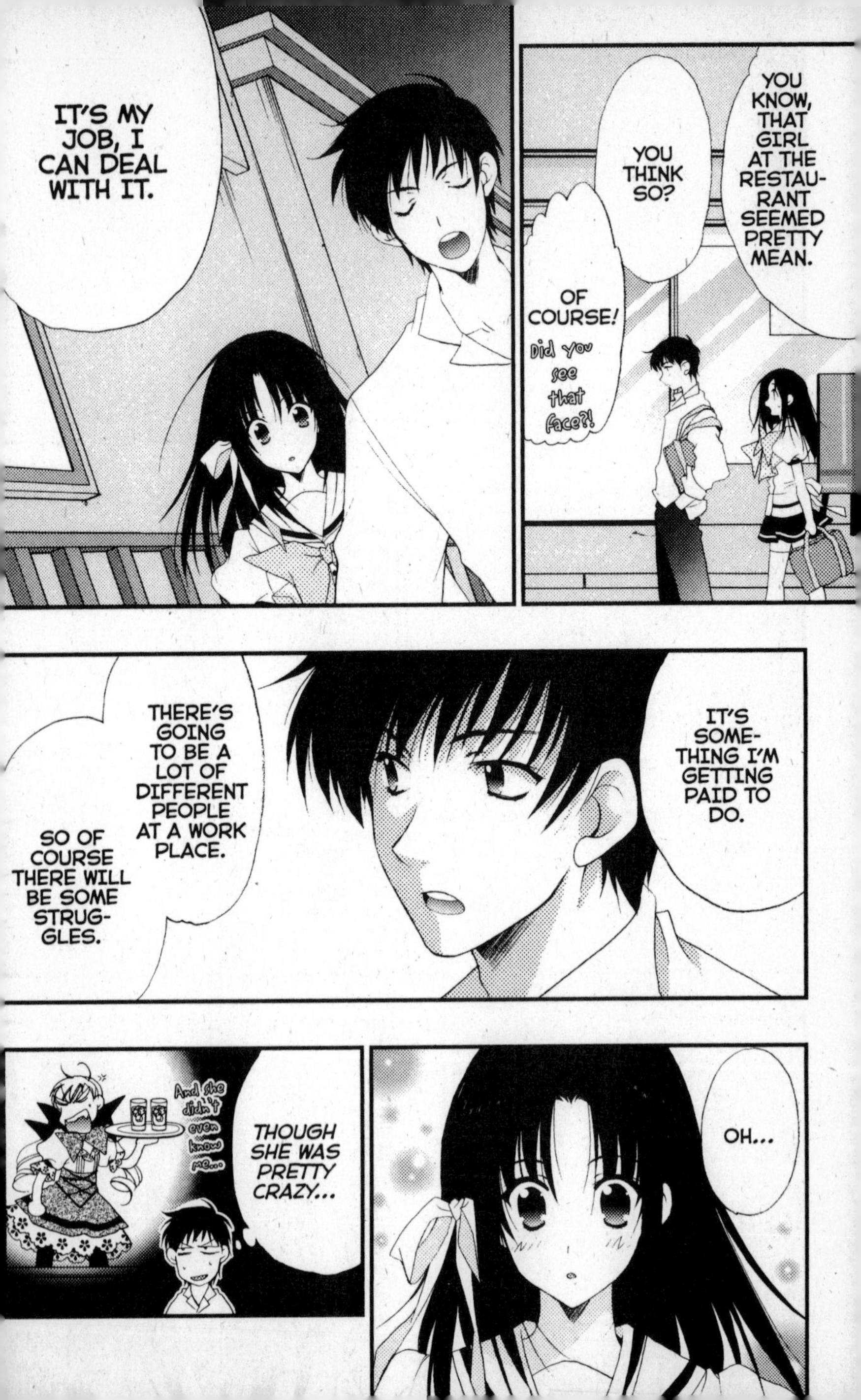
YOU KNOW, THAT GIRL AT THE RESTAURANT SEEMED PRETTY MEAN.
YOU THINK SO?
OF COURSE!
Did you see that face?!
IT'S MY JOB, I CAN DEAL WITH IT.
IT'S SOMETHING I'M GETTING PAID TO DO.
THERE'S GOING TO BE A LOT OF DIFFERENT PEOPLE AT A WORK PLACE.
SO OF COURSE THERE WILL BE SOME STRUGGLES.
OH...
THOUGH SHE WAS PRETTY CRAZY...
And she didn't even know me...

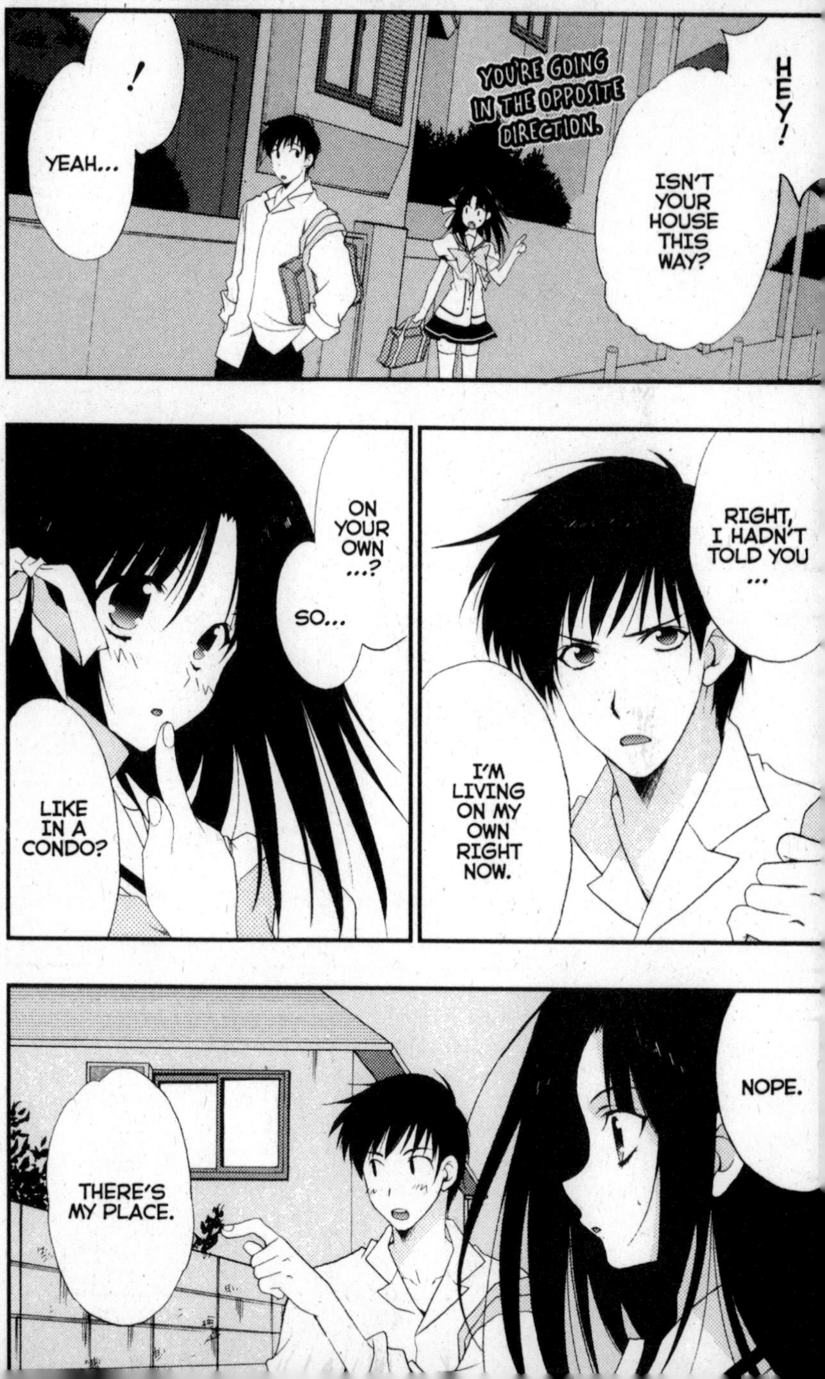
HEY!
ISN'T YOUR HOUSE THIS WAY?
YOU'RE GOING IN THE OPPOSITE DIRECTION.
!
YEAH...
RIGHT, I HADN'T TOLD YOU ...
I'M LIVING ON MY OWN RIGHT NOW.
ON YOUR OWN ...?
SO...
LIKE IN A CONDO?
NOPE.
THERE'S MY PLACE.

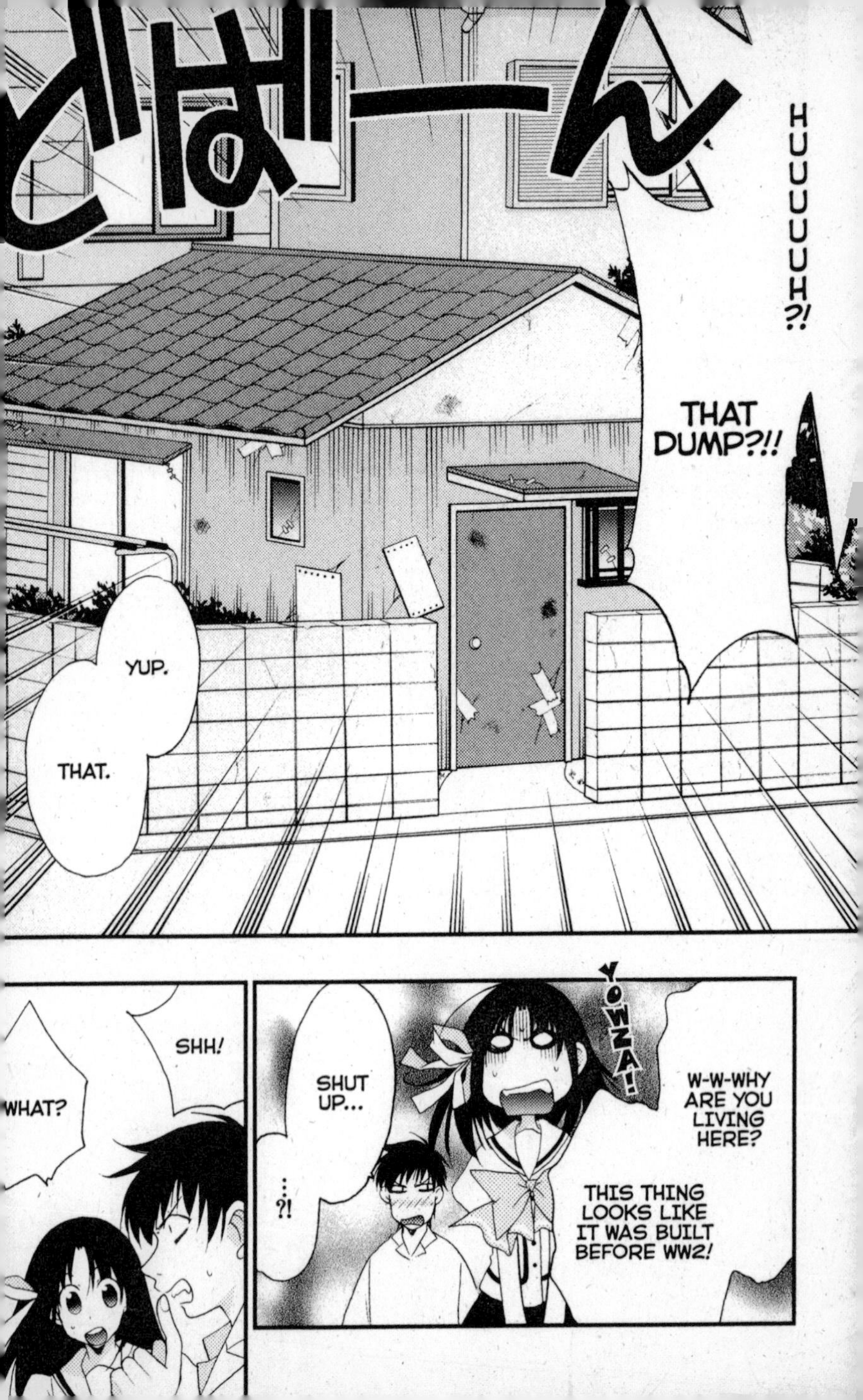
どばーん
HUUUUUH?!
THAT DUMP?!!
YUP.
THAT.
YOWZA!
W-W-WHY ARE YOU LIVING HERE?
THIS THING LOOKS LIKE IT WAS BUILT BEFORE WW2!
SHUT UP...
...?!
SHH!
WHAT?

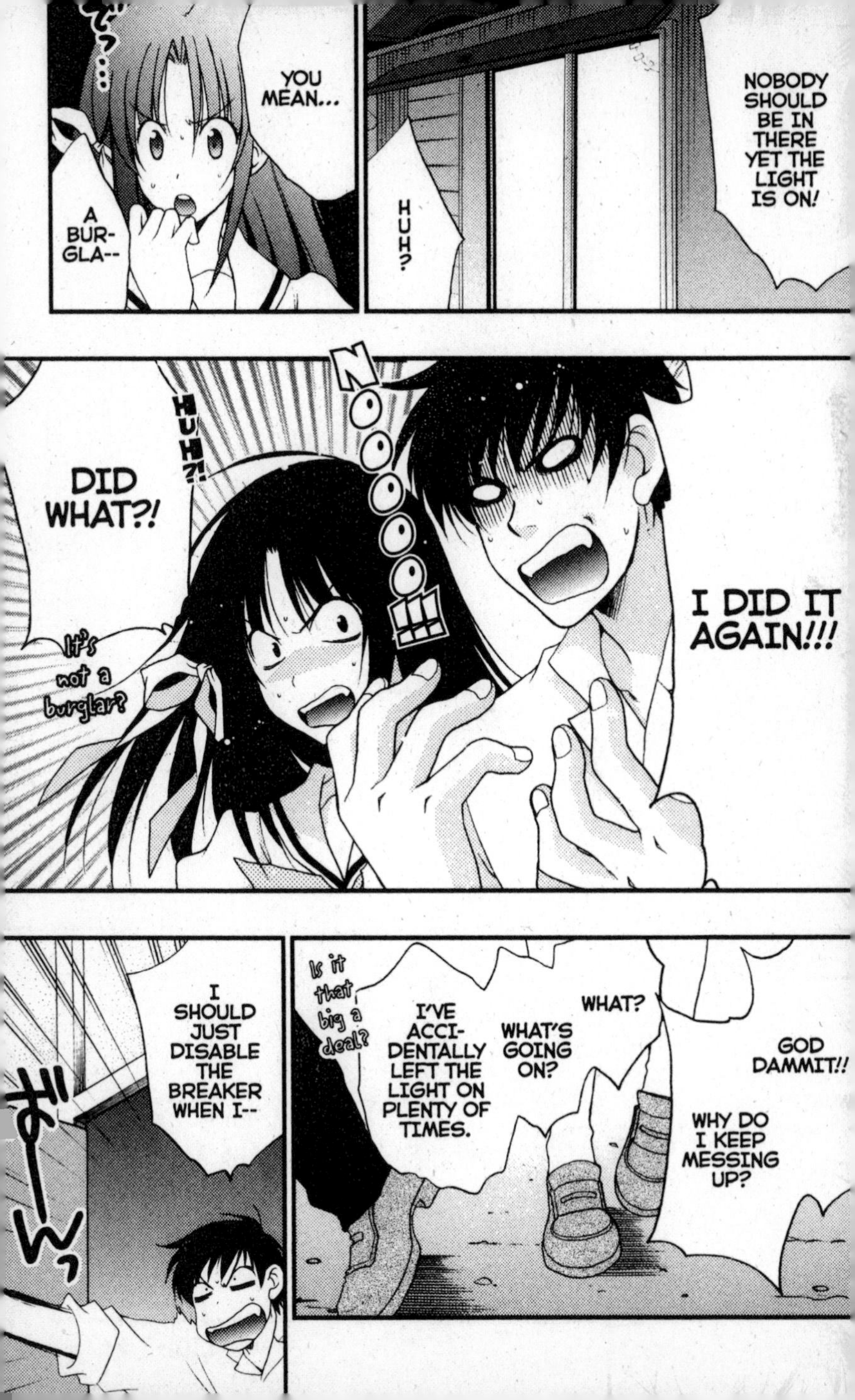
NOBODY SHOULD BE IN THERE YET THE LIGHT IS ON!
HUH?
YOU MEAN...
A BUR-GLA--
I DID IT AGAIN!!!
NOOOOO!!!
HUH?!
DID WHAT?!
It's not a burglar?
GOD DAMMIT!!
WHY DO I KEEP MESSING UP?
WHAT?
WHAT'S GOING ON?
I'VE ACCI-DENTALLY LEFT THE LIGHT ON PLENTY OF TIMES.
Is it that big a deal?
I SHOULD JUST DISABLE THE BREAKER WHEN I--

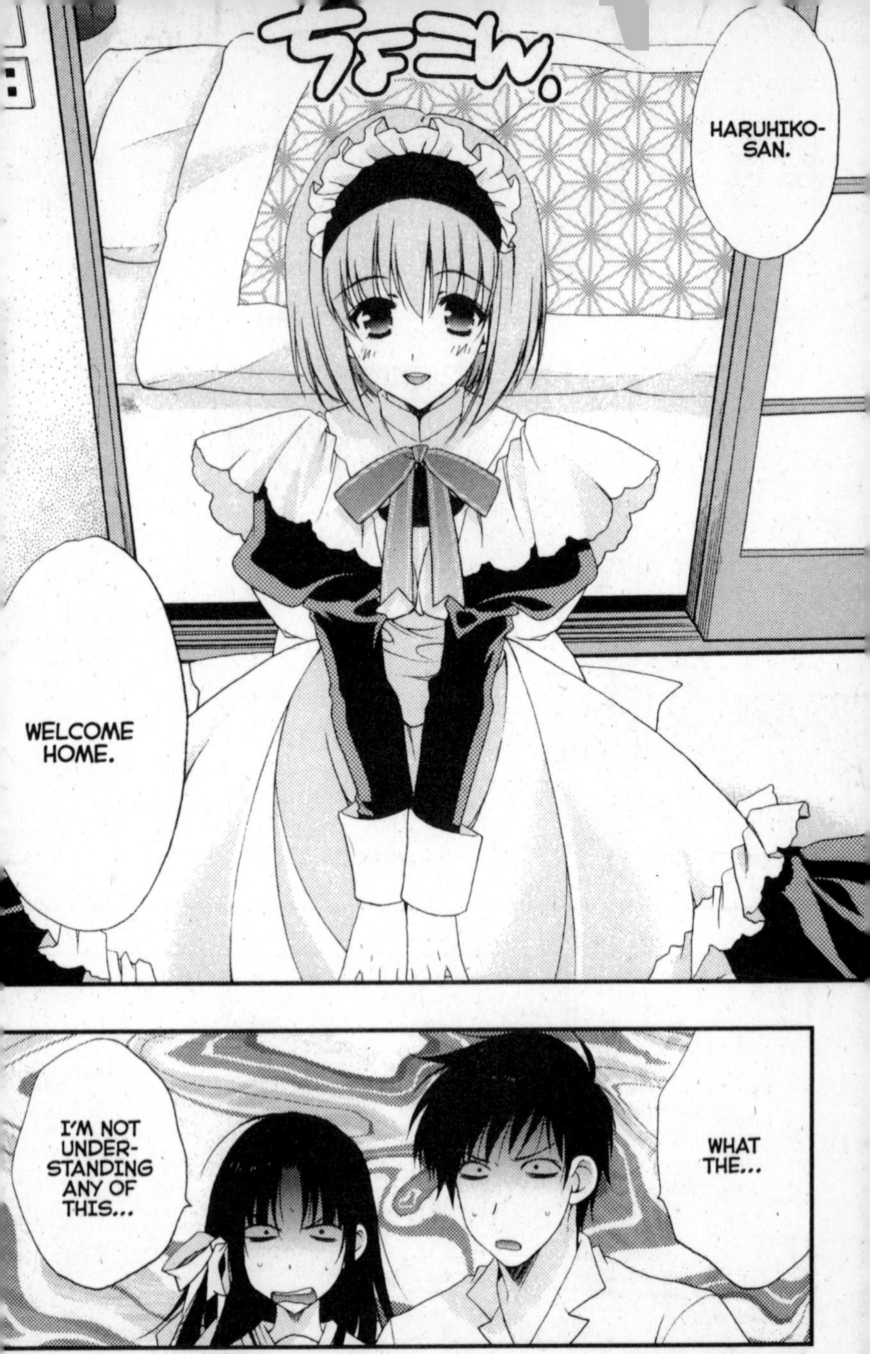
ちょこん。
HARUHIKO-SAN.
WELCOME HOME.
WHAT THE...
I'M NOT UNDER-STANDING ANY OF THIS...

Life-1 ✤ END

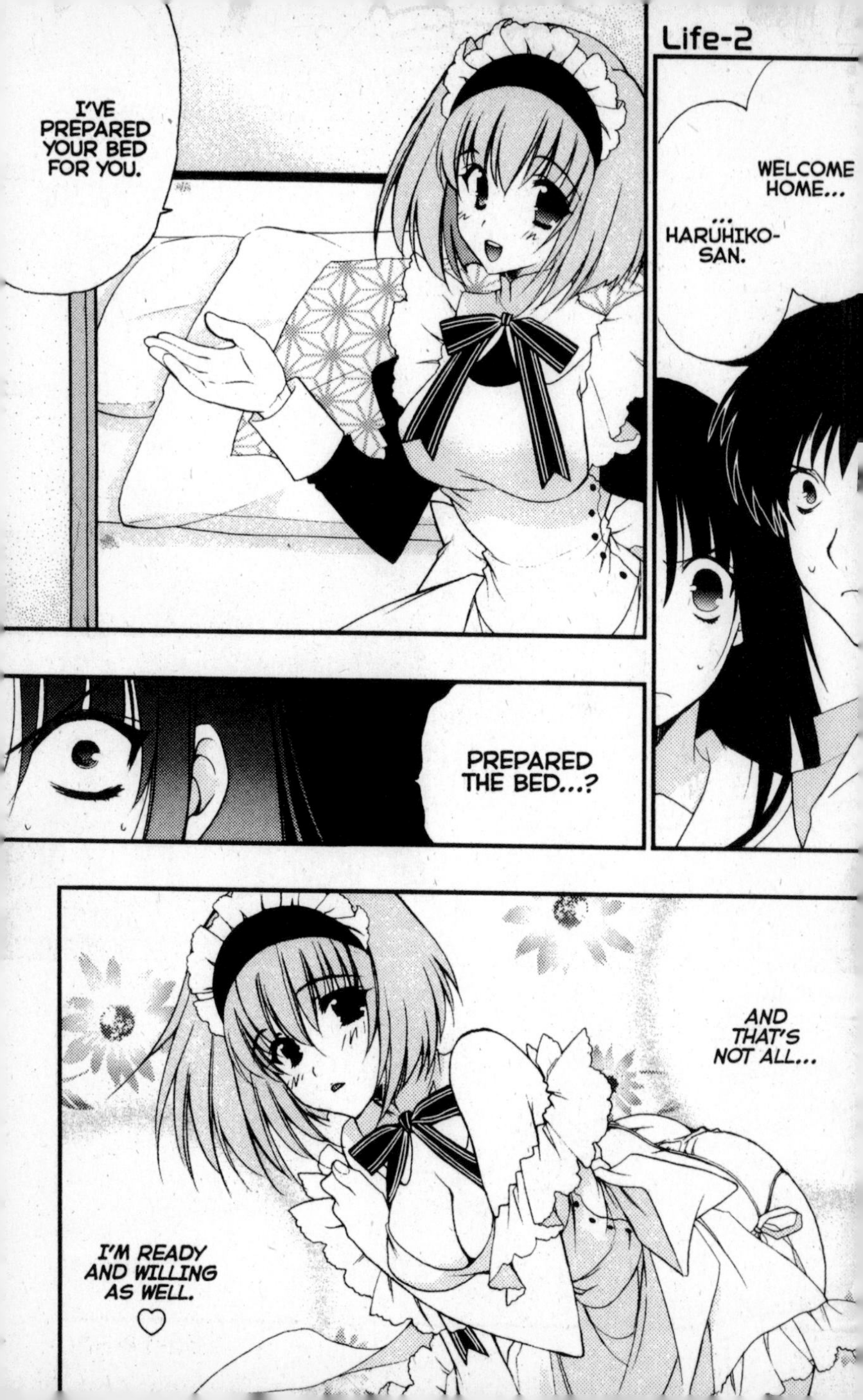
WELCOME HOME...
... HARUHIKO-SAN.
I'VE PREPARED YOUR BED FOR YOU.
PREPARED THE BED...?
AND THAT'S NOT ALL...
I'M READY AND WILLING AS WELL. ♡

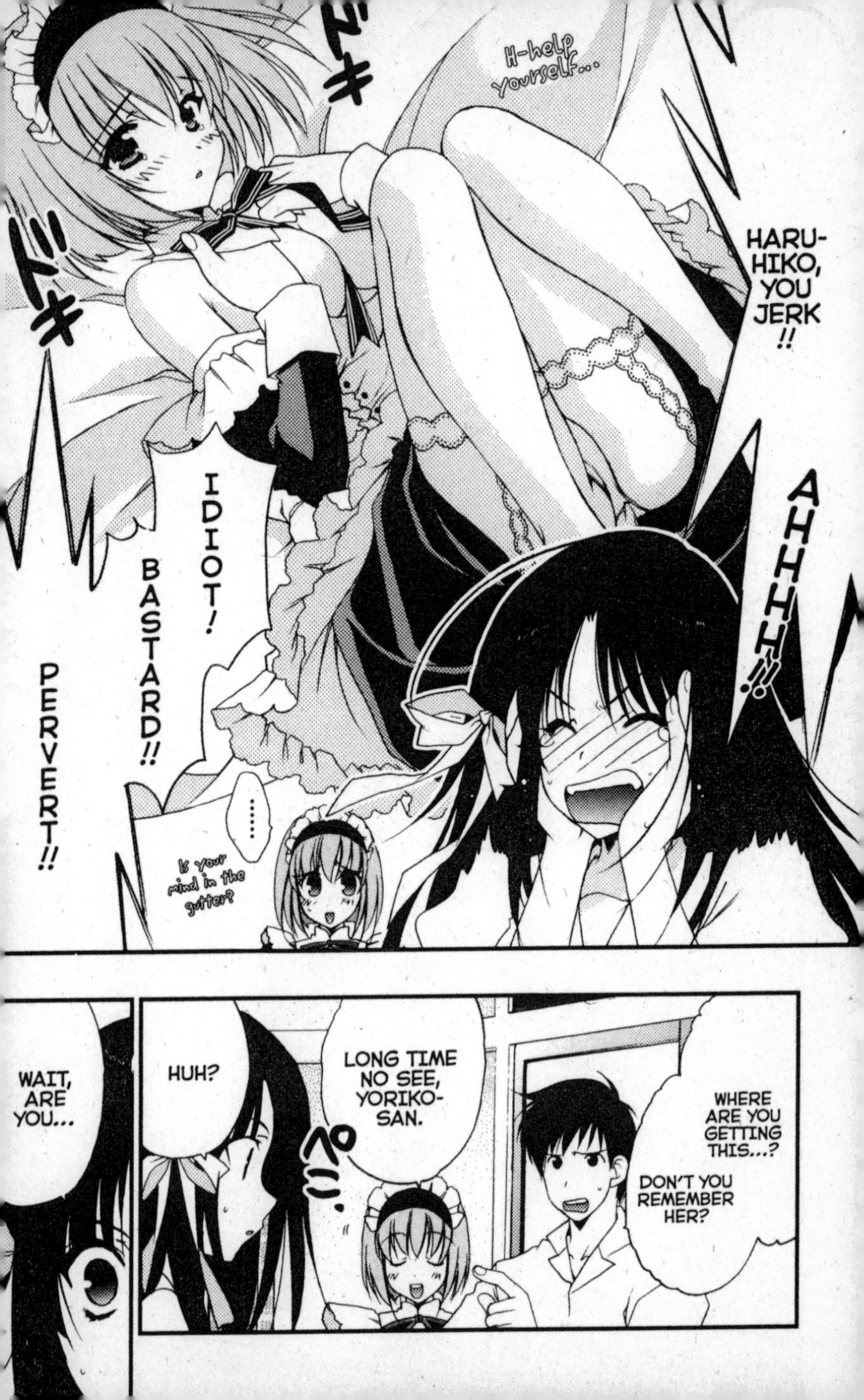
ドキ
H-help yourself...
HARU-HIKO, YOU JERK!!
AHHHHH!!
ドキ
IDIOT! BASTARD!! PERVERT!!
......
Is your mind in the gutter?
WHERE ARE YOU GETTING THIS...?
DON'T YOU REMEMBER HER?
LONG TIME NO SEE, YORIKO-SAN.
ぺこ
HUH?
WAIT, ARE YOU...

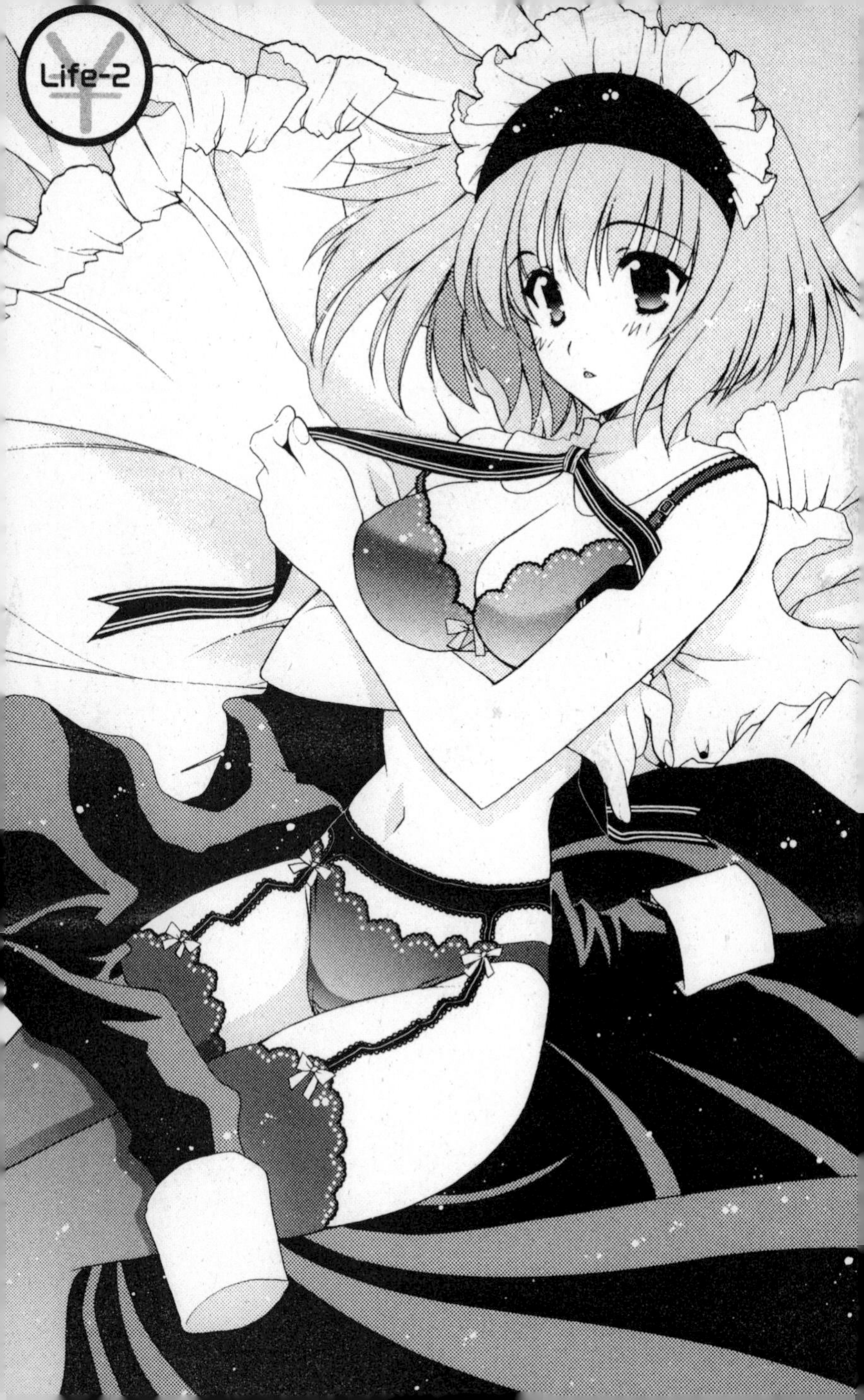
Life-2

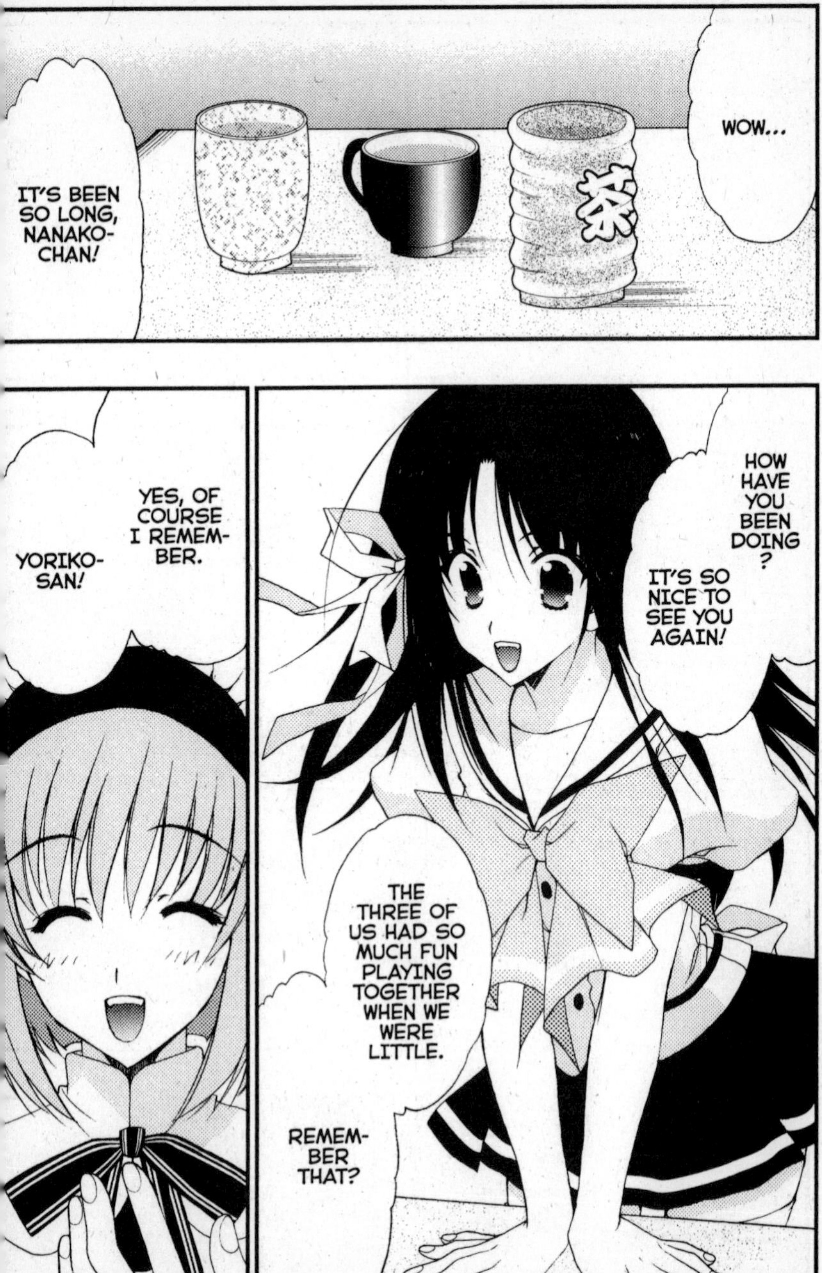
WOW...
IT'S BEEN SO LONG, NANAKO-CHAN!
HOW HAVE YOU BEEN DOING?
IT'S SO NICE TO SEE YOU AGAIN!
THE THREE OF US HAD SO MUCH FUN PLAYING TOGETHER WHEN WE WERE LITTLE.
REMEMBER THAT?
YES, OF COURSE I REMEMBER.
YORIKO-SAN!

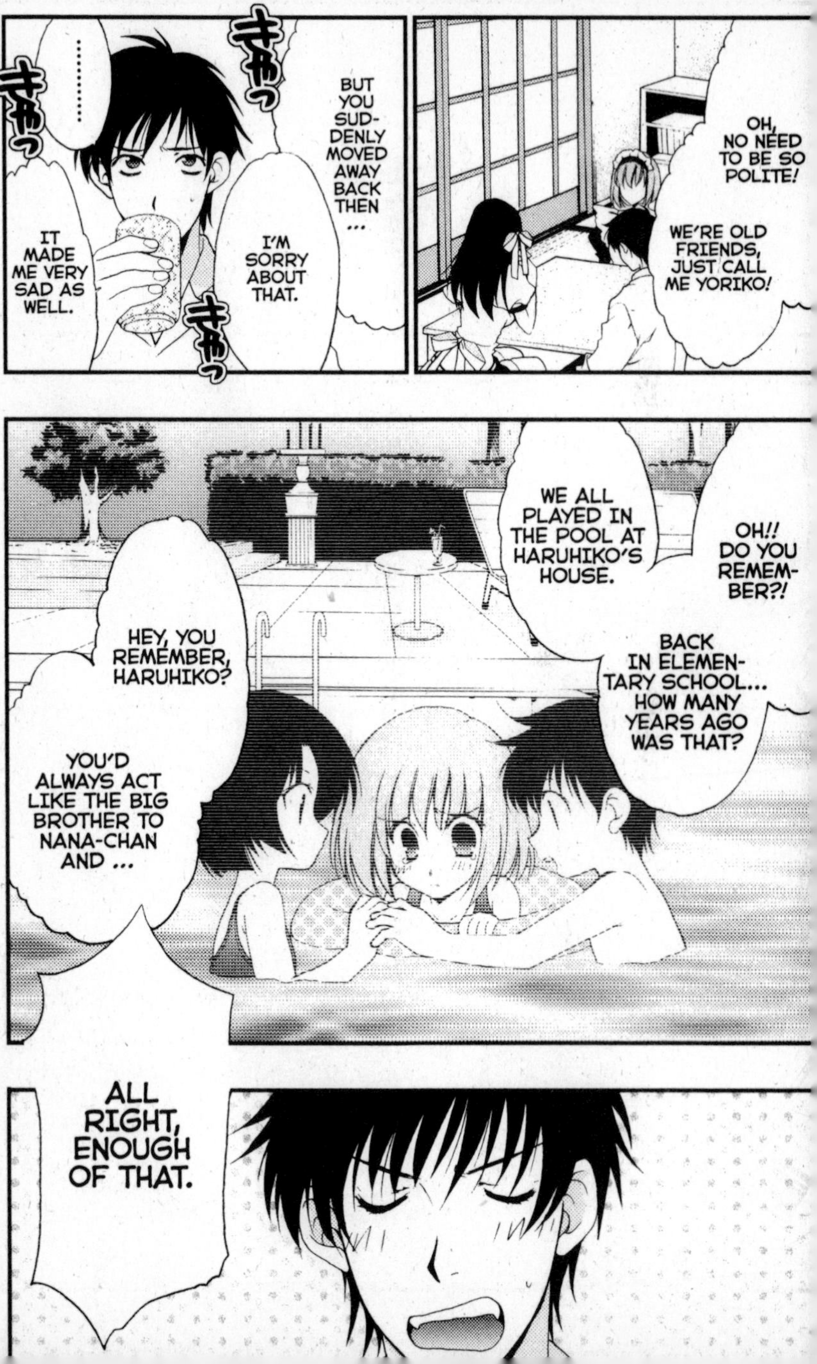
OH, NO NEED TO BE SO POLITE!
WE'RE OLD FRIENDS, JUST CALL ME YORIKO!
きゃっ
BUT YOU SUDDENLY MOVED AWAY BACK THEN ...
......
きゃっ
I'M SORRY ABOUT THAT.
IT MADE ME VERY SAD AS WELL.
きゃっ
OH!! DO YOU REMEMBER?!
WE ALL PLAYED IN THE POOL AT HARUHIKO'S HOUSE.
BACK IN ELEMENTARY SCHOOL... HOW MANY YEARS AGO WAS THAT?
HEY, YOU REMEMBER, HARUHIKO?
YOU'D ALWAYS ACT LIKE THE BIG BROTHER TO NANA-CHAN AND ...
ALL RIGHT, ENOUGH OF THAT.

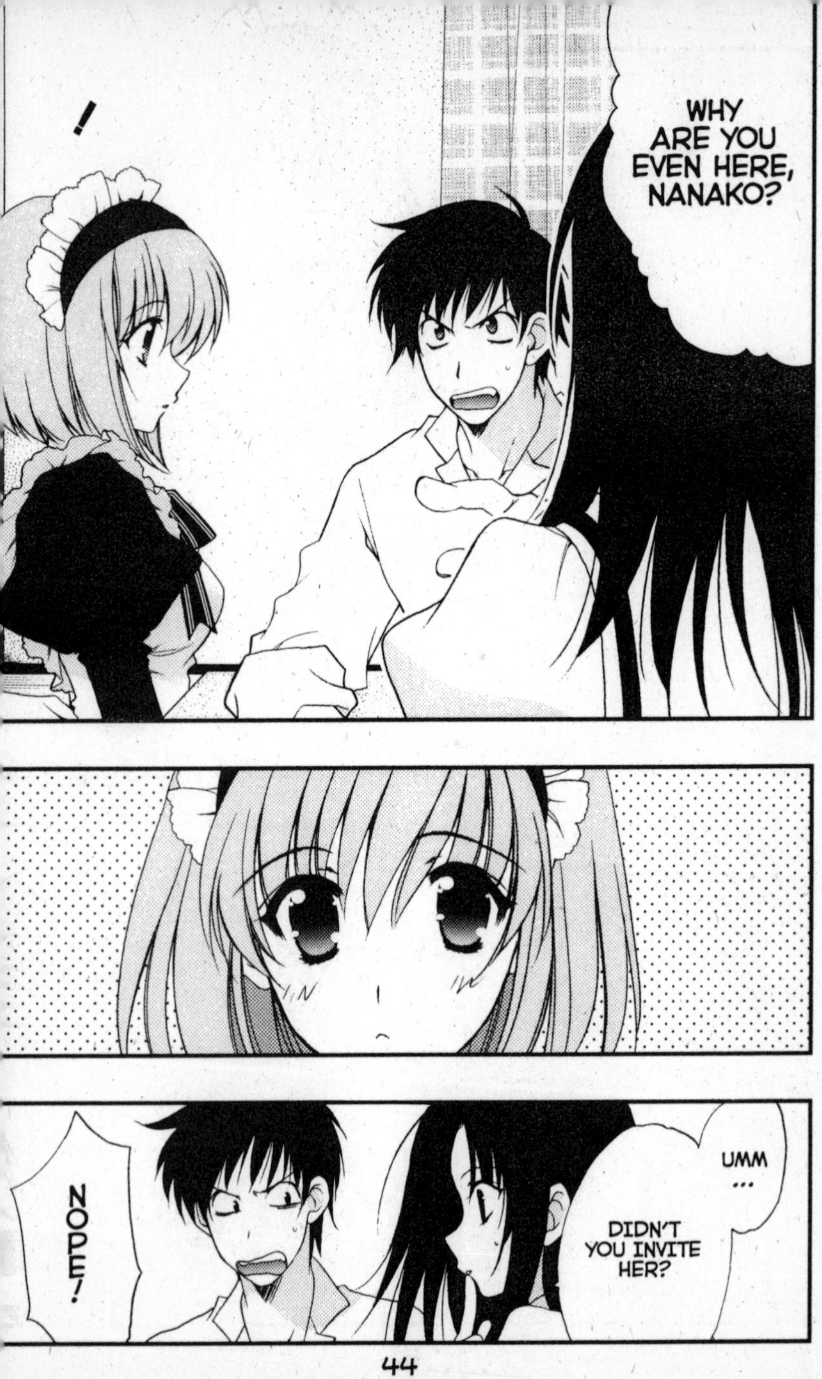
WHY ARE YOU EVEN HERE, NANAKO?
!
UMM ...
DIDN'T YOU INVITE HER?
NOPE!

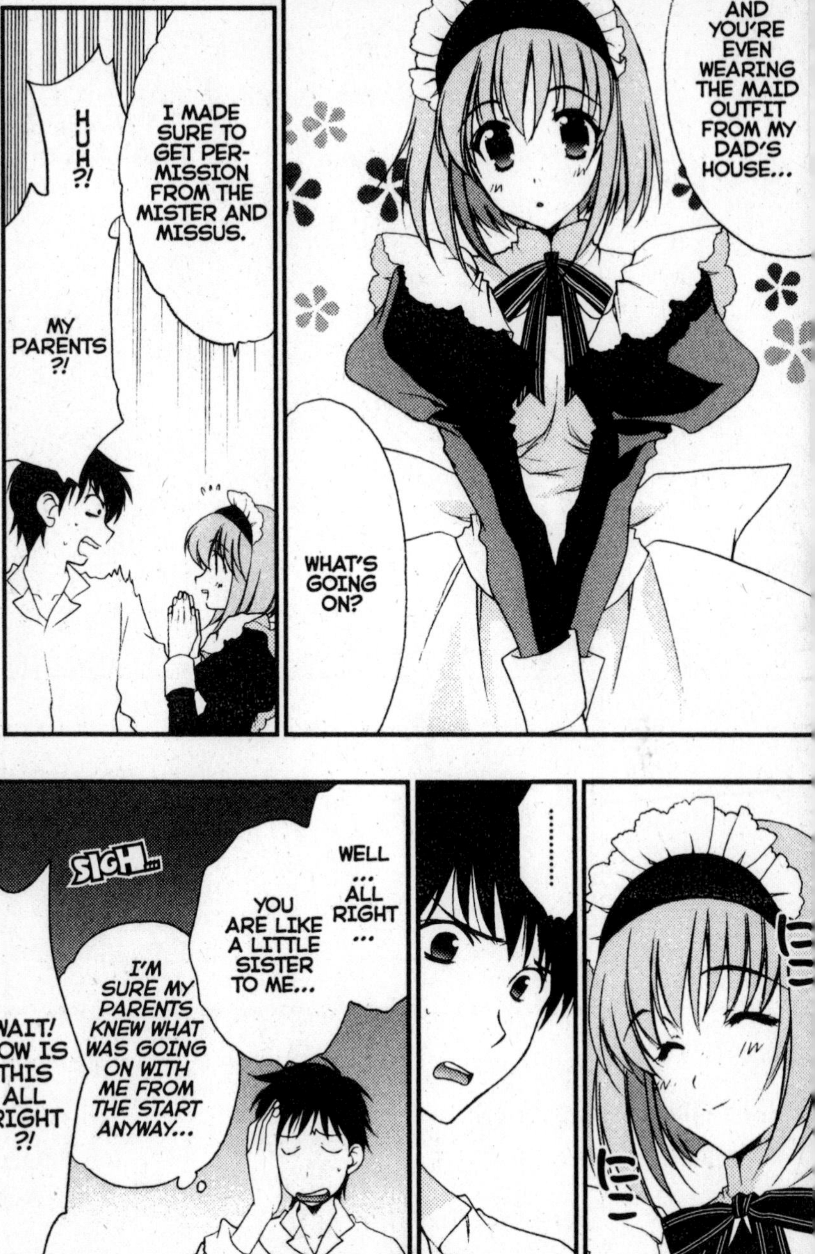
AND YOU'RE EVEN WEARING THE MAID OUTFIT FROM MY DAD'S HOUSE...
WHAT'S GOING ON?
I MADE SURE TO GET PERMISSION FROM THE MISTER AND MISSUS.
HUH?!
MY PARENTS?!
......
WELL ... ALL RIGHT ...
YOU ARE LIKE A LITTLE SISTER TO ME...
SIGH...
I'M SURE MY PARENTS KNEW WHAT WAS GOING ON WITH ME FROM THE START ANYWAY...
WAIT! HOW IS THIS ALL RIGHT?!

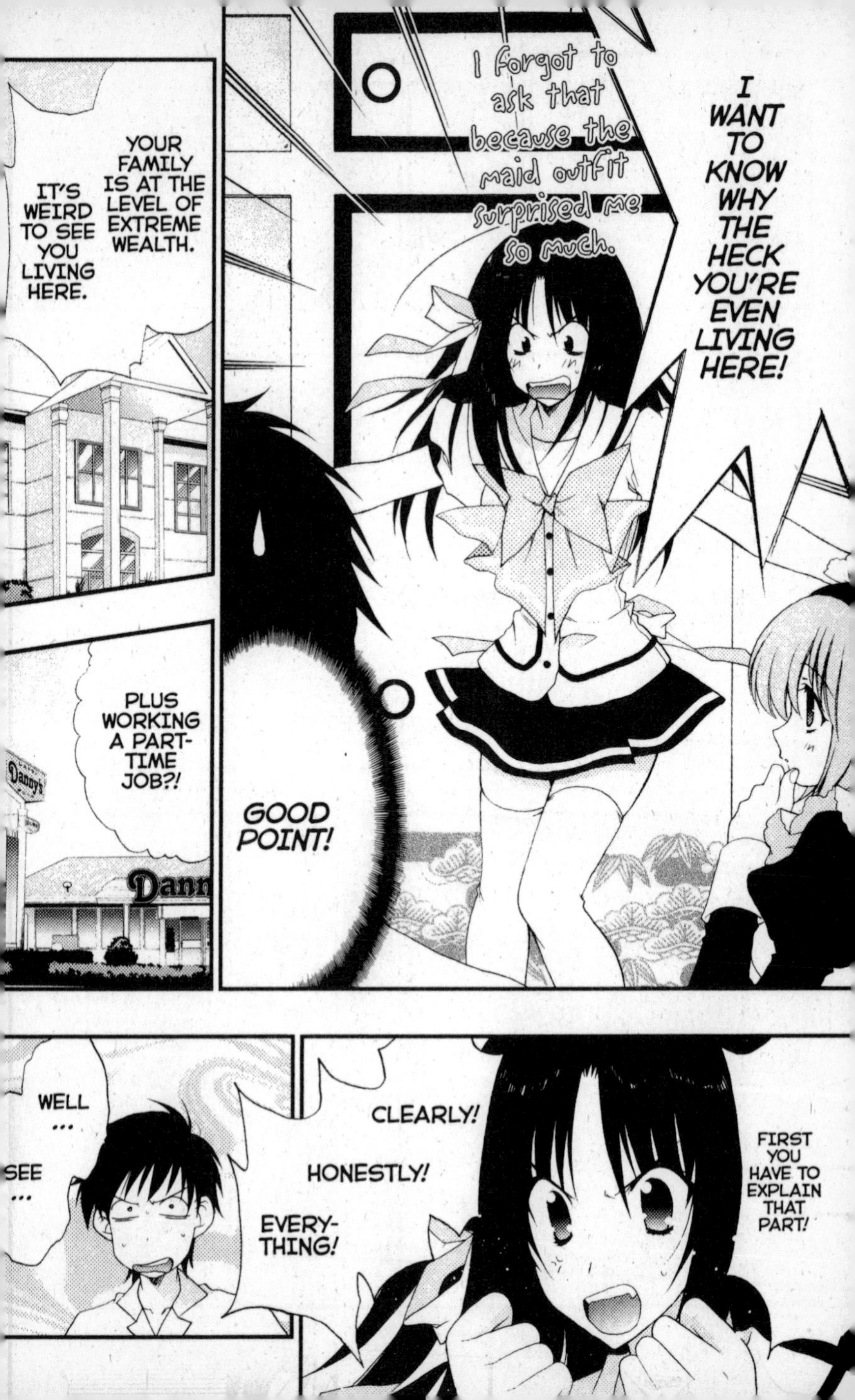
I WANT TO KNOW WHY THE HECK YOU'RE EVEN LIVING HERE!
I forgot to ask that because the maid outfit surprised me so much.
GOOD POINT!
YOUR FAMILY IS AT THE LEVEL OF EXTREME WEALTH.
IT'S WEIRD TO SEE YOU LIVING HERE.
PLUS WORKING A PART-TIME JOB?!
Danny's
Dann
FIRST YOU HAVE TO EXPLAIN THAT PART!
CLEARLY!
HONESTLY!
EVERY-THING!
WELL ...
SEE ...

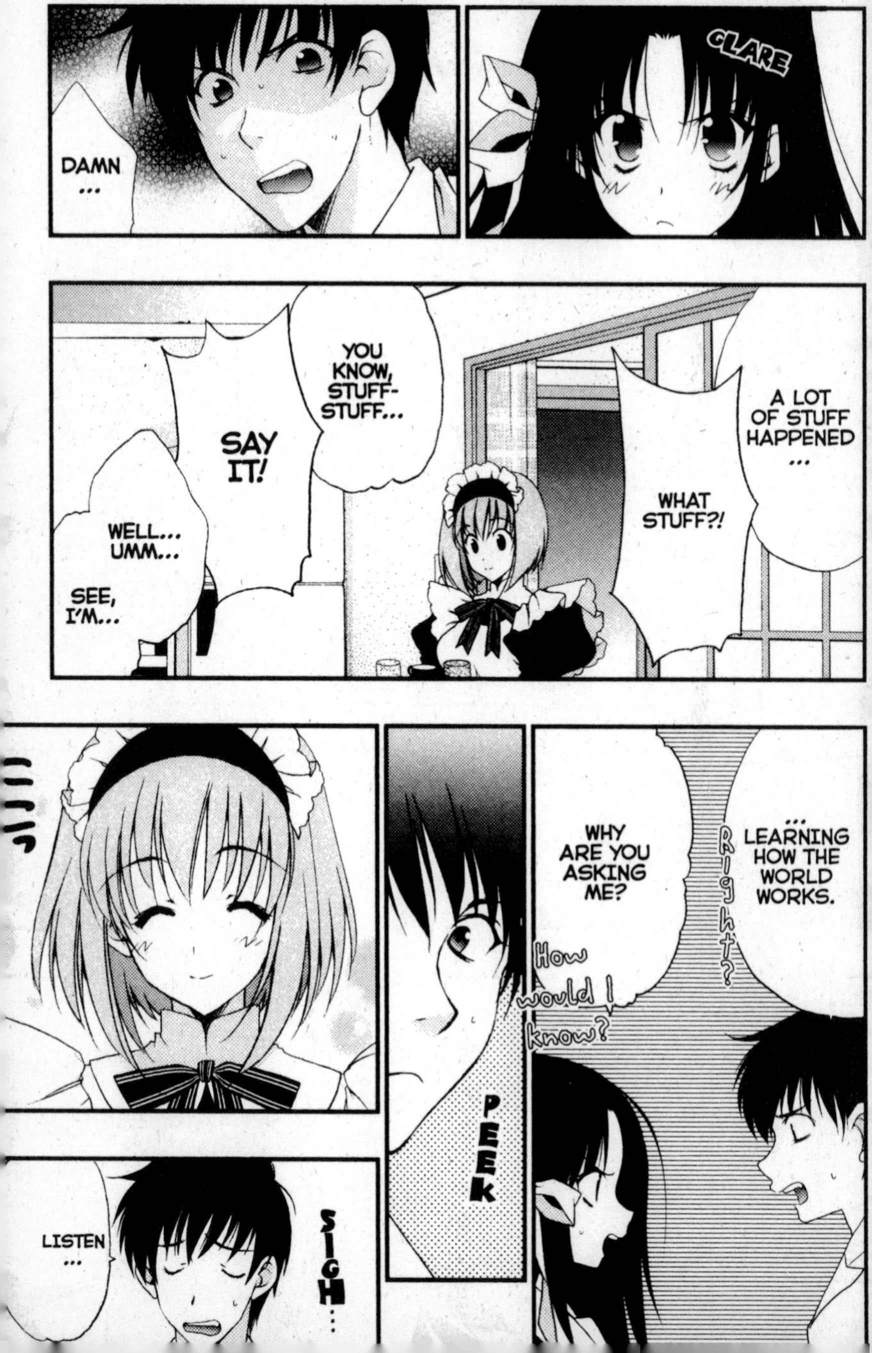
GLARE
DAMN ...
A LOT OF STUFF HAPPENED ...
WHAT STUFF?!
YOU KNOW, STUFF-STUFF...
SAY IT!
WELL... UMM...
SEE, I'M...
... LEARNING HOW THE WORLD WORKS.
Right?
WHY ARE YOU ASKING ME?
How would I know?
PEEK
SIGH...
LISTEN ...

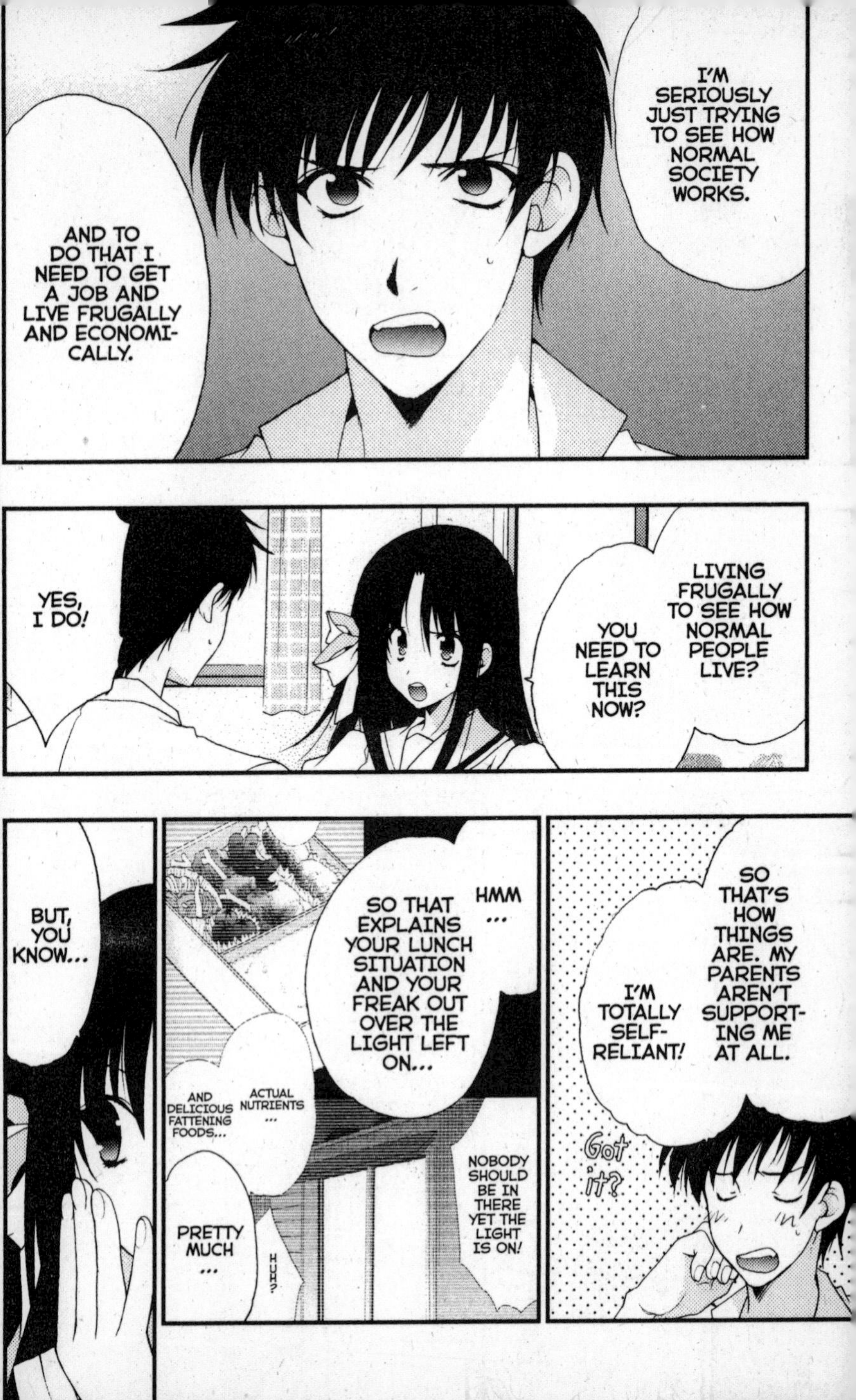

I'M SERIOUSLY JUST TRYING TO SEE HOW NORMAL SOCIETY WORKS.
AND TO DO THAT I NEED TO GET A JOB AND LIVE FRUGALLY AND ECONOMI-CALLY.
LIVING FRUGALLY TO SEE HOW NORMAL PEOPLE LIVE?
YOU NEED TO LEARN THIS NOW?
YES, I DO!
SO THAT'S HOW THINGS ARE. MY PARENTS AREN'T SUPPORT-ING ME AT ALL.
I'M TOTALLY SELF-RELIANT!
Got it?
HMM...
SO THAT EXPLAINS YOUR LUNCH SITUATION AND YOUR FREAK OUT OVER THE LIGHT LEFT ON...
NOBODY SHOULD BE IN THERE YET THE LIGHT IS ON!
ACTUAL NUTRIENTS...
AND DELICIOUS FATTENING FOODS...
HUH?
PRETTY MUCH...
BUT, YOU KNOW...

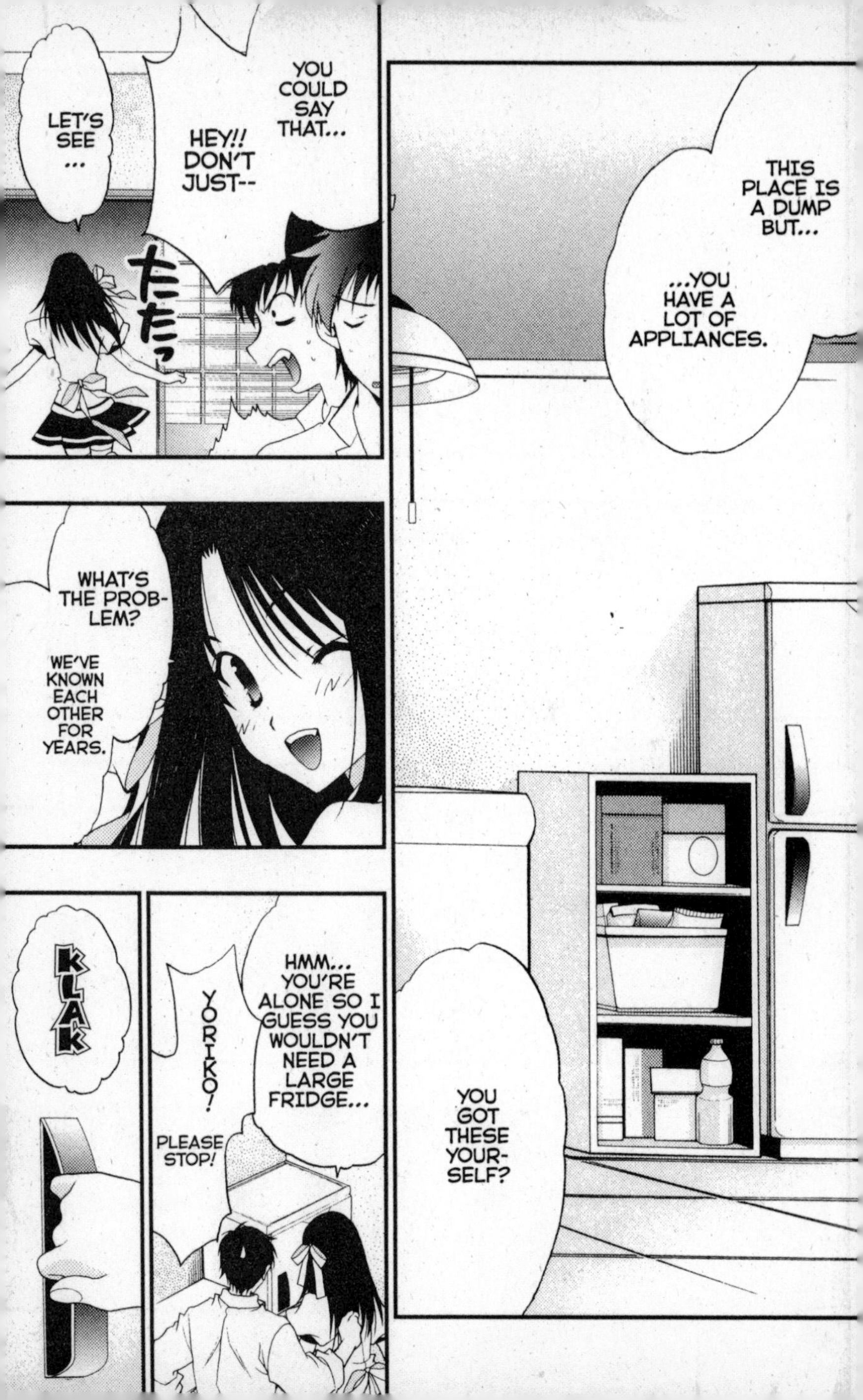
THIS PLACE IS A DUMP BUT...
...YOU HAVE A LOT OF APPLIANCES.
YOU GOT THESE YOURSELF?
YOU COULD SAY THAT...
HEY!! DON'T JUST--
LET'S SEE ...
たたっ
WHAT'S THE PROB-LEM?
WE'VE KNOWN EACH OTHER FOR YEARS.
HMM... YOU'RE ALONE SO I GUESS YOU WOULDN'T NEED A LARGE FRIDGE...
YORIKO!
PLEASE STOP!
KLAK

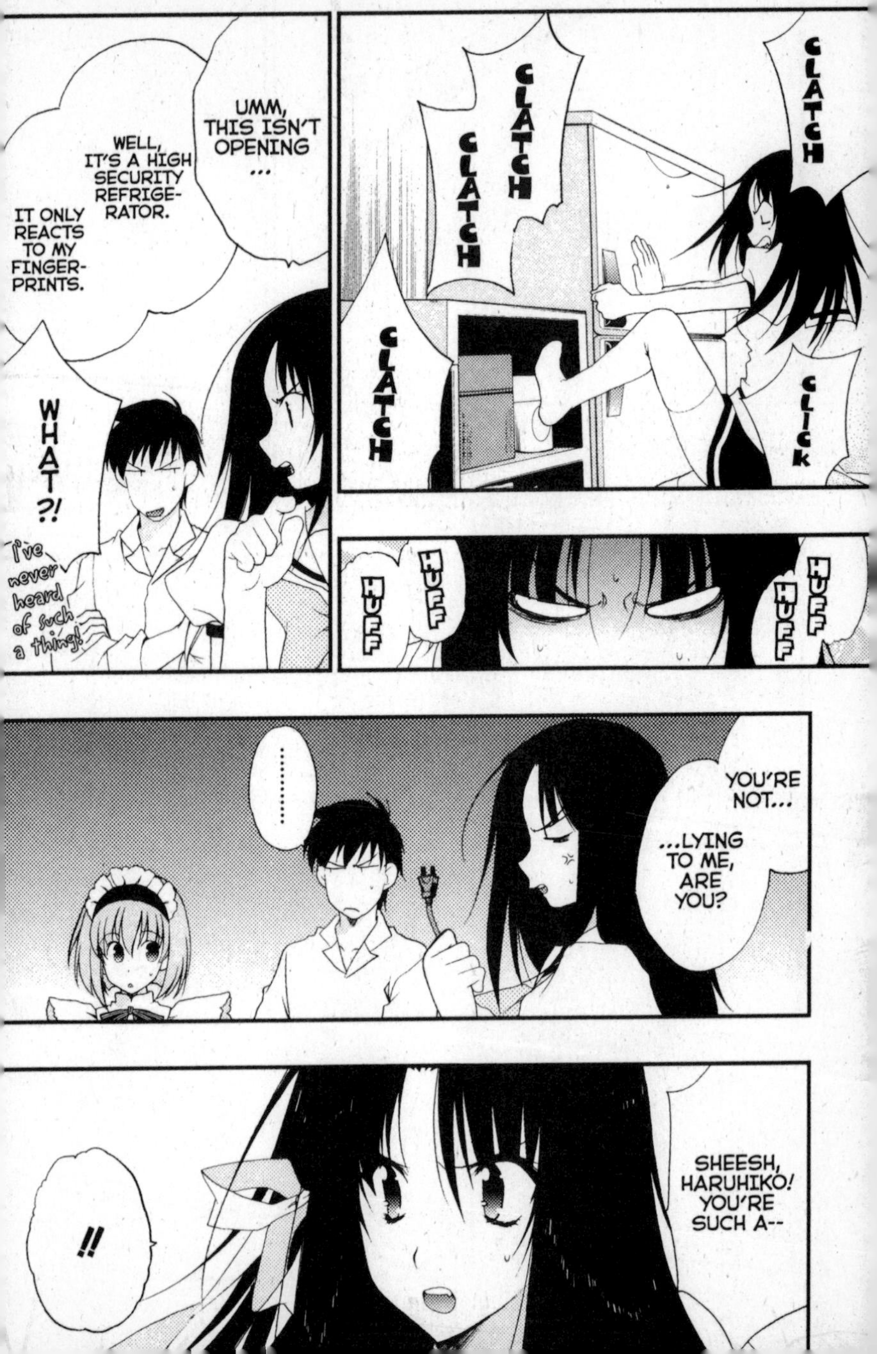
CLATCH
CLATCH
CLATCH
CLATCH
CLICK
HUFF HUFF
HUFF HUFF
UMM, THIS ISN'T OPENING...
WELL, IT'S A HIGH SECURITY REFRIGERATOR.
IT ONLY REACTS TO MY FINGERPRINTS.
WHAT?!
I've never heard of such a thing!
YOU'RE NOT...
...LYING TO ME, ARE YOU?
....
SHEESH, HARUHIKO! YOU'RE SUCH A--
!!

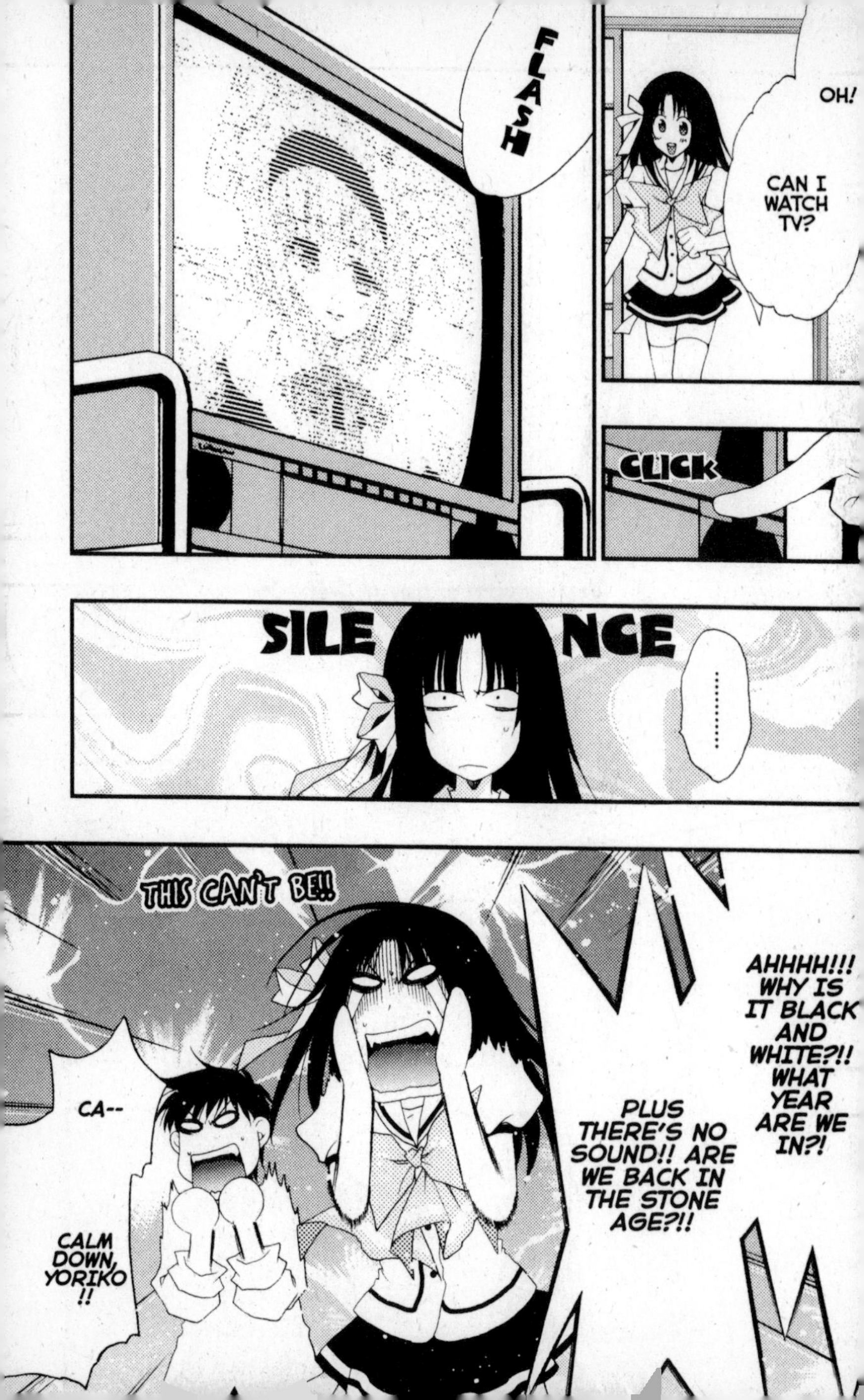
OH!
CAN I WATCH TV?
CLICK
FLASH
SILENCE
......
AHHHH!!! WHY IS IT BLACK AND WHITE?!! WHAT YEAR ARE WE IN?!
PLUS THERE'S NO SOUND!! ARE WE BACK IN THE STONE AGE?!!
THIS CAN'T BE!!
CA--
CALM DOWN, YORIKO !!

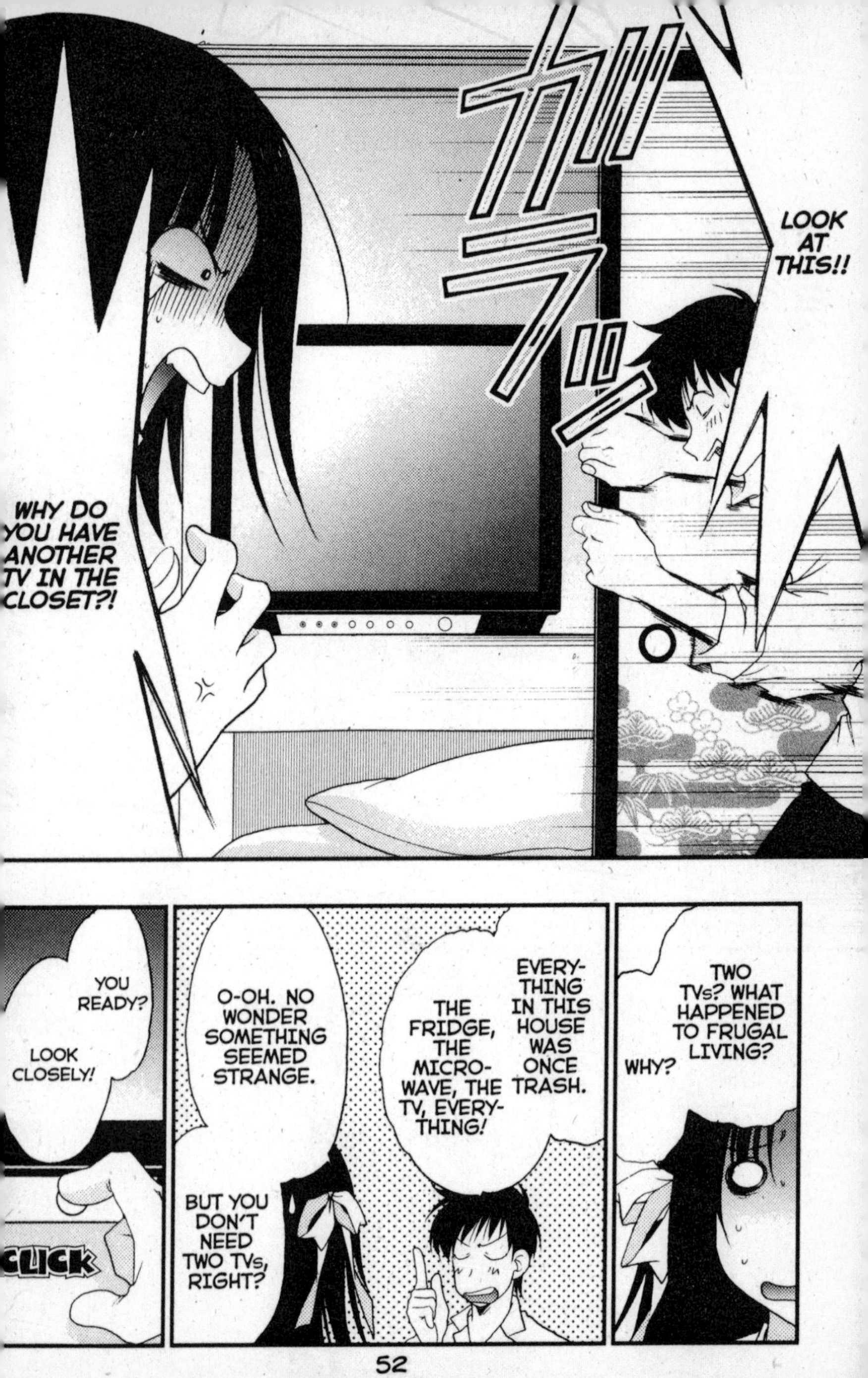
LOOK AT THIS!!
WHY DO YOU HAVE ANOTHER TV IN THE CLOSET?!
TWO TVs? WHAT HAPPENED TO FRUGAL LIVING?
WHY?
EVERY-THING IN THIS HOUSE WAS ONCE TRASH.
THE FRIDGE, THE MICRO-WAVE, THE TV, EVERY-THING!
O-OH. NO WONDER SOMETHING SEEMED STRANGE.
BUT YOU DON'T NEED TWO TVs, RIGHT?
YOU READY?
LOOK CLOSELY!
CLICK

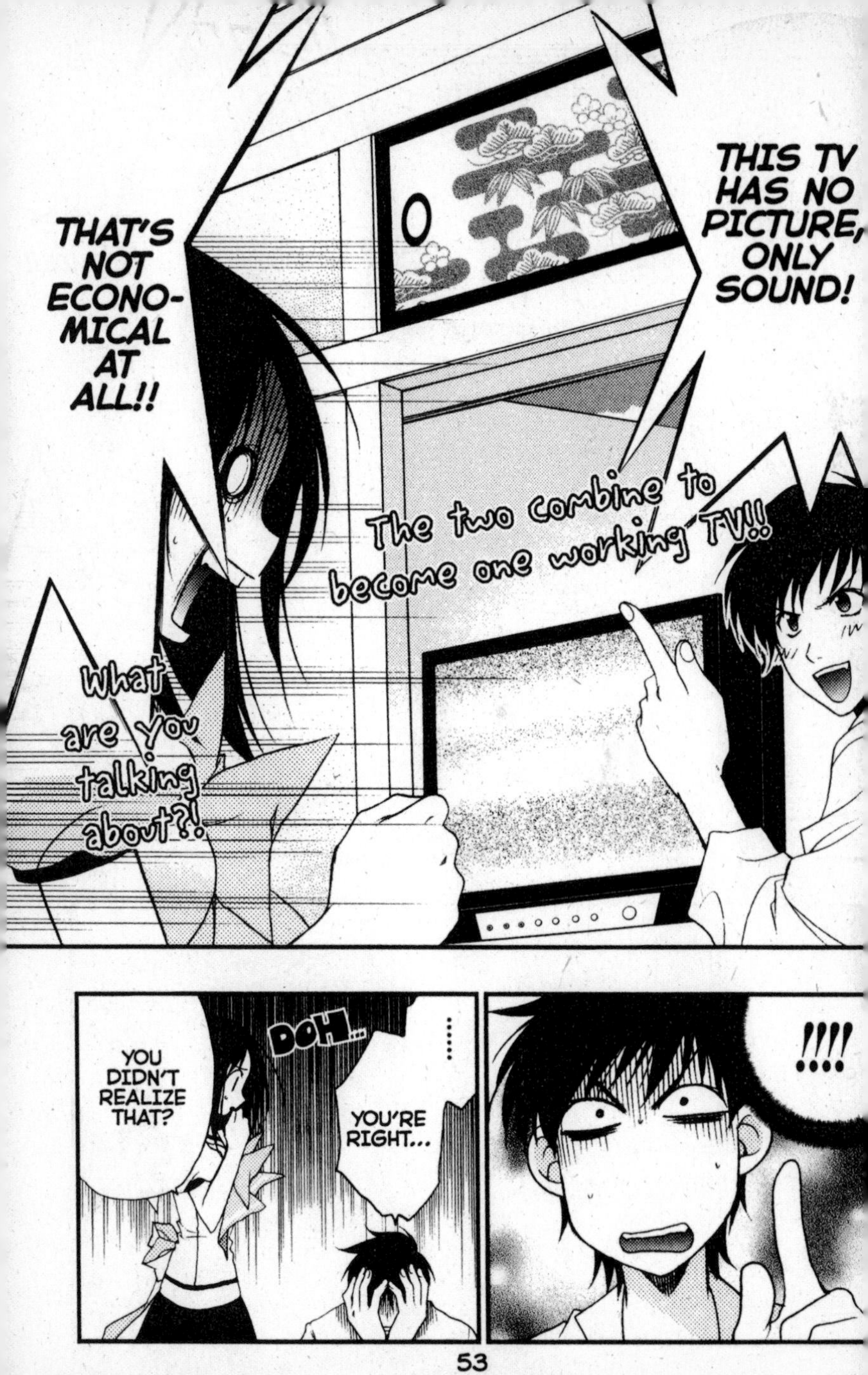
THIS TV HAS NO PICTURE, ONLY SOUND!
The two combine to become one working TV!!
THAT'S NOT ECONOMICAL AT ALL!!
What are you talking about?!
!!!!
......
DOH...
YOU'RE RIGHT...
YOU DIDN'T REALIZE THAT?

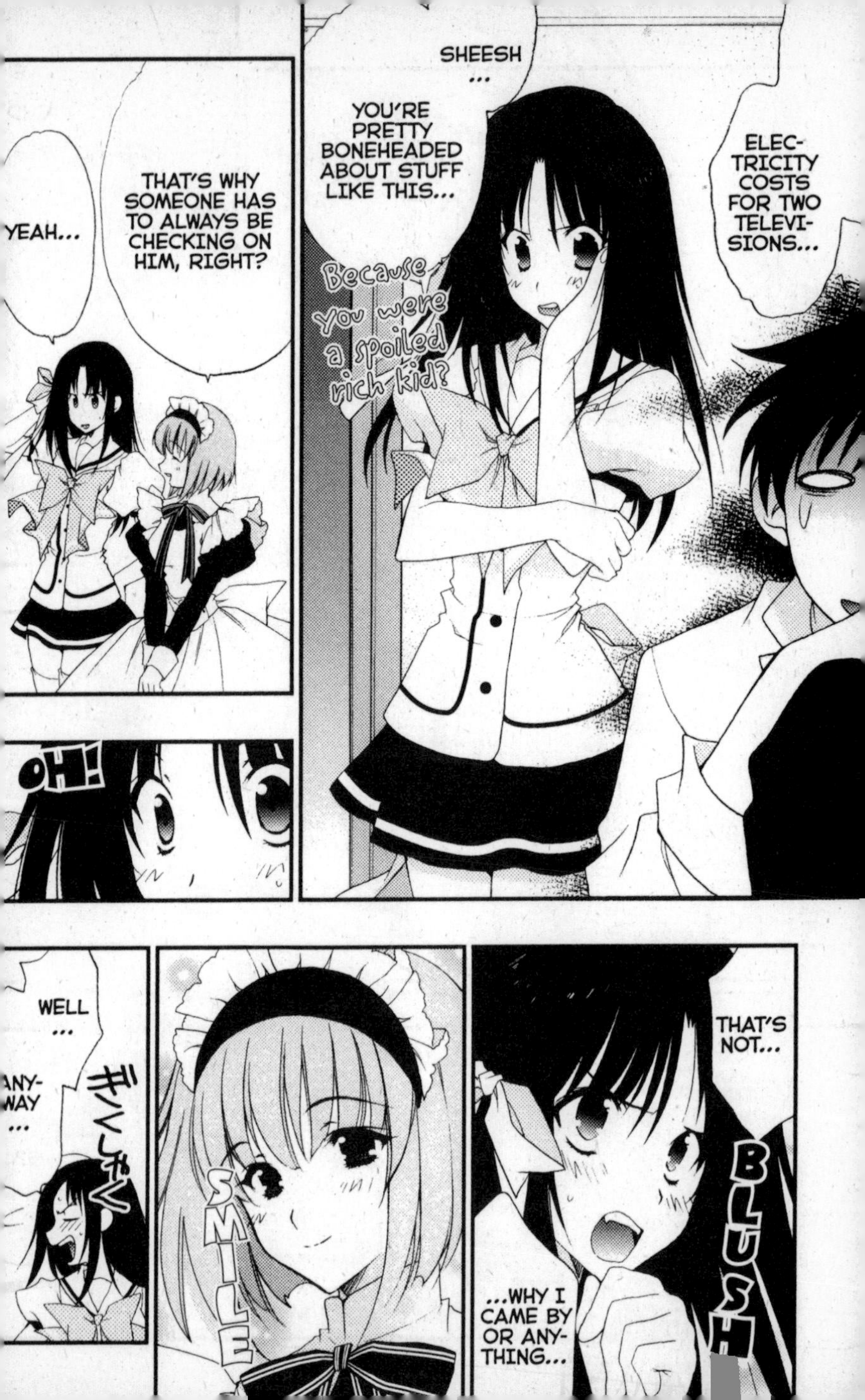
ELECTRICITY COSTS FOR TWO TELEVISIONS...
SHEESH...
YOU'RE PRETTY BONEHEADED ABOUT STUFF LIKE THIS...
Because you were a spoiled rich kid?
THAT'S WHY SOMEONE HAS TO ALWAYS BE CHECKING ON HIM, RIGHT?
YEAH...
OH!
THAT'S NOT...
BLUSH
...WHY I CAME BY OR ANYTHING...
SMILE
WELL...
ANYWAY...
ぎくしゃく

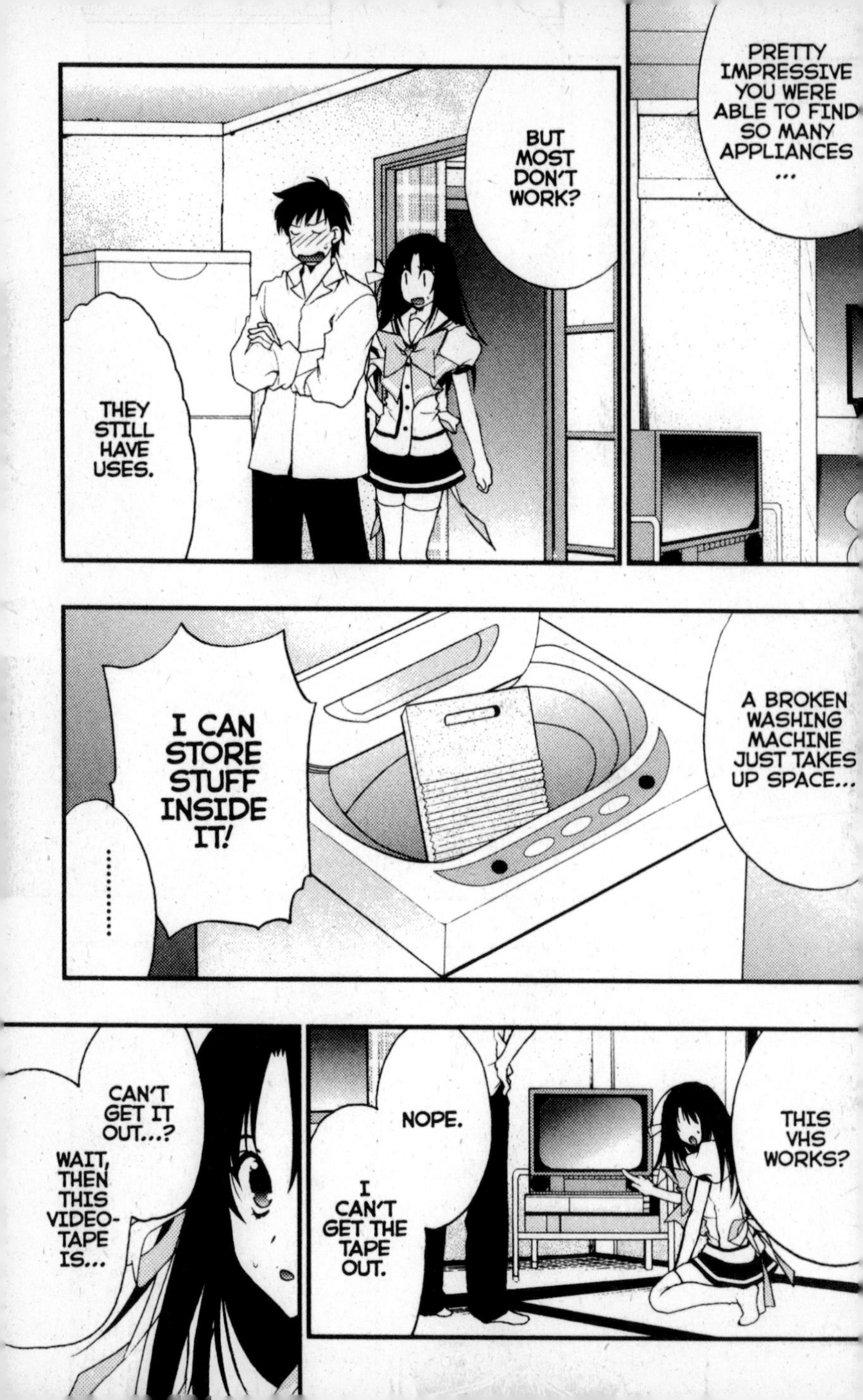
PRETTY IMPRESSIVE YOU WERE ABLE TO FIND SO MANY APPLIANCES ...
BUT MOST DON'T WORK?
THEY STILL HAVE USES.
A BROKEN WASHING MACHINE JUST TAKES UP SPACE...
I CAN STORE STUFF INSIDE IT!
....
THIS VHS WORKS?
NOPE.
I CAN'T GET THE TAPE OUT.
CAN'T GET IT OUT...?
WAIT, THEN THIS VIDEO-TAPE IS...

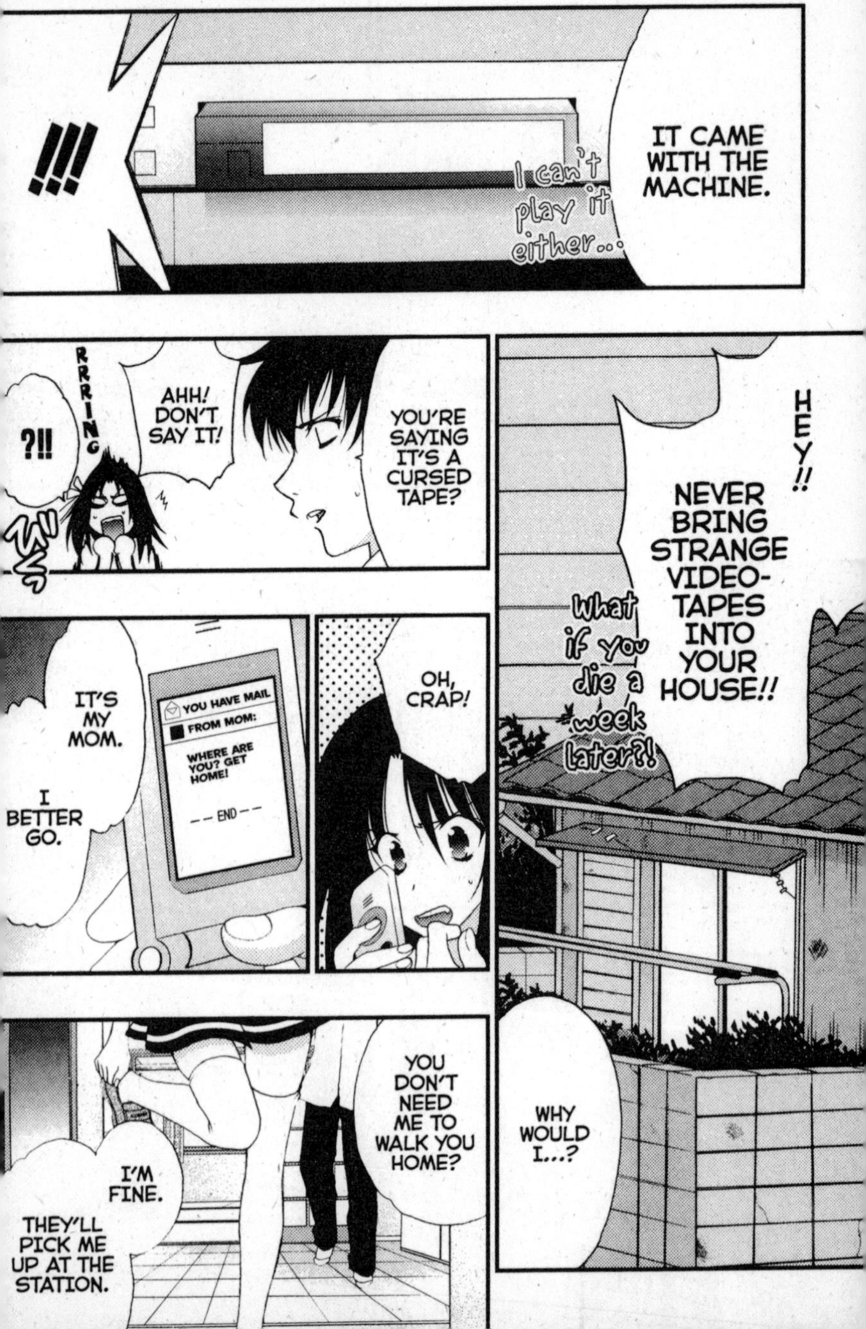
IT CAME WITH THE MACHINE.
I can't play it either...
!!!!
HEY!!
NEVER BRING STRANGE VIDEO-TAPES INTO YOUR HOUSE!!
What if you die a week later?!
WHY WOULD I...?
YOU'RE SAYING IT'S A CURSED TAPE?
AHH! DON'T SAY IT!
RRRING
?!!
OH, CRAP!
YOU HAVE MAIL
FROM MOM:
WHERE ARE YOU? GET HOME!
--- END ---
IT'S MY MOM.
I BETTER GO.
YOU DON'T NEED ME TO WALK YOU HOME?
I'M FINE.
THEY'LL PICK ME UP AT THE STATION.

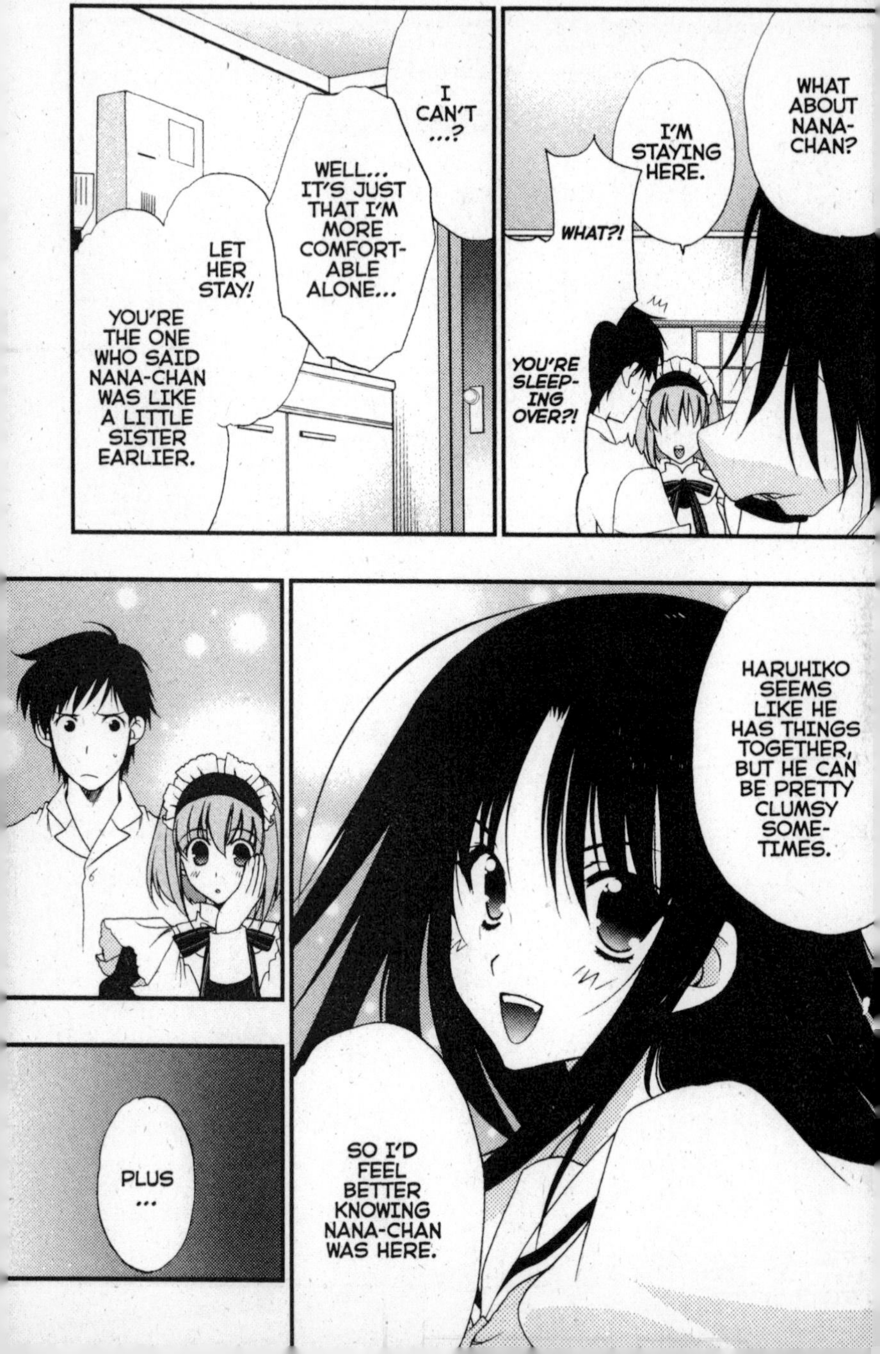
WHAT ABOUT NANA-CHAN?
I'M STAYING HERE.
WHAT?!
YOU'RE SLEEP-ING OVER?!
I CAN'T ...?
WELL... IT'S JUST THAT I'M MORE COMFORT-ABLE ALONE...
LET HER STAY!
YOU'RE THE ONE WHO SAID NANA-CHAN WAS LIKE A LITTLE SISTER EARLIER.
HARUHIKO SEEMS LIKE HE HAS THINGS TOGETHER, BUT HE CAN BE PRETTY CLUMSY SOME-TIMES.
SO I'D FEEL BETTER KNOWING NANA-CHAN WAS HERE.
PLUS ...

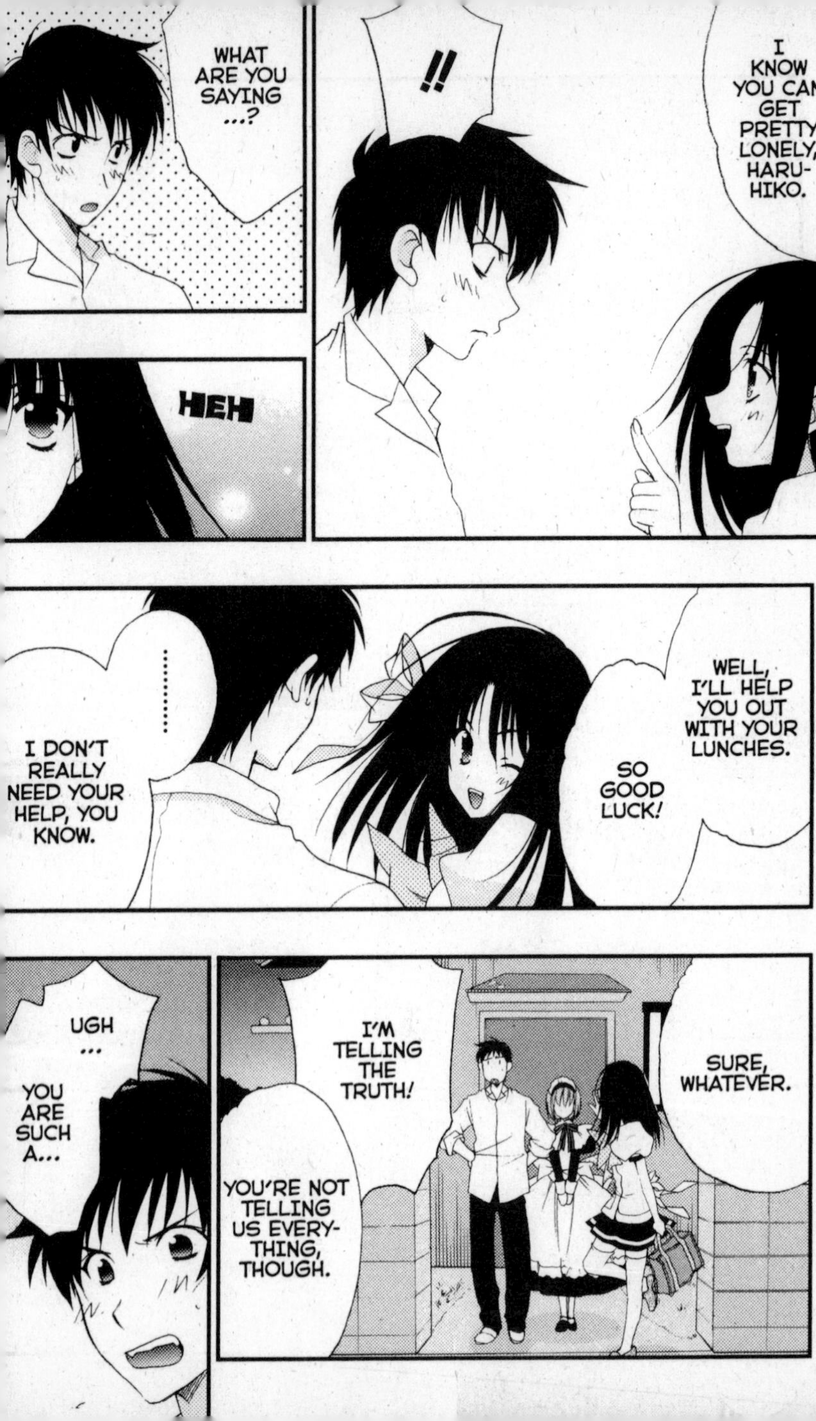
I KNOW YOU CAN GET PRETTY LONELY, HARU-HIKO.
!!
WHAT ARE YOU SAYING ...?
HEH
WELL, I'LL HELP YOU OUT WITH YOUR LUNCHES.
SO GOOD LUCK!
....
I DON'T REALLY NEED YOUR HELP, YOU KNOW.
SURE, WHATEVER.
I'M TELLING THE TRUTH!
YOU'RE NOT TELLING US EVERY-THING, THOUGH.
UGH ...
YOU ARE SUCH A...

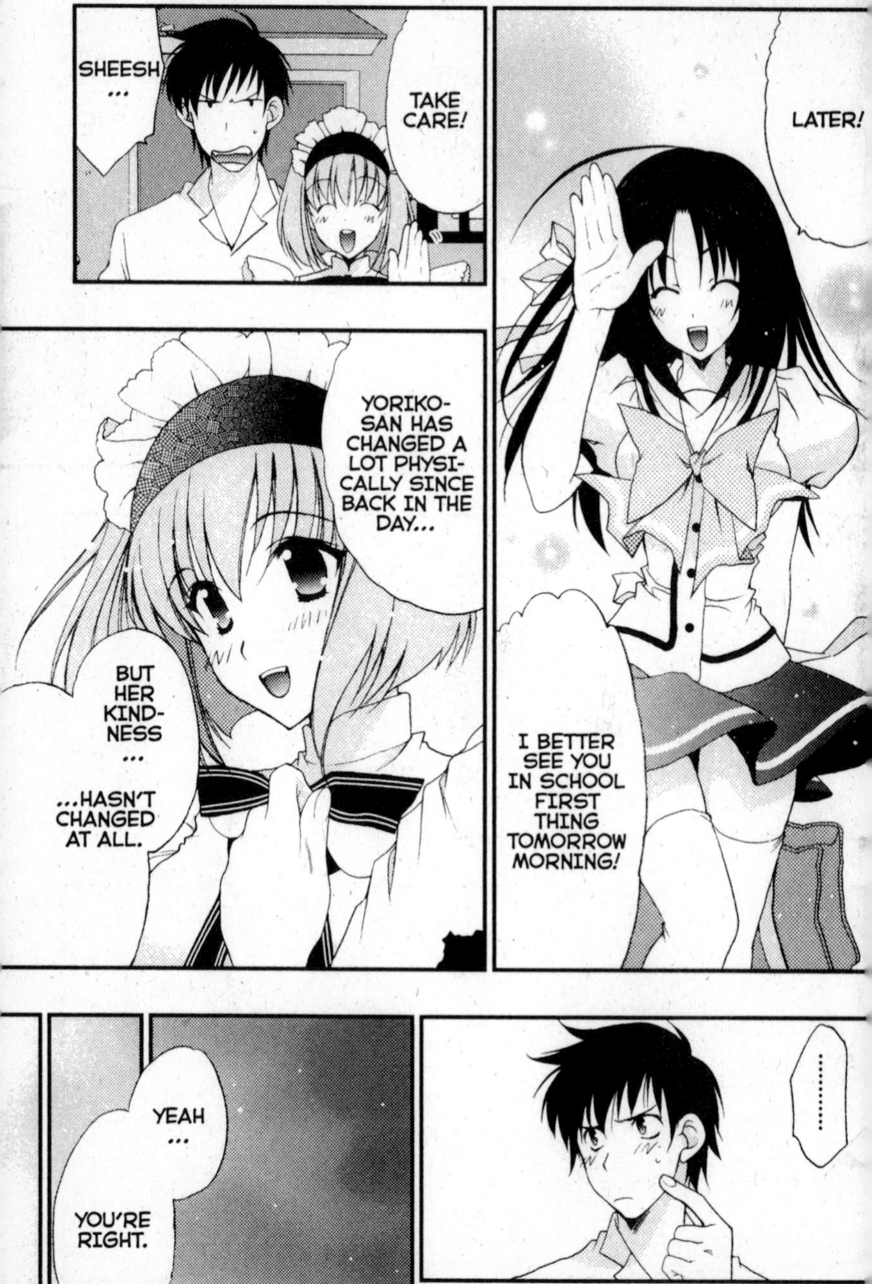
LATER!
I BETTER SEE YOU IN SCHOOL FIRST THING TOMORROW MORNING!
TAKE CARE!
SHEESH...
YORIKO-SAN HAS CHANGED A LOT PHYSICALLY SINCE BACK IN THE DAY...
BUT HER KINDNESS...
...HASN'T CHANGED AT ALL.
....
YEAH...
YOU'RE RIGHT.

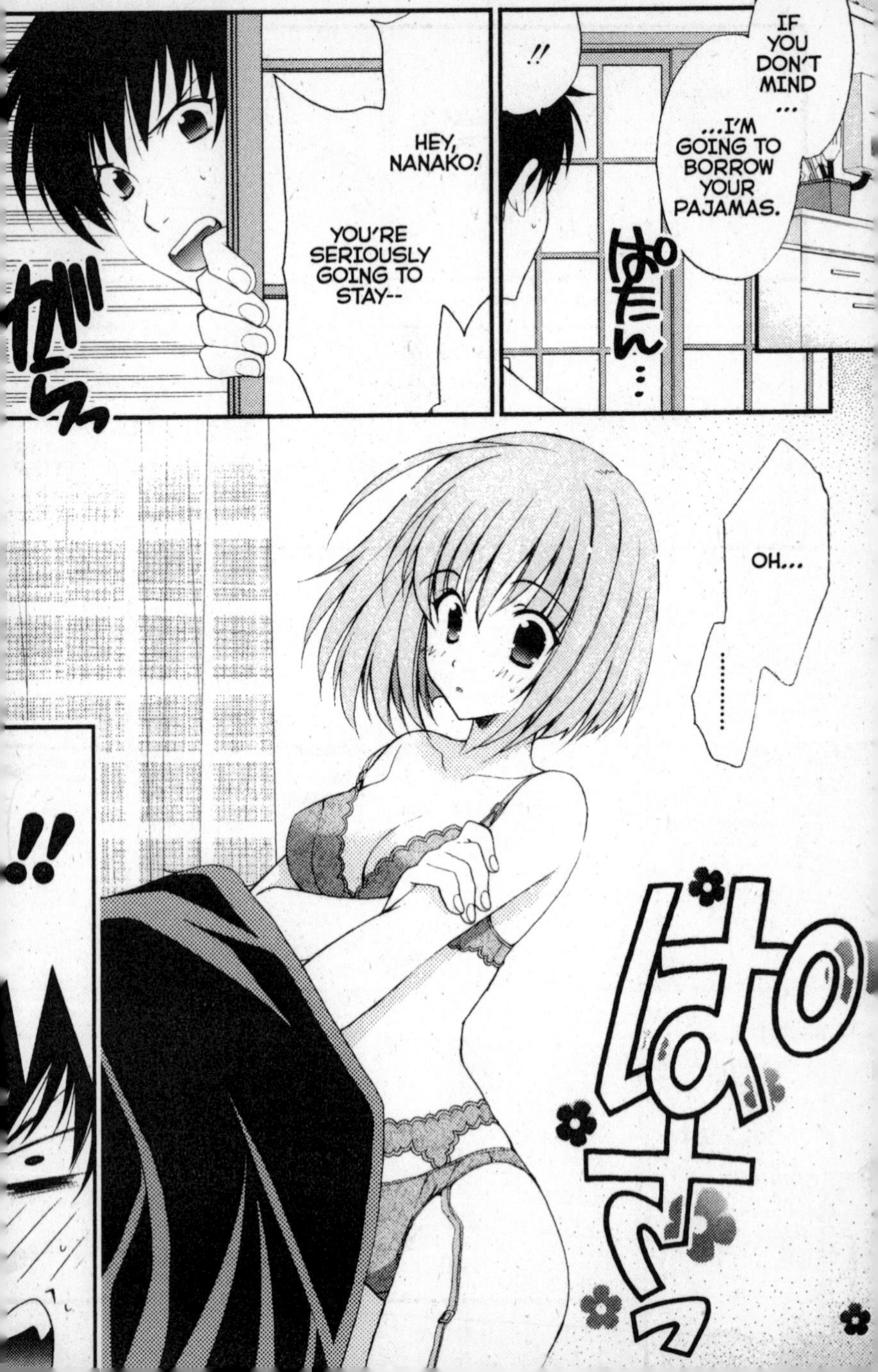
IF YOU DON'T MIND ...
...I'M GOING TO BORROW YOUR PAJAMAS.
!!
ぱたん…
HEY, NANAKO!
YOU'RE SERIOUSLY GOING TO STAY--
がらっ
OH...
......
ぱぁっ
!!

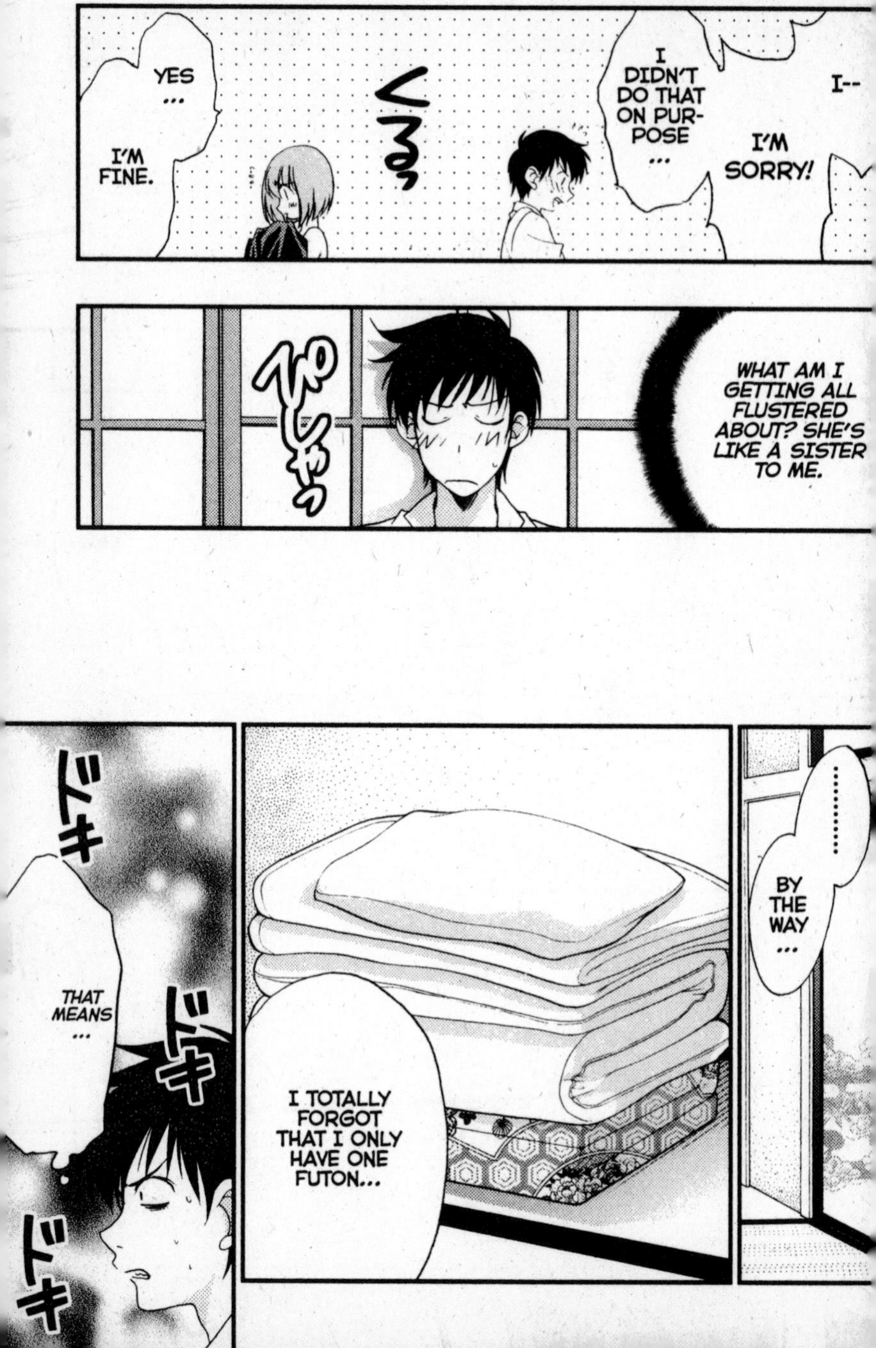
I--
I'M SORRY!
I DIDN'T DO THAT ON PUR-POSE...
くるっ
YES... I'M FINE.
WHAT AM I GETTING ALL FLUSTERED ABOUT? SHE'S LIKE A SISTER TO ME.
ぴしゃっ
....
BY THE WAY...
I TOTALLY FORGOT THAT I ONLY HAVE ONE FUTON...
ドキ
ドキ
ドキ
THAT MEANS...

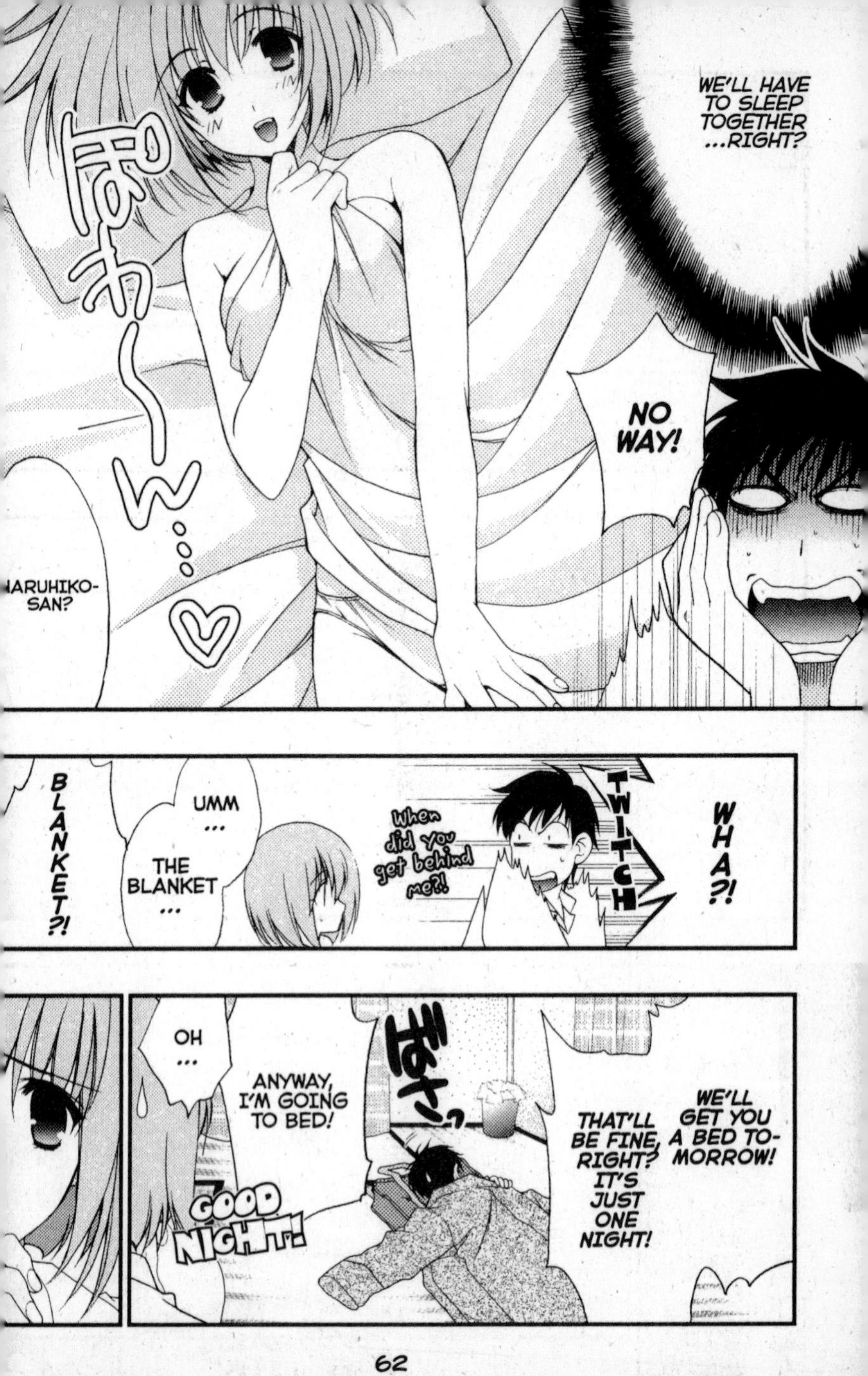
WE'LL HAVE TO SLEEP TOGETHER ...RIGHT?
NO WAY!
ぽわ～ん…♡
HARUHIKO-SAN?
WHA?!
TWITCH
When did you get behind me?!
UMM ... THE BLANKET ...
BLANKET?!
WE'LL GET YOU A BED TO-MORROW!
THAT'LL BE FINE, RIGHT? IT'S JUST ONE NIGHT!
ばさっ
ANYWAY, I'M GOING TO BED!
OH ...
GOOD NIGHT!

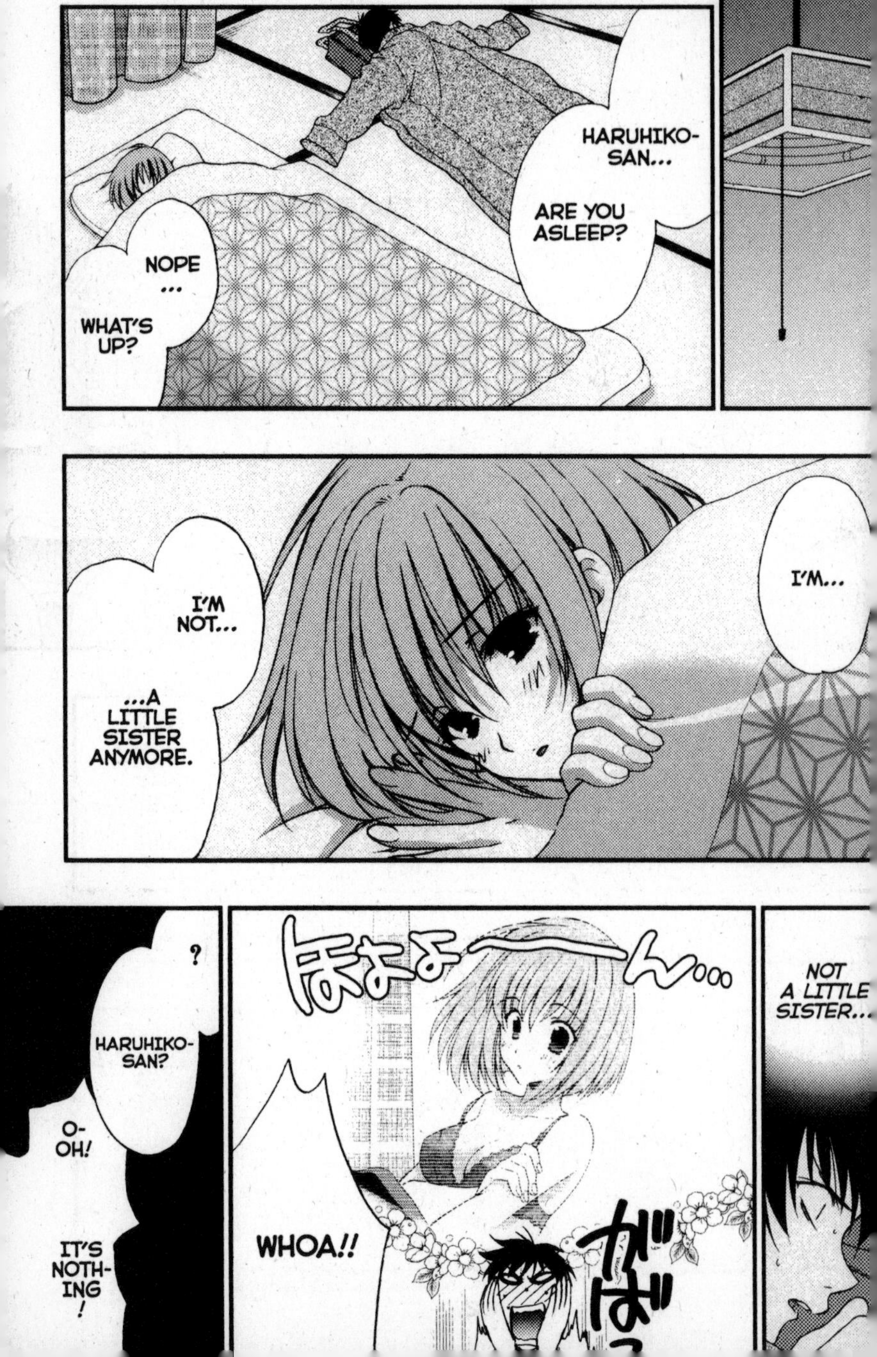
HARUHIKO-SAN...
ARE YOU ASLEEP?
NOPE ... WHAT'S UP?
I'M...
I'M NOT...
...A LITTLE SISTER ANYMORE.
NOT A LITTLE SISTER...
ほよよ〜〜ん...
WHOA!!
がばっ
?
HARUHIKO-SAN?
O-OH!
IT'S NOTH-ING!

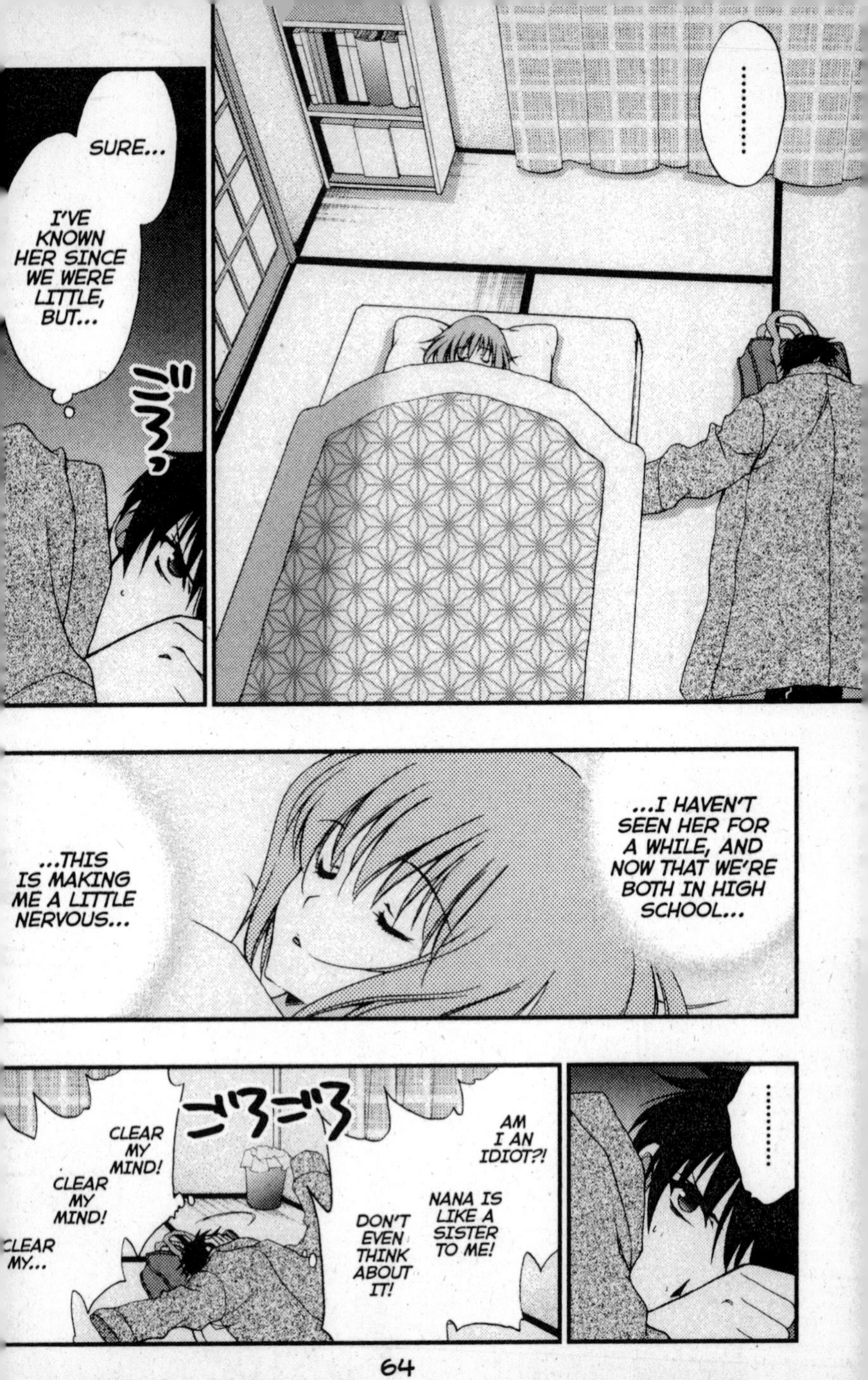
......
SURE...
I'VE KNOWN HER SINCE WE WERE LITTLE, BUT...
...I HAVEN'T SEEN HER FOR A WHILE, AND NOW THAT WE'RE BOTH IN HIGH SCHOOL...
...THIS IS MAKING ME A LITTLE NERVOUS...
......
AM I AN IDIOT?!
NANA IS LIKE A SISTER TO ME!
DON'T EVEN THINK ABOUT IT!
ごろごろ
CLEAR MY MIND!
CLEAR MY MIND!
CLEAR MY...

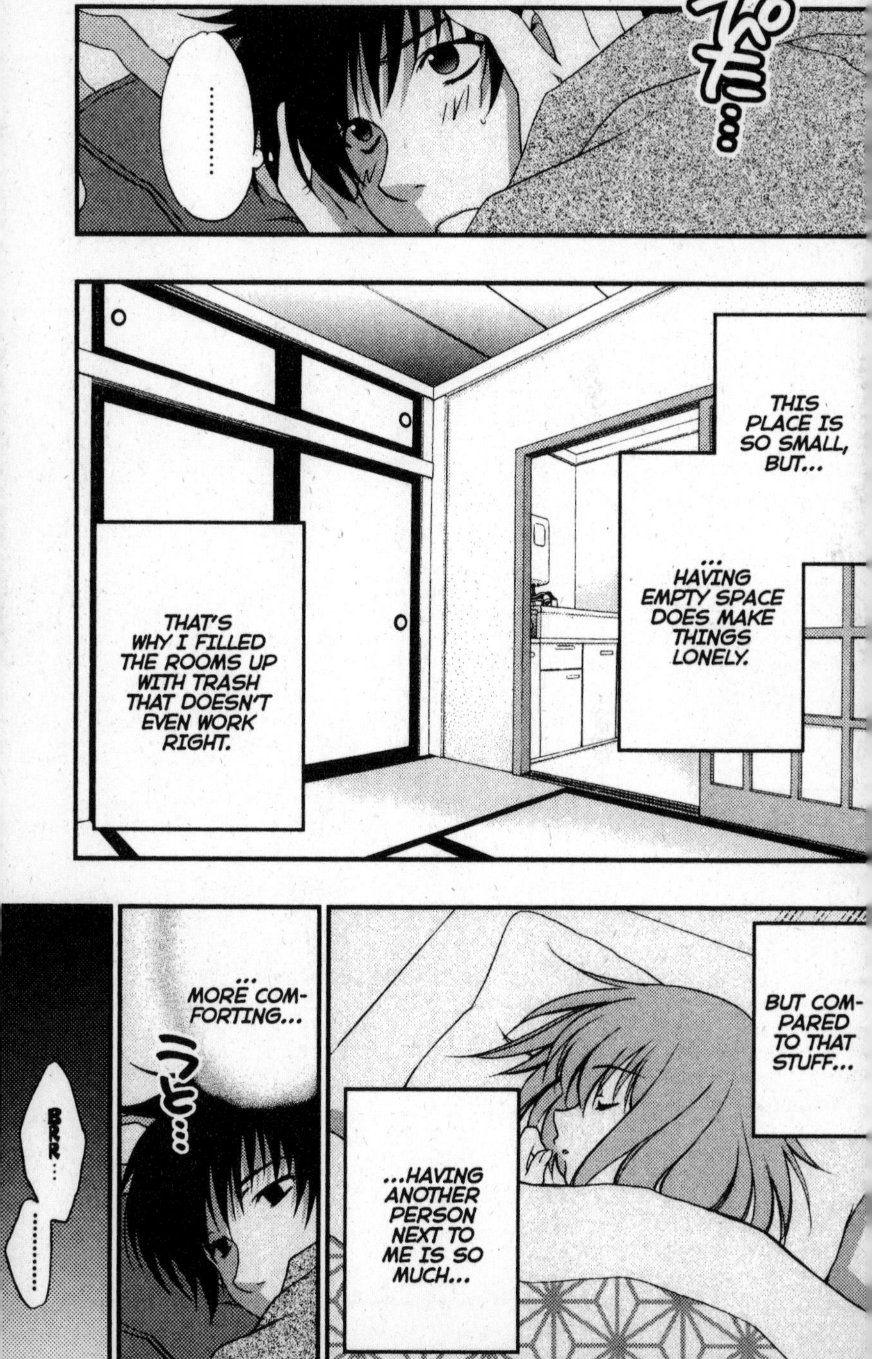

....
THIS PLACE IS SO SMALL, BUT...
...HAVING EMPTY SPACE DOES MAKE THINGS LONELY.
THAT'S WHY I FILLED THE ROOMS UP WITH TRASH THAT DOESN'T EVEN WORK RIGHT.
BUT COMPARED TO THAT STUFF...
...HAVING ANOTHER PERSON NEXT TO ME IS SO MUCH...
...MORE COM-FORTING...
BRRR...
....

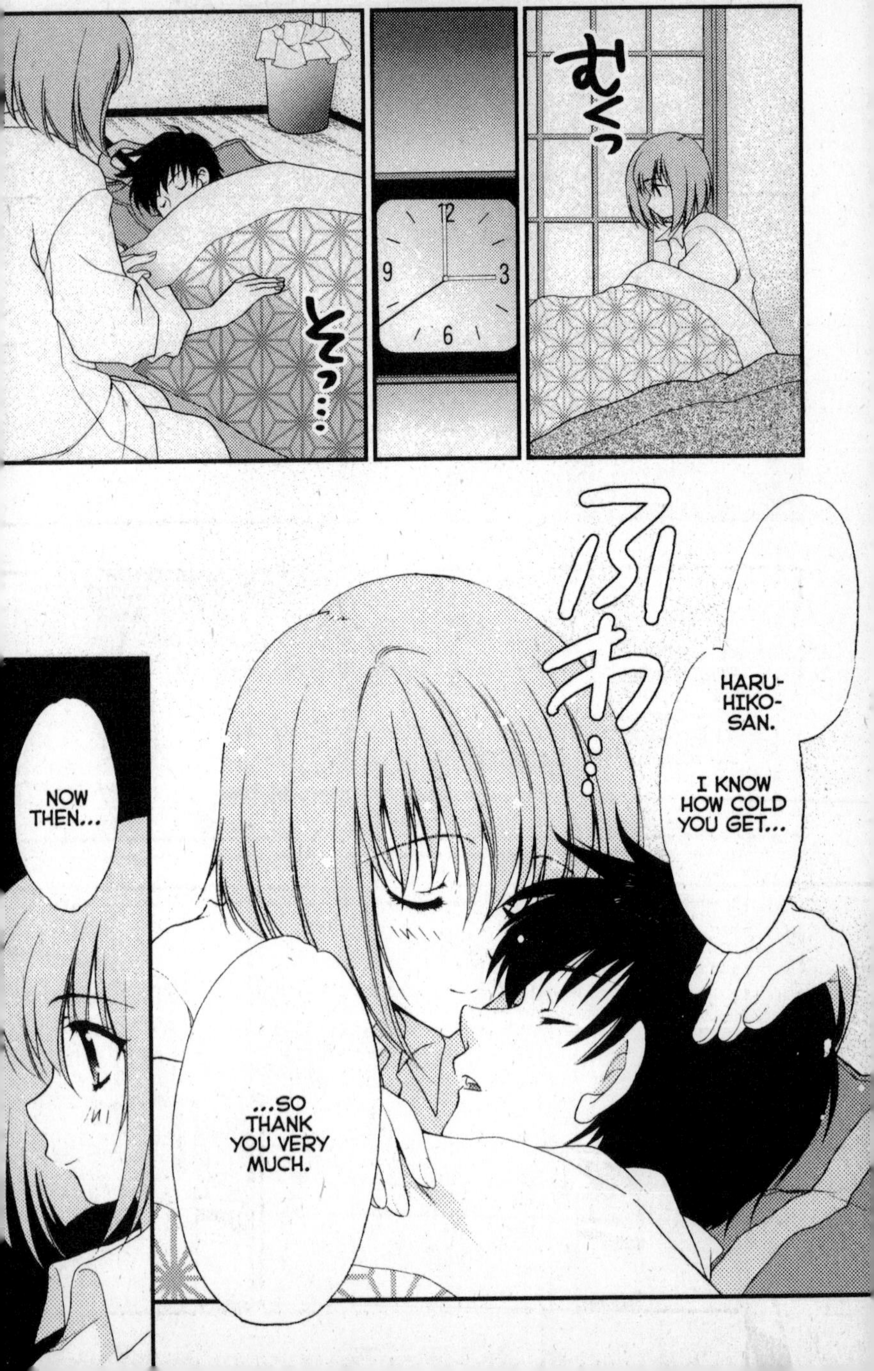
むくっ
そっ…
ふわ…
HARU-HIKO-SAN.
I KNOW HOW COLD YOU GET...
...SO THANK YOU VERY MUCH.
NOW THEN...

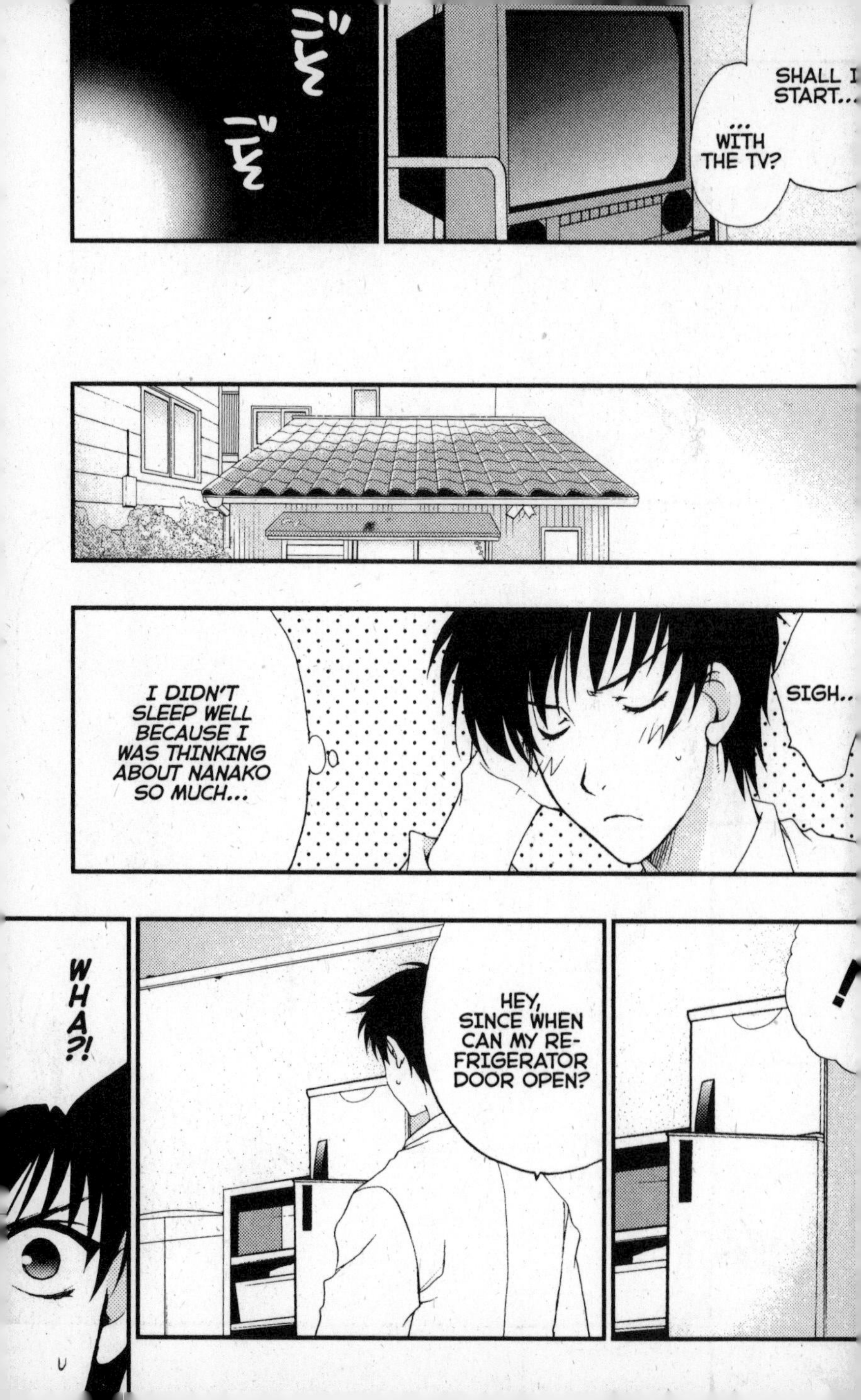
SHALL I START...
...WITH THE TV?
SIGH...
I DIDN'T SLEEP WELL BECAUSE I WAS THINKING ABOUT NANAKO SO MUCH...
!
HEY, SINCE WHEN CAN MY RE-FRIGERATOR DOOR OPEN?
WHA?!

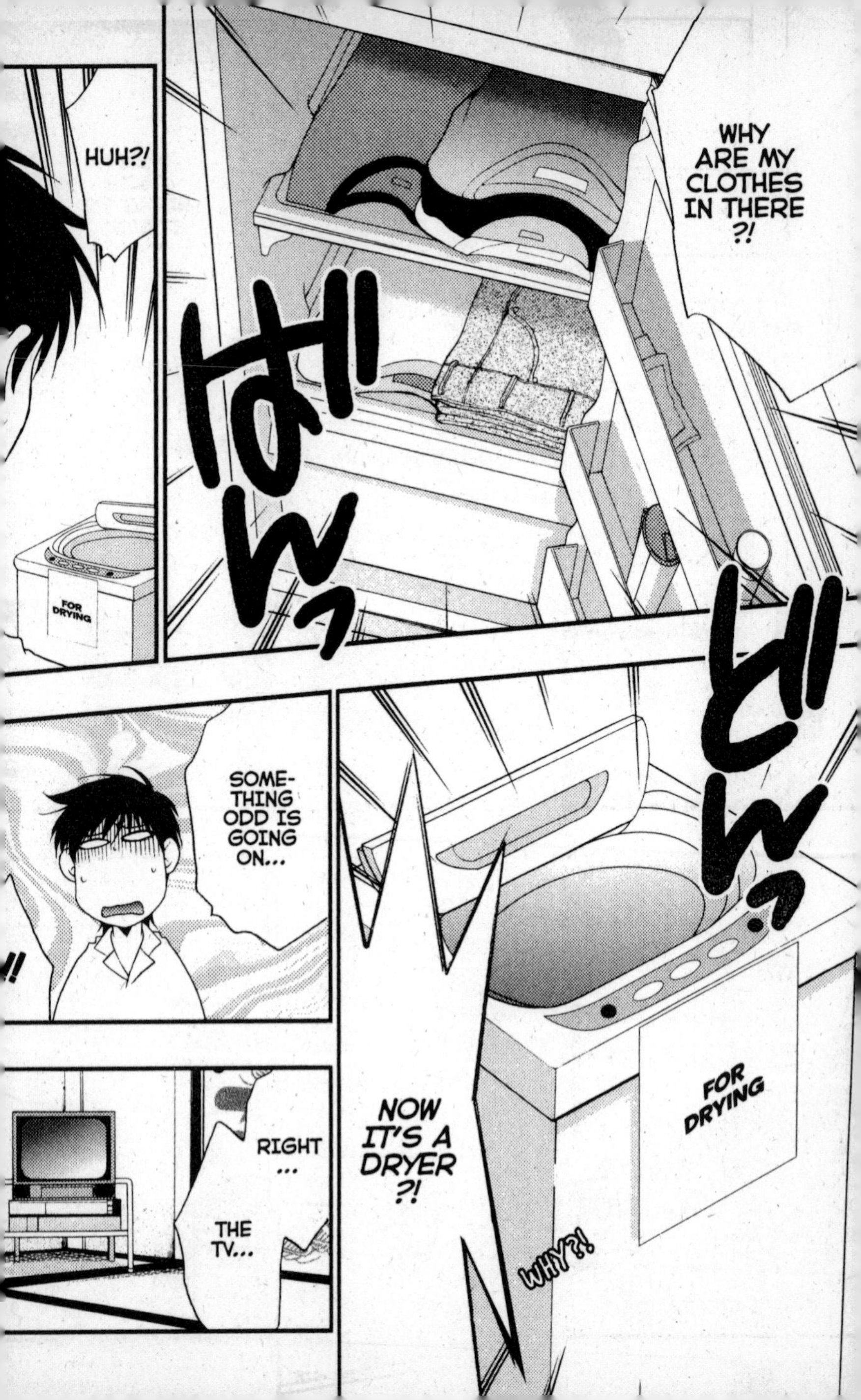
WHY ARE MY CLOTHES IN THERE ?!
ばんっ
HUH?!
FOR DRYING
どんっ
FOR DRYING
NOW IT'S A DRYER ?!
WHY?!
SOME-THING ODD IS GOING ON...
RIGHT ...
THE TV...

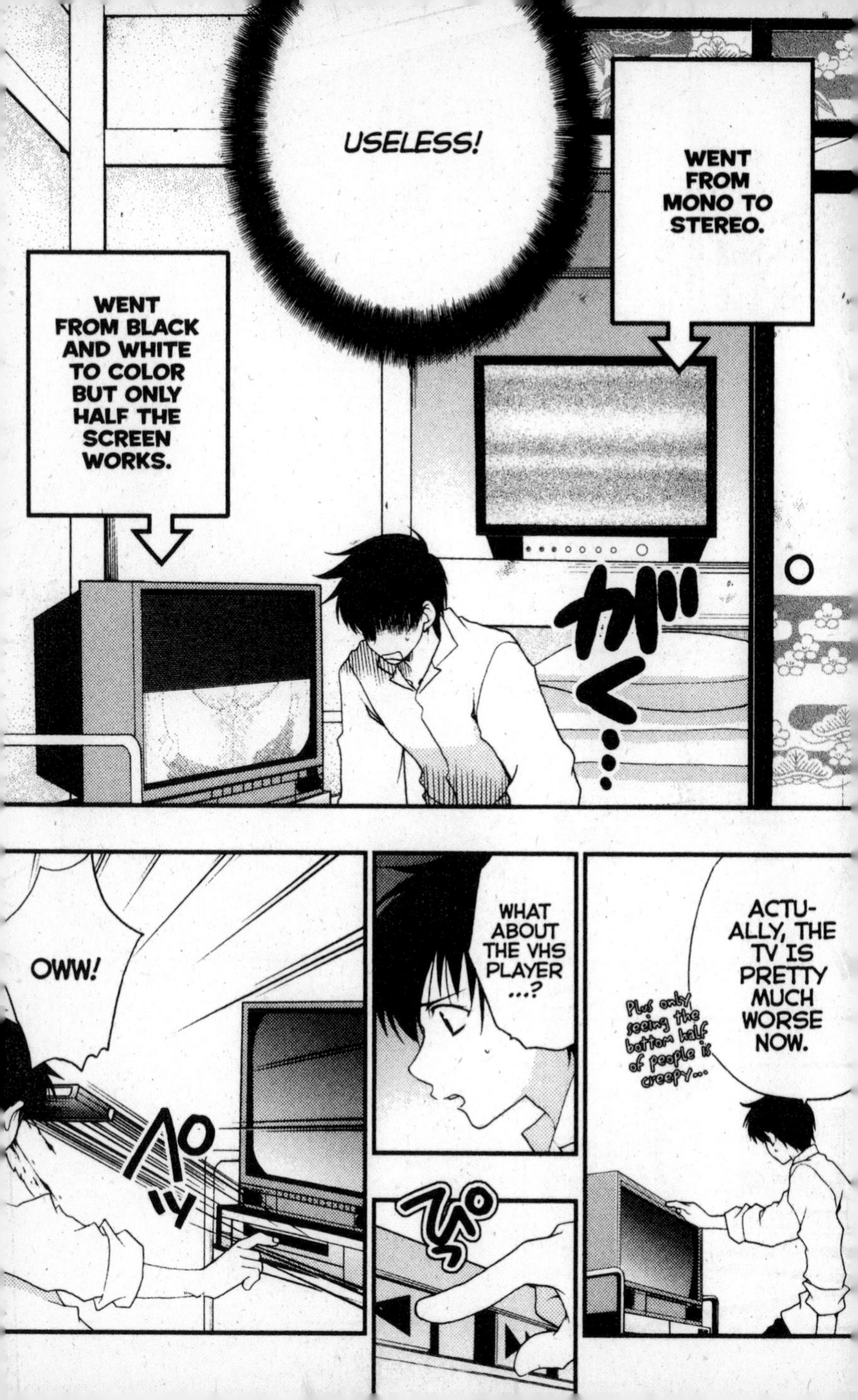
WENT FROM MONO TO STEREO.
USELESS!
WENT FROM BLACK AND WHITE TO COLOR BUT ONLY HALF THE SCREEN WORKS.
がく…
ACTU-ALLY, THE TV IS PRETTY MUCH WORSE NOW.
Plus only seeing the bottom half of people is creepy...
WHAT ABOUT THE VHS PLAYER ...?
OWW!

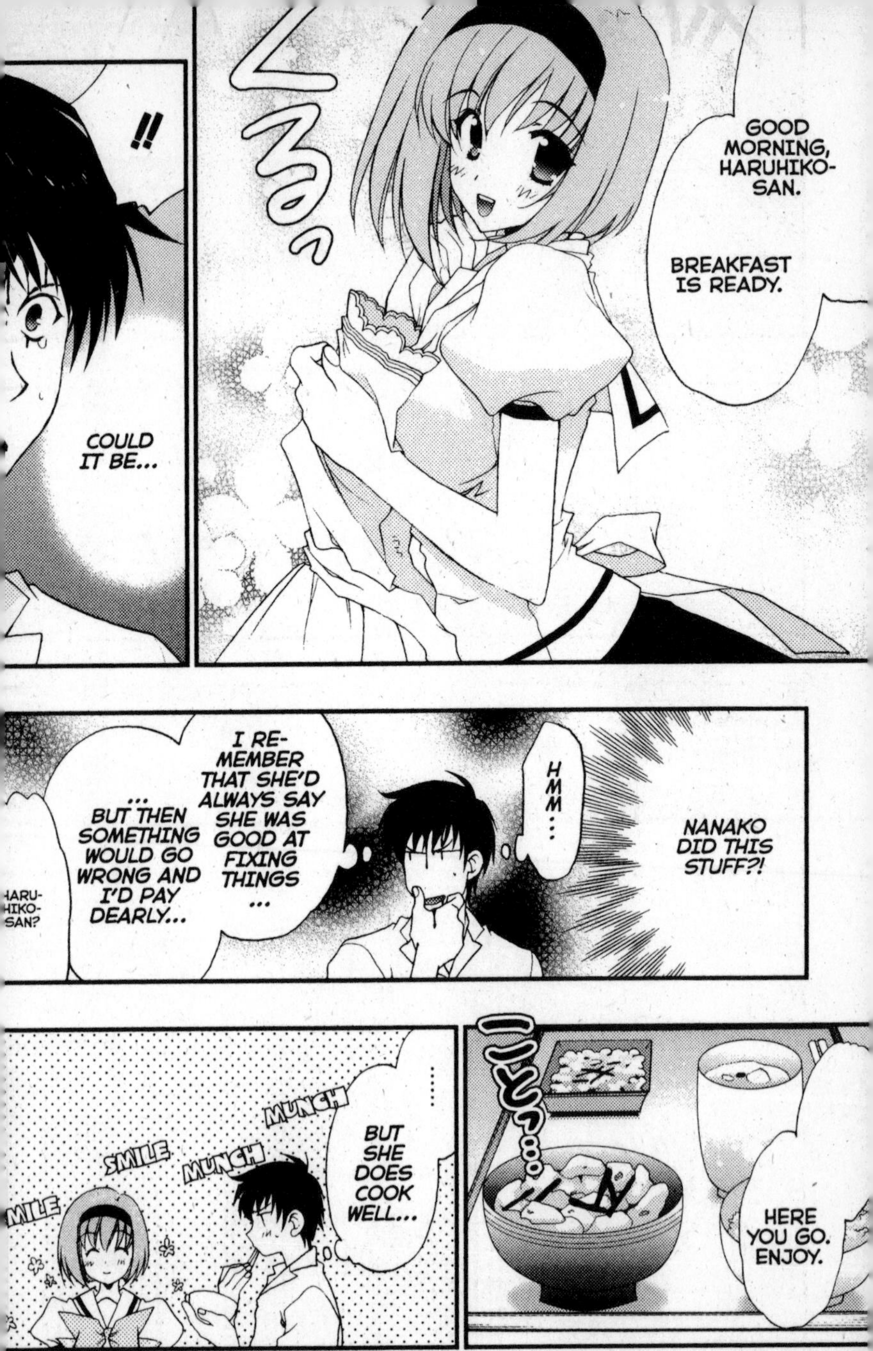
GOOD MORNING, HARUHIKO-SAN.
BREAKFAST IS READY.
くるっ
!!
COULD IT BE...
NANAKO DID THIS STUFF?!
HMM...
I RE-MEMBER THAT SHE'D ALWAYS SAY SHE WAS GOOD AT FIXING THINGS ...
... BUT THEN SOMETHING WOULD GO WRONG AND I'D PAY DEARLY...
HARU-HIKO-SAN?
HERE YOU GO. ENJOY.
ことっ…
...
BUT SHE DOES COOK WELL...
MUNCH
MUNCH
SMILE
SMILE

Life-2 ♣ END

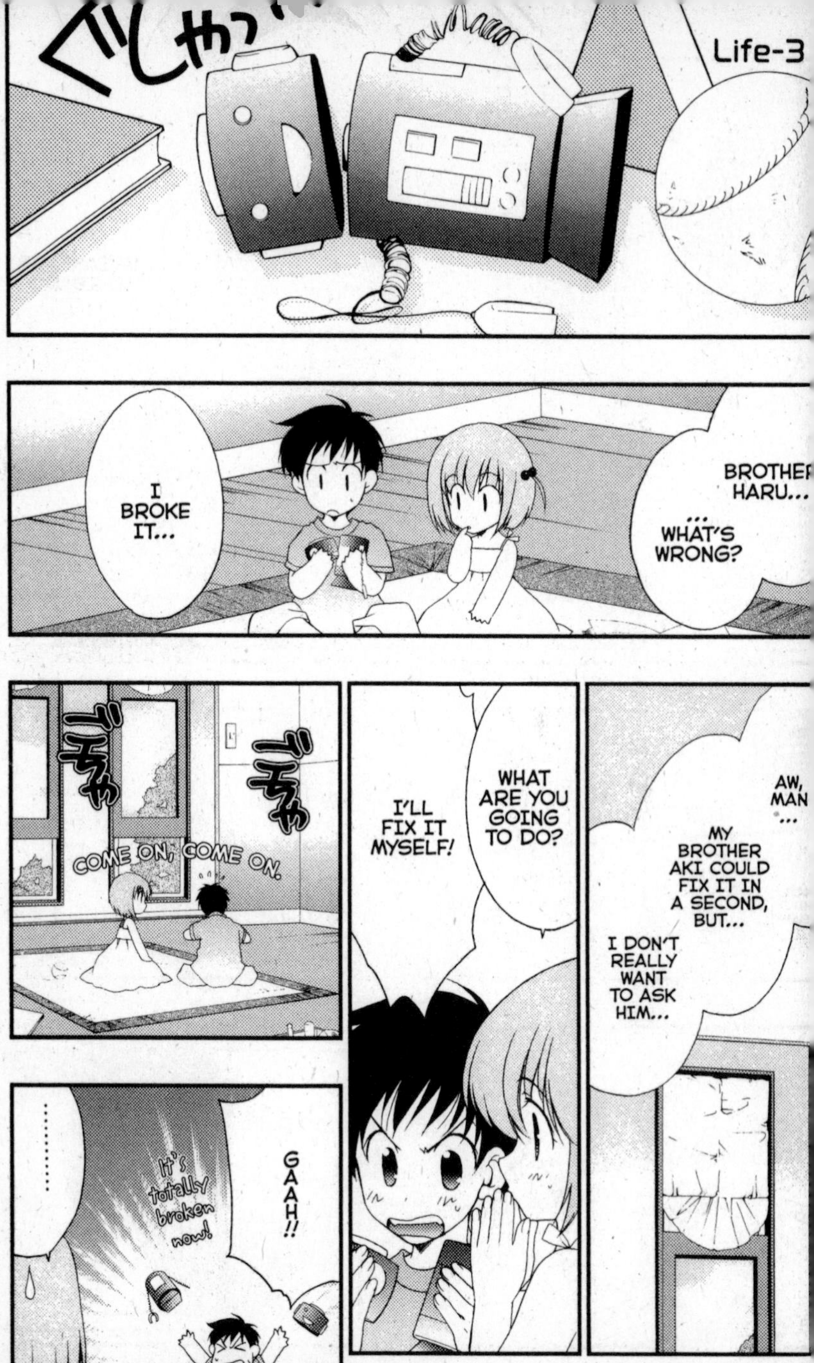
ぐしゃっ
BROTHER HARU... ... WHAT'S WRONG?
I BROKE IT...
AW, MAN...
MY BROTHER AKI COULD FIX IT IN A SECOND, BUT...
I DON'T REALLY WANT TO ASK HIM...
WHAT ARE YOU GOING TO DO?
I'LL FIX IT MYSELF!
ごちゃ
ごちゃ
COME ON, COME ON.
GAAH!!
It's totally broken now!
....

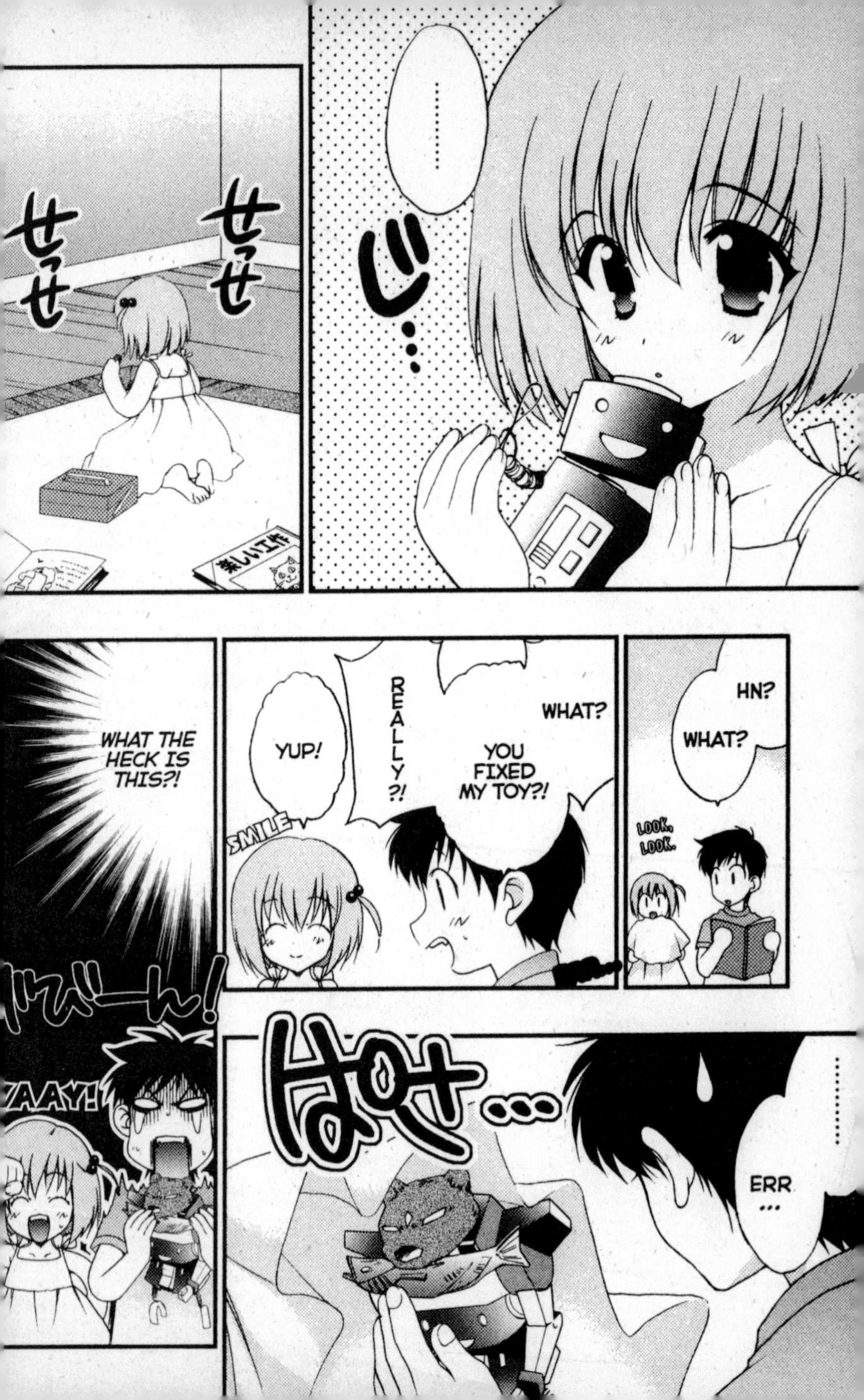

......
じ…
せっせ
せっせ
HN?
WHAT?
LOOK, LOOK.
WHAT?
YOU FIXED MY TOY?!
REALLY?!
YUP!
SMILE
......
ERR...
はっ…
WHAT THE HECK IS THIS?!
びーん!
AAY!

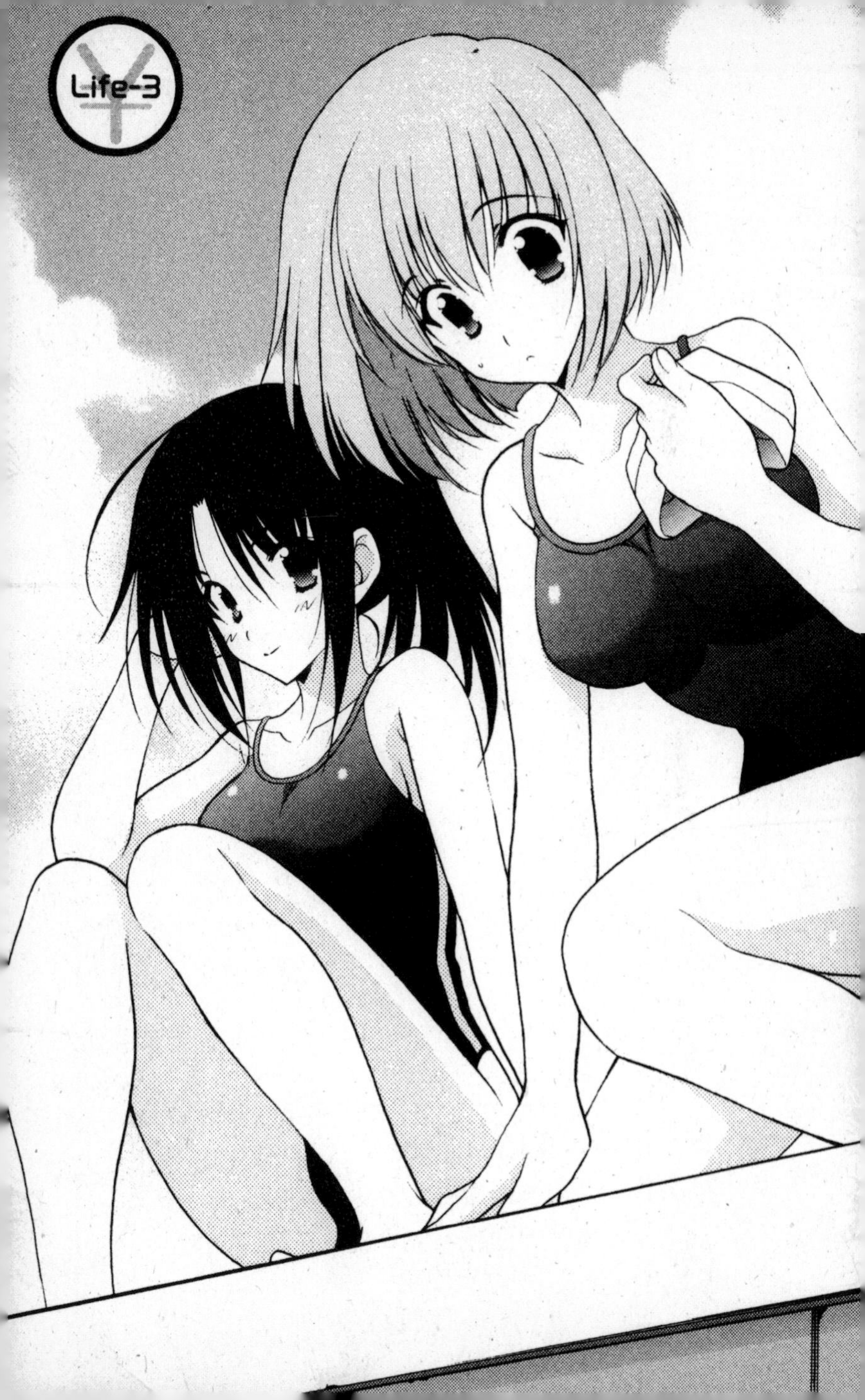
Life-3

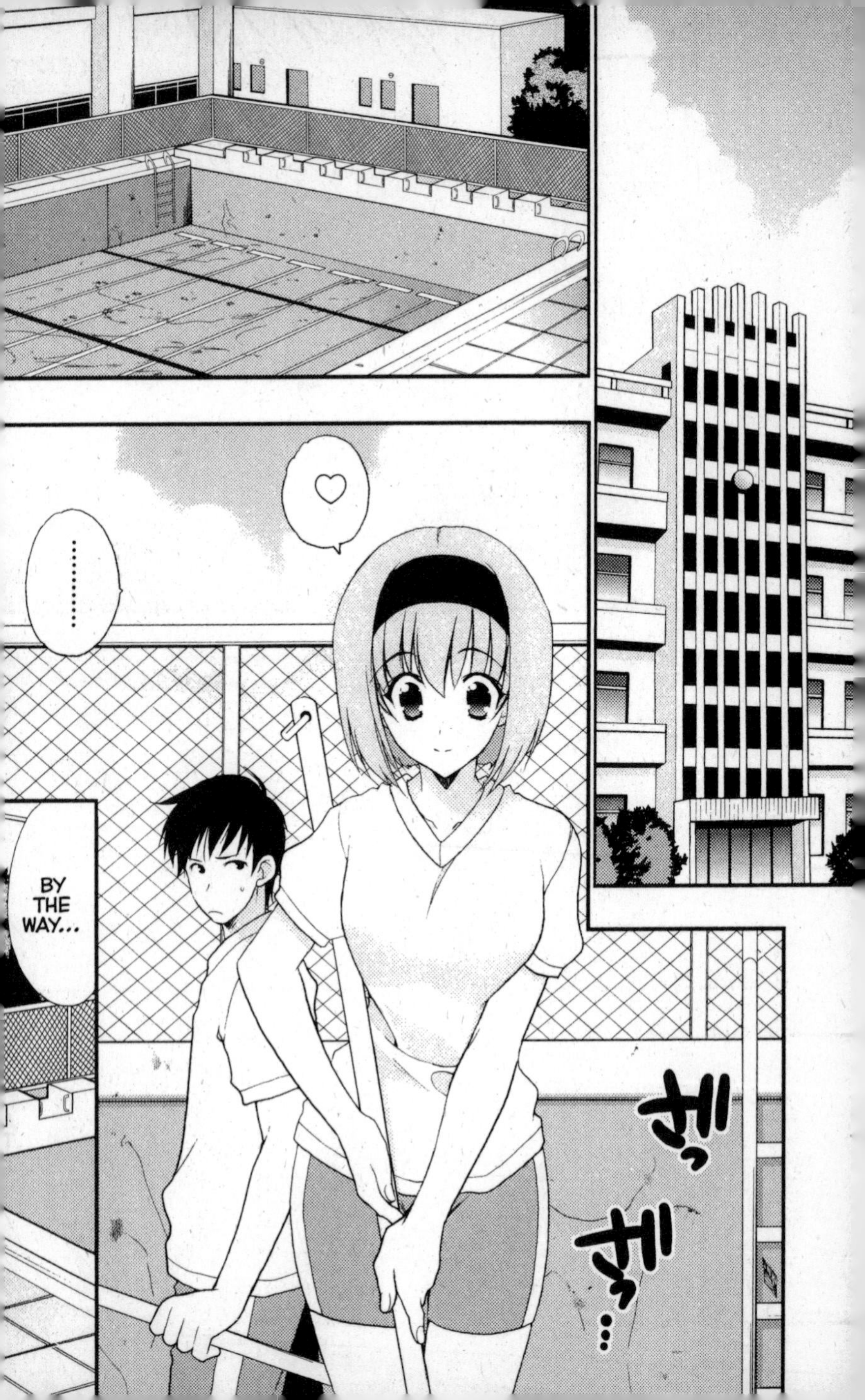
♡
......
ざっ
ざっ…
BY THE WAY...

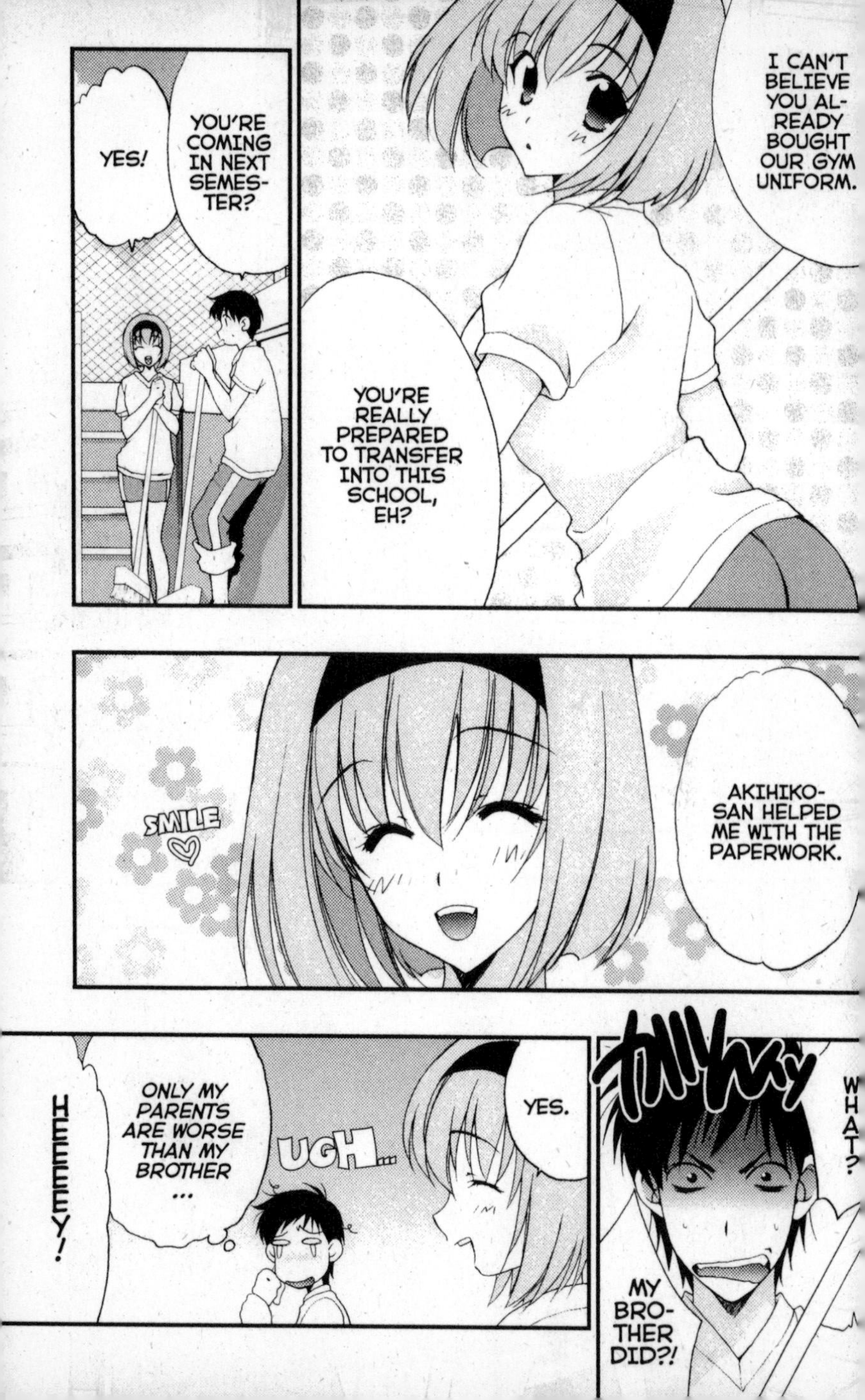
I CAN'T BELIEVE YOU AL-READY BOUGHT OUR GYM UNIFORM.
YOU'RE REALLY PREPARED TO TRANSFER INTO THIS SCHOOL, EH?
YOU'RE COMING IN NEXT SEMES-TER?
YES!
AKIHIKO-SAN HELPED ME WITH THE PAPERWORK.
SMILE
WHAT?
MY BRO-THER DID?!
YES.
UGH...
ONLY MY PARENTS ARE WORSE THAN MY BROTHER ...
HEEEEY!

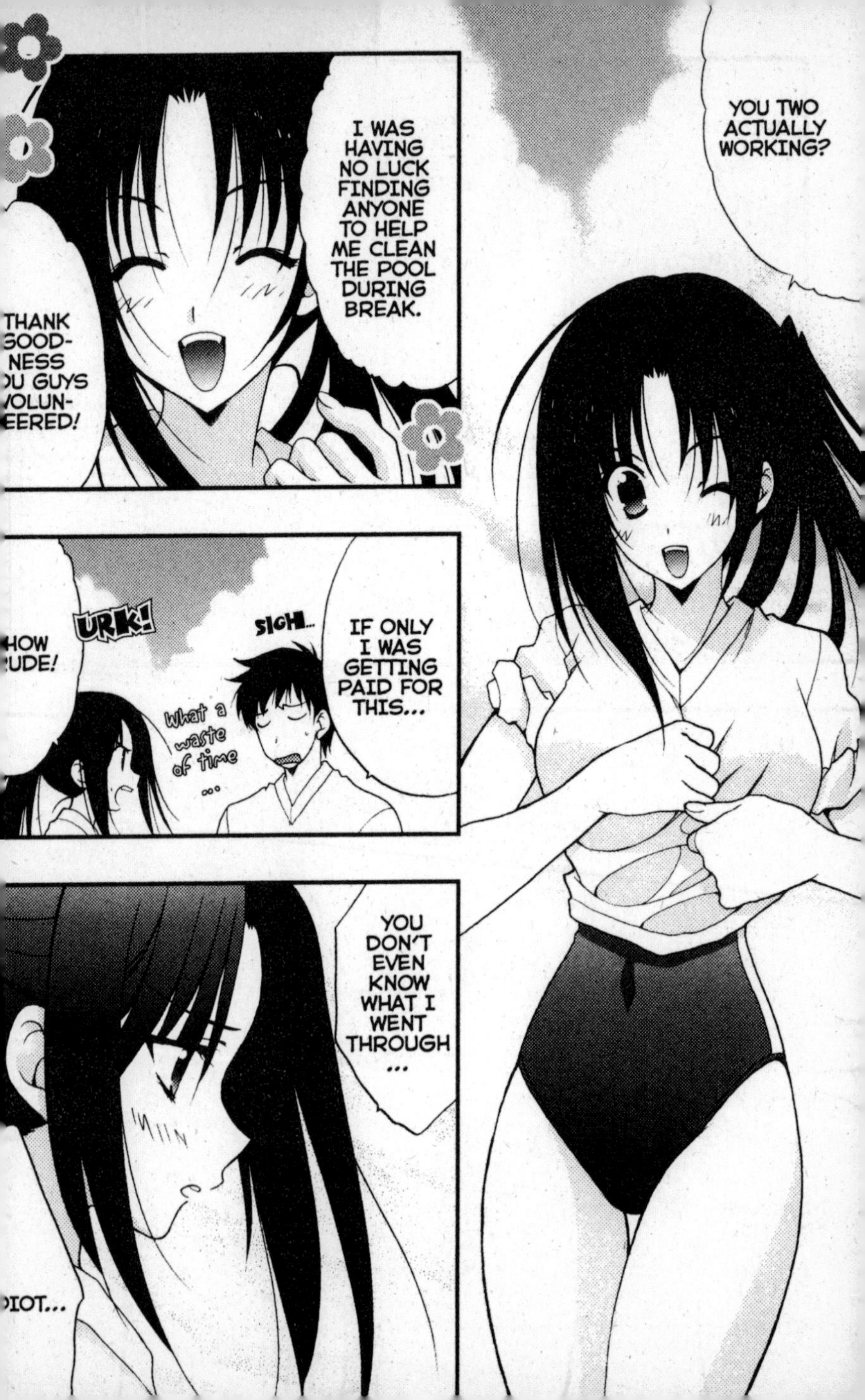
YOU TWO ACTUALLY WORKING?
I WAS HAVING NO LUCK FINDING ANYONE TO HELP ME CLEAN THE POOL DURING BREAK.
THANK GOOD- NESS OU GUYS OLUN- EERED!
IF ONLY I WAS GETTING PAID FOR THIS...
SIGH...
What a waste of time ...
URK!
HOW UDE!
YOU DON'T EVEN KNOW WHAT I WENT THROUGH ...
IOT...

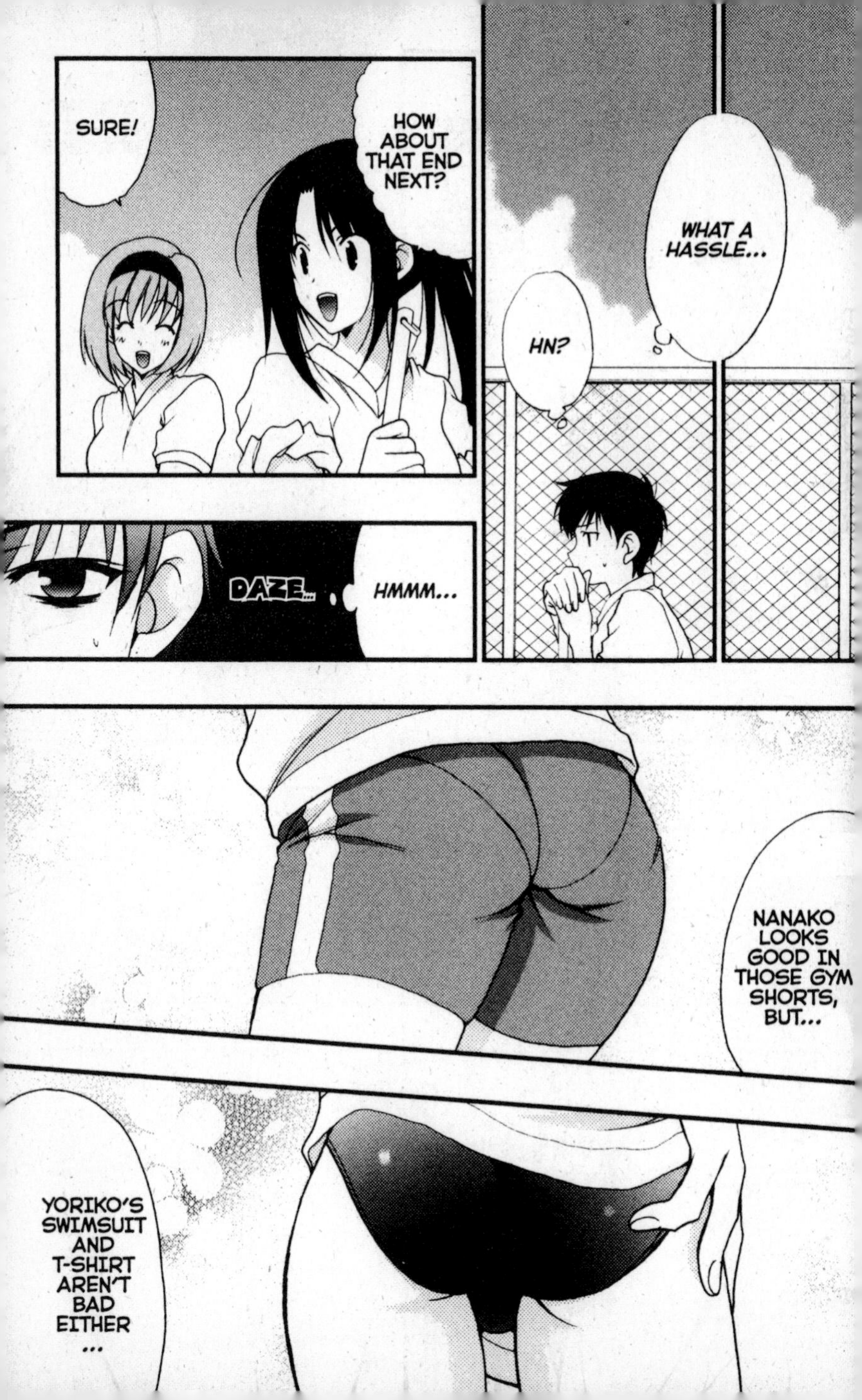
WHAT A HASSLE...
HN?
HOW ABOUT THAT END NEXT?
SURE!
HMMM...
DAZE...
NANAKO LOOKS GOOD IN THOSE GYM SHORTS, BUT...
YORIKO'S SWIMSUIT AND T-SHIRT AREN'T BAD EITHER ...

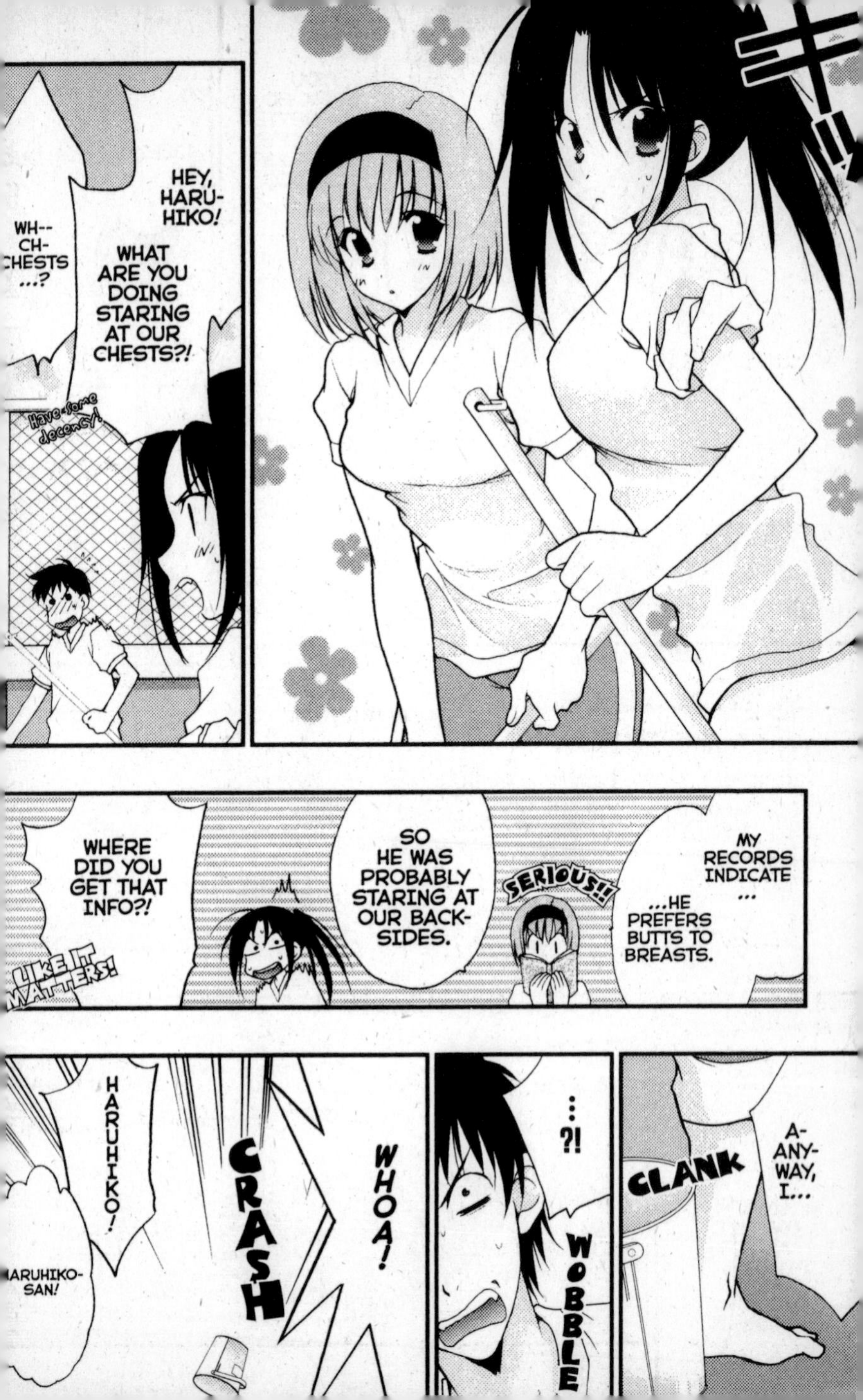
HEY, HARU-HIKO!
WHAT ARE YOU DOING STARING AT OUR CHESTS?!
WH-- CH-CHESTS ...?
Have some decency!
MY RECORDS INDICATE ...
...HE PREFERS BUTTS TO BREASTS.
SERIOUS!!
SO HE WAS PROBABLY STARING AT OUR BACK-SIDES.
WHERE DID YOU GET THAT INFO?!
LIKE IT MATTERS!
A-ANY-WAY, I...
CLANK
...?!
WOBBLE
WHOA!
CRASH
HARUHIKO!
HARUHIKO-SAN!

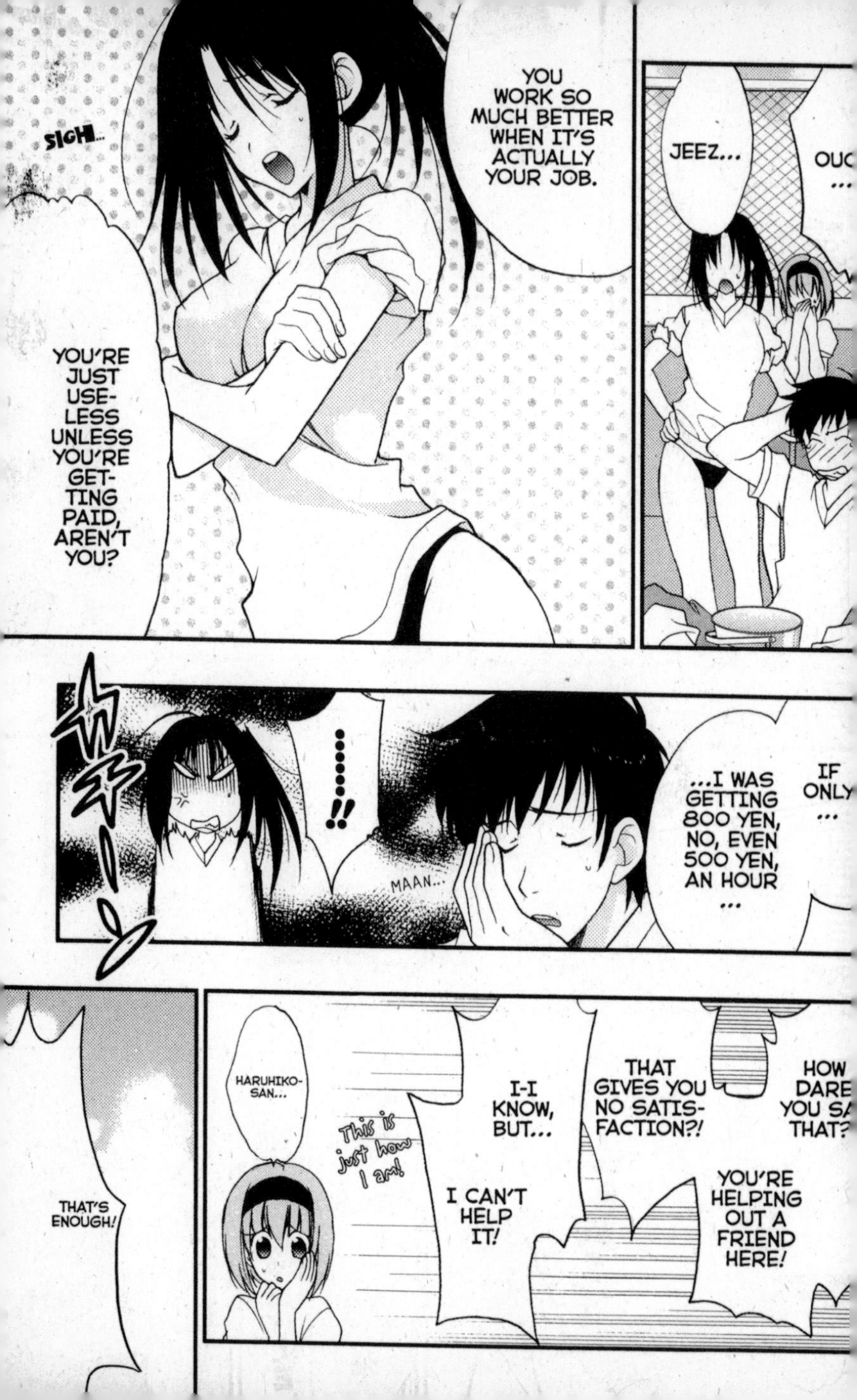
OUC...
JEEZ...
YOU WORK SO MUCH BETTER WHEN IT'S ACTUALLY YOUR JOB.
SIGH...
YOU'RE JUST USE-LESS UNLESS YOU'RE GET-TING PAID, AREN'T YOU?
IF ONLY...
...I WAS GETTING 800 YEN, NO, EVEN 500 YEN, AN HOUR...
MAAN...
......!!
HOW DARE YOU SA THAT?
YOU'RE HELPING OUT A FRIEND HERE!
THAT GIVES YOU NO SATIS-FACTION?!
I-I KNOW, BUT...
I CAN'T HELP IT!
This is just how I am!
HARUHIKO-SAN...
THAT'S ENOUGH!

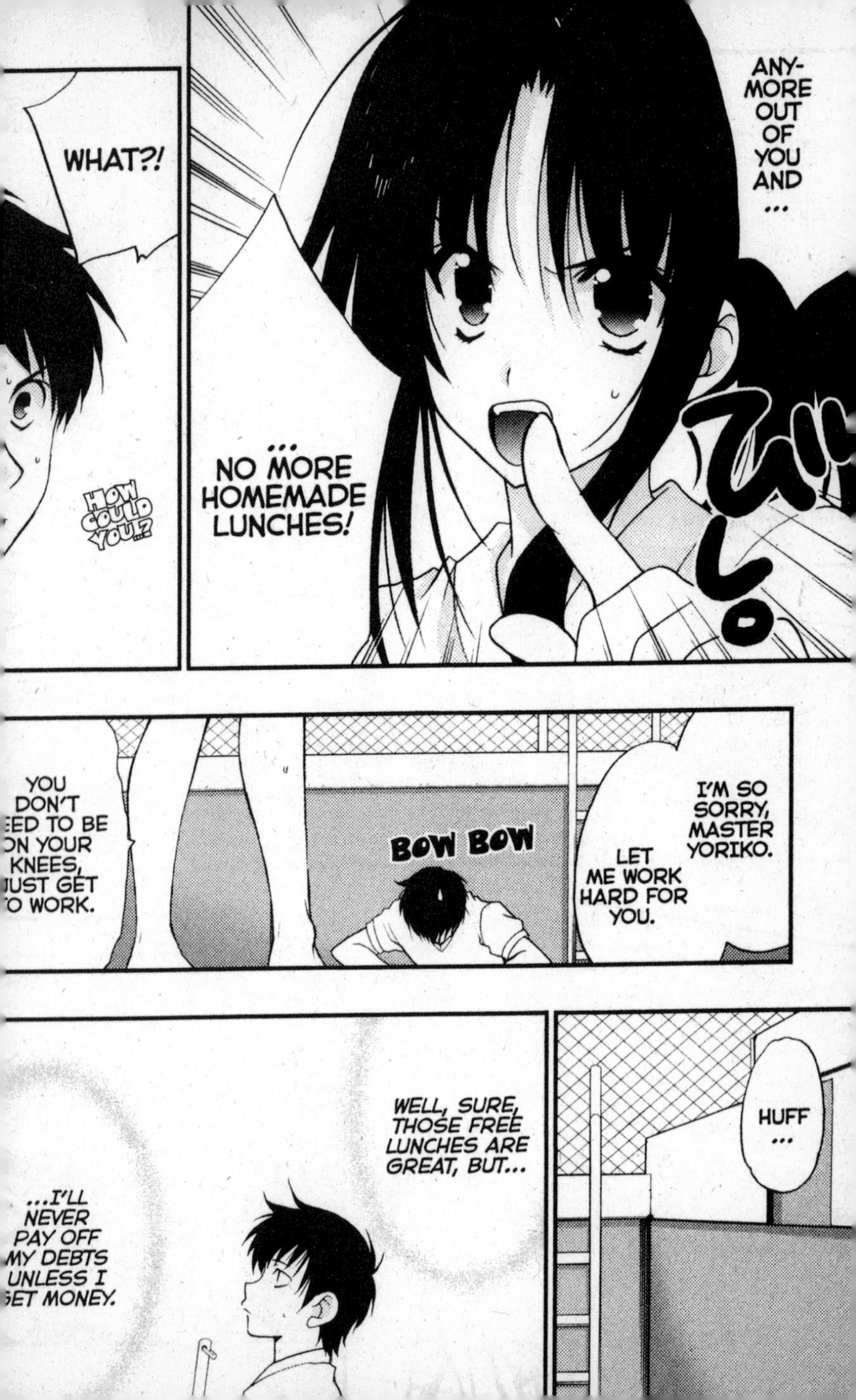
ANY-MORE OUT OF YOU AND ...
... NO MORE HOMEMADE LUNCHES!
WHAT?!
HOW COULD YOU!?
I'M SO SORRY, MASTER YORIKO.
LET ME WORK HARD FOR YOU.
BOW BOW
YOU DON'T EED TO BE ON YOUR KNEES, UST GET O WORK.
HUFF ...
WELL, SURE, THOSE FREE LUNCHES ARE GREAT, BUT...
...I'LL NEVER PAY OFF MY DEBTS UNLESS I ET MONEY.

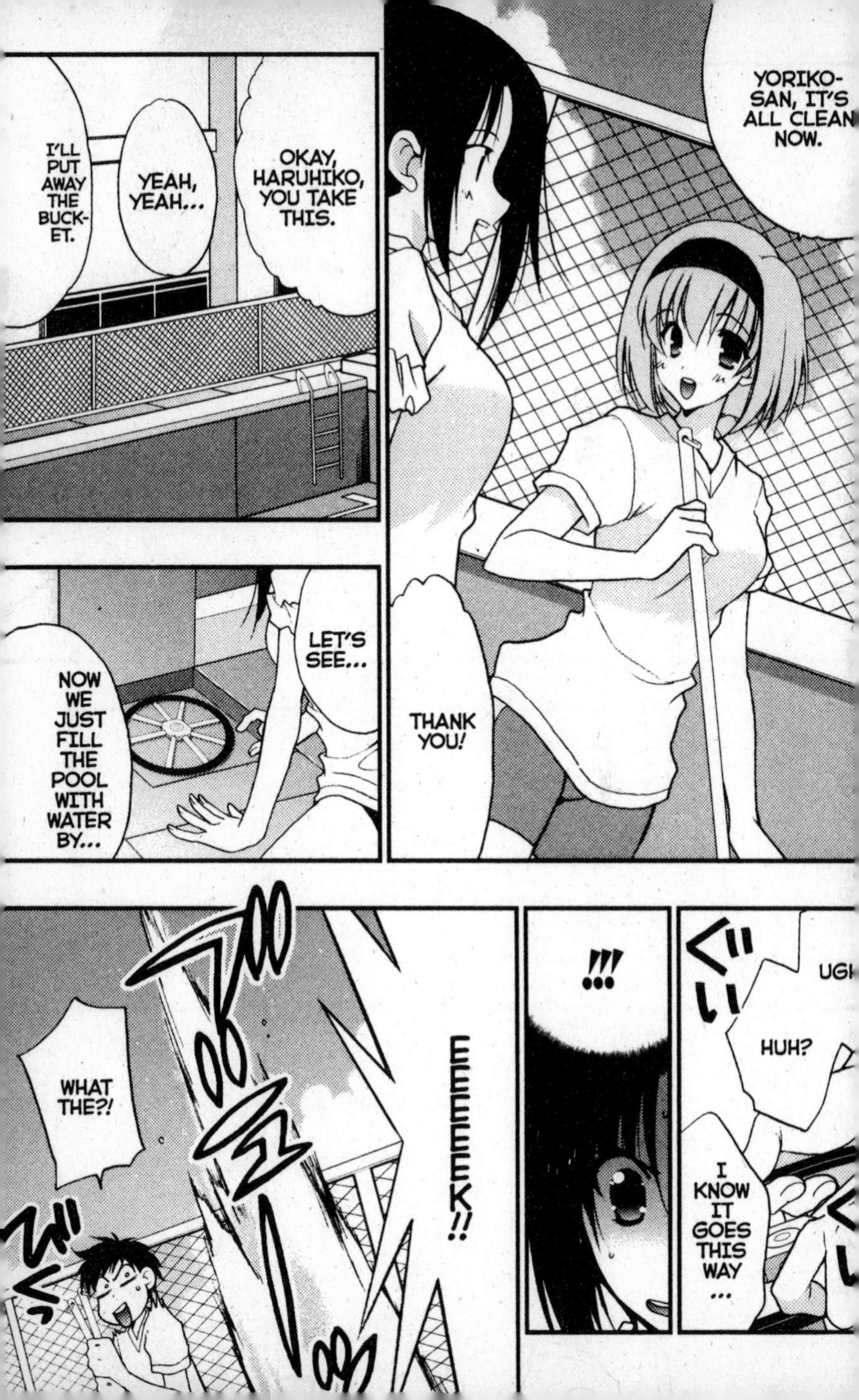

YORIKO-SAN, IT'S ALL CLEAN NOW.
THANK YOU!
OKAY, HARUHIKO, YOU TAKE THIS.
YEAH, YEAH...
I'LL PUT AWAY THE BUCK-ET.
LET'S SEE...
NOW WE JUST FILL THE POOL WITH WATER BY...
ぐい
HUH?
I KNOW IT GOES THIS WAY...
!!!
EEEEEEK!!
WHAT THE?!

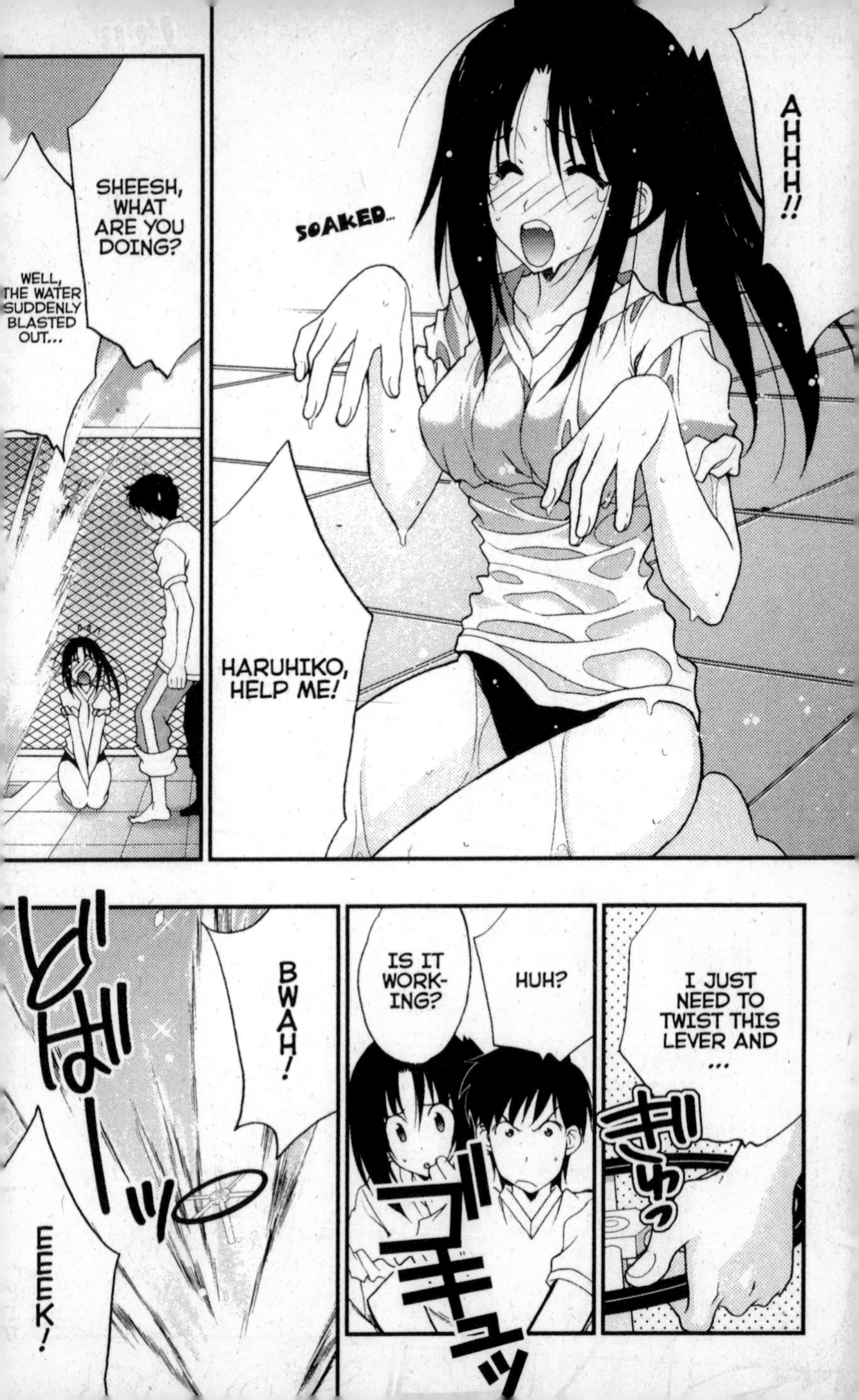
AHHH!!
SOAKED...
HARUHIKO, HELP ME!
SHEESH, WHAT ARE YOU DOING?
WELL, THE WATER SUDDENLY BLASTED OUT...
I JUST NEED TO TWIST THIS LEVER AND ...
ぎゅっ
ゴキュッ
HUH?
IS IT WORKING-ING?
BWAH!
どばーッ
EEEK!

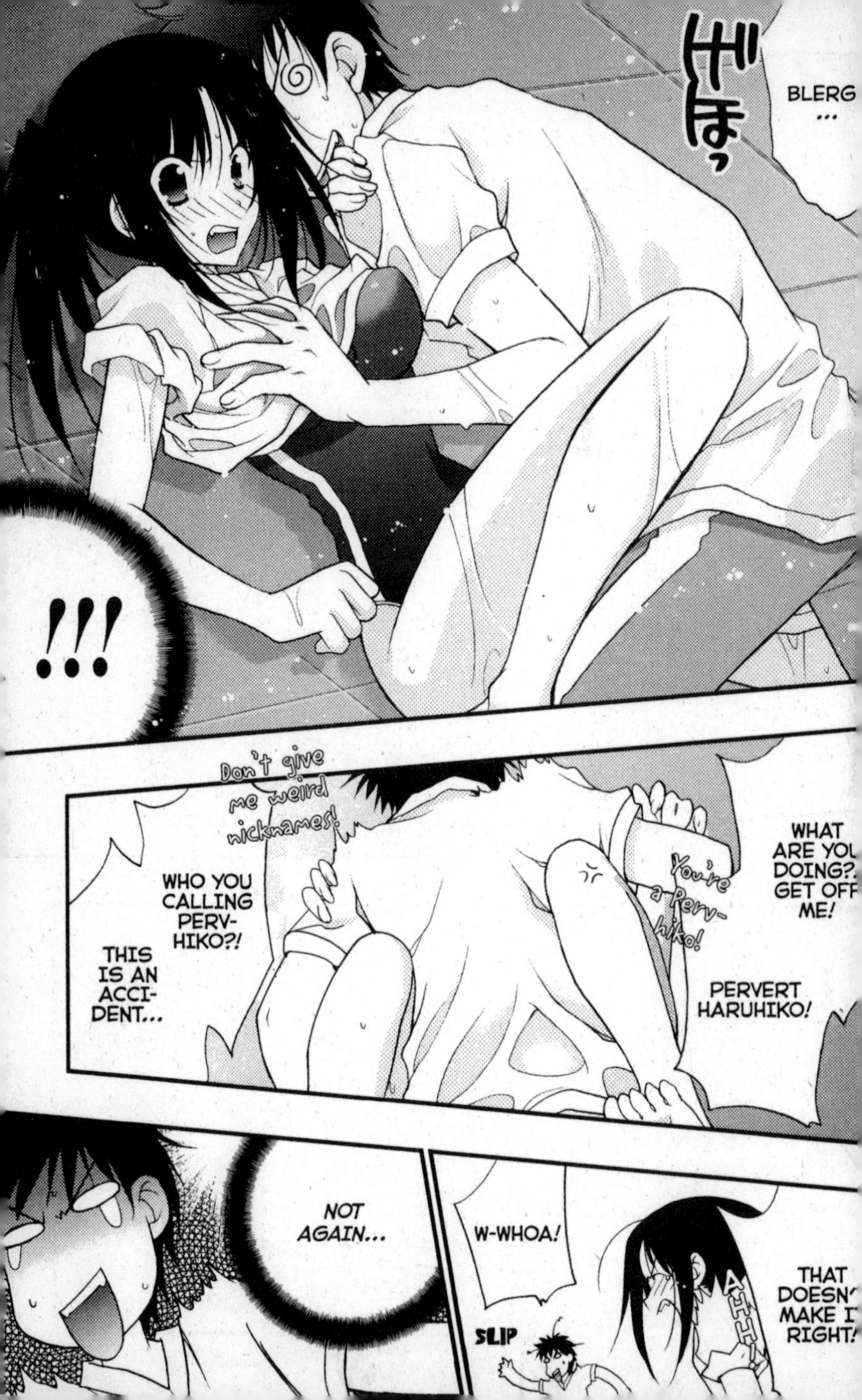
げほっ
BLERG ...
!!!
WHAT ARE YOU DOING?! GET OFF ME!
You're a Perv-hiko!
PERVERT HARUHIKO!
Don't give me weird nicknames!
WHO YOU CALLING PERV-HIKO?!
THIS IS AN ACCI-DENT...
THAT DOESN' MAKE I RIGHT!
AHHH!
SLIP
W-WHOA!
NOT AGAIN...

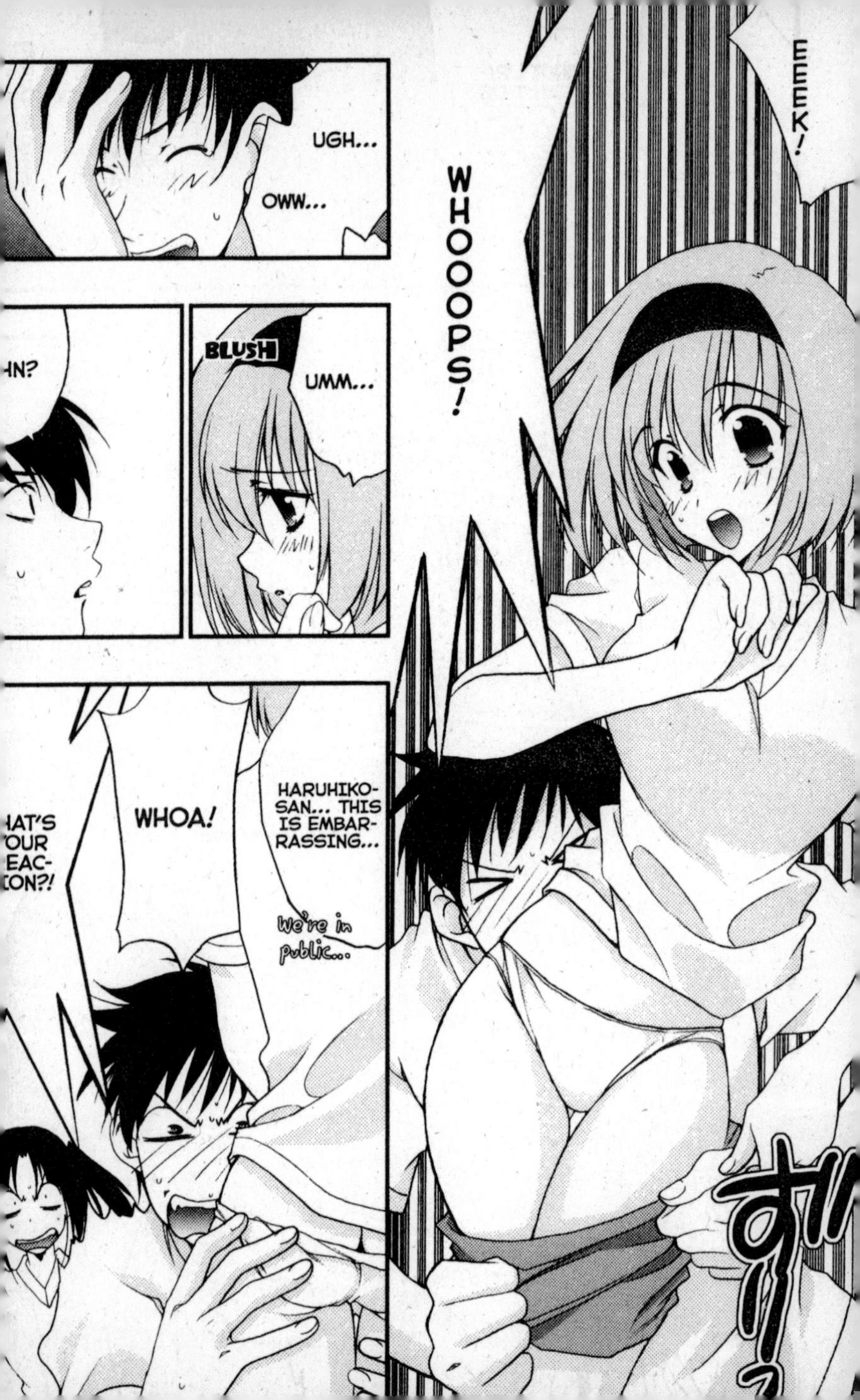
EEEK!
WHOOOPS!
す
UGH...
OWW...
BLUSH
UMM...
HN?
HARUHIKO-SAN... THIS IS EMBARRASSING...
we're in public...
WHOA!
HAT'S OUR EAC- ION?!

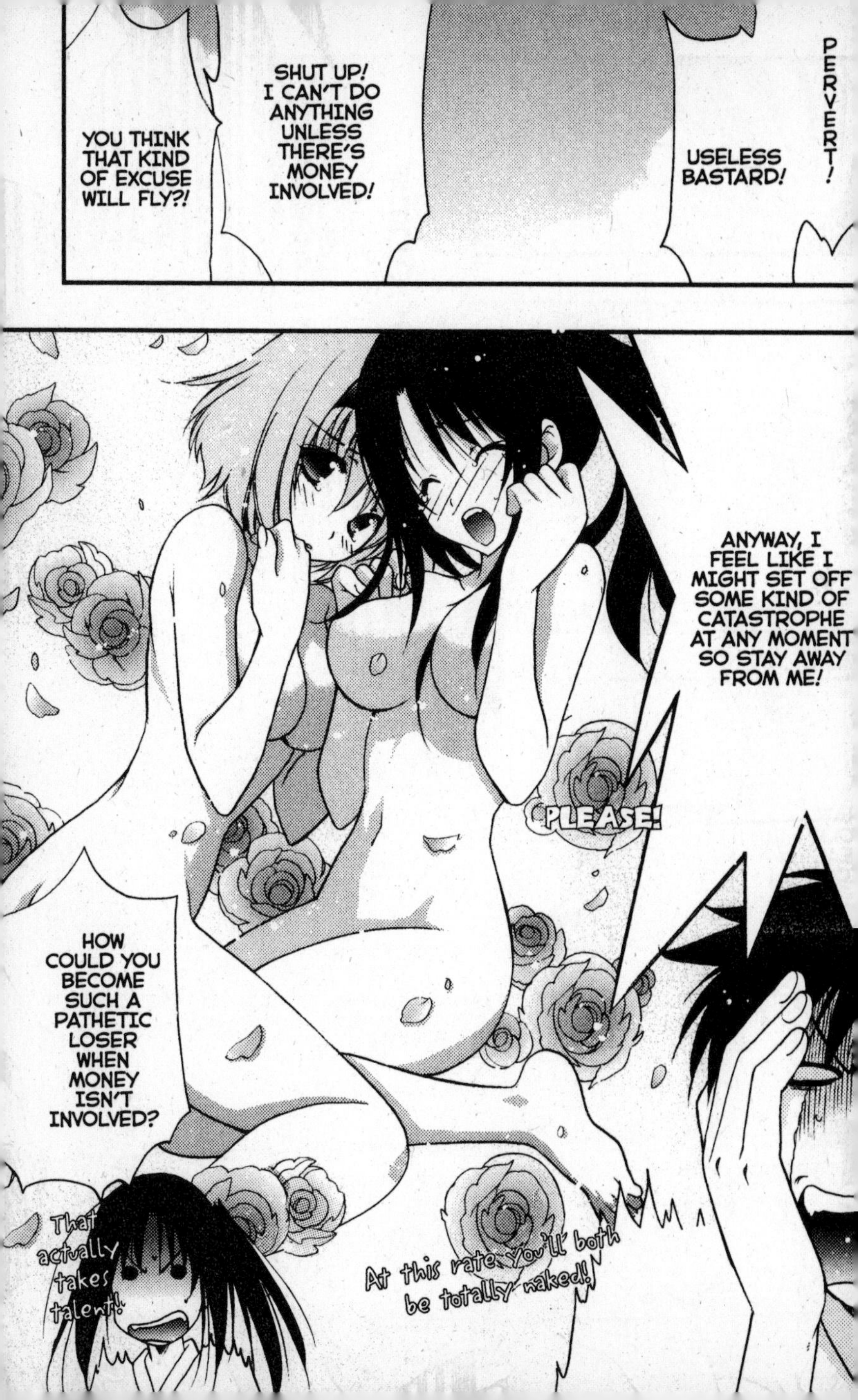
PERVERT!
USELESS BASTARD!
SHUT UP! I CAN'T DO ANYTHING UNLESS THERE'S MONEY INVOLVED!
YOU THINK THAT KIND OF EXCUSE WILL FLY?!
ANYWAY, I FEEL LIKE I MIGHT SET OFF SOME KIND OF CATASTROPHE AT ANY MOMENT SO STAY AWAY FROM ME!
PLEASE!
HOW COULD YOU BECOME SUCH A PATHETIC LOSER WHEN MONEY ISN'T INVOLVED?
At this rate you'll both be totally naked!
That actually takes talent!

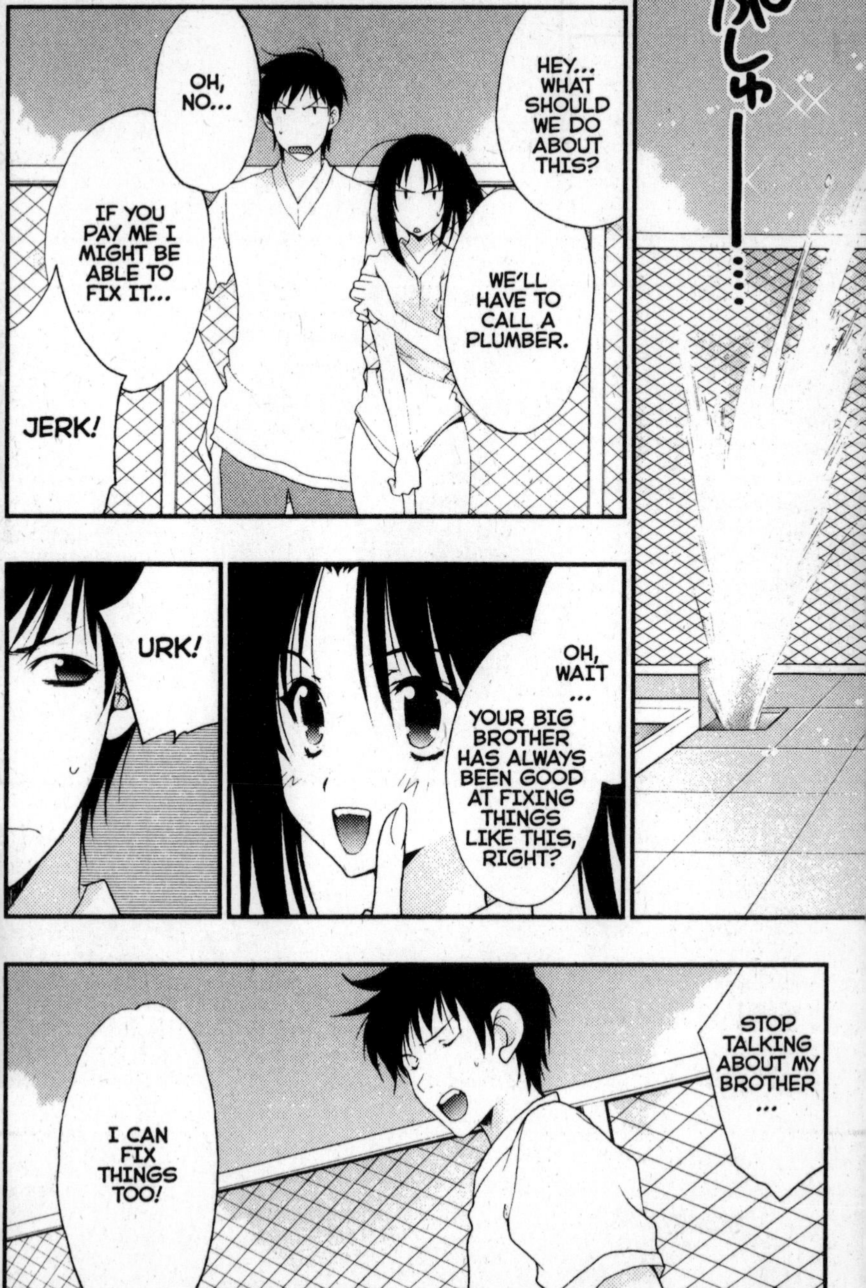
ぷしゅー……
HEY... WHAT SHOULD WE DO ABOUT THIS?
WE'LL HAVE TO CALL A PLUMBER.
OH, NO...
IF YOU PAY ME I MIGHT BE ABLE TO FIX IT...
JERK!
OH, WAIT ... YOUR BIG BROTHER HAS ALWAYS BEEN GOOD AT FIXING THINGS LIKE THIS, RIGHT?
URK!
STOP TALKING ABOUT MY BROTHER ...
I CAN FIX THINGS TOO!

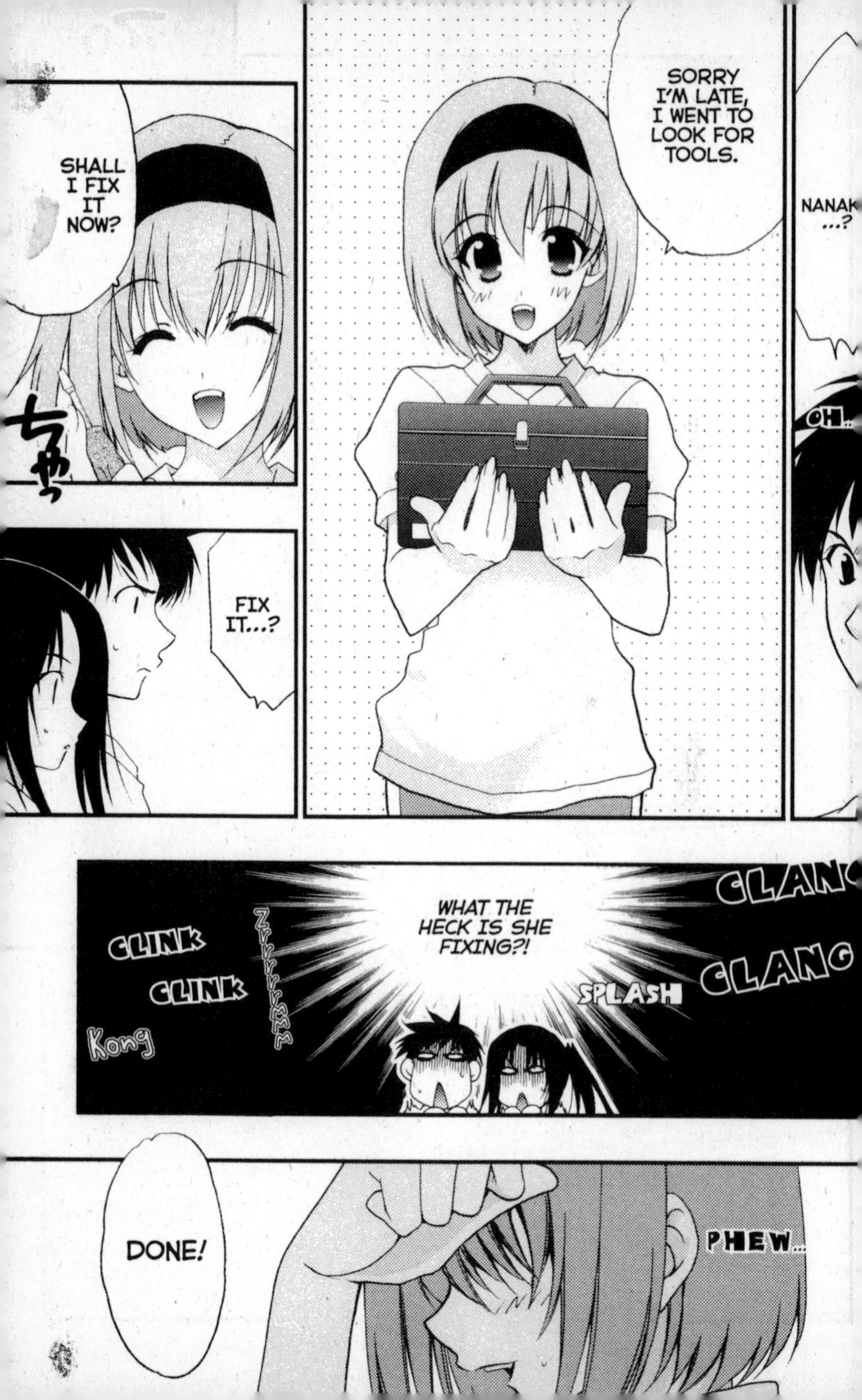
NANAK
...?
OH...
SORRY I'M LATE, I WENT TO LOOK FOR TOOLS.
SHALL I FIX IT NOW?
ちゃっ
FIX IT...?
CLANG
CLANG
SPLASH
WHAT THE HECK IS SHE FIXING?!
Zrrrrrmmm
CLINK
CLINK
Kong
PHEW...
DONE!

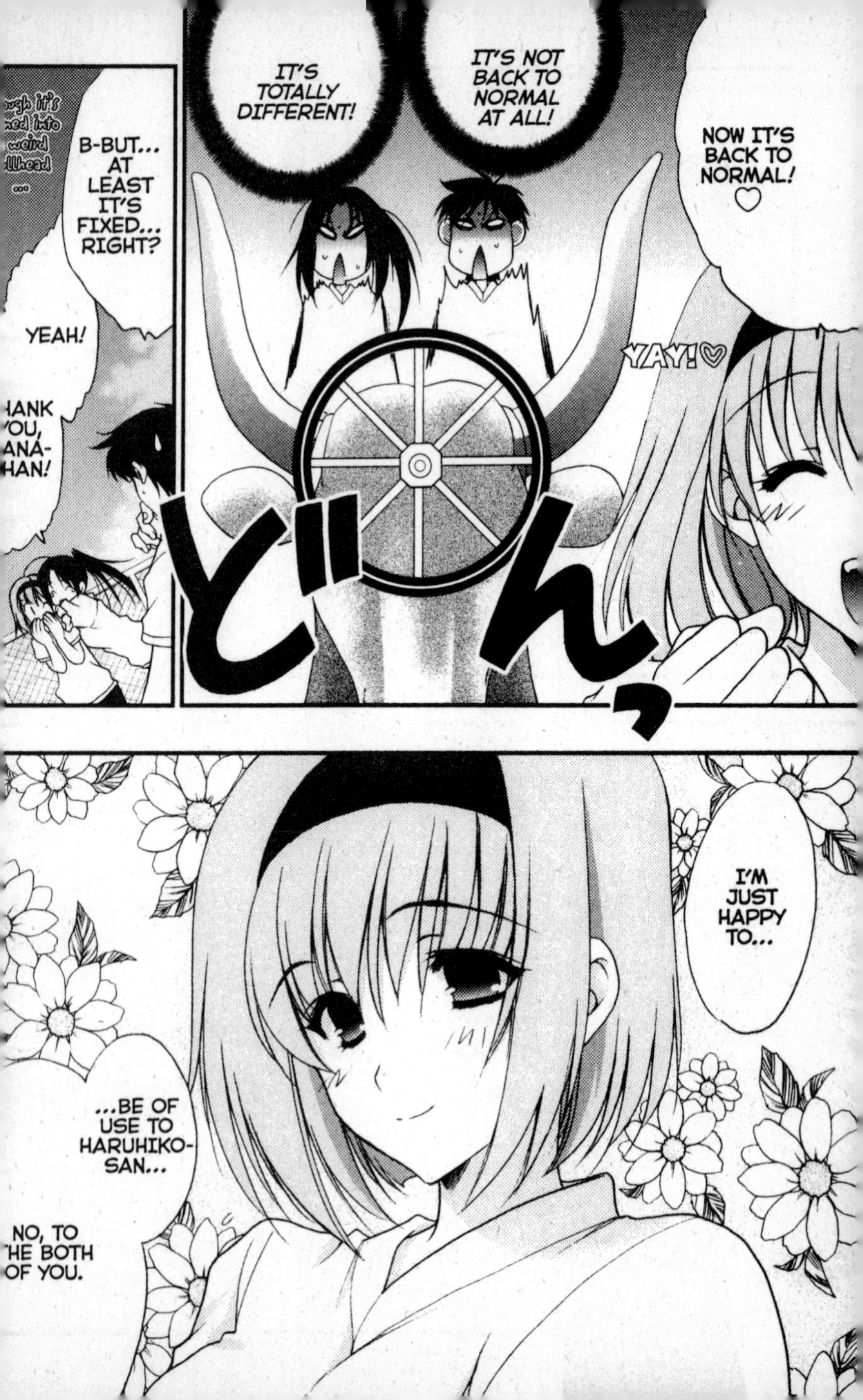
NOW IT'S BACK TO NORMAL! ♡
IT'S NOT BACK TO NORMAL AT ALL!
IT'S TOTALLY DIFFERENT!
YAY! ♡
どん、
B-BUT... AT LEAST IT'S FIXED... RIGHT?
YEAH!
HANK YOU, ANA-HAN!
I'M JUST HAPPY TO...
...BE OF USE TO HARUHIKO-SAN...
NO, TO HE BOTH OF YOU.

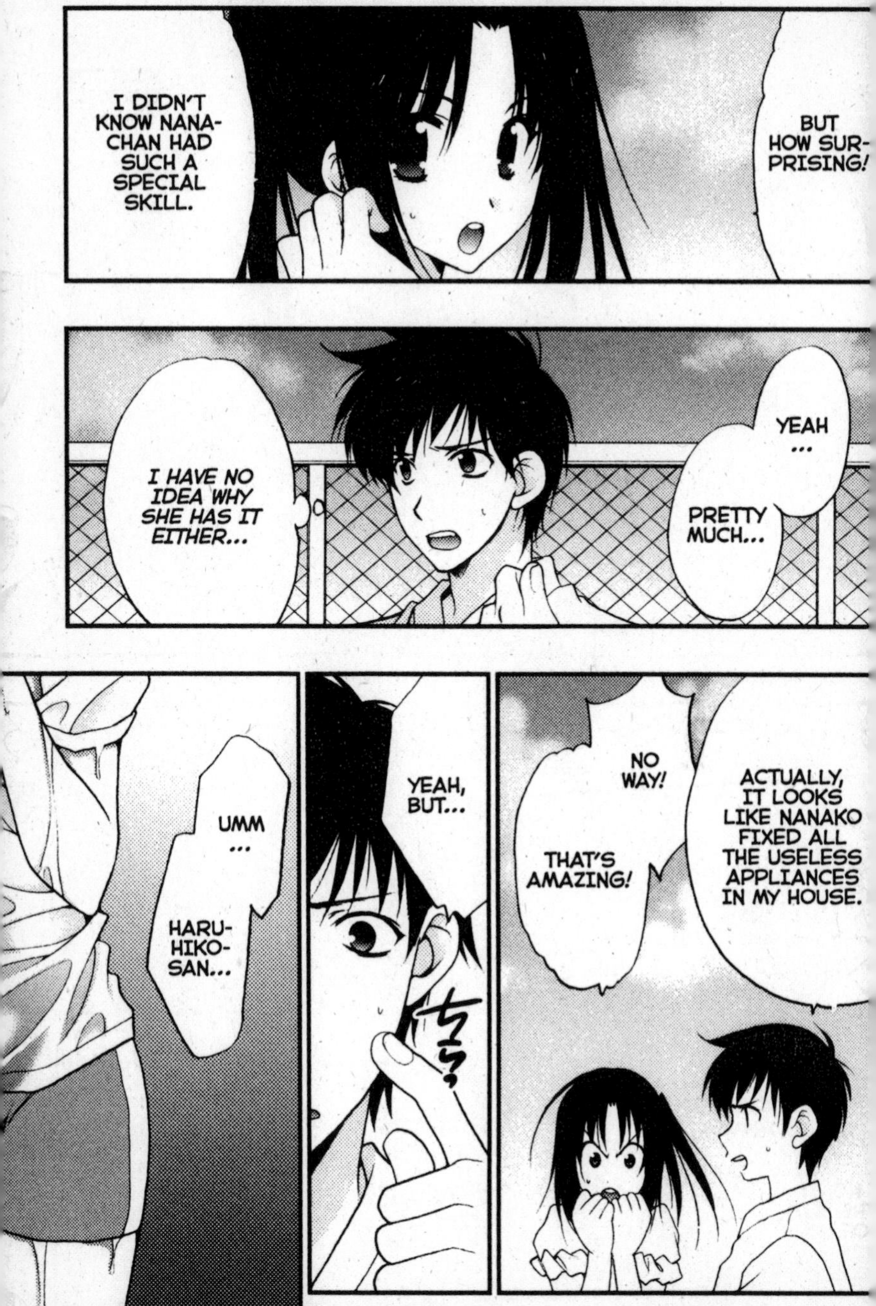
BUT HOW SURPRISING!
I DIDN'T KNOW NANA-CHAN HAD SUCH A SPECIAL SKILL.
YEAH ...
PRETTY MUCH...
I HAVE NO IDEA WHY SHE HAS IT EITHER...
ACTUALLY, IT LOOKS LIKE NANAKO FIXED ALL THE USELESS APPLIANCES IN MY HOUSE.
NO WAY!
THAT'S AMAZING!
YEAH, BUT...
UMM ...
HARUHIKO-SAN...

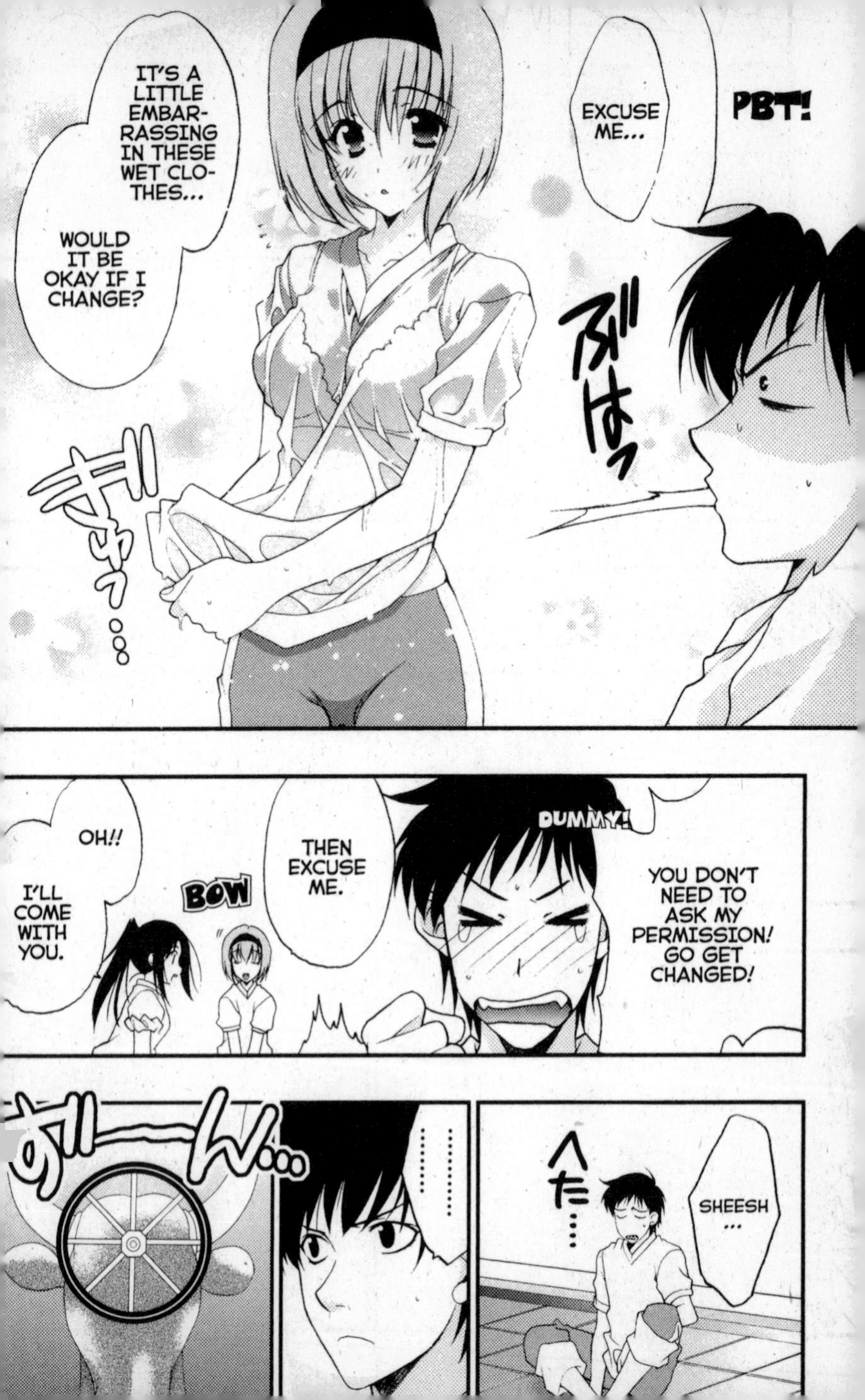
PBT!
EXCUSE ME...
ぶはっ
IT'S A LITTLE EMBARRASSING IN THESE WET CLOTHES...
WOULD IT BE OKAY IF I CHANGE?
ぎゅっ...
DUMMY!
YOU DON'T NEED TO ASK MY PERMISSION! GO GET CHANGED!
THEN EXCUSE ME.
BOW
OH!!
I'LL COME WITH YOU.
SHEESH...
へた...
......

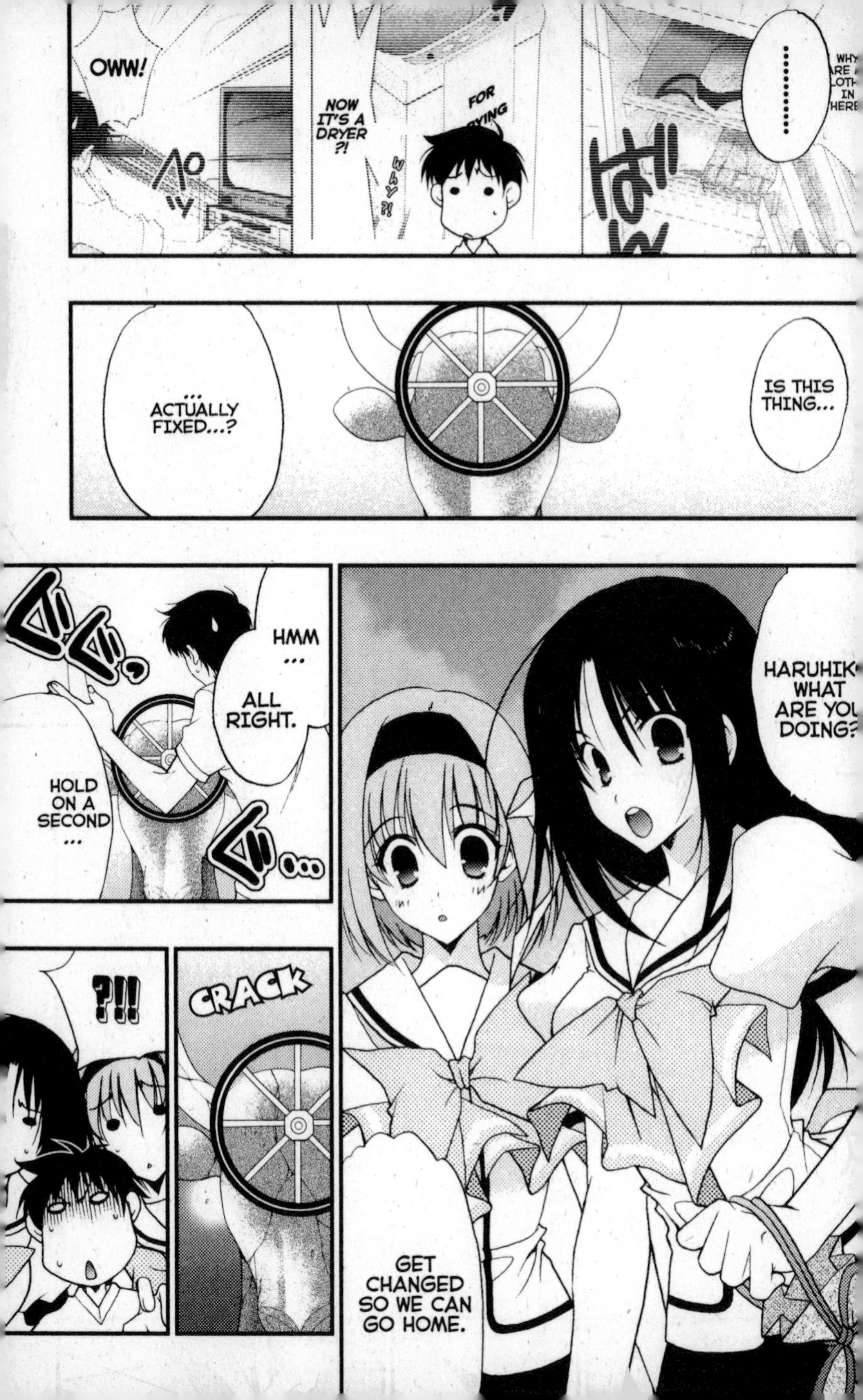
......
WHY ARE LOTH IN HERE
FOR
NOW IT'S A DRYER ?!
WHY ?!
OWW!
IS THIS THING...
...ACTUALLY FIXED...?
HARUHIK WHAT ARE YO DOING?
GET CHANGED SO WE CAN GO HOME.
HMM ... ALL RIGHT.
HOLD ON A SECOND ...
CRACK
?!!

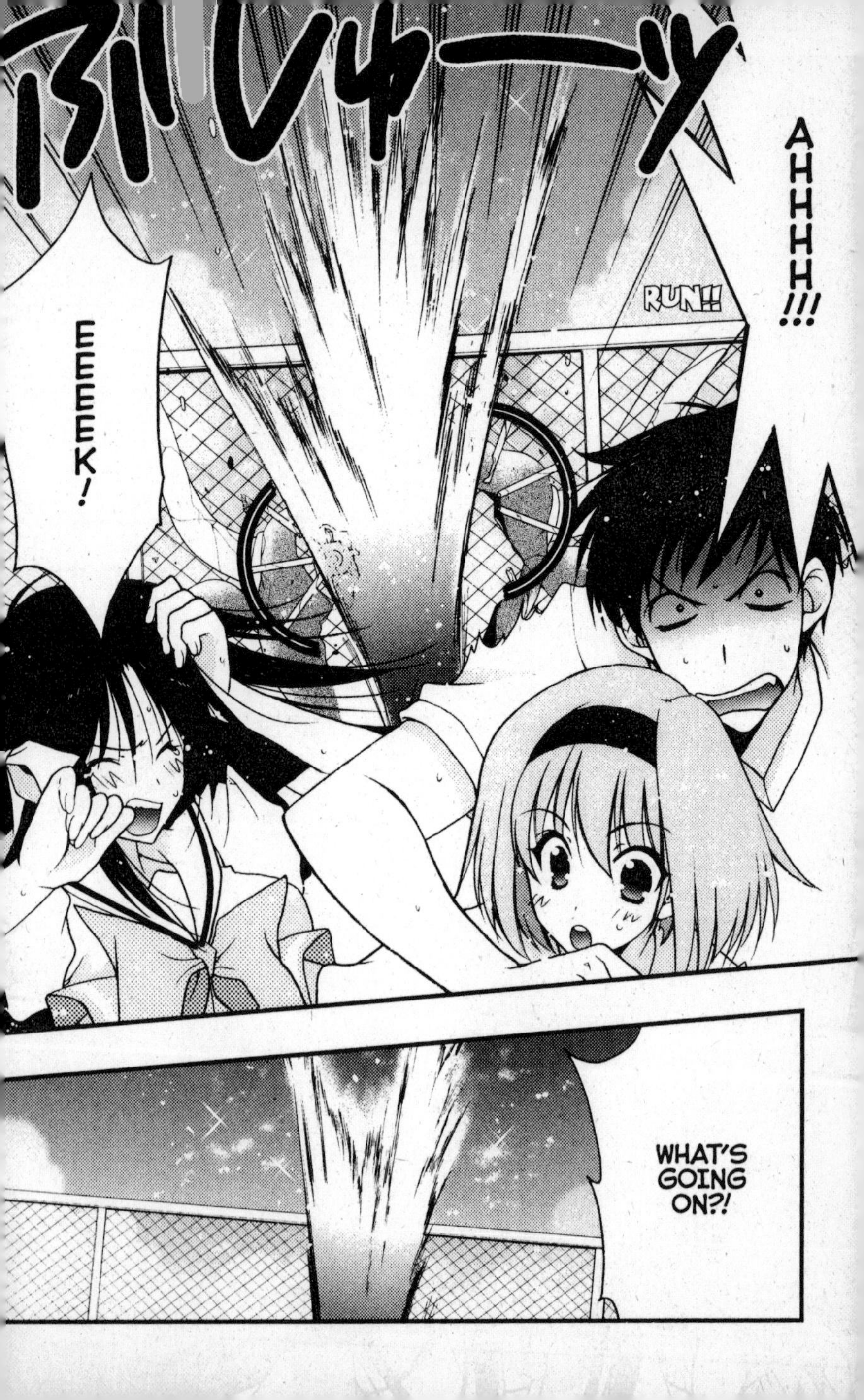
ぶしゅーーッ
AHHHH!!!
RUN!!
EEEEEK!
WHAT'S GOING ON?!

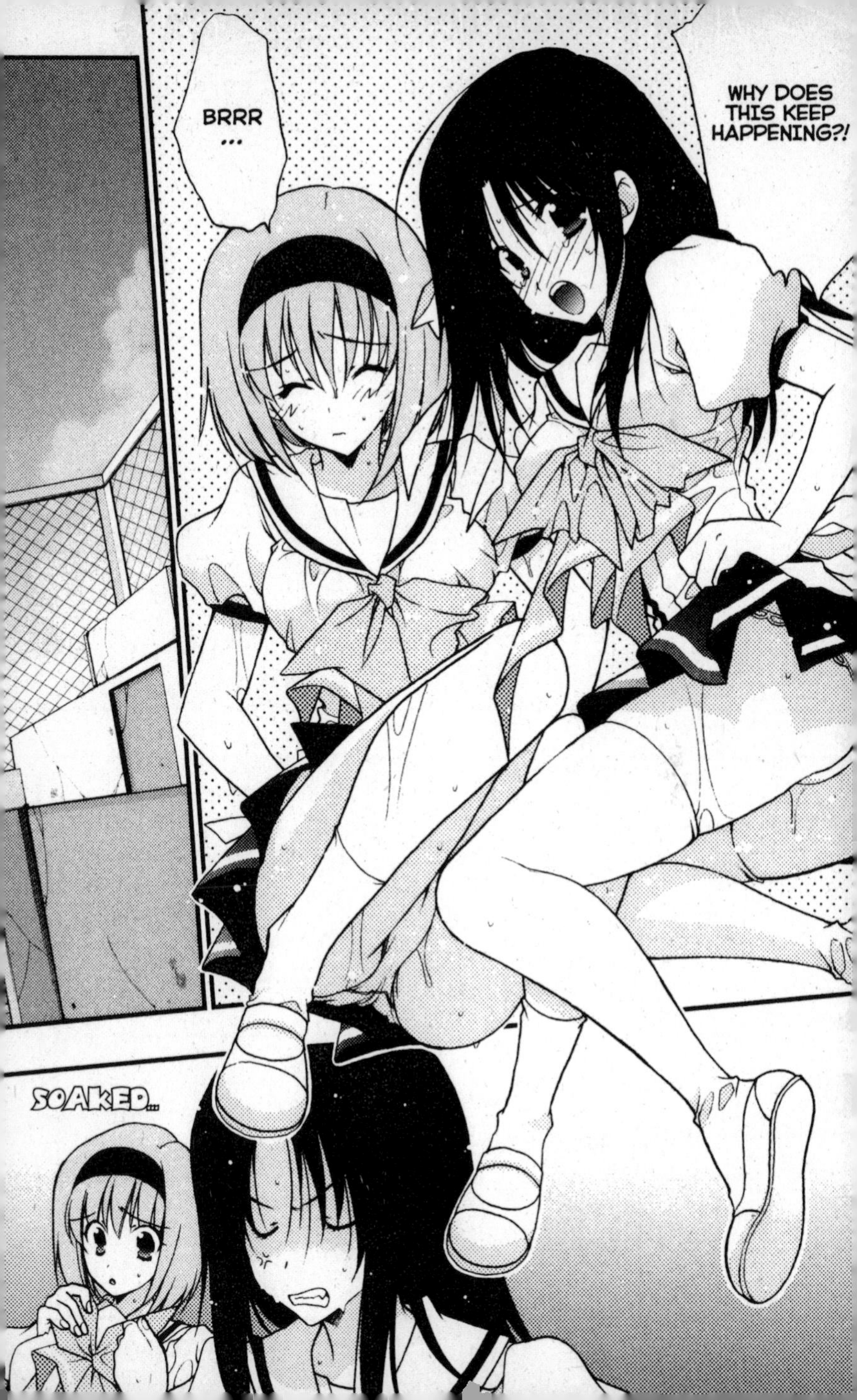
WHY DOES THIS KEEP HAPPENING?!
BRRR ...
SOAKED...

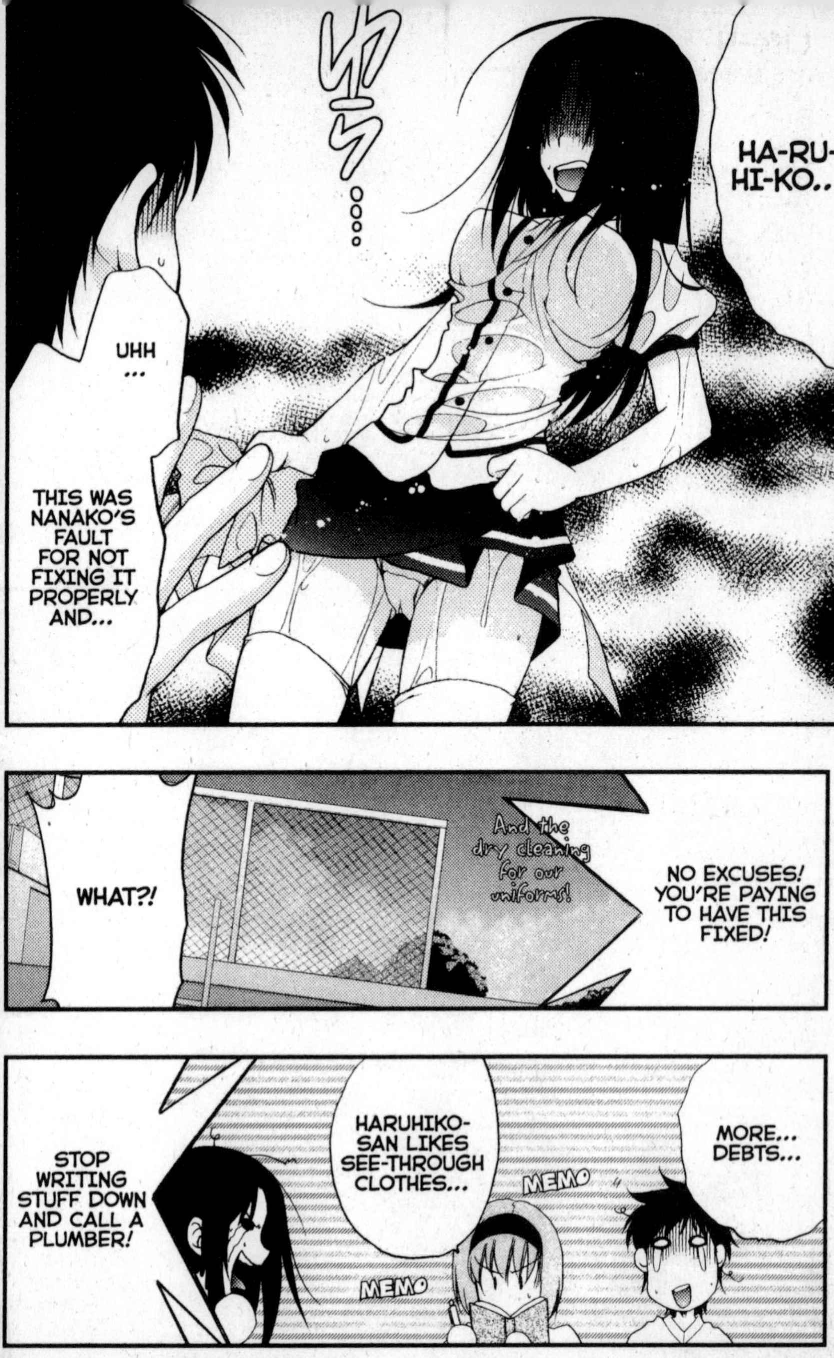
ゆら
oooo
HA-RU-HI-KO...
UHH ...
THIS WAS NANAKO'S FAULT FOR NOT FIXING IT PROPERLY AND...
NO EXCUSES! YOU'RE PAYING TO HAVE THIS FIXED!
And the dry cleaning for our uniforms!
WHAT?!
MORE... DEBTS...
HARUHIKO-SAN LIKES SEE-THROUGH CLOTHES...
MEMO
MEMO
STOP WRITING STUFF DOWN AND CALL A PLUMBER!

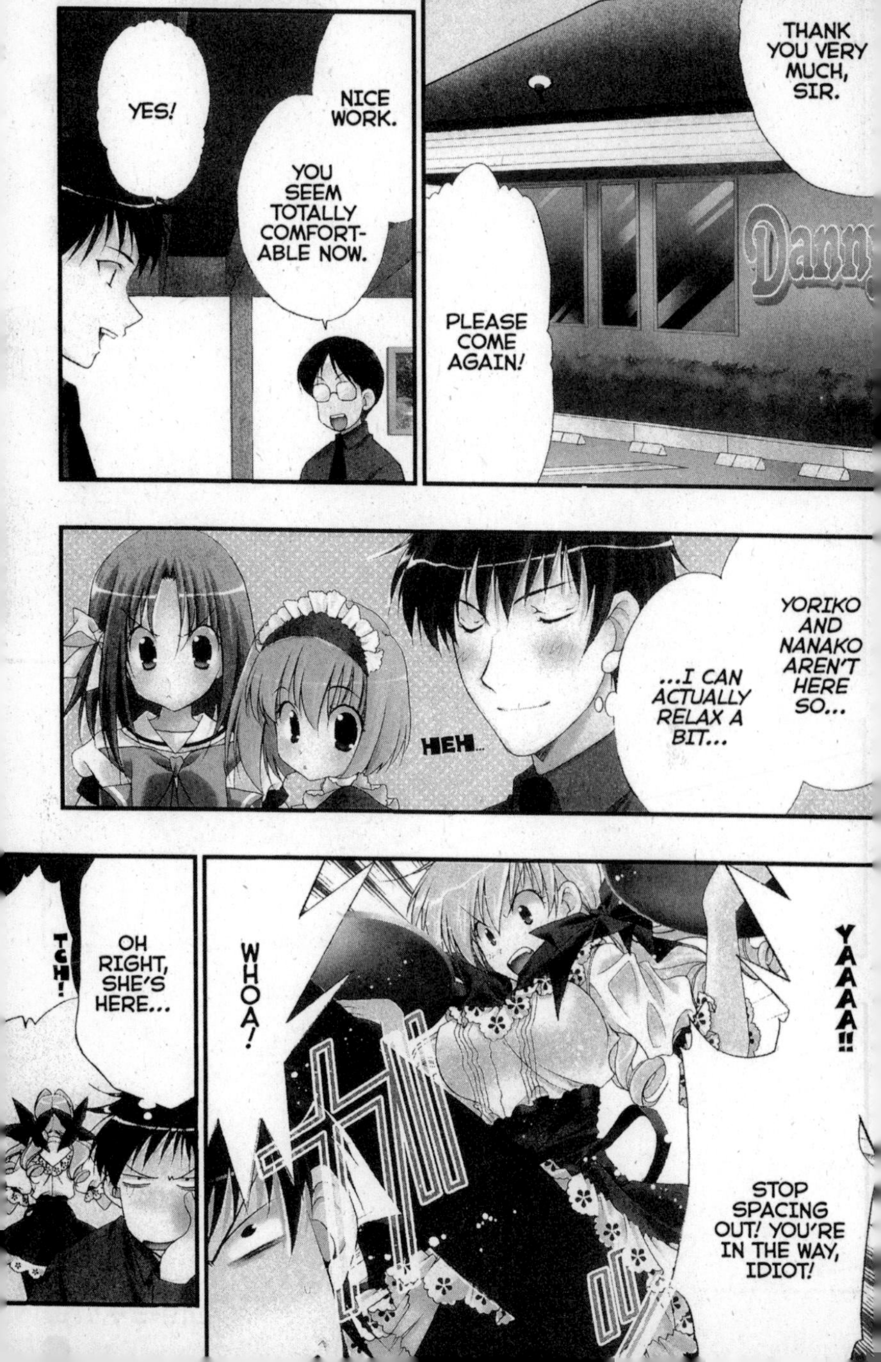
THANK YOU VERY MUCH, SIR.
PLEASE COME AGAIN!
NICE WORK.
YOU SEEM TOTALLY COMFORT-ABLE NOW.
YES!
YORIKO AND NANAKO AREN'T HERE SO...
...I CAN ACTUALLY RELAX A BIT...
HEH...
YAAAAA!!
STOP SPACING OUT! YOU'RE IN THE WAY, IDIOT!
WHOA!
OH RIGHT, SHE'S HERE...
TCH!

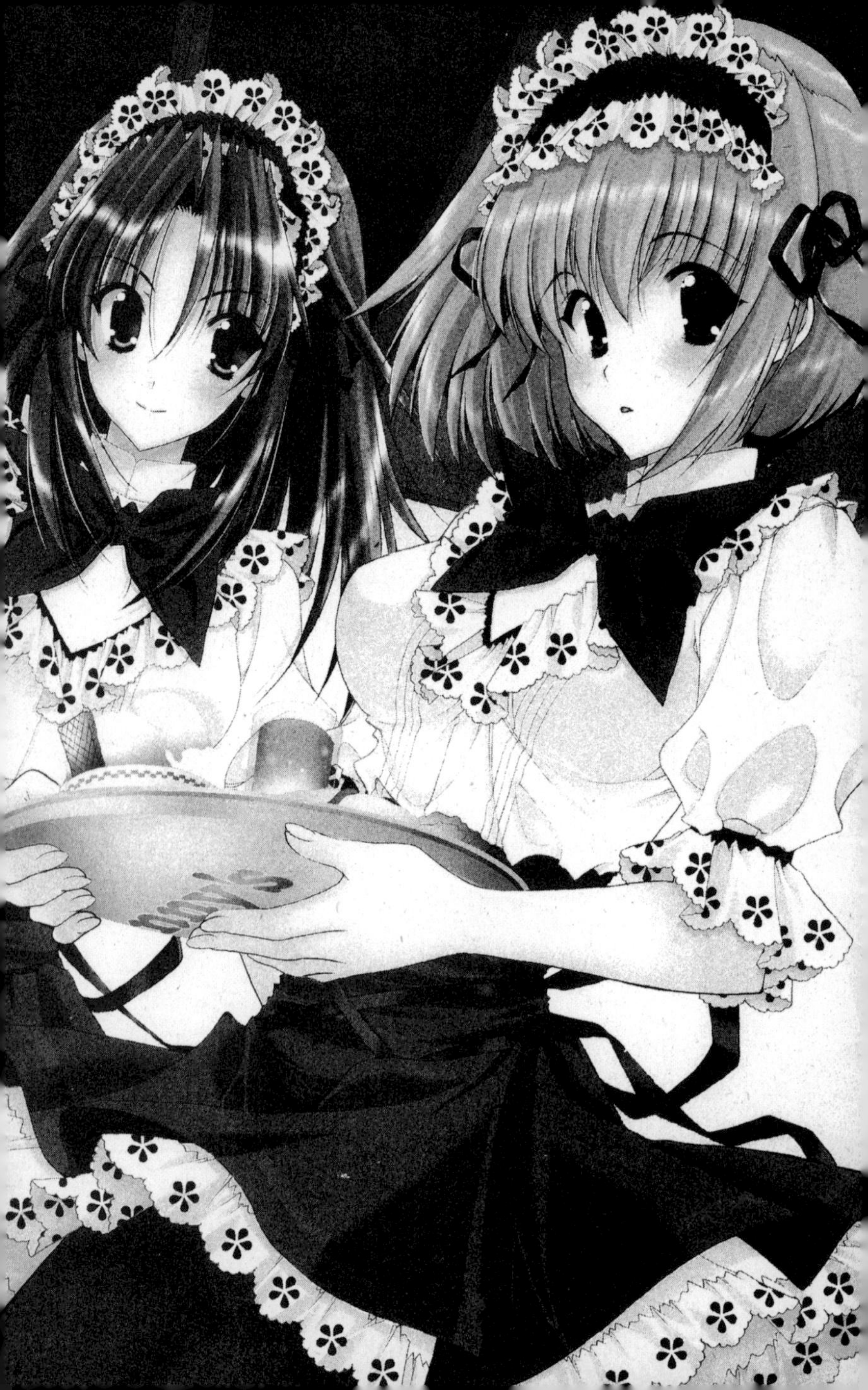

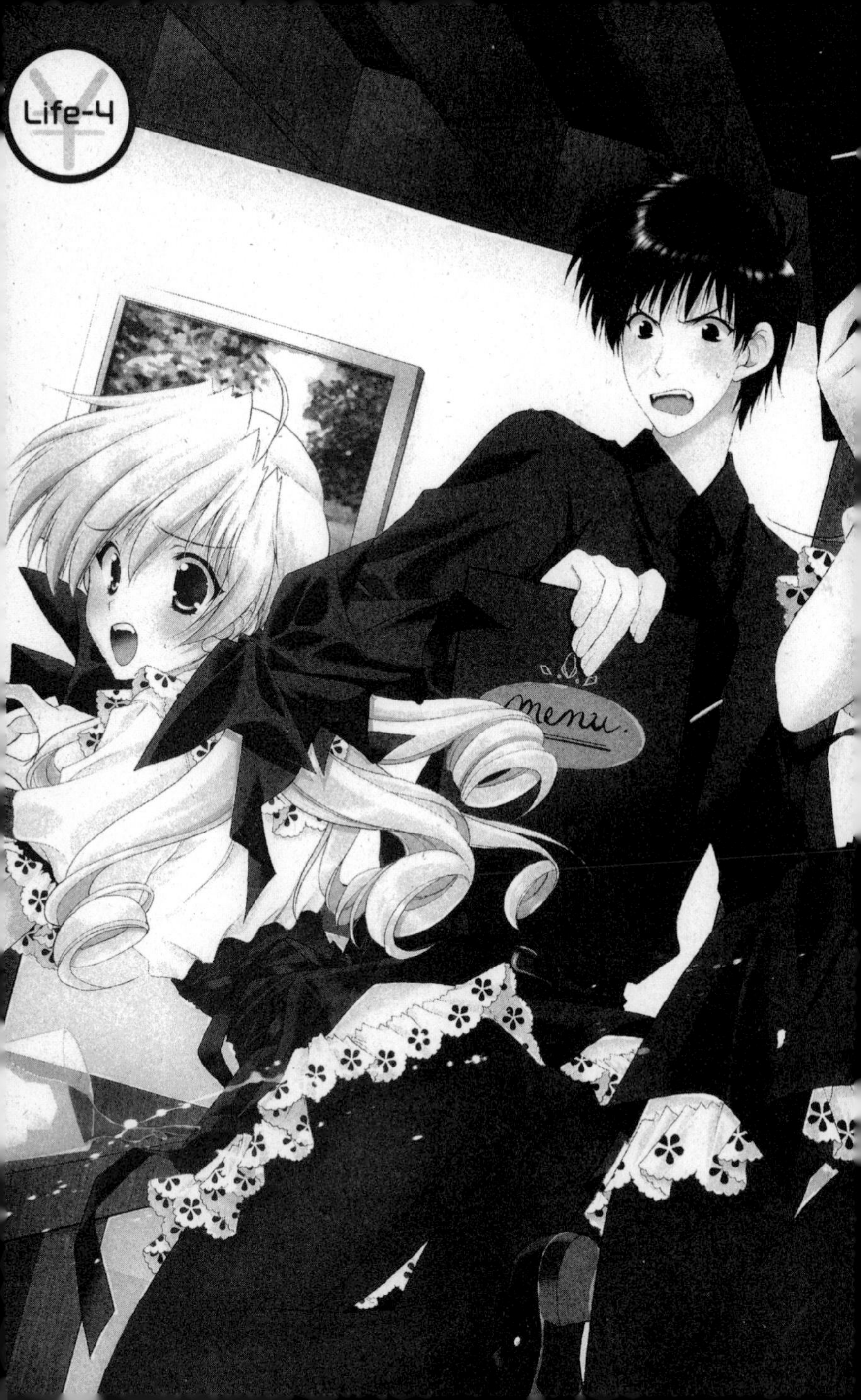
Life-4
menu.

セイビング・ライフ
SAVING LIFE

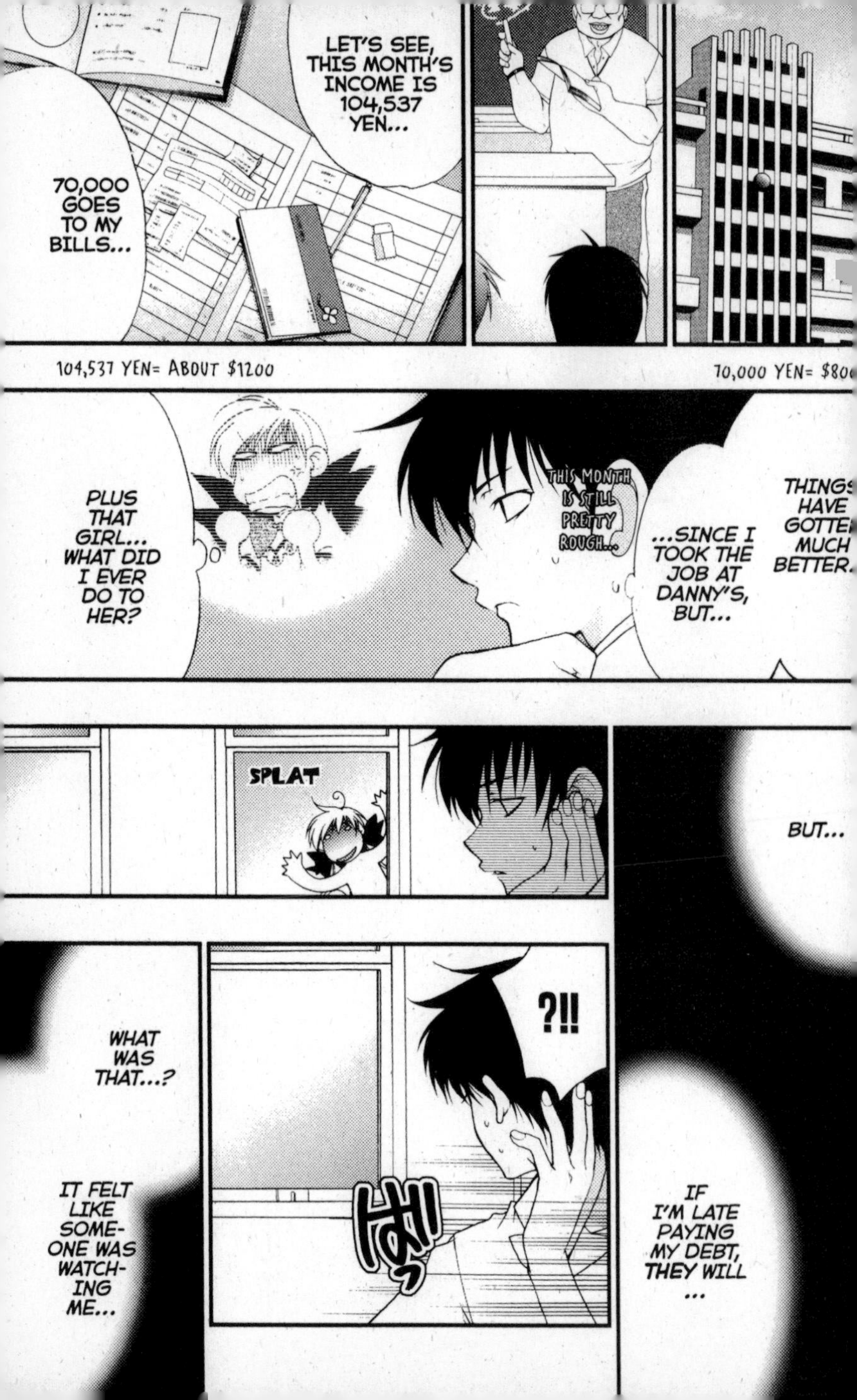
LET'S SEE, THIS MONTH'S INCOME IS 104,537 YEN...
70,000 GOES TO MY BILLS...
70,000 YEN= $80
104,537 YEN= ABOUT $1200
THINGS HAVE GOTTE MUCH BETTER.
...SINCE I TOOK THE JOB AT DANNY'S, BUT...
THIS MONTH IS STILL PRETTY ROUGH...
PLUS THAT GIRL... WHAT DID I EVER DO TO HER?
BUT...
IF I'M LATE PAYING MY DEBT, THEY WILL ...
SPLAT
?!!
はっ
WHAT WAS THAT...?
IT FELT LIKE SOMEONE WAS WATCHING ME...

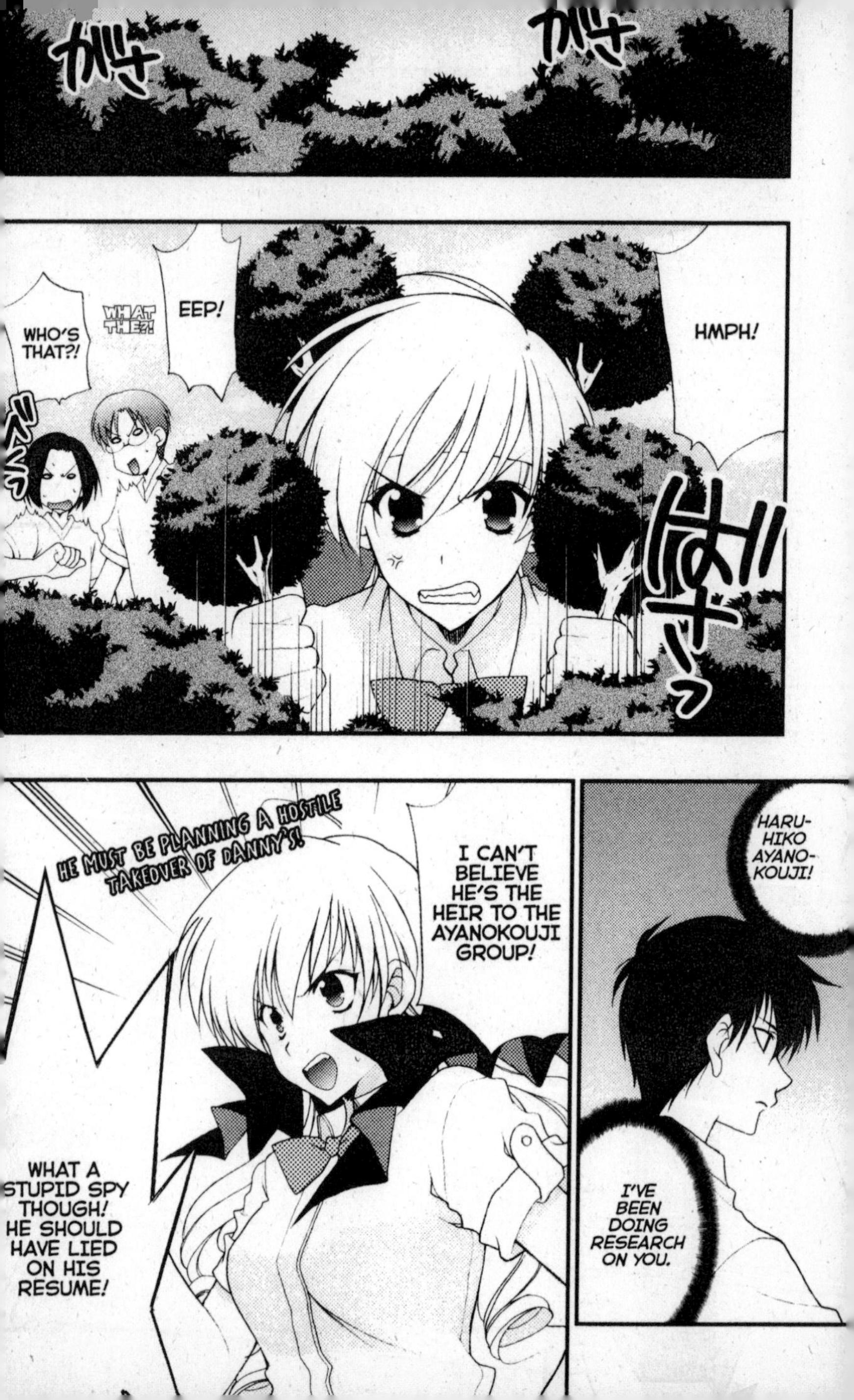
がさ
がさ
HMPH!
はっ
EEP!
WHAT THE?!
WHO'S THAT?!
HARU-HIKO AYANO-KOUJI!
I'VE BEEN DOING RESEARCH ON YOU.
I CAN'T BELIEVE HE'S THE HEIR TO THE AYANOKOUJI GROUP!
HE MUST BE PLANNING A HOSTILE TAKEOVER OF DANNY'S!
WHAT A STUPID SPY THOUGH! HE SHOULD HAVE LIED ON HIS RESUME!

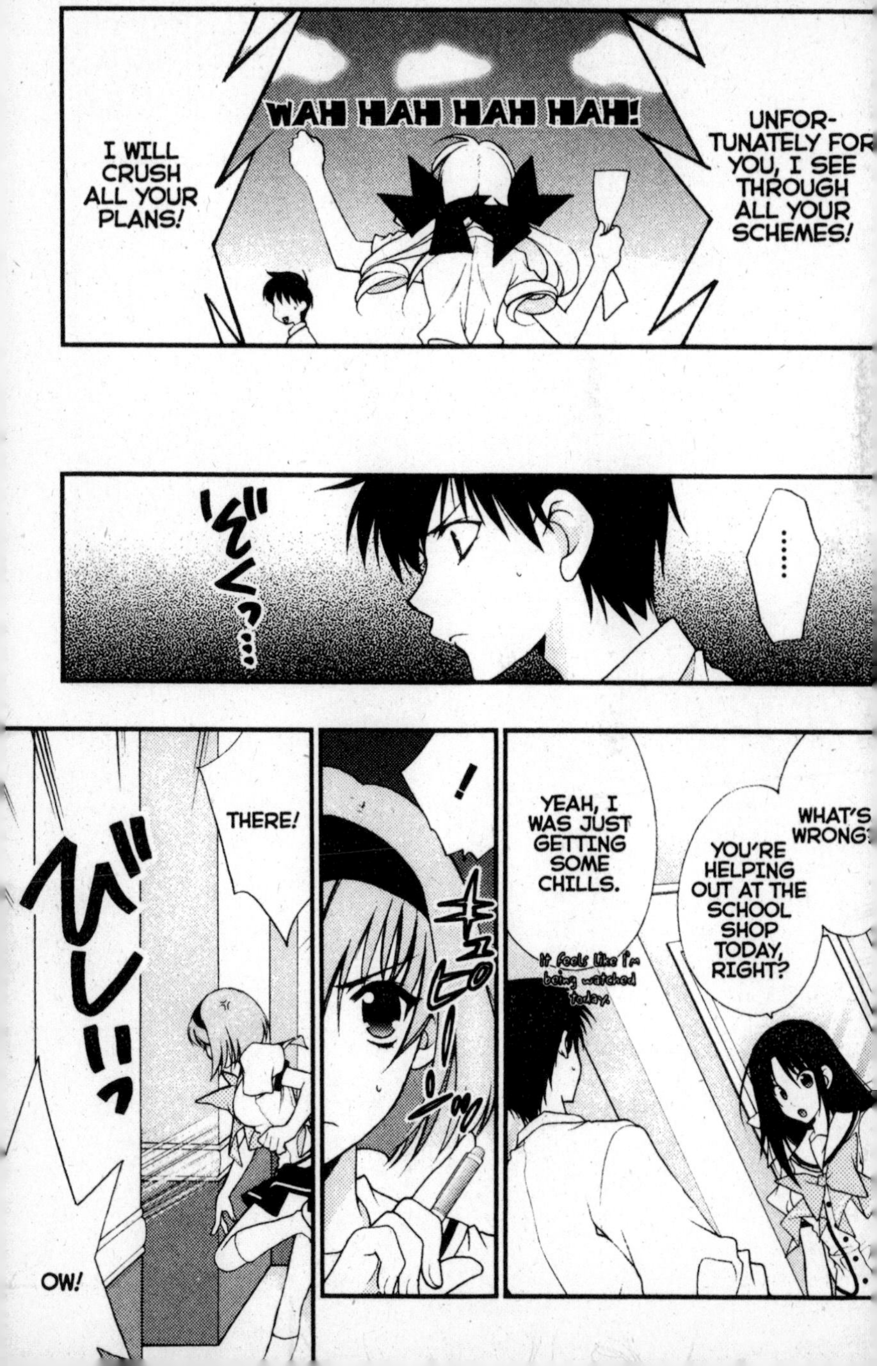
UNFOR-TUNATELY FOR YOU, I SEE THROUGH ALL YOUR SCHEMES!
WAH HAH HAH HAH!
I WILL CRUSH ALL YOUR PLANS!
......
ぞくっ…
WHAT'S WRONG?
YOU'RE HELPING OUT AT THE SCHOOL SHOP TODAY, RIGHT?
YEAH, I WAS JUST GETTING SOME CHILLS.
It feels like I'm being watched today.
!
THERE!
OW!

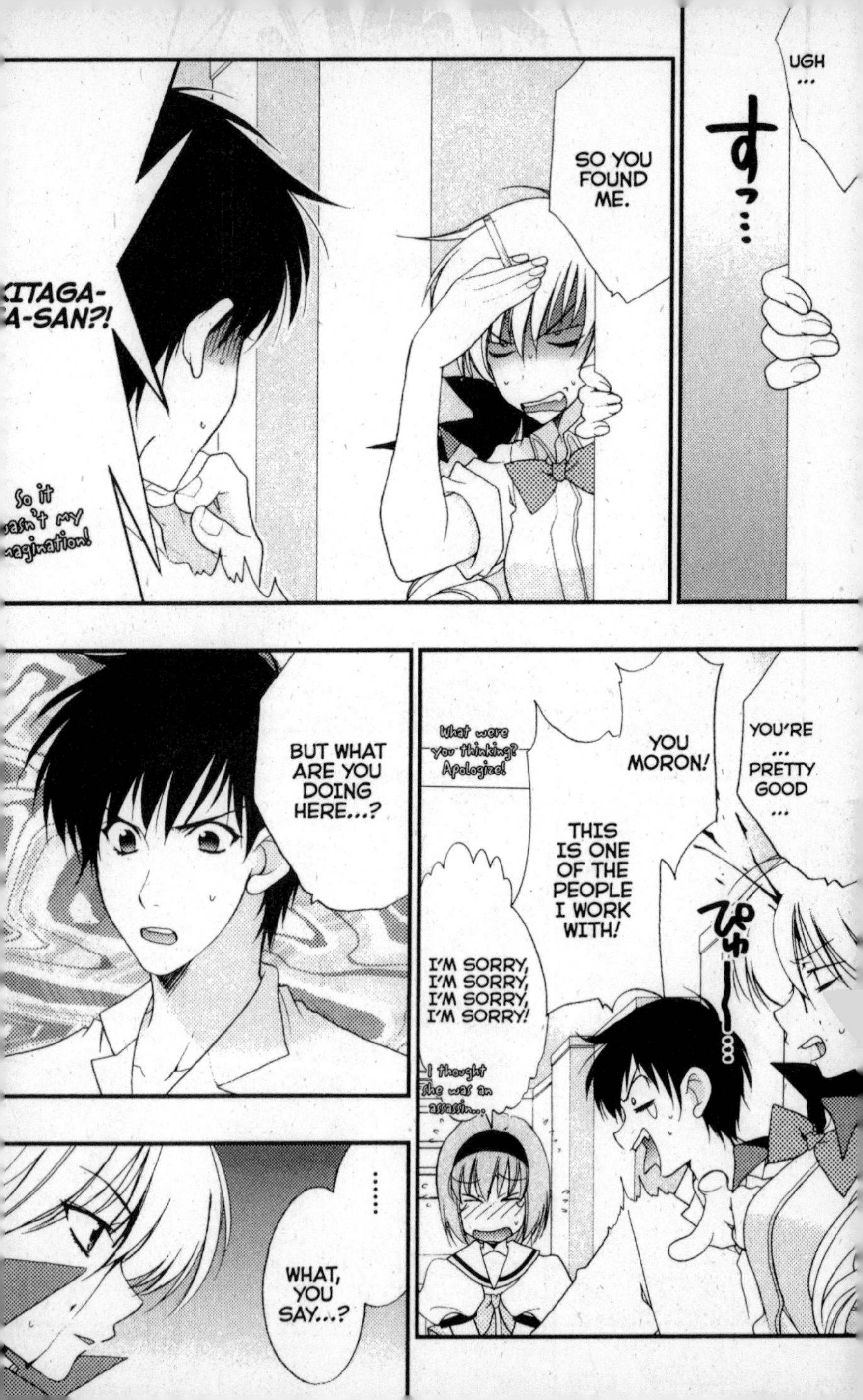
UGH ...
すっ…
SO YOU FOUND ME.
ITAGA-
A-SAN?!
So it
asn't my
nagination!
YOU'RE ... PRETTY GOOD ...
YOU MORON!
THIS IS ONE OF THE PEOPLE I WORK WITH!
ぴゅ〜〜…
What were you thinking? Apologize!
I'M SORRY, I'M SORRY, I'M SORRY, I'M SORRY!
I thought she was an assassin...
BUT WHAT ARE YOU DOING HERE...?
......
WHAT, YOU SAY...?

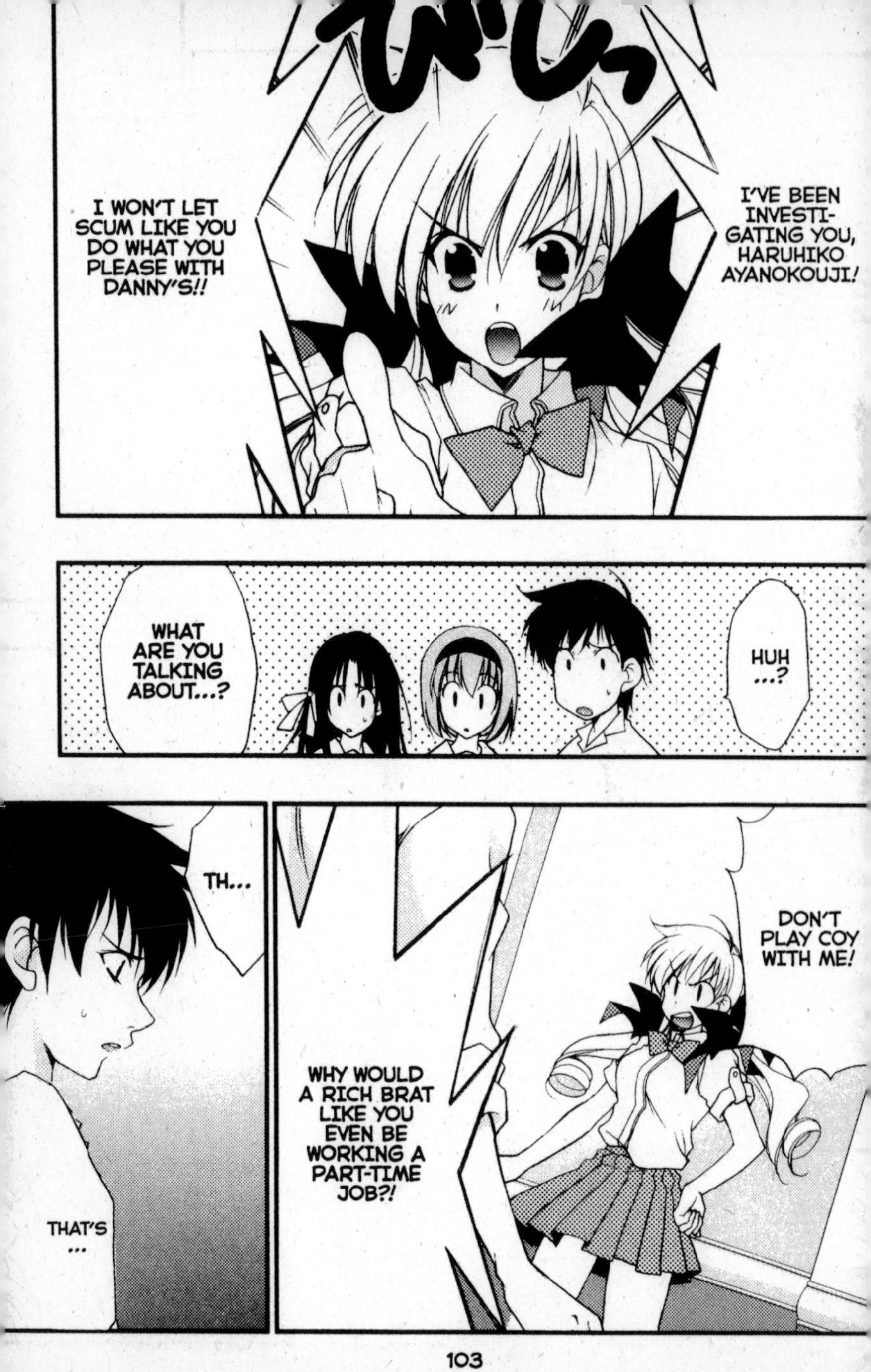
びしっ
I'VE BEEN INVESTI-GATING YOU, HARUHIKO AYANOKOUJI!
I WON'T LET SCUM LIKE YOU DO WHAT YOU PLEASE WITH DANNY'S!!
HUH ...?
WHAT ARE YOU TALKING ABOUT...?
DON'T PLAY COY WITH ME!
WHY WOULD A RICH BRAT LIKE YOU EVEN BE WORKING A PART-TIME JOB?!
TH...
THAT'S ...

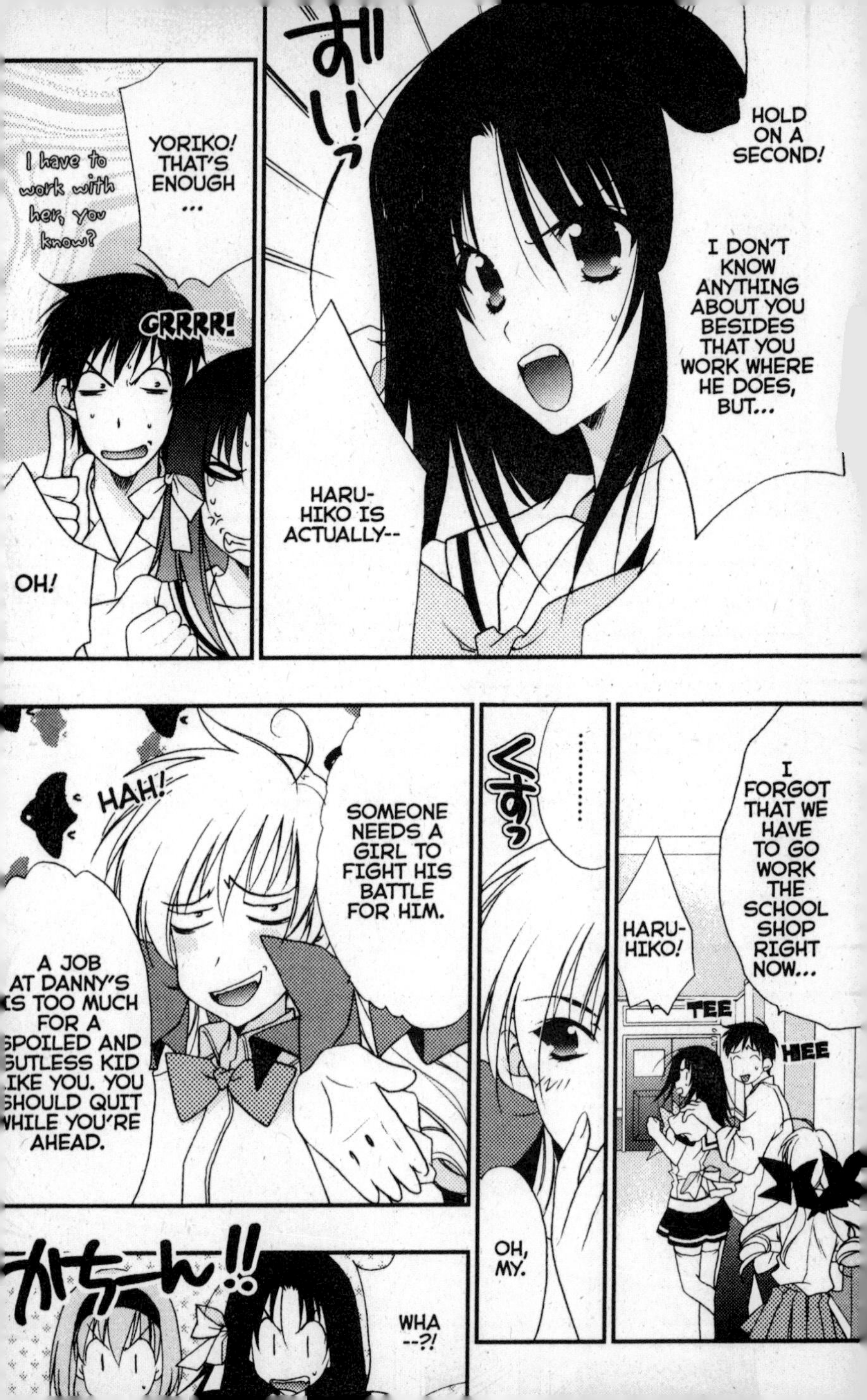
ずいっ
HOLD ON A SECOND!
I DON'T KNOW ANYTHING ABOUT YOU BESIDES THAT YOU WORK WHERE HE DOES, BUT...
HARU-HIKO IS ACTUALLY--
YORIKO! THAT'S ENOUGH ...
I have to work with her, you know?
GRRRR!
OH!
I FORGOT THAT WE HAVE TO GO WORK THE SCHOOL SHOP RIGHT NOW...
HARU-HIKO!
TEE
HEE
......
くすっ
OH, MY.
HAH!
SOMEONE NEEDS A GIRL TO FIGHT HIS BATTLE FOR HIM.
A JOB AT DANNY'S IS TOO MUCH FOR A SPOILED AND GUTLESS KID LIKE YOU. YOU SHOULD QUIT WHILE YOU'RE AHEAD.
かちーん!!
WHA --?!

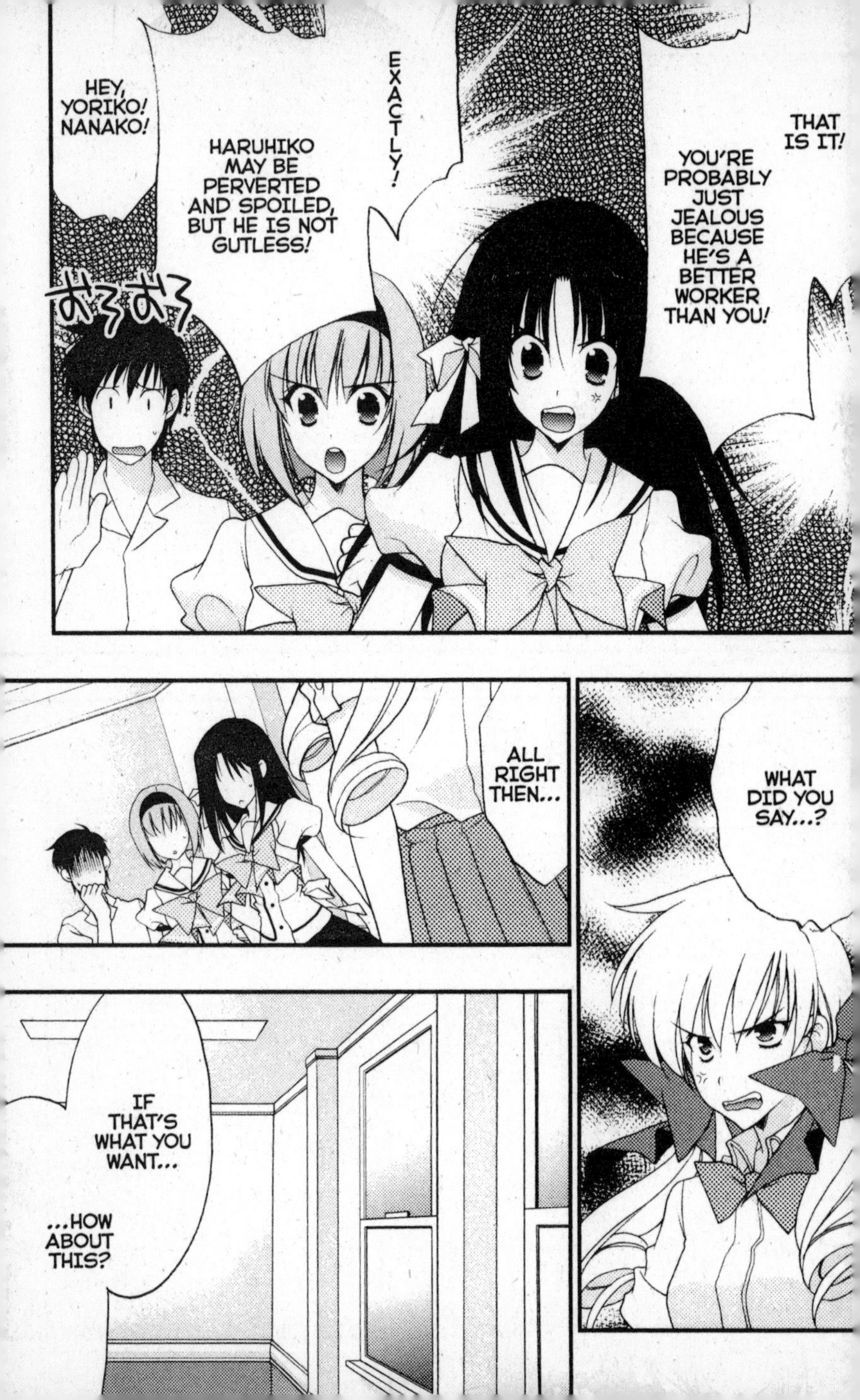
THAT IS IT!
YOU'RE PROBABLY JUST JEALOUS BECAUSE HE'S A BETTER WORKER THAN YOU!
EXACTLY!
HARUHIKO MAY BE PERVERTED AND SPOILED, BUT HE IS NOT GUTLESS!
HEY, YORIKO! NANAKO!
おろおろ
WHAT DID YOU SAY...?
ALL RIGHT THEN...
IF THAT'S WHAT YOU WANT...
...HOW ABOUT THIS?

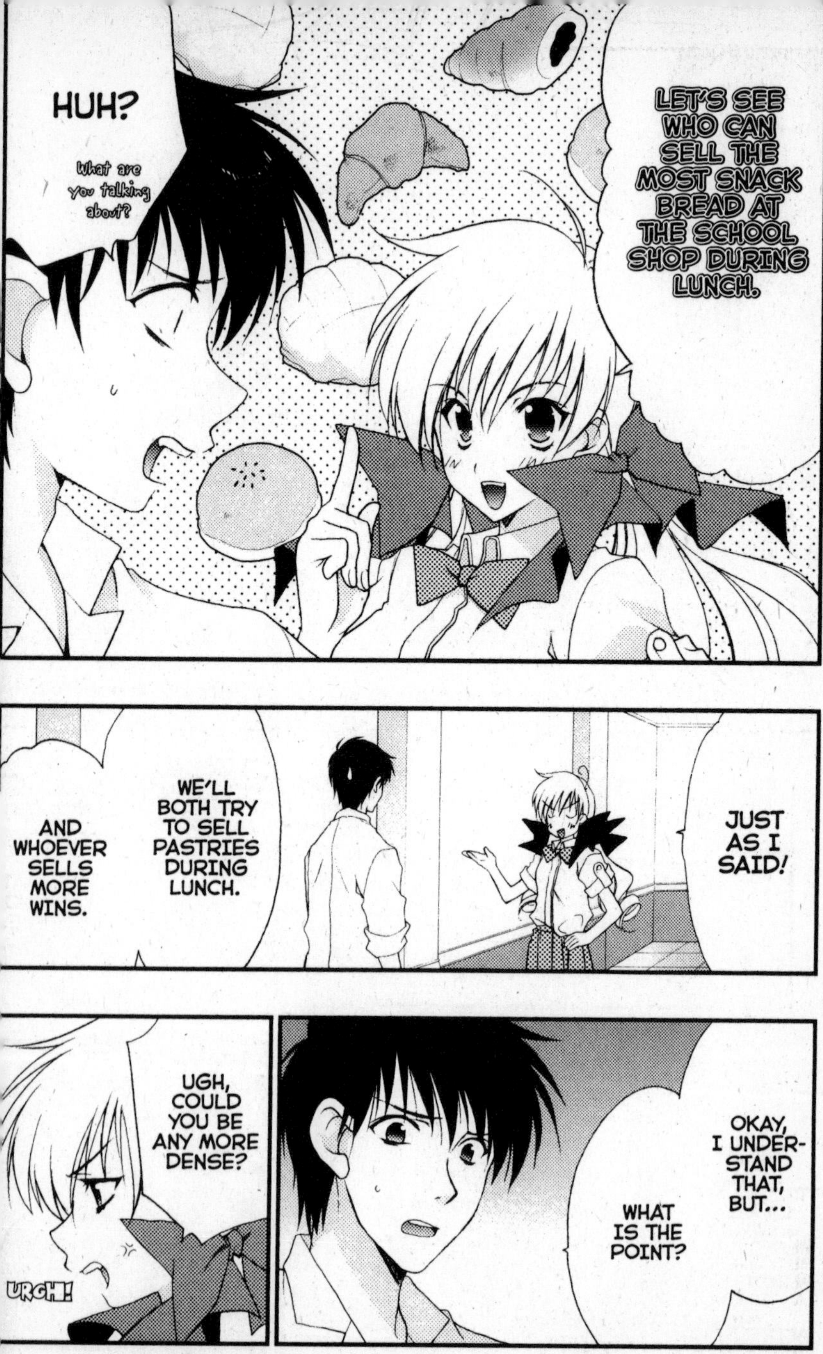
LET'S SEE WHO CAN SELL THE MOST SNACK BREAD AT THE SCHOOL SHOP DURING LUNCH.
HUH?
What are you talking about?
JUST AS I SAID!
WE'LL BOTH TRY TO SELL PASTRIES DURING LUNCH.
AND WHOEVER SELLS MORE WINS.
OKAY, I UNDER-STAND THAT, BUT...
WHAT IS THE POINT?
UGH, COULD YOU BE ANY MORE DENSE?
URGH!

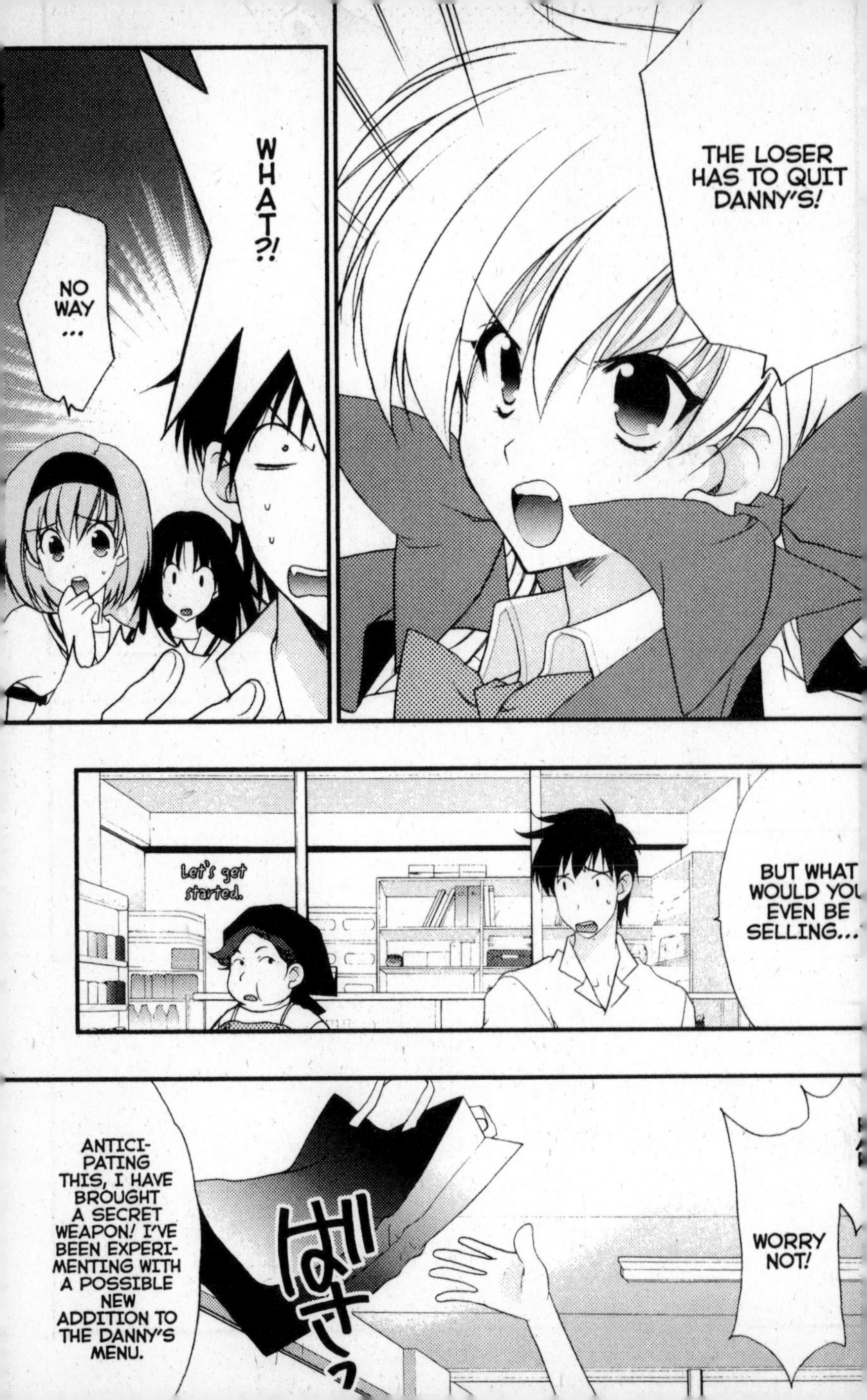
THE LOSER HAS TO QUIT DANNY'S!
WHAT?!
NO WAY...
BUT WHAT WOULD YOU EVEN BE SELLING...
Let's get started.
WORRY NOT!
ANTICI-PATING THIS, I HAVE BROUGHT A SECRET WEAPON! I'VE BEEN EXPERI-MENTING WITH A POSSIBLE NEW ADDITION TO THE DANNY'S MENU.

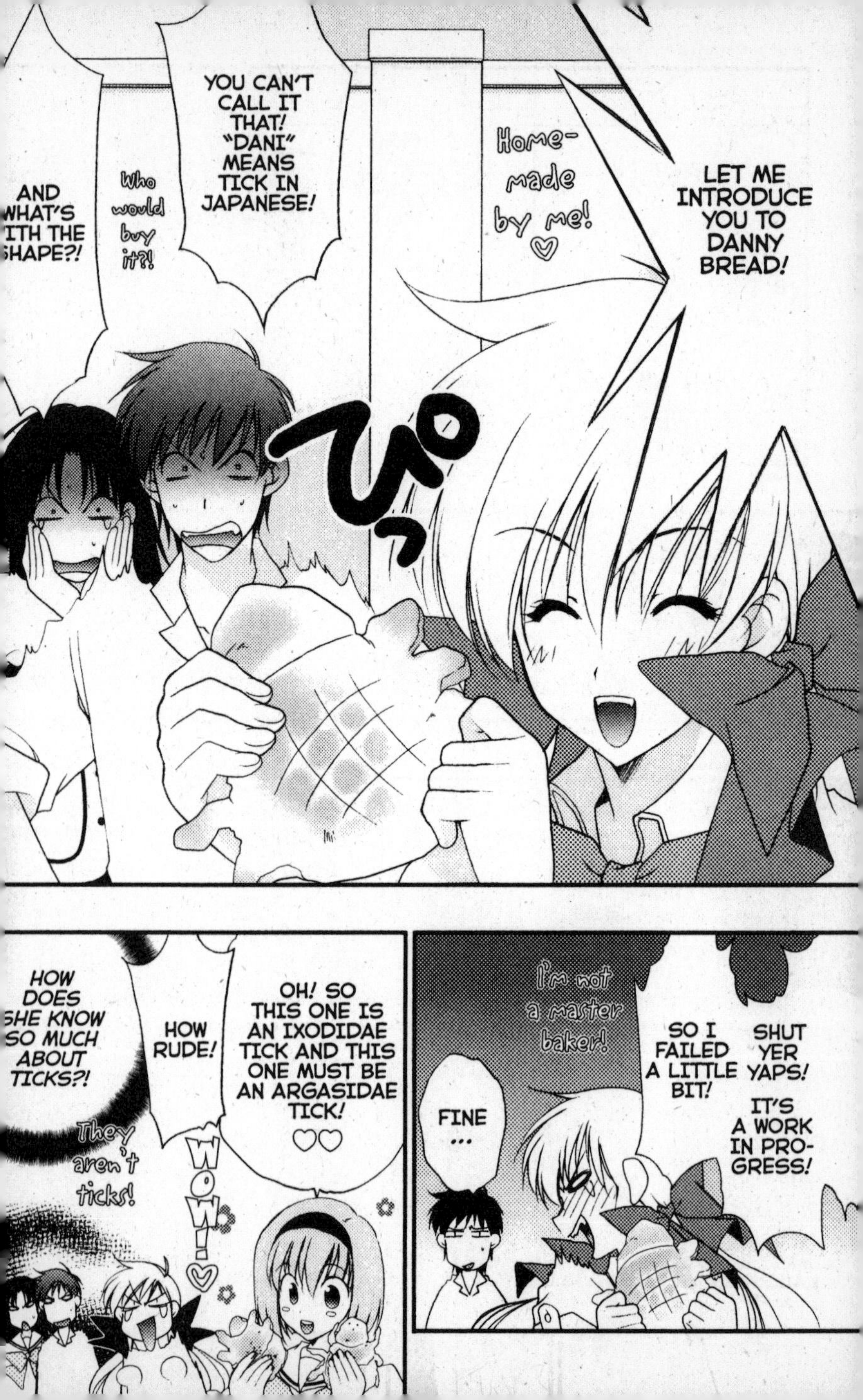
LET ME INTRODUCE YOU TO DANNY BREAD!
Home-made by me! ♡
ぴっ
YOU CAN'T CALL IT THAT! "DANI" MEANS TICK IN JAPANESE!
Who would buy it?!
AND WHAT'S ITH THE SHAPE?!
SHUT YER YAPS!
IT'S A WORK IN PRO-GRESS!
SO I FAILED A LITTLE BIT!
I'm not a master baker!
FINE ...
OH! SO THIS ONE IS AN IXODIDAE TICK AND THIS ONE MUST BE AN ARGASIDAE TICK! ♡♡
WOW! ♡
HOW RUDE!
HOW DOES SHE KNOW SO MUCH ABOUT TICKS?!
They aren't ticks!

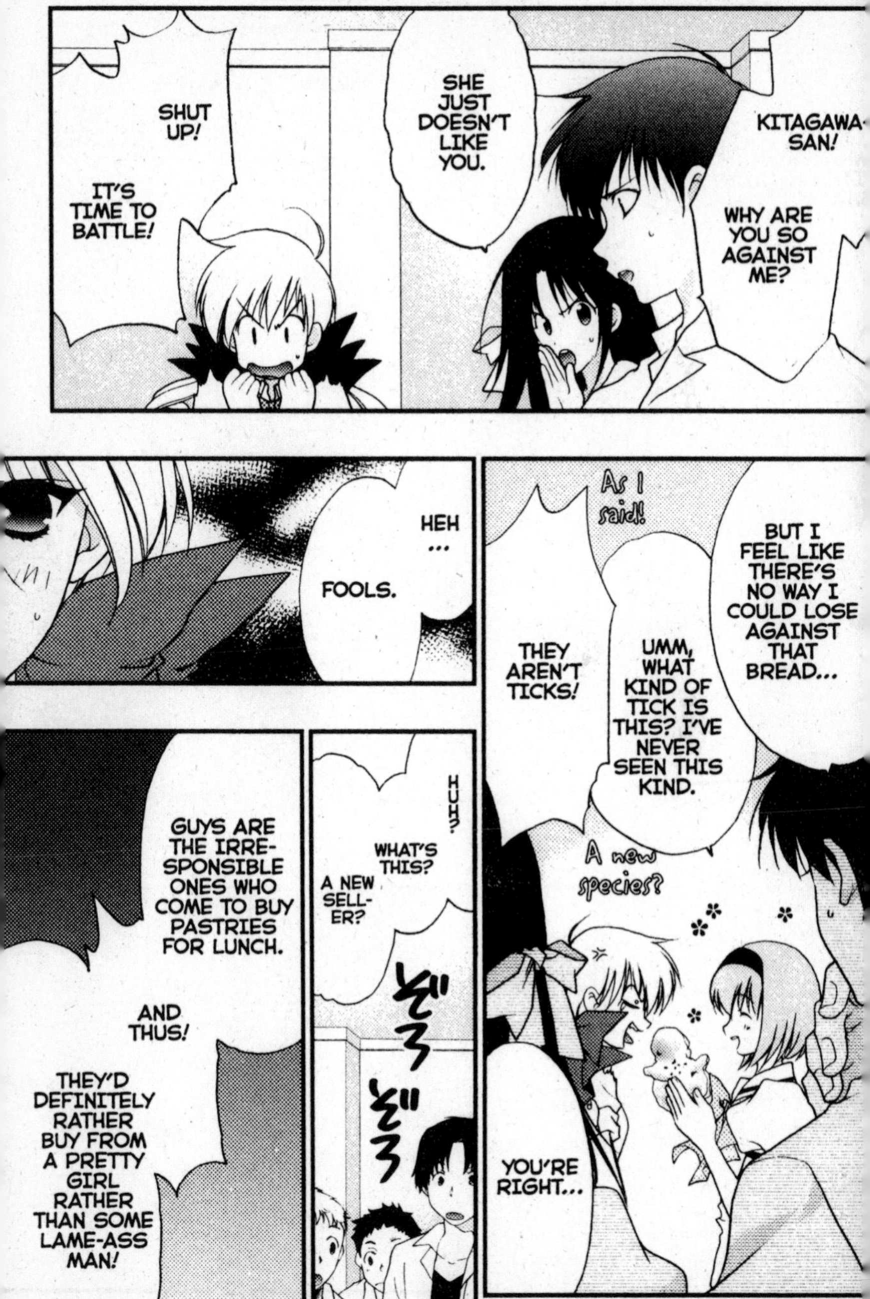
KITAGAWA-SAN!
WHY ARE YOU SO AGAINST ME?
SHE JUST DOESN'T LIKE YOU.
SHUT UP!
IT'S TIME TO BATTLE!
BUT I FEEL LIKE THERE'S NO WAY I COULD LOSE AGAINST THAT BREAD...
As I said!
UMM, WHAT KIND OF TICK IS THIS? I'VE NEVER SEEN THIS KIND.
THEY AREN'T TICKS!
A new species?
YOU'RE RIGHT...
HEH...
FOOLS.
HUH?
WHAT'S THIS?
A NEW SELL-ER?
ぞろ
ぞろ
GUYS ARE THE IRRE-SPONSIBLE ONES WHO COME TO BUY PASTRIES FOR LUNCH.
AND THUS!
THEY'D DEFINITELY RATHER BUY FROM A PRETTY GIRL RATHER THAN SOME LAME-ASS MAN!

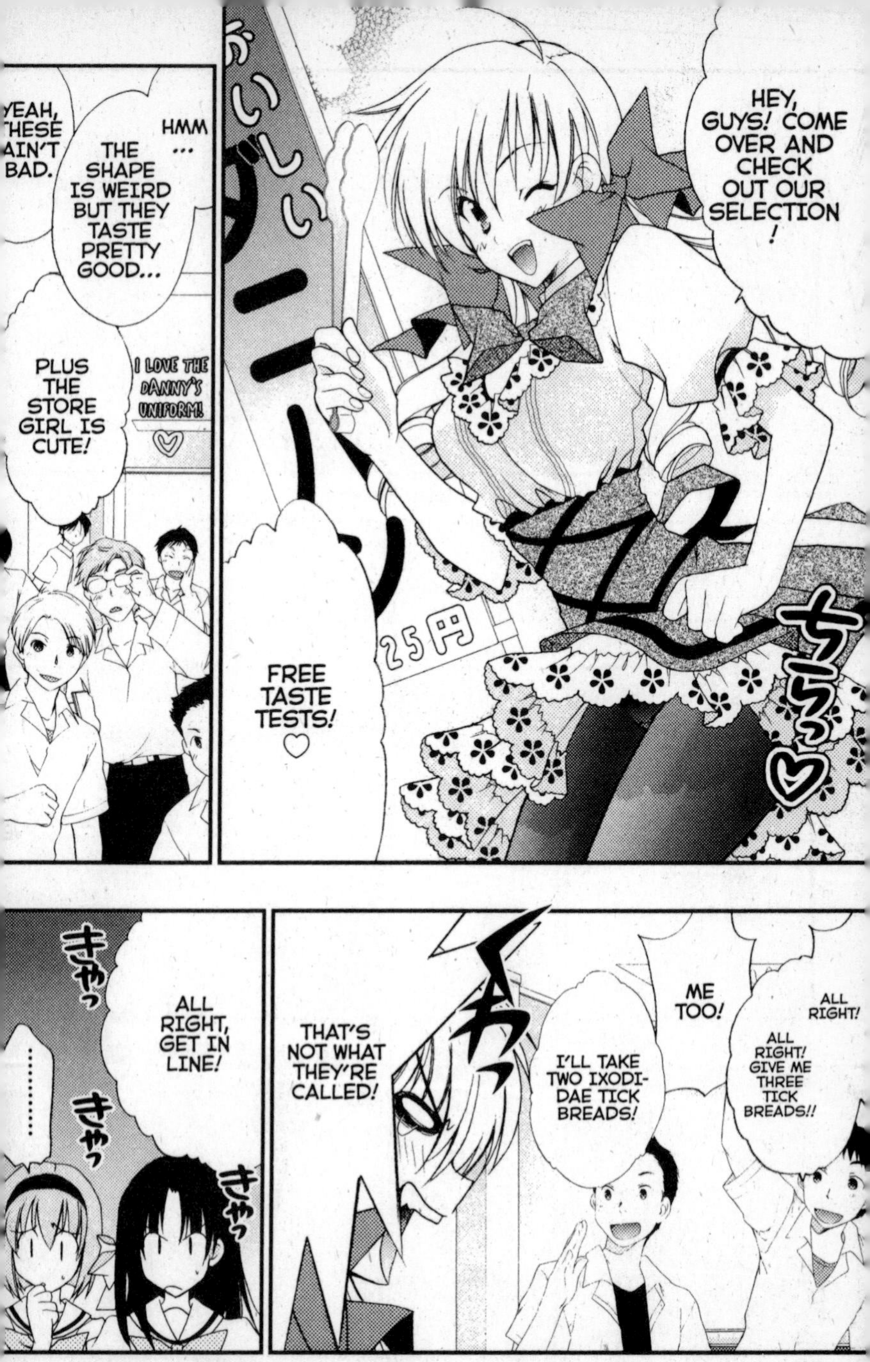
HEY, GUYS! COME OVER AND CHECK OUT OUR SELECTION!
ちらっ♡
FREE TASTE TESTS! ♡
25円
HMM...
THE SHAPE IS WEIRD BUT THEY TASTE PRETTY GOOD...
YEAH, THESE AIN'T BAD.
I LOVE THE DANNY'S UNIFORM! ♡
PLUS THE STORE GIRL IS CUTE!
ALL RIGHT!
ALL RIGHT! GIVE ME THREE TICK BREADS!!
ME TOO!
I'LL TAKE TWO IXODIDAE TICK BREADS!
THAT'S NOT WHAT THEY'RE CALLED!
ALL RIGHT, GET IN LINE!
きゃっ
きゃっ
きゃっ
......

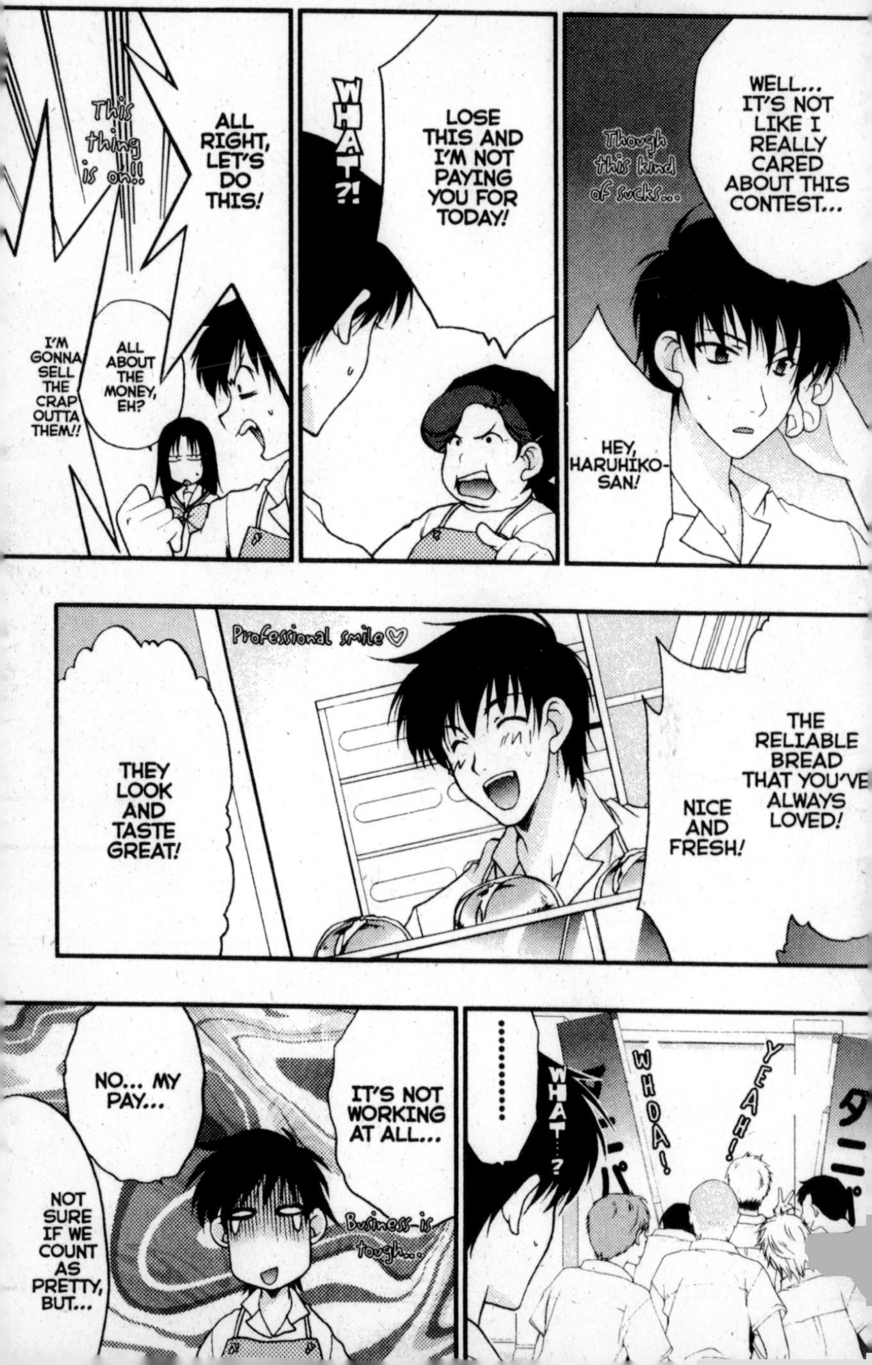
WELL... IT'S NOT LIKE I REALLY CARED ABOUT THIS CONTEST...
Though this kind of sucks...
HEY, HARUHIKO-SAN!
LOSE THIS AND I'M NOT PAYING YOU FOR TODAY!
WHAT?!
ALL RIGHT, LET'S DO THIS!
This thing is on!!
ALL ABOUT THE MONEY, EH?
I'M GONNA SELL THE CRAP OUTTA THEM!!
THE RELIABLE BREAD THAT YOU'VE ALWAYS LOVED!
NICE AND FRESH!
Professional smile♡
THEY LOOK AND TASTE GREAT!
YEAH!
WHOA!
WHAT...?
....
IT'S NOT WORKING AT ALL...
NO... MY PAY...
Business is tough...
NOT SURE IF WE COUNT AS PRETTY, BUT...

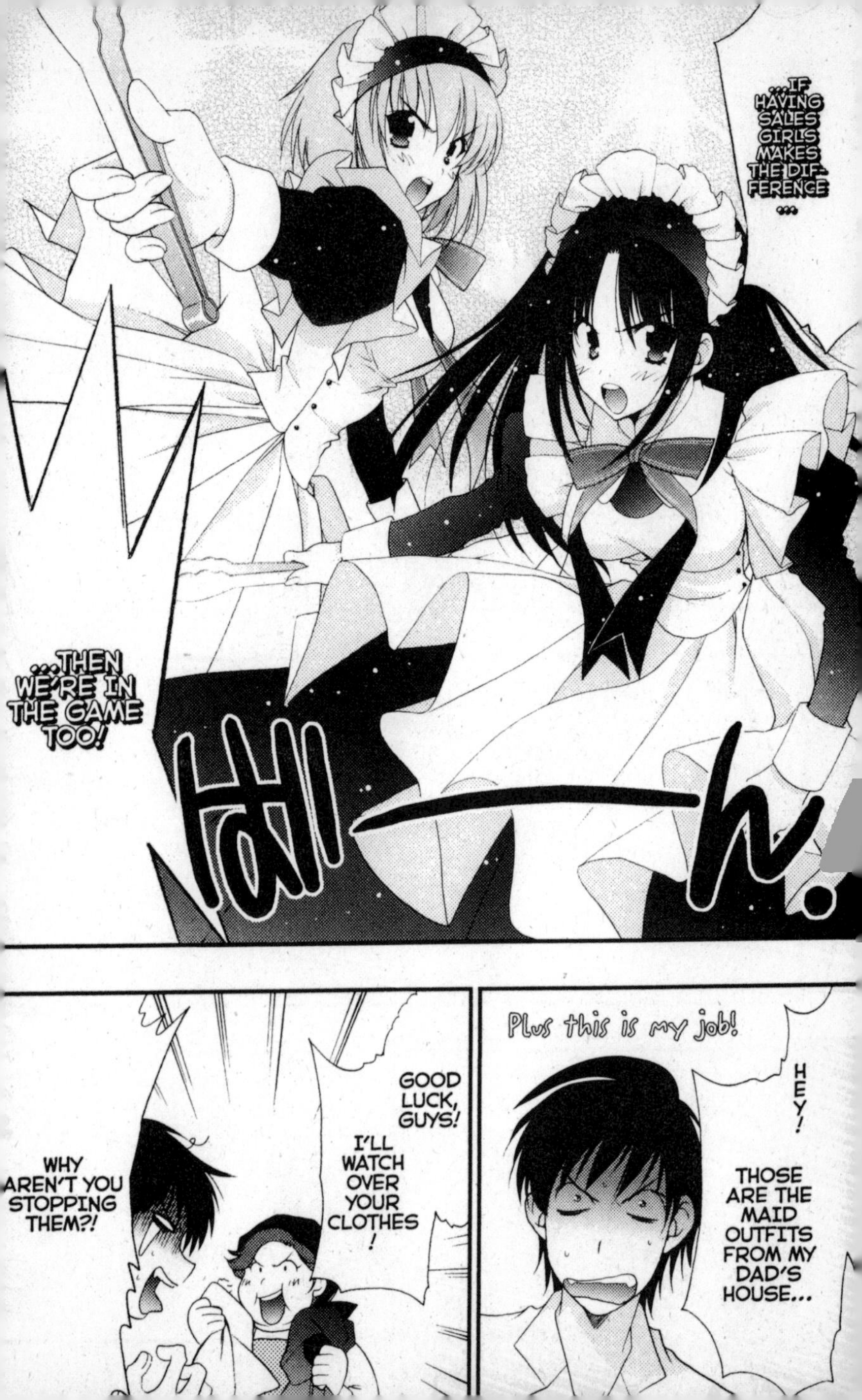
...IF HAVING SALES GIRLS MAKES THE DIF-FERENCE...
...THEN WE'RE IN THE GAME TOO!
Plus this is my job!
HEY!
THOSE ARE THE MAID OUTFITS FROM MY DAD'S HOUSE...
GOOD LUCK, GUYS!
I'LL WATCH OVER YOUR CLOTHES!
WHY AREN'T YOU STOPPING THEM?!

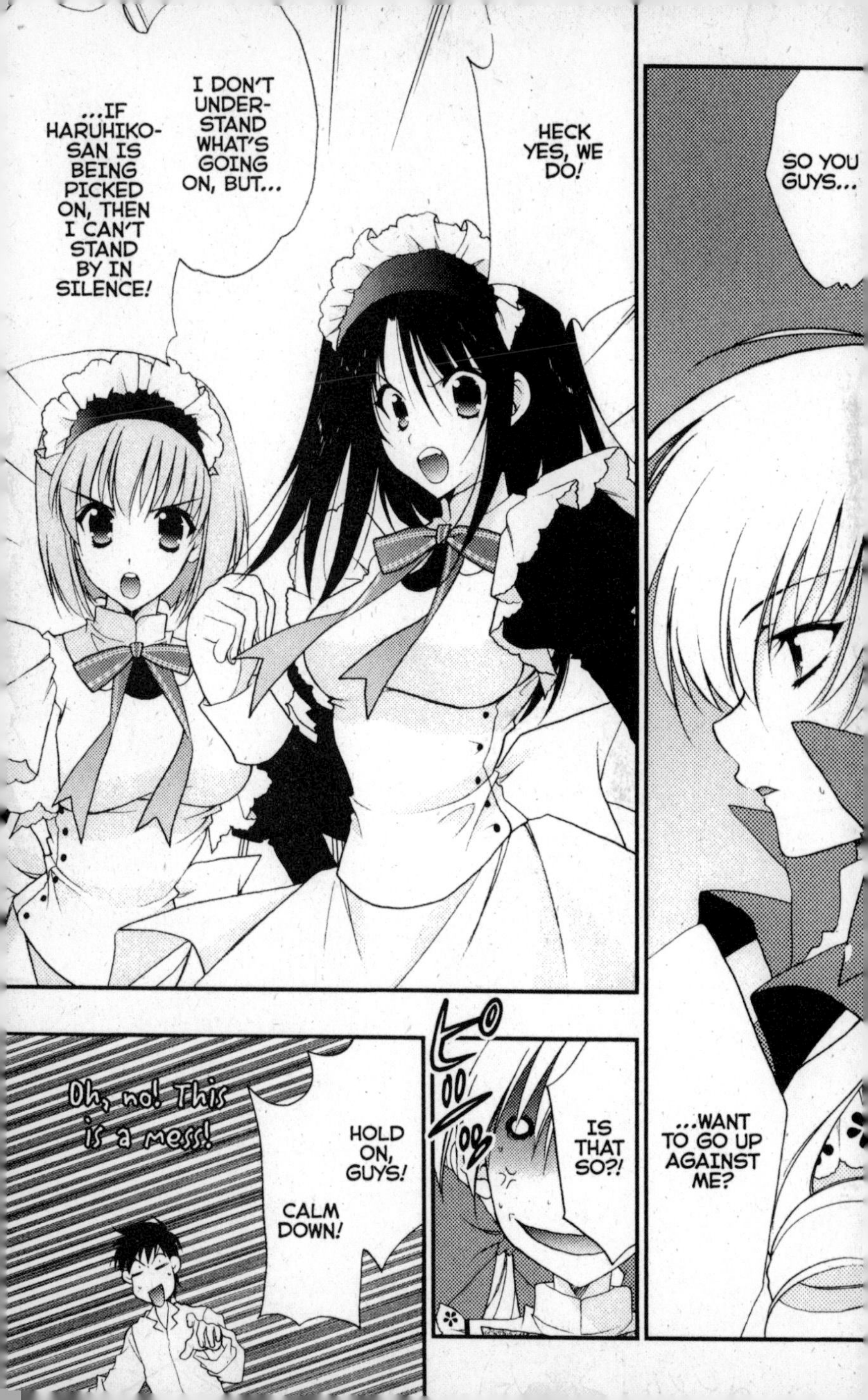
SO YOU GUYS...
...WANT TO GO UP AGAINST ME?
HECK YES, WE DO!
I DON'T UNDERSTAND WHAT'S GOING ON, BUT...
...IF HARUHIKO-SAN IS BEING PICKED ON, THEN I CAN'T STAND BY IN SILENCE!
IS THAT SO?!
HOLD ON, GUYS!
CALM DOWN!
Oh, no! This is a mess!

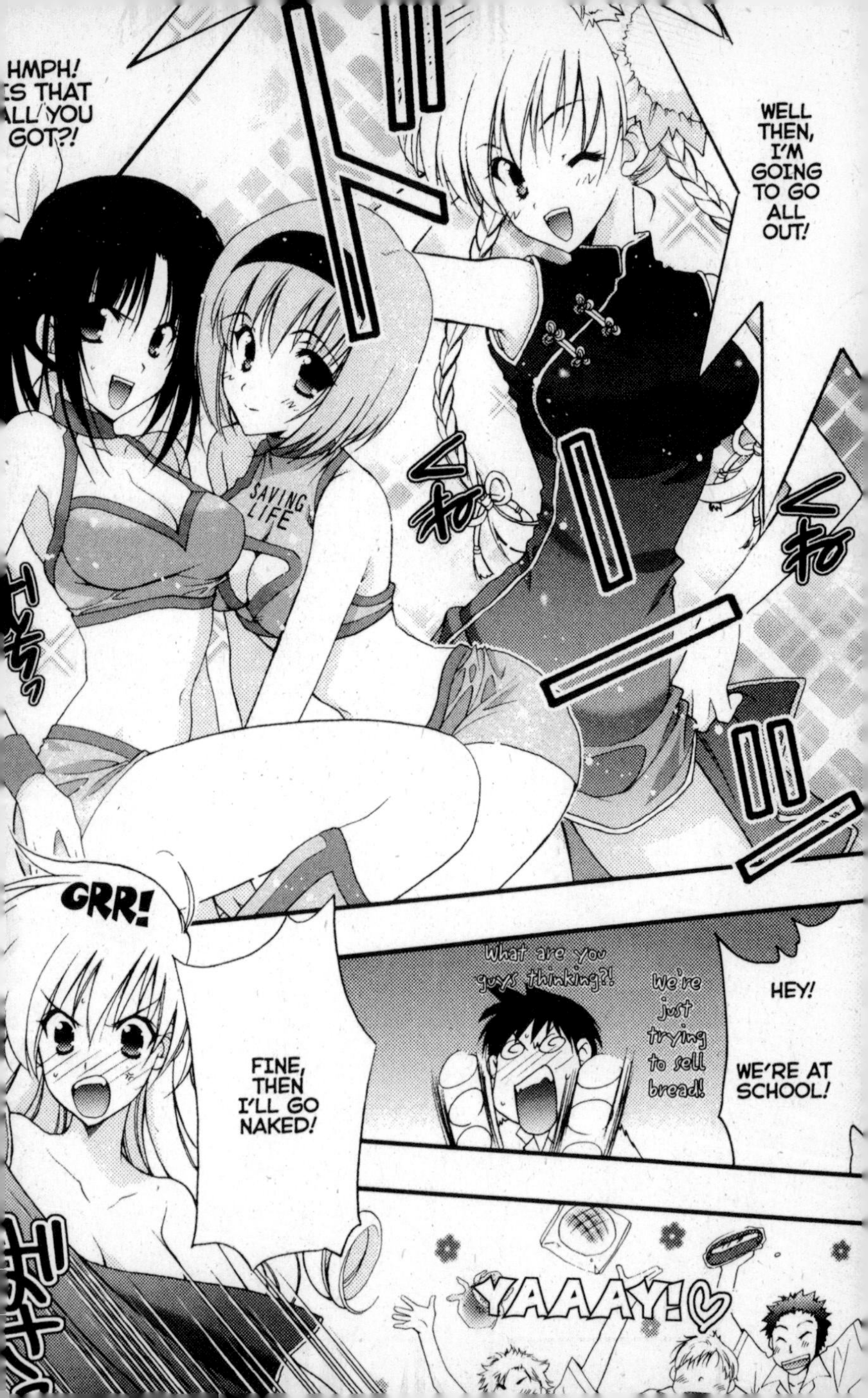
WELL THEN, I'M GOING TO GO ALL OUT!
HMPH! IS THAT ALL YOU GOT?!
くね
くね
HEY!
WE'RE AT SCHOOL!
What are you guys thinking?!
We're just trying to sell bread!
YAAAAY!♡
GRR!
FINE, THEN I'LL GO NAKED!

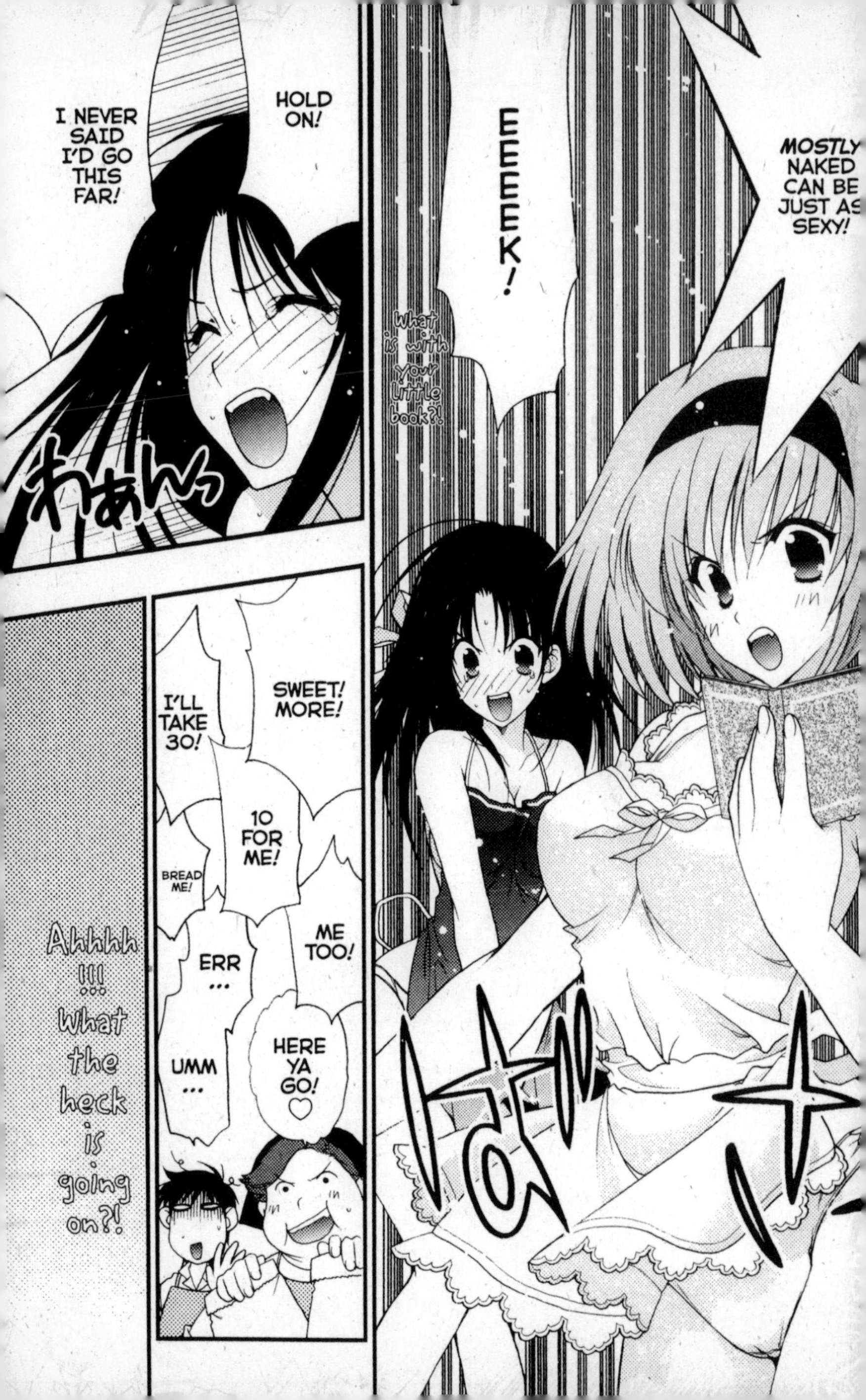
MOSTLY NAKED CAN BE JUST AS SEXY!
EEEEK!
what is with your little book?!
HOLD ON!
I NEVER SAID I'D GO THIS FAR!
わぁんっ
SWEET! MORE!
I'LL TAKE 30!
10 FOR ME!
BREAD ME!
ME TOO!
ERR ...
HERE YA GO! ♡
UMM ...
Ahhhh !!! what the heck is going on?!

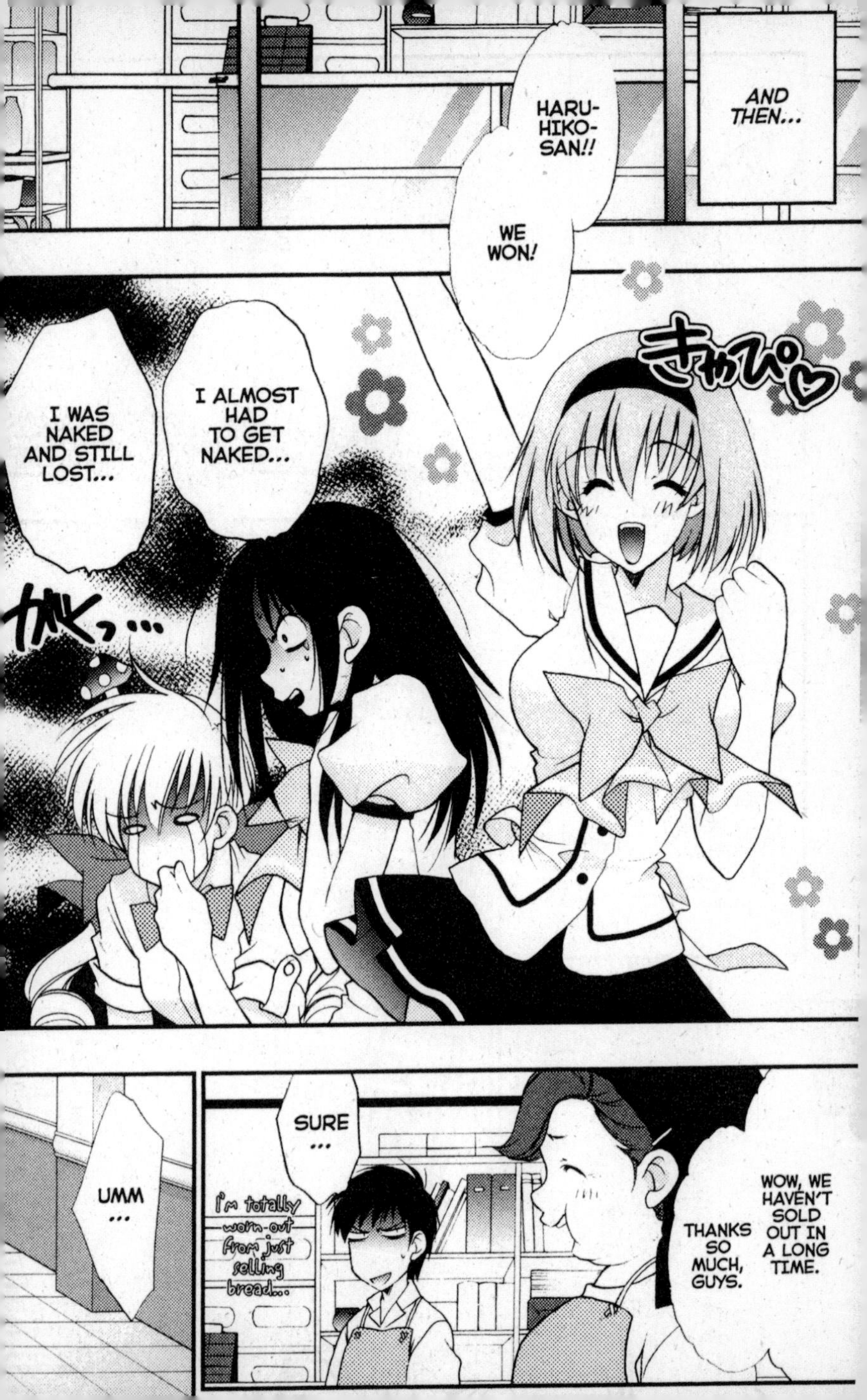
AND THEN...
HARU-HIKO-SAN!!
WE WON!
きゃぴ♡
I ALMOST HAD TO GET NAKED...
I WAS NAKED AND STILL LOST...
がくっ...
WOW, WE HAVEN'T SOLD OUT IN A LONG TIME.
THANKS SO MUCH, GUYS.
SURE ...
I'm totally worn-out from just selling bread...
UMM ...

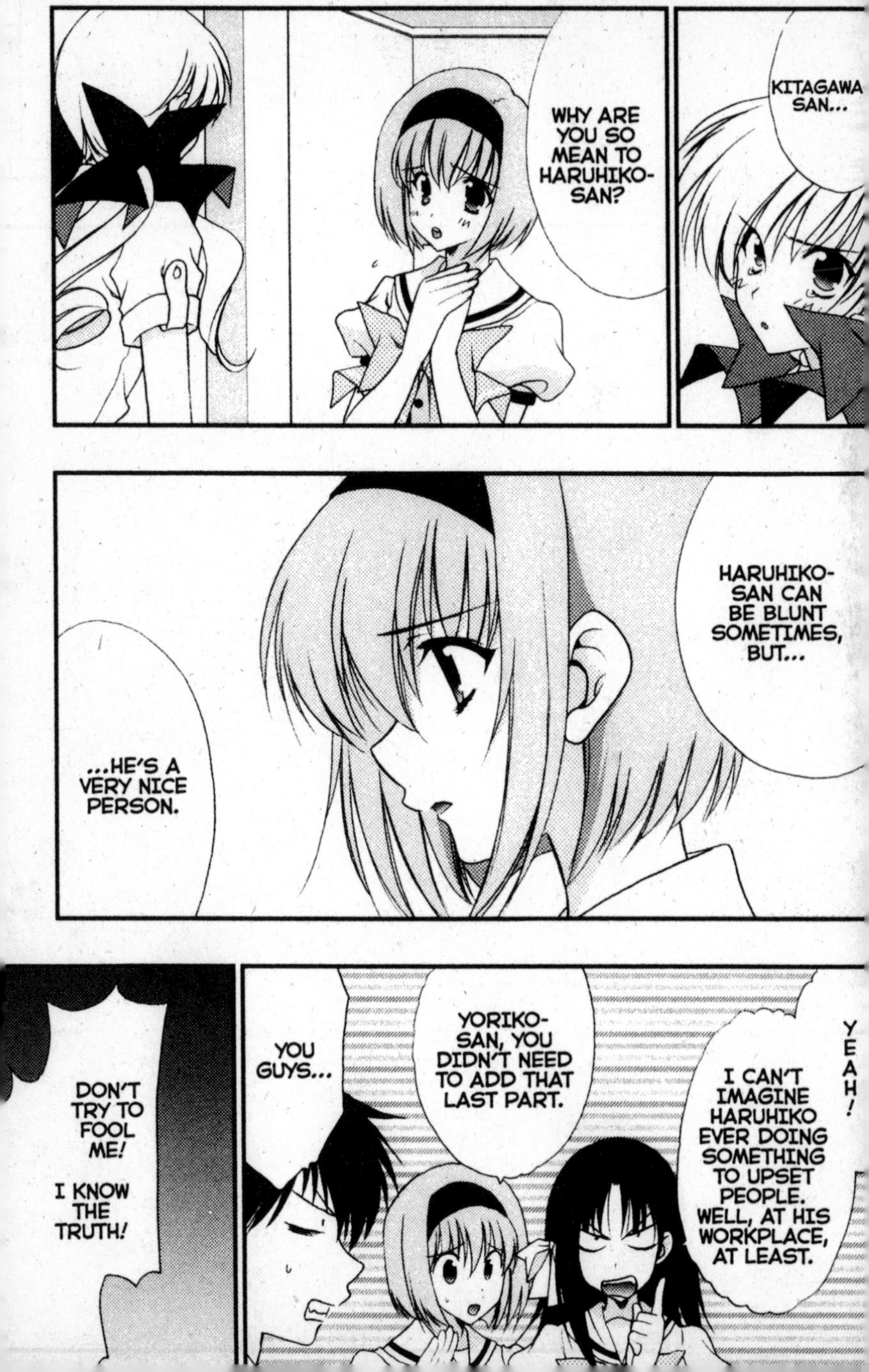
KITAGAWA SAN...
WHY ARE YOU SO MEAN TO HARUHIKO-SAN?
HARUHIKO-SAN CAN BE BLUNT SOMETIMES, BUT...
...HE'S A VERY NICE PERSON.
YEAH!
I CAN'T IMAGINE HARUHIKO EVER DOING SOMETHING TO UPSET PEOPLE. WELL, AT HIS WORKPLACE, AT LEAST.
YORIKO-SAN, YOU DIDN'T NEED TO ADD THAT LAST PART.
YOU GUYS...
DON'T TRY TO FOOL ME!
I KNOW THE TRUTH!

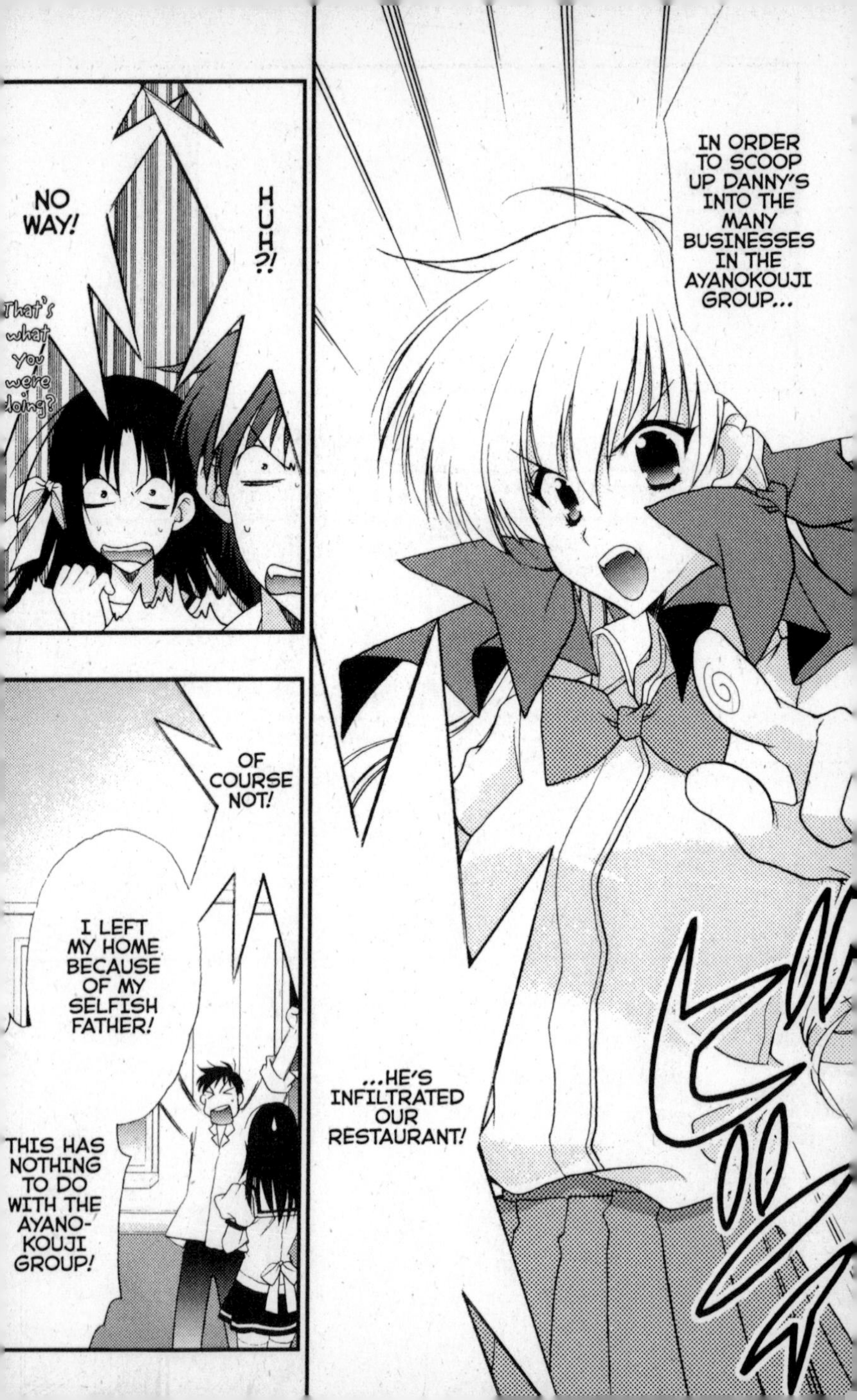
IN ORDER TO SCOOP UP DANNY'S INTO THE MANY BUSINESSES IN THE AYANOKOUJI GROUP...
...HE'S INFILTRATED OUR RESTAURANT!
HUH?!
NO WAY!
That's what you were doing?
OF COURSE NOT!
I LEFT MY HOME BECAUSE OF MY SELFISH FATHER!
THIS HAS NOTHING TO DO WITH THE AYANO-KOUJI GROUP!

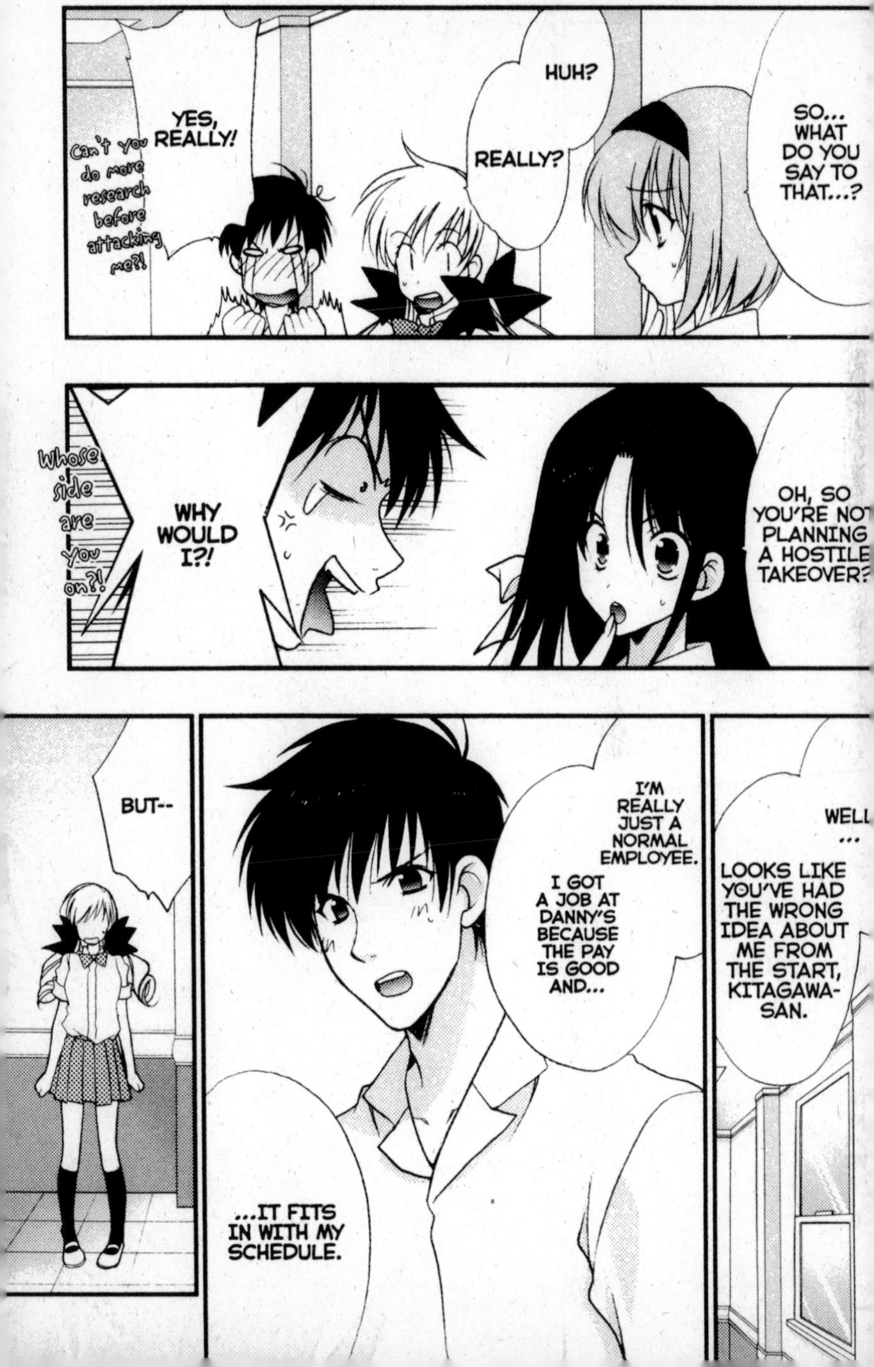
SO... WHAT DO YOU SAY TO THAT...?
HUH?
REALLY?
YES, REALLY!
Can't you do more research before attacking me?!
OH, SO YOU'RE NOT PLANNING A HOSTILE TAKEOVER?
WHY WOULD I?!
Whose side are you on?!
WELL... LOOKS LIKE YOU'VE HAD THE WRONG IDEA ABOUT ME FROM THE START, KITAGAWA-SAN.
I'M REALLY JUST A NORMAL EMPLOYEE.
I GOT A JOB AT DANNY'S BECAUSE THE PAY IS GOOD AND...
...IT FITS IN WITH MY SCHEDULE.
BUT--

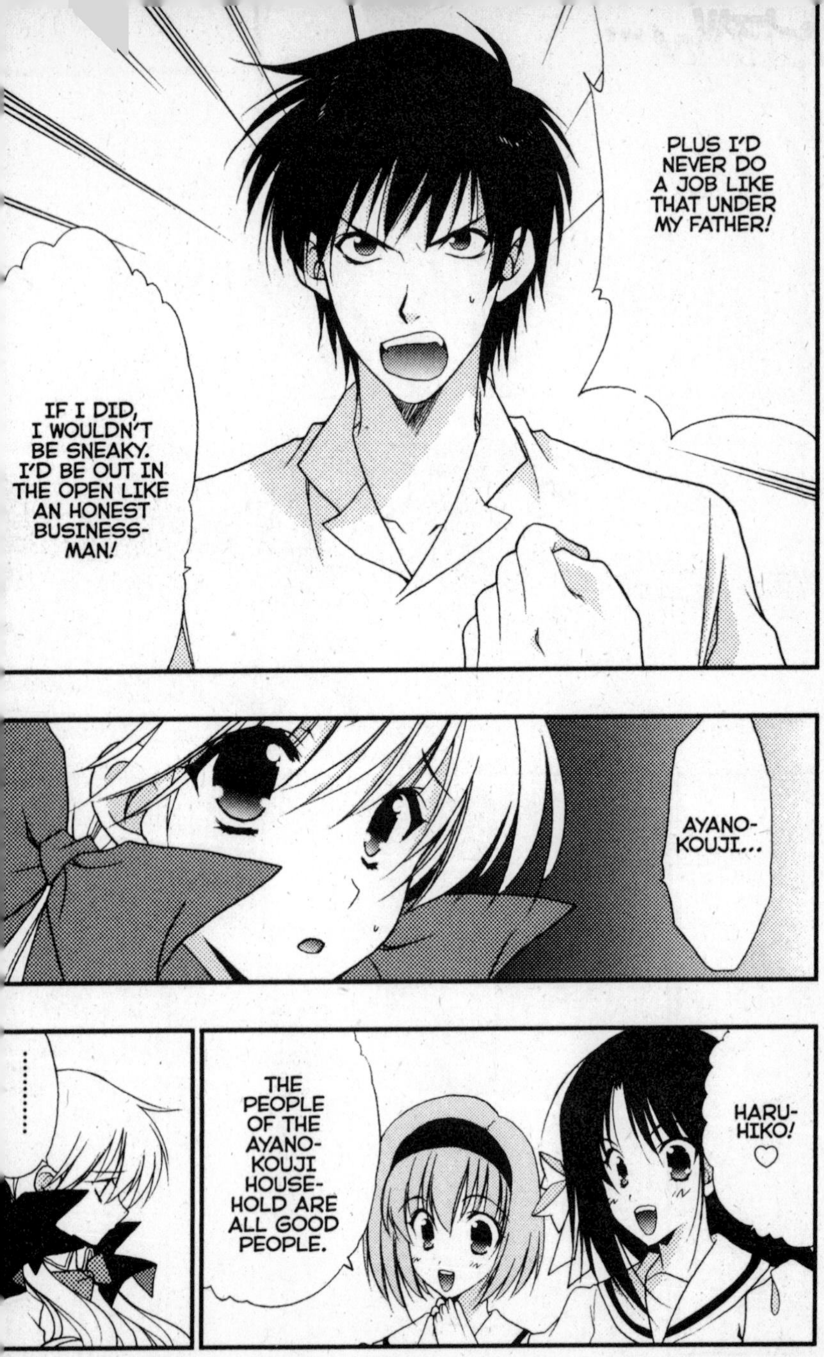
PLUS I'D NEVER DO A JOB LIKE THAT UNDER MY FATHER!
IF I DID, I WOULDN'T BE SNEAKY. I'D BE OUT IN THE OPEN LIKE AN HONEST BUSINESS-MAN!
AYANO-KOUJI...
HARU-HIKO! ♡
THE PEOPLE OF THE AYANO-KOUJI HOUSE-HOLD ARE ALL GOOD PEOPLE.
....

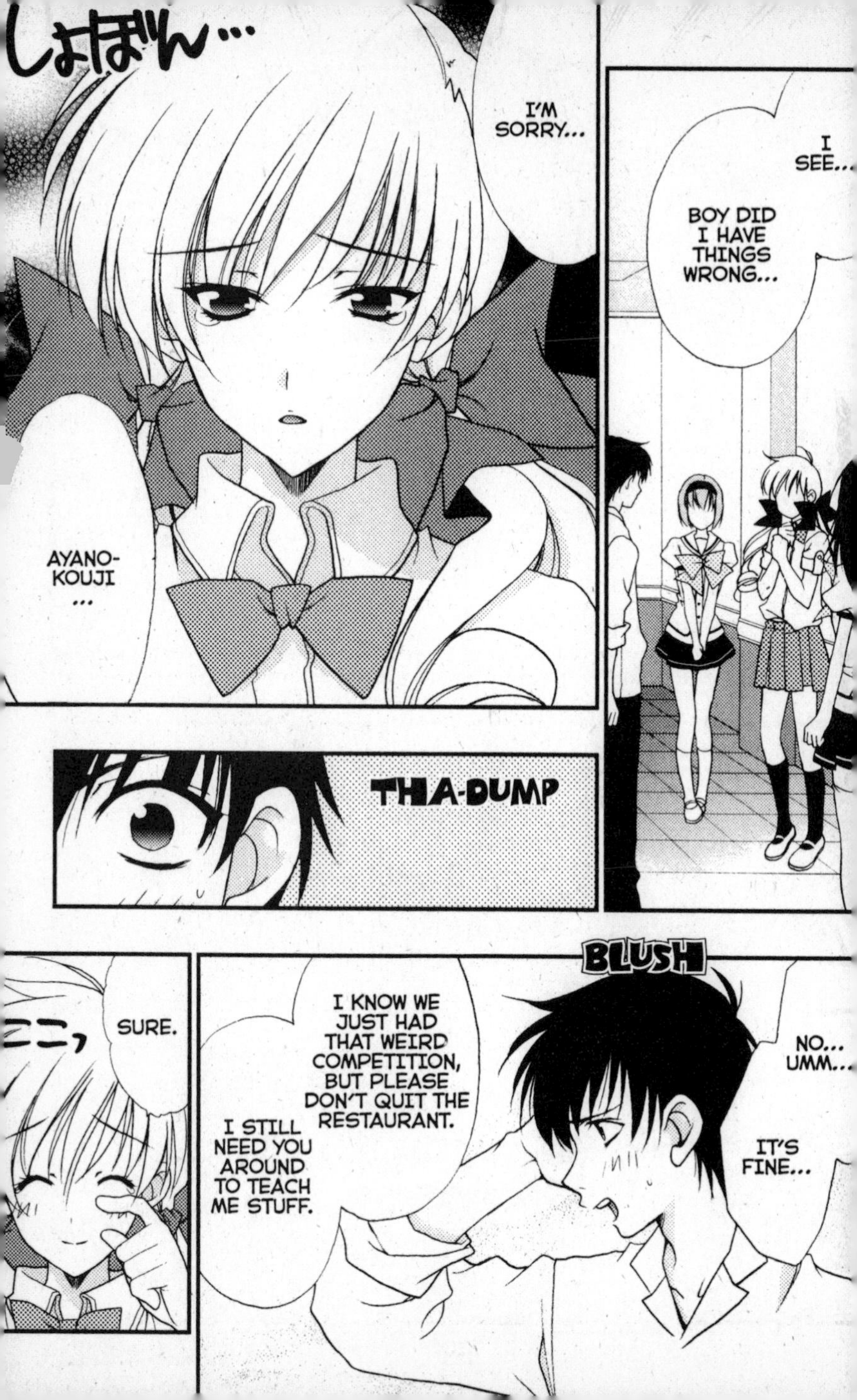
I SEE...
BOY DID I HAVE THINGS WRONG...
しょぼん…
I'M SORRY...
AYANO-KOUJI ...
THA-DUMP
BLUSH
NO... UMM...
IT'S FINE...
I KNOW WE JUST HAD THAT WEIRD COMPETITION, BUT PLEASE DON'T QUIT THE RESTAURANT.
I STILL NEED YOU AROUND TO TEACH ME STUFF.
SURE.
ニコッ

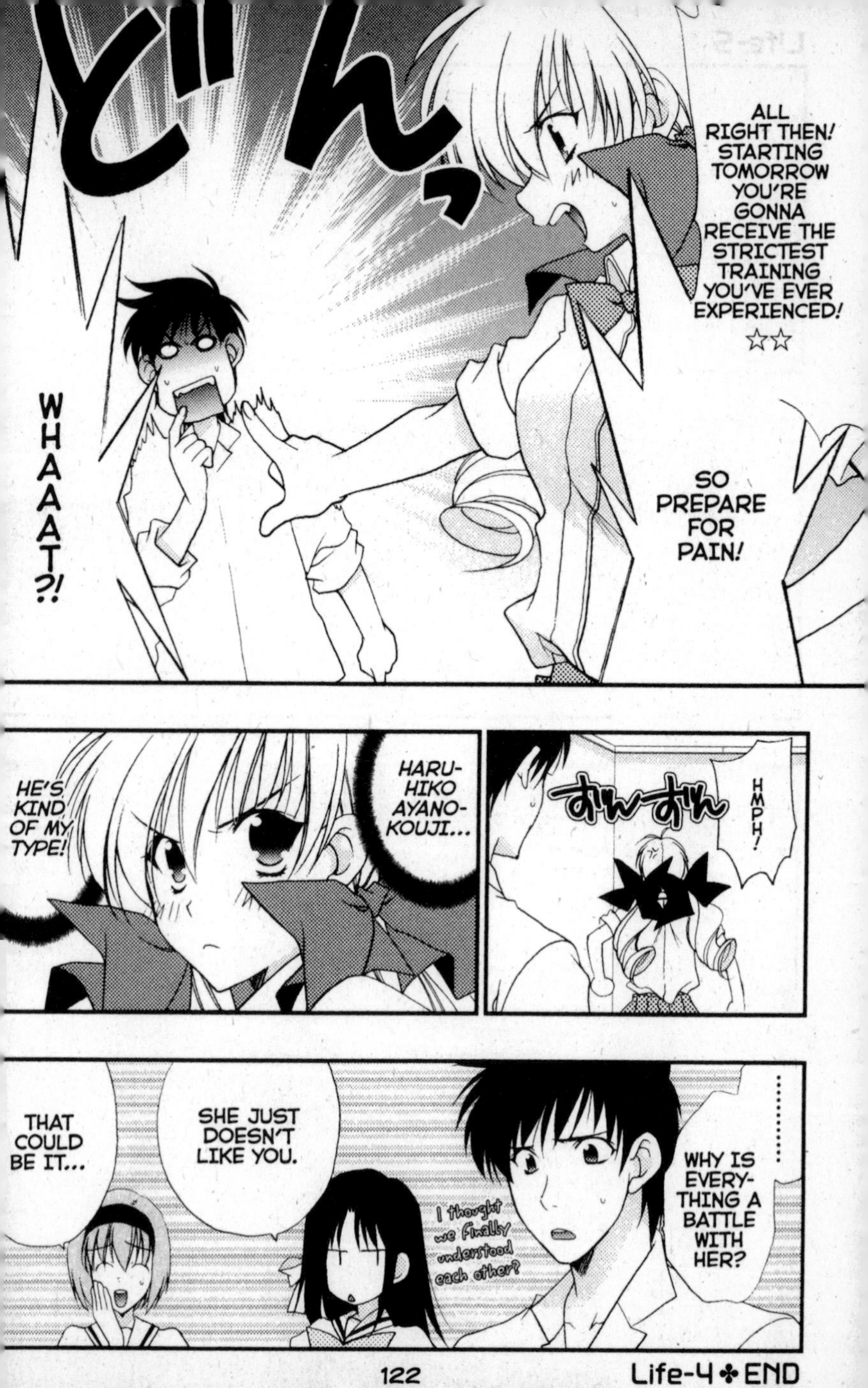
どん,
ALL RIGHT THEN! STARTING TOMORROW YOU'RE GONNA RECEIVE THE STRICTEST TRAINING YOU'VE EVER EXPERIENCED! ☆☆
SO PREPARE FOR PAIN!
WHAAAAT?!
HMPH!
HARU-HIKO AYANO-KOUJI...
HE'S KIND OF MY TYPE!
......
WHY IS EVERY-THING A BATTLE WITH HER?
I thought we finally understood each other?
SHE JUST DOESN'T LIKE YOU.
THAT COULD BE IT...

Life-4 ✤ END

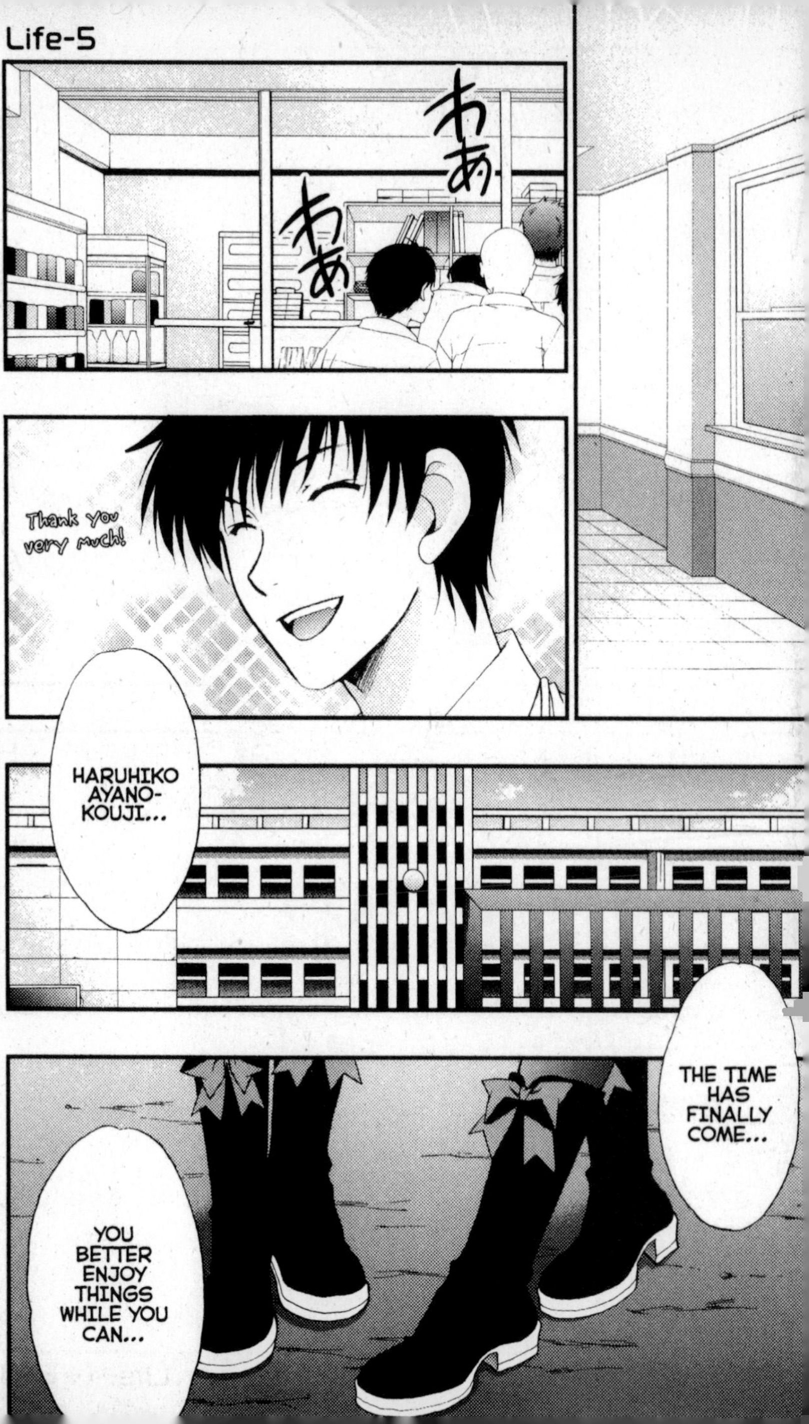
わあ
わあ
Thank you very much!
HARUHIKO AYANO-KOUJI...
THE TIME HAS FINALLY COME...
YOU BETTER ENJOY THINGS WHILE YOU CAN...

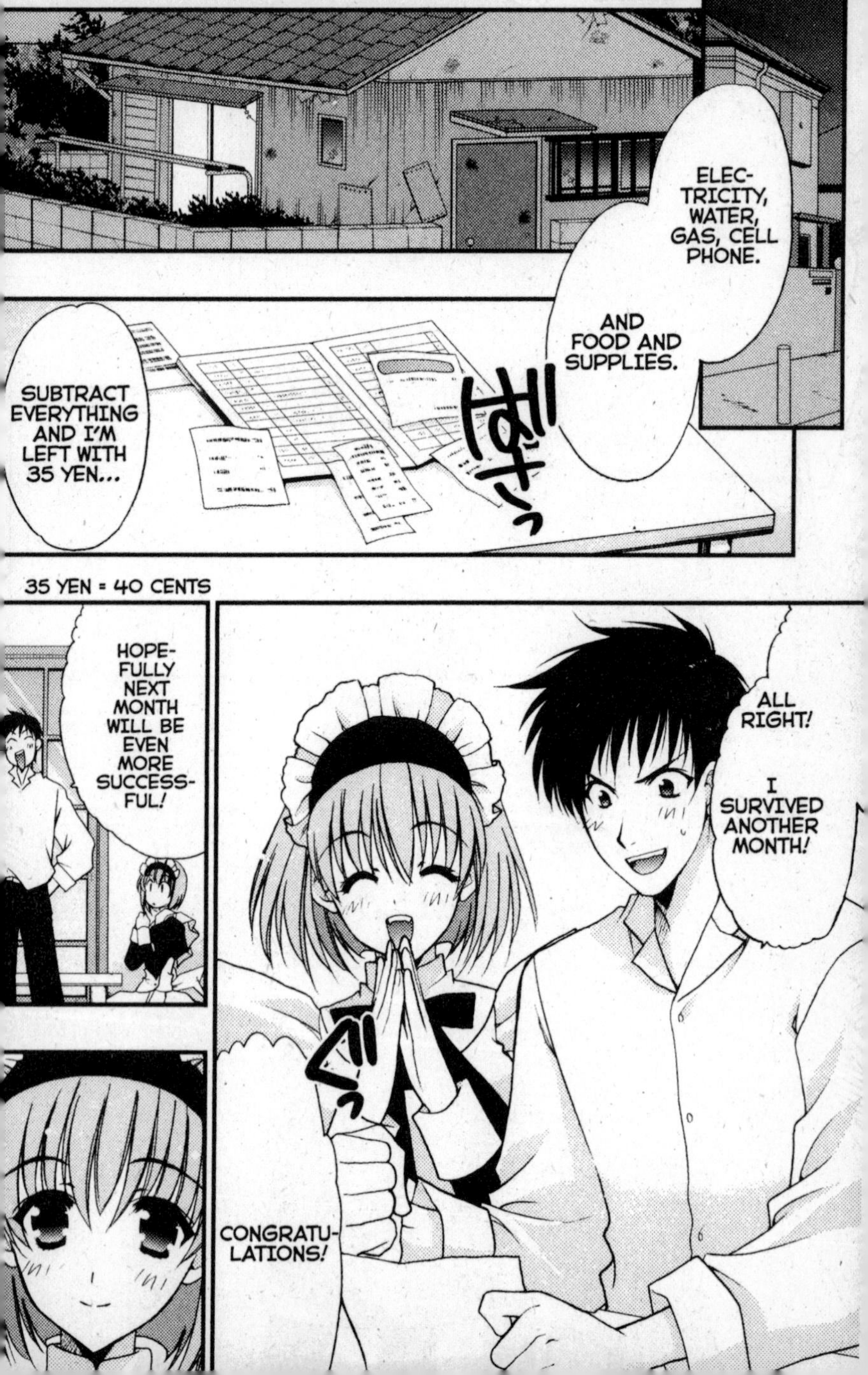
ELEC-TRICITY, WATER, GAS, CELL PHONE.
AND FOOD AND SUPPLIES.
SUBTRACT EVERYTHING AND I'M LEFT WITH 35 YEN...
35 YEN = 40 CENTS
ALL RIGHT!
I SURVIVED ANOTHER MONTH!
CONGRATU-LATIONS!
HOPE-FULLY NEXT MONTH WILL BE EVEN MORE SUCCESS-FUL!

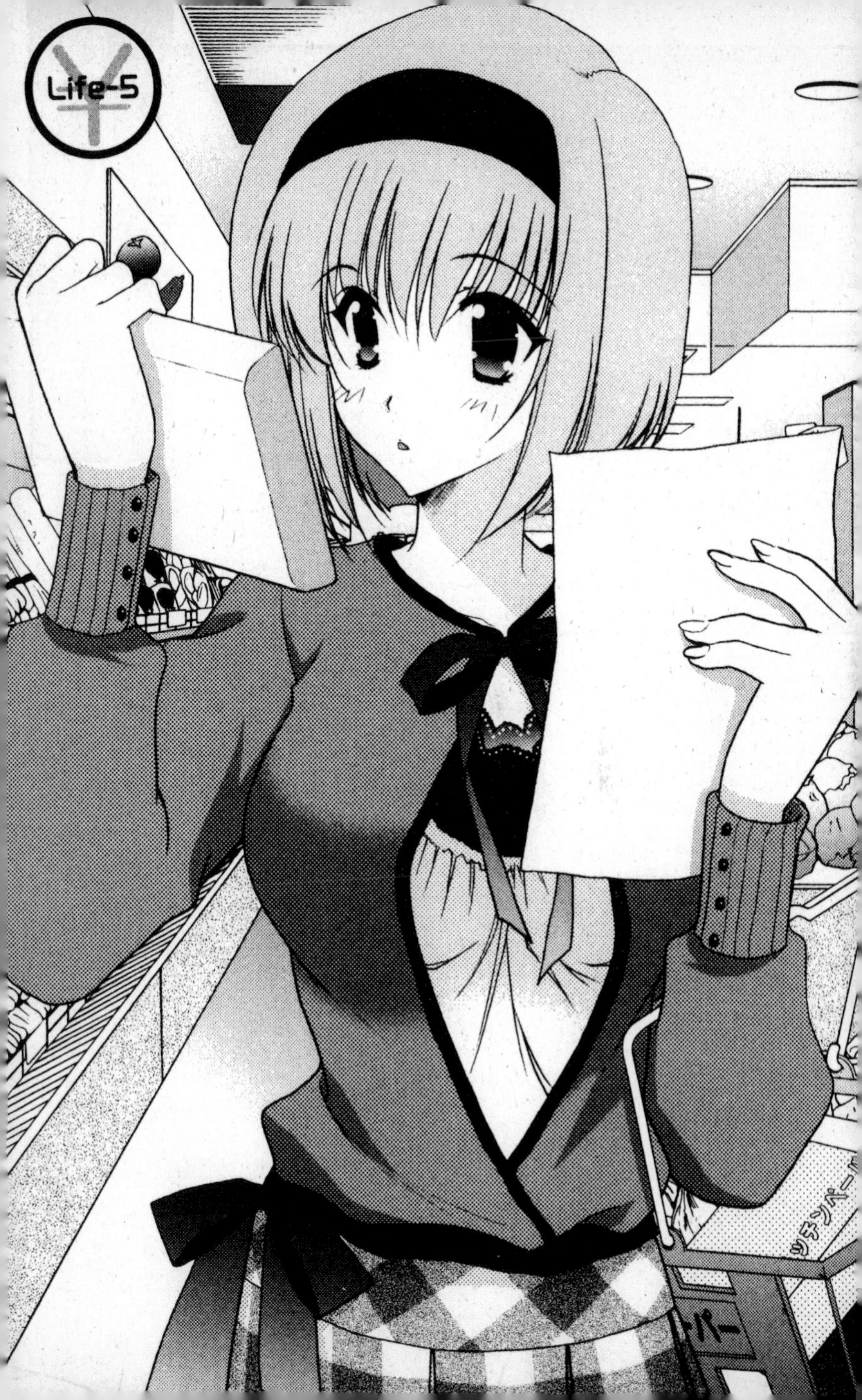
Life-5
ッチンペー

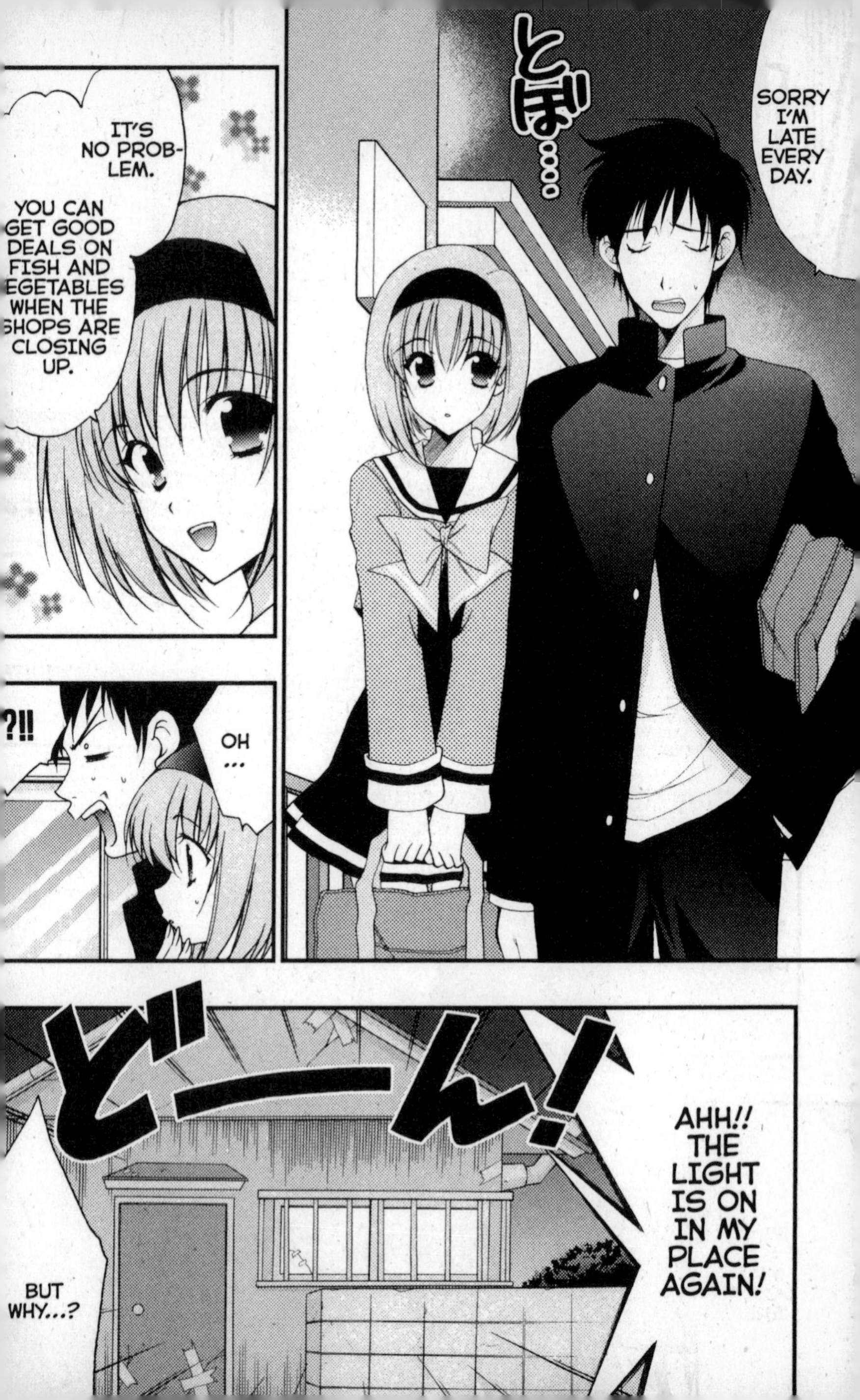

SORRY I'M LATE EVERY DAY.
とぼ…
IT'S NO PROB-LEM.
YOU CAN GET GOOD DEALS ON FISH AND EGETABLES WHEN THE SHOPS ARE CLOSING UP.
OH ...
?!!
どーん!
AHH!! THE LIGHT IS ON IN MY PLACE AGAIN!
BUT WHY...?

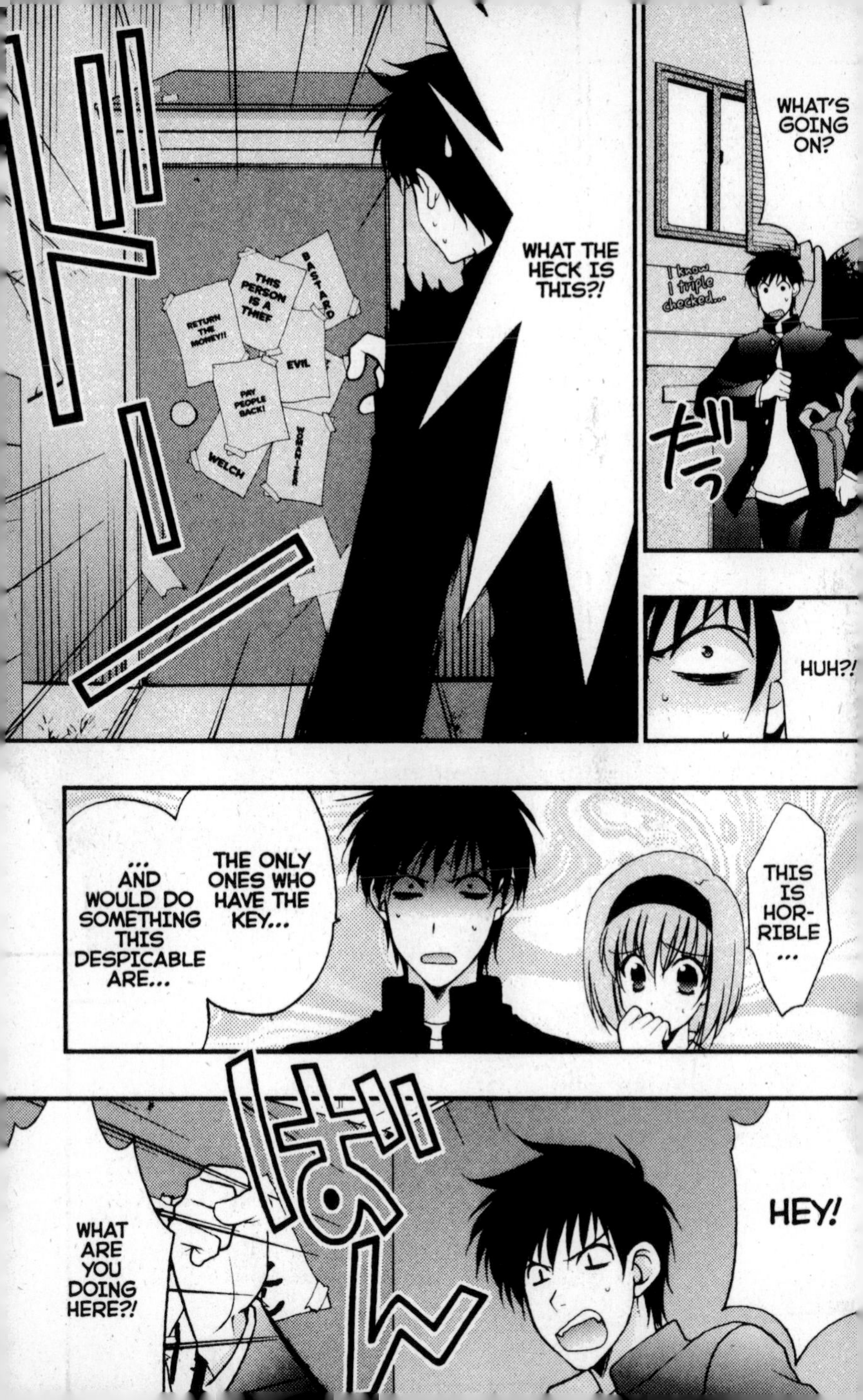
WHAT'S GOING ON?
I know I triple checked...
だっ
HUH?!
WHAT THE HECK IS THIS?!
ドーン
BASTARD
THIS PERSON IS A THIEF
RETURN THE MONEY!!
EVIL
PAY PEOPLE BACK!
WOMANIZER
WELCH
THIS IS HORRIBLE...
THE ONLY ONES WHO HAVE THE KEY...
...AND WOULD DO SOMETHING THIS DESPICABLE ARE...
HEY!
ばん
WHAT ARE YOU DOING HERE?!

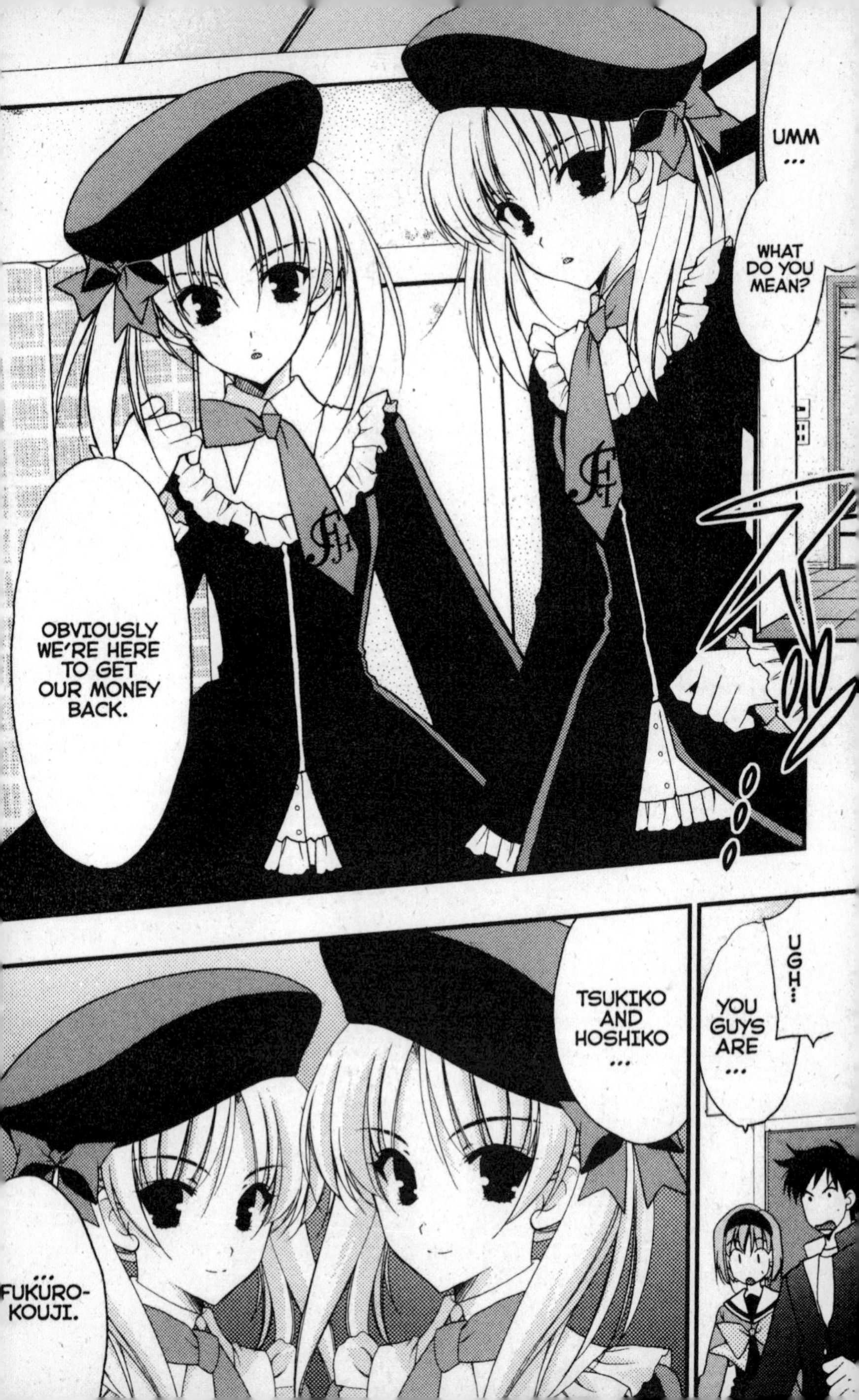
UMM ...
WHAT DO YOU MEAN?
OBVIOUSLY WE'RE HERE TO GET OUR MONEY BACK.
UGH...
YOU GUYS ARE ...
TSUKIKO AND HOSHIKO ...
... FUKURO-KOUJI.

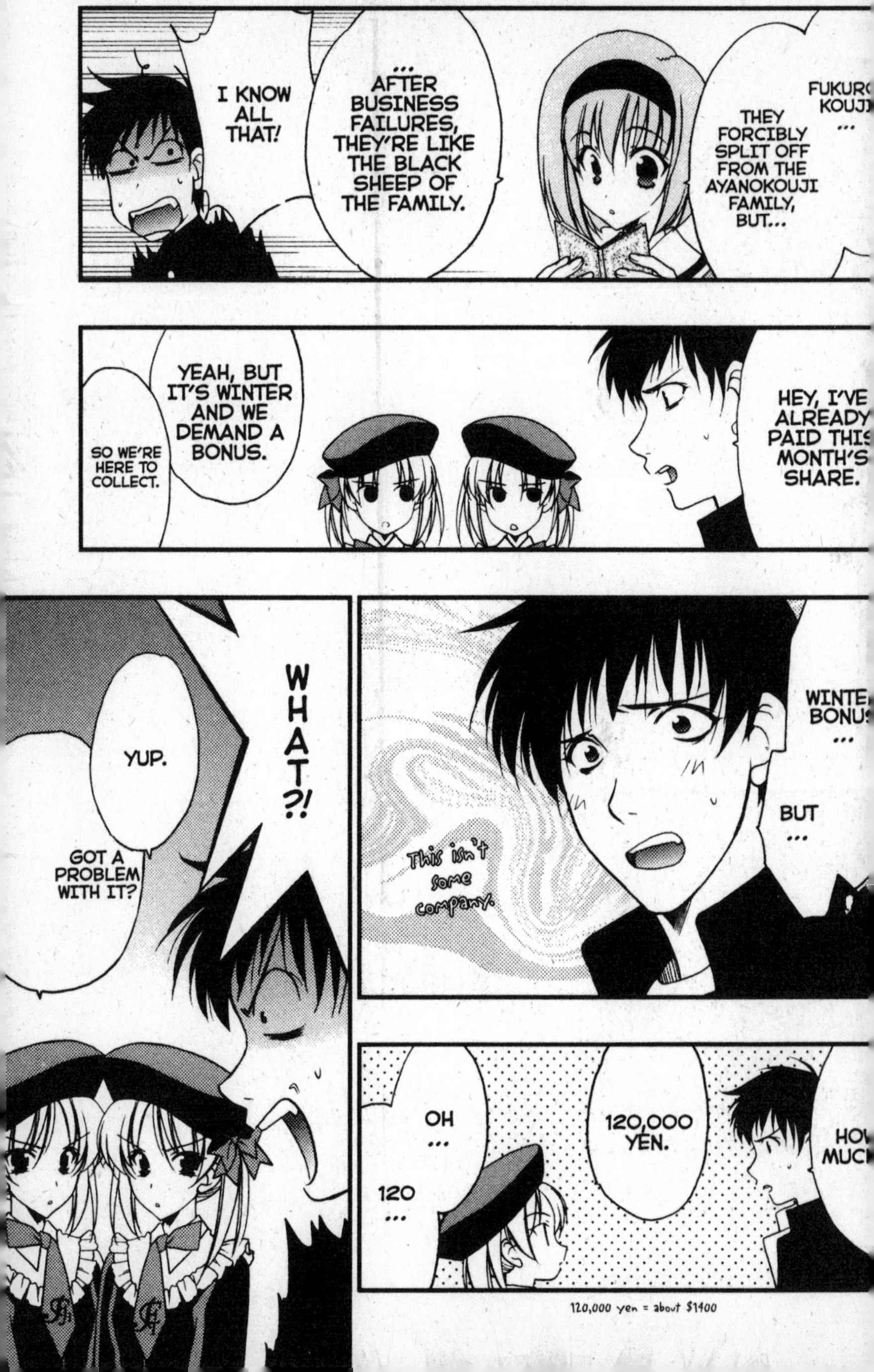
FUKURO KOUJI ...
THEY FORCIBLY SPLIT OFF FROM THE AYANOKOUJI FAMILY, BUT...
... AFTER BUSINESS FAILURES, THEY'RE LIKE THE BLACK SHEEP OF THE FAMILY.
I KNOW ALL THAT!
HEY, I'VE ALREADY PAID THIS MONTH'S SHARE.
YEAH, BUT IT'S WINTER AND WE DEMAND A BONUS.
SO WE'RE HERE TO COLLECT.
WINTE BONU ...
BUT ...
This isn't some company.
HOW MUCH
120,000 YEN.
OH ... 120 ...
WHAT?!
YUP.
GOT A PROBLEM WITH IT?
120,000 yen = about $1400

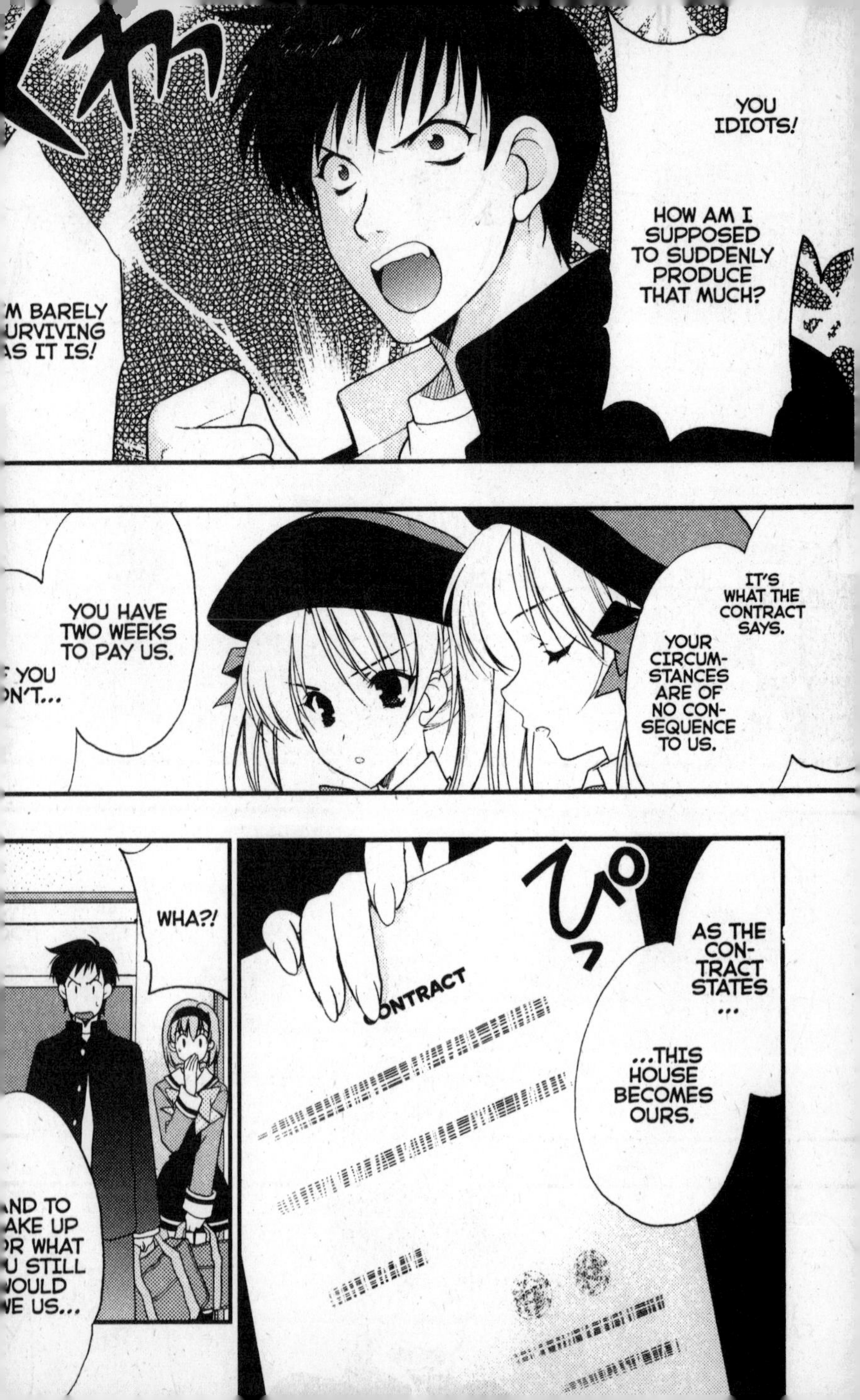
YOU IDIOTS!
HOW AM I SUPPOSED TO SUDDENLY PRODUCE THAT MUCH?
'M BARELY URVIVING AS IT IS!
IT'S WHAT THE CONTRACT SAYS.
YOUR CIRCUM-STANCES ARE OF NO CON-SEQUENCE TO US.
YOU HAVE TWO WEEKS TO PAY US.
F YOU ON'T...
AS THE CON-TRACT STATES...
...THIS HOUSE BECOMES OURS.
CONTRACT
WHA?!
ND TO AKE UP OR WHAT U STILL VOULD VE US...

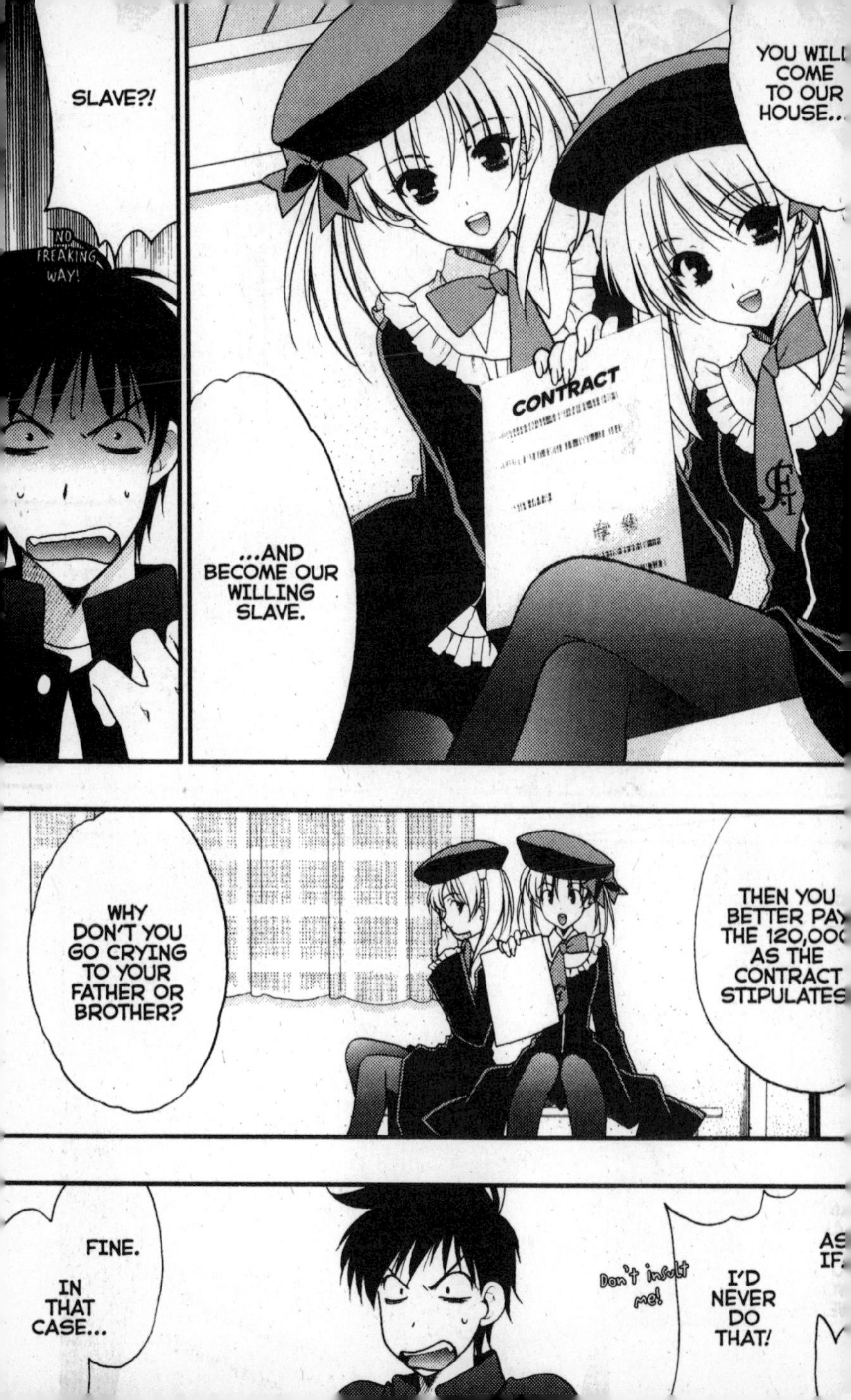

YOU WILL COME TO OUR HOUSE..
CONTRACT
...AND BECOME OUR WILLING SLAVE.
SLAVE?!
NO FREAKING WAY!
THEN YOU BETTER PAY THE 120,000 AS THE CONTRACT STIPULATES
WHY DON'T YOU GO CRYING TO YOUR FATHER OR BROTHER?
AS IF.
I'D NEVER DO THAT!
Don't insult me!
FINE.
IN THAT CASE...

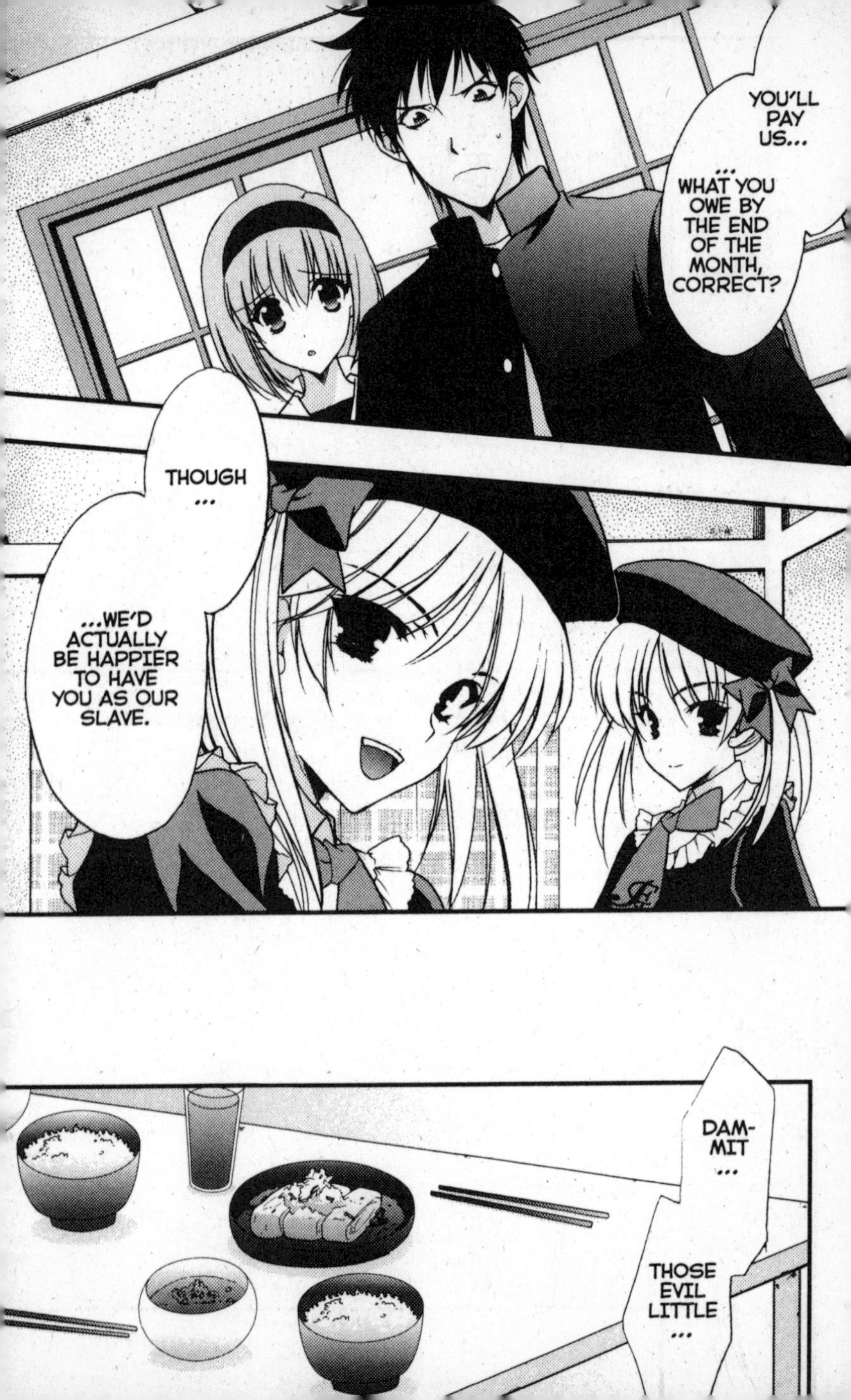
YOU'LL PAY US...
...WHAT YOU OWE BY THE END OF THE MONTH, CORRECT?
THOUGH...
...WE'D ACTUALLY BE HAPPIER TO HAVE YOU AS OUR SLAVE.
DAM-MIT...
THOSE EVIL LITTLE...

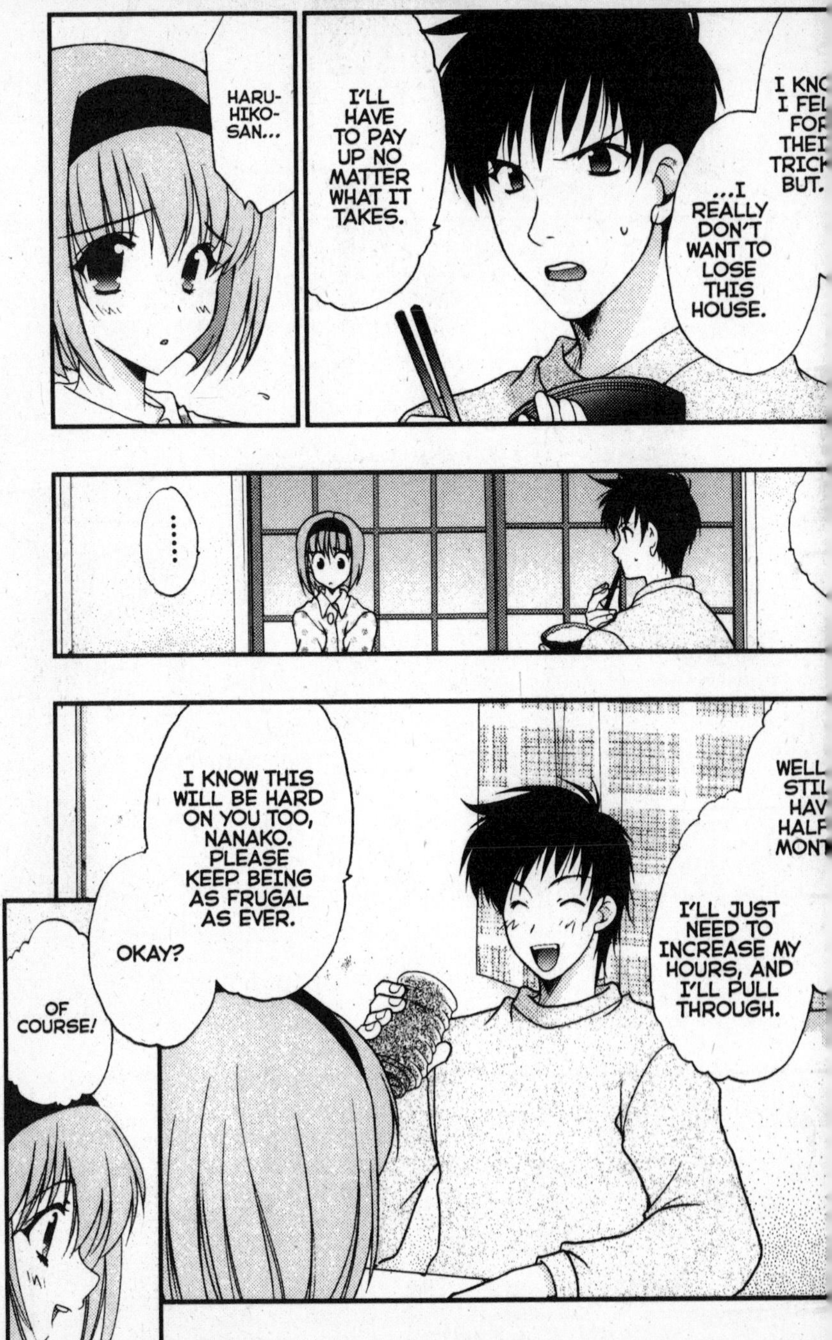

I KNO I FEL FOR THEI TRICK BUT.
...I REALLY DON'T WANT TO LOSE THIS HOUSE.
I'LL HAVE TO PAY UP NO MATTER WHAT IT TAKES.
HARU-HIKO-SAN...
......
WELL STIL HAV HALF MONT
I'LL JUST NEED TO INCREASE MY HOURS, AND I'LL PULL THROUGH.
I KNOW THIS WILL BE HARD ON YOU TOO, NANAKO. PLEASE KEEP BEING AS FRUGAL AS EVER.
OKAY?
OF COURSE!

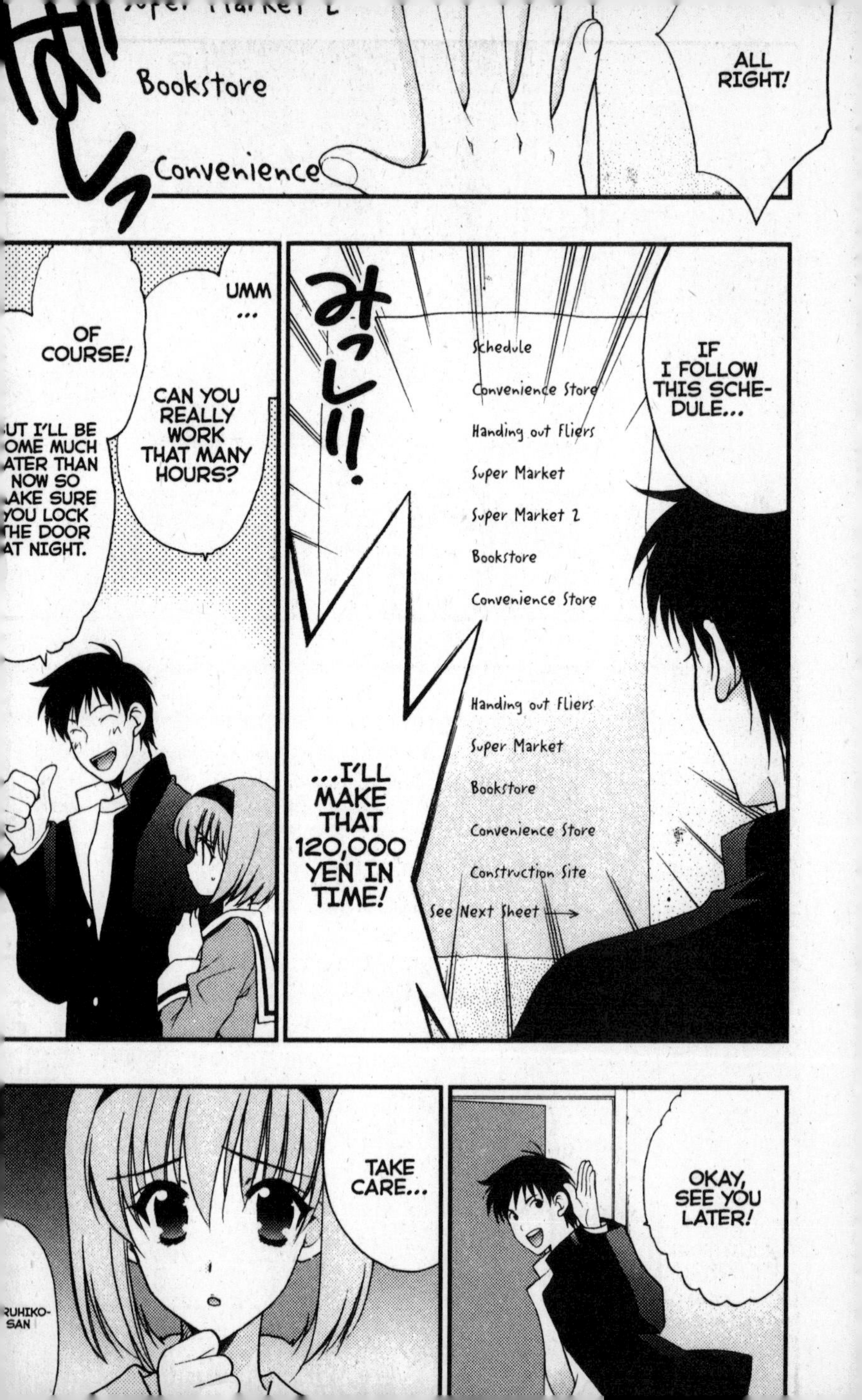
ALL RIGHT!
Bookstore
Convenience
ばしっ
IF I FOLLOW THIS SCHEDULE...
Schedule
Convenience Store
Handing out Fliers
Super Market
Super Market 2
Bookstore
Convenience Store
Handing out Fliers
Super Market
Bookstore
Convenience Store
Construction Site
See Next Sheet →
みっしり!
...I'LL MAKE THAT 120,000 YEN IN TIME!
UMM ...
CAN YOU REALLY WORK THAT MANY HOURS?
OF COURSE!
UT I'LL BE OME MUCH ATER THAN NOW SO AKE SURE YOU LOCK THE DOOR AT NIGHT.
OKAY, SEE YOU LATER!
TAKE CARE...
RUHIKO-SAN

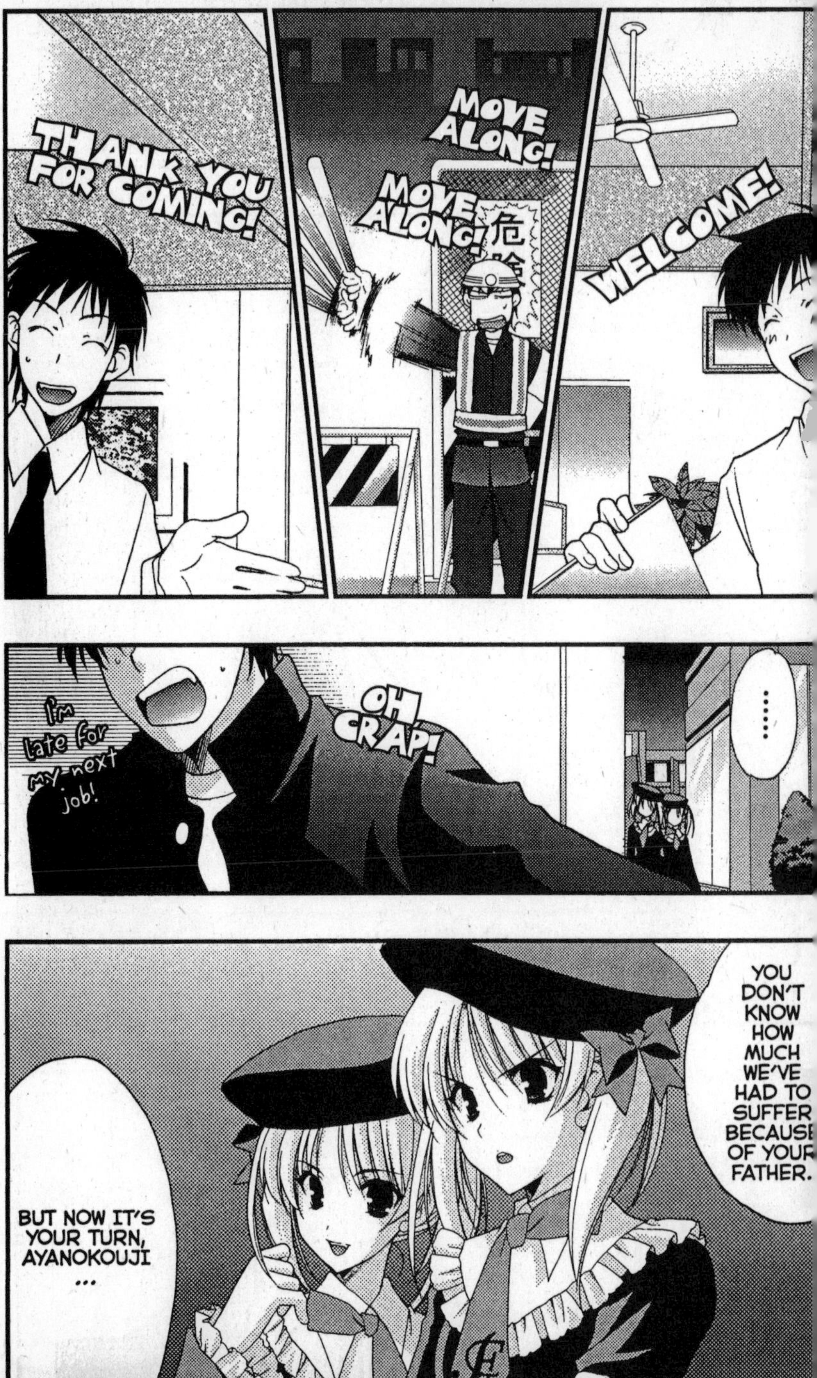
WELCOME!
MOVE ALONG!
MOVE ALONG!
THANK YOU FOR COMING!
......
OH CRAP!
I'm late for my next job!
YOU DON'T KNOW HOW MUCH WE'VE HAD TO SUFFER BECAUSE OF YOUR FATHER.
BUT NOW IT'S YOUR TURN, AYANOKOUJI ...

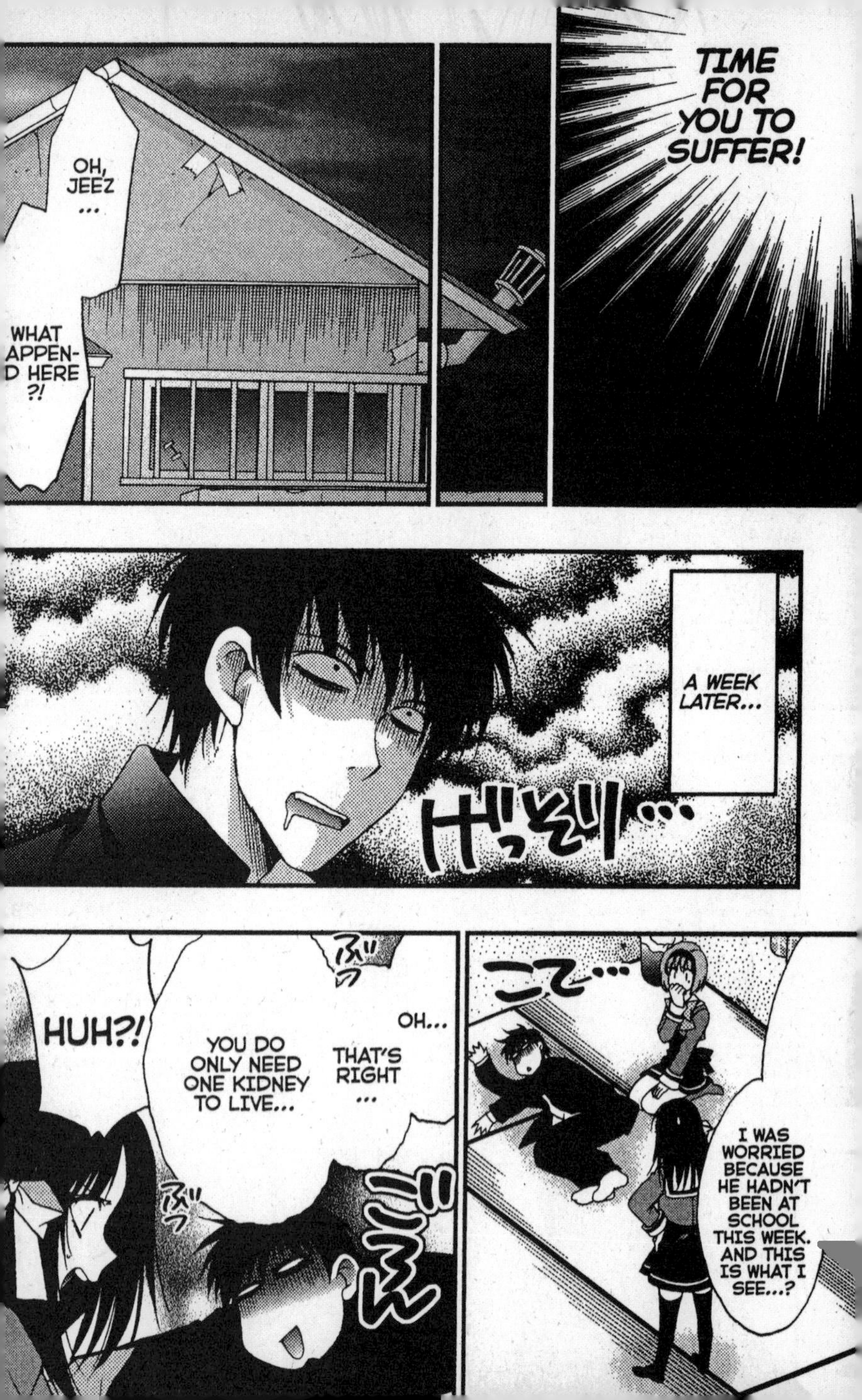
TIME FOR YOU TO SUFFER!
OH, JEEZ ...
WHAT HAPPEN-D HERE ?!
A WEEK LATER...
げっそり…
こて…
I WAS WORRIED BECAUSE HE HADN'T BEEN AT SCHOOL THIS WEEK. AND THIS IS WHAT I SEE...?
ぷ
OH... THAT'S RIGHT ...
YOU DO ONLY NEED ONE KIDNEY TO LIVE...
HUH?!
ごろん
ぷ

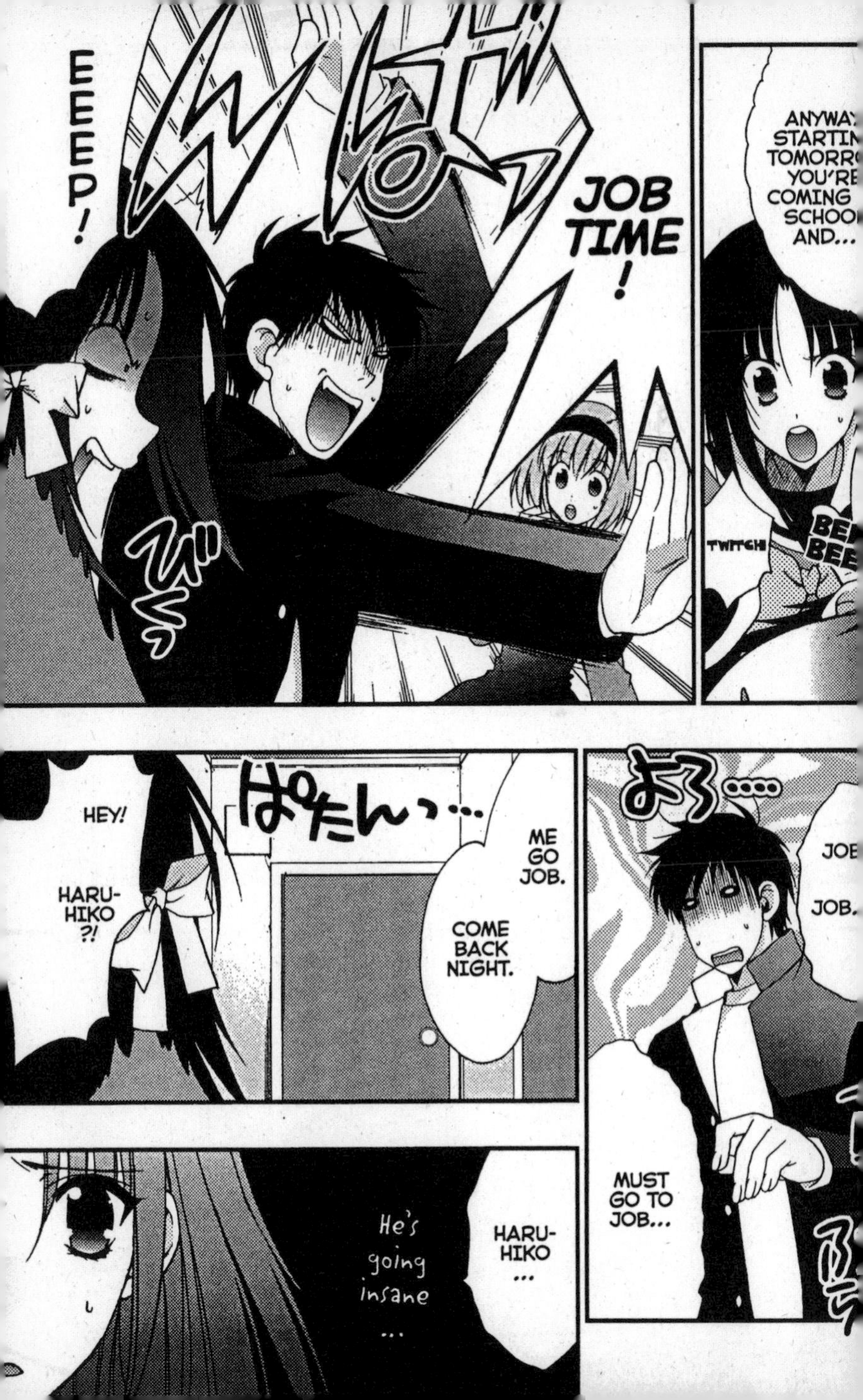

ANYWAY STARTIN TOMORRO YOU'RE COMING SCHOO AND...
TWITCH
JOB TIME!
EEEP!
よろ….
JOB
JOB.
MUST GO TO JOB...
ぱたんっ…
ME GO JOB.
COME BACK NIGHT.
HEY!
HARU-HIKO?!
HARU-HIKO...
He's going insane...

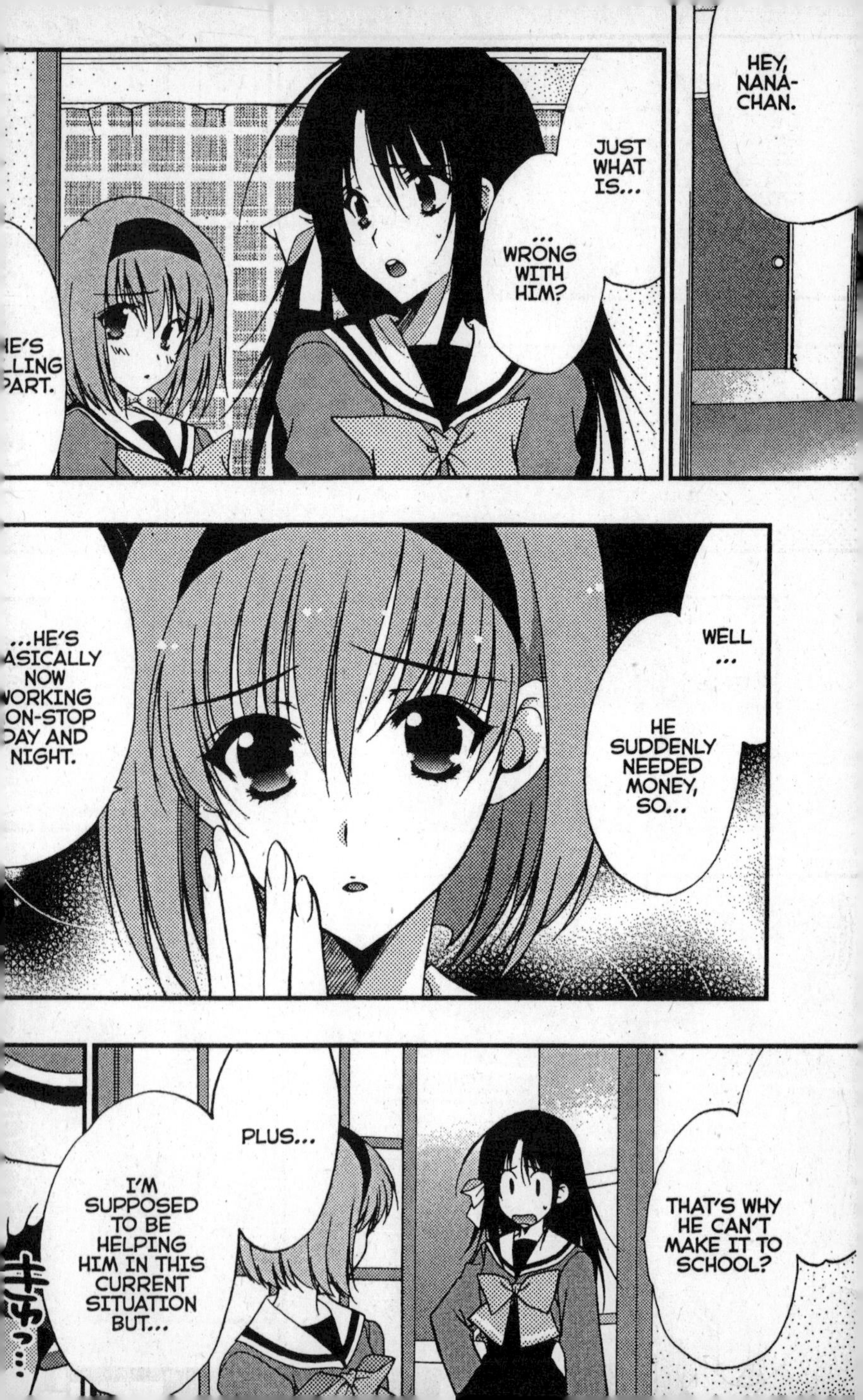
HEY, NANA-CHAN.
JUST WHAT IS...
...WRONG WITH HIM?
HE'S LLING PART.
WELL...
HE SUDDENLY NEEDED MONEY, SO...
...HE'S ASICALLY NOW ORKING ON-STOP AY AND NIGHT.
THAT'S WHY HE CAN'T MAKE IT TO SCHOOL?
PLUS...
I'M SUPPOSED TO BE HELPING HIM IN THIS CURRENT SITUATION BUT...

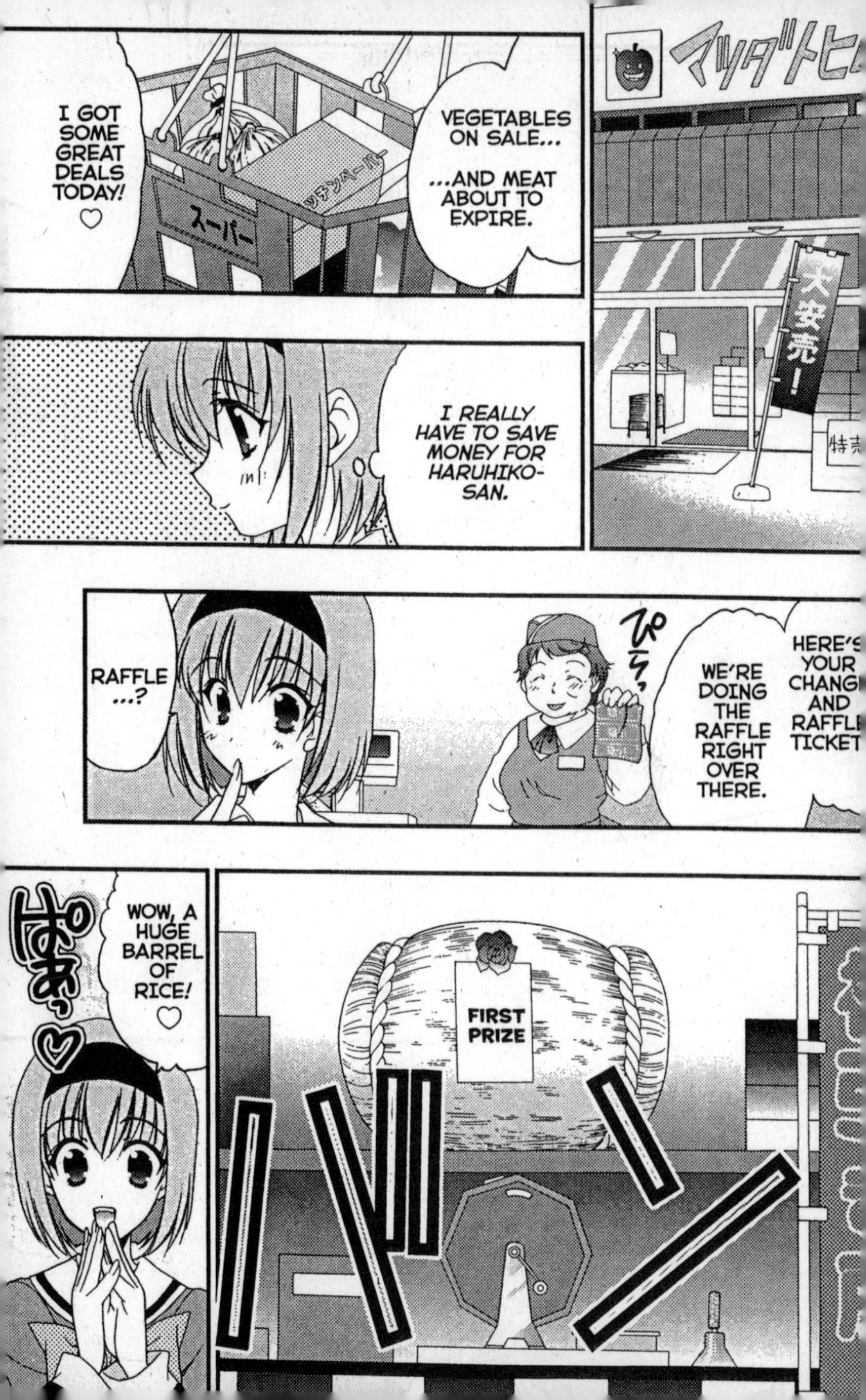
大安売！
VEGETABLES ON SALE...
...AND MEAT ABOUT TO EXPIRE.
スーパー
I GOT SOME GREAT DEALS TODAY! ♡
I REALLY HAVE TO SAVE MONEY FOR HARUHIKO-SAN.
HERE'S YOUR CHANG AND RAFFL TICKET
ぴらっ
WE'RE DOING THE RAFFLE RIGHT OVER THERE.
RAFFLE ...?
ドーン
FIRST PRIZE
ぱあっ♡
WOW, A HUGE BARREL OF RICE! ♡

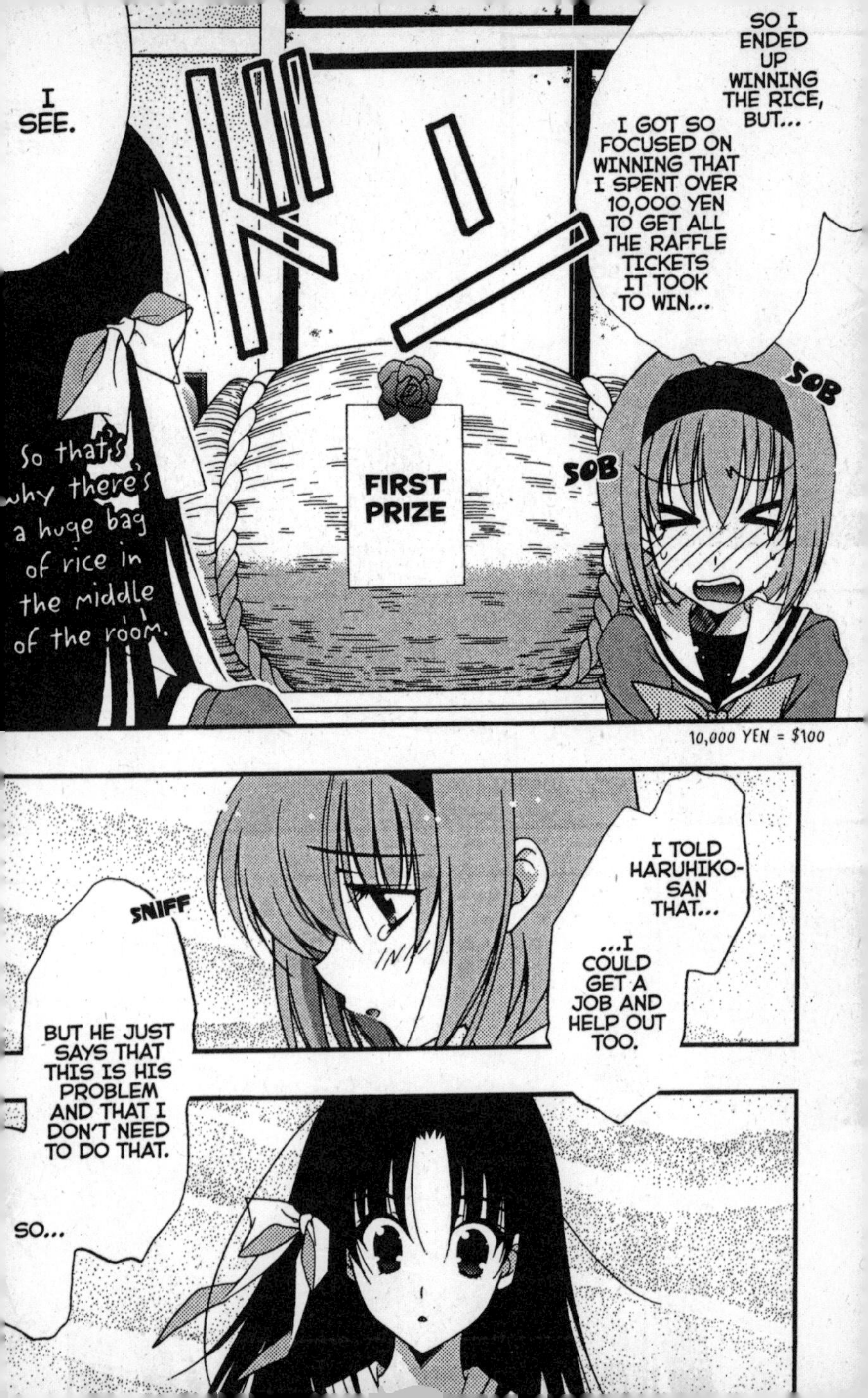
SO I ENDED UP WINNING THE RICE, BUT...
I GOT SO FOCUSED ON WINNING THAT I SPENT OVER 10,000 YEN TO GET ALL THE RAFFLE TICKETS IT TOOK TO WIN...
SOB
SOB
FIRST PRIZE
I SEE.
So that's why there's a huge bag of rice in the middle of the room.
10,000 YEN = $100
I TOLD HARUHIKO-SAN THAT...
...I COULD GET A JOB AND HELP OUT TOO.
SNIFF
BUT HE JUST SAYS THAT THIS IS HIS PROBLEM AND THAT I DON'T NEED TO DO THAT.
SO...

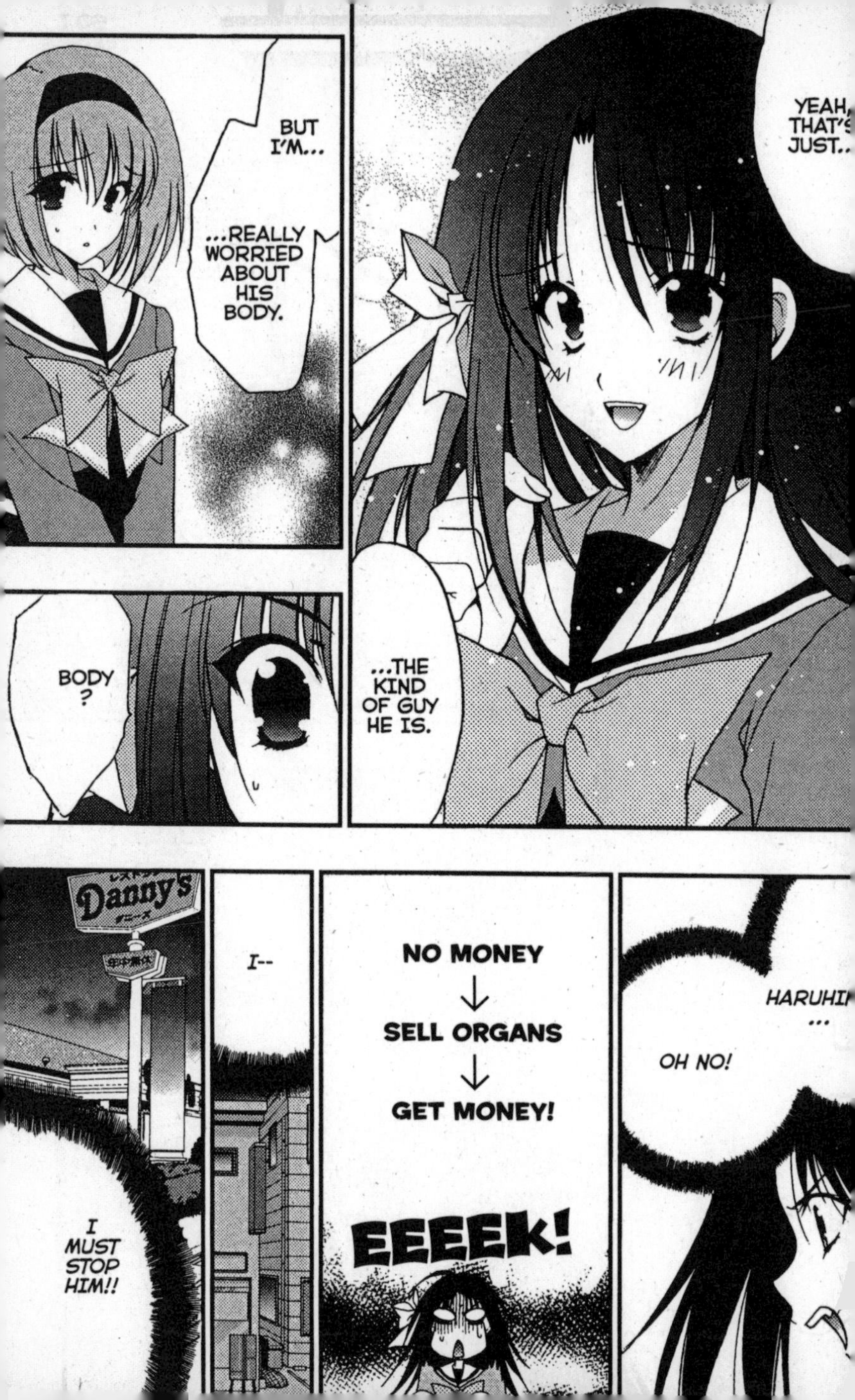

YEAH, THAT'S JUST...
...THE KIND OF GUY HE IS.
BUT I'M...
...REALLY WORRIED ABOUT HIS BODY.
BODY?
HARUHI...
OH NO!
NO MONEY ↓ SELL ORGANS ↓ GET MONEY!
EEEEK!
I--
Danny's
I MUST STOP HIM!!

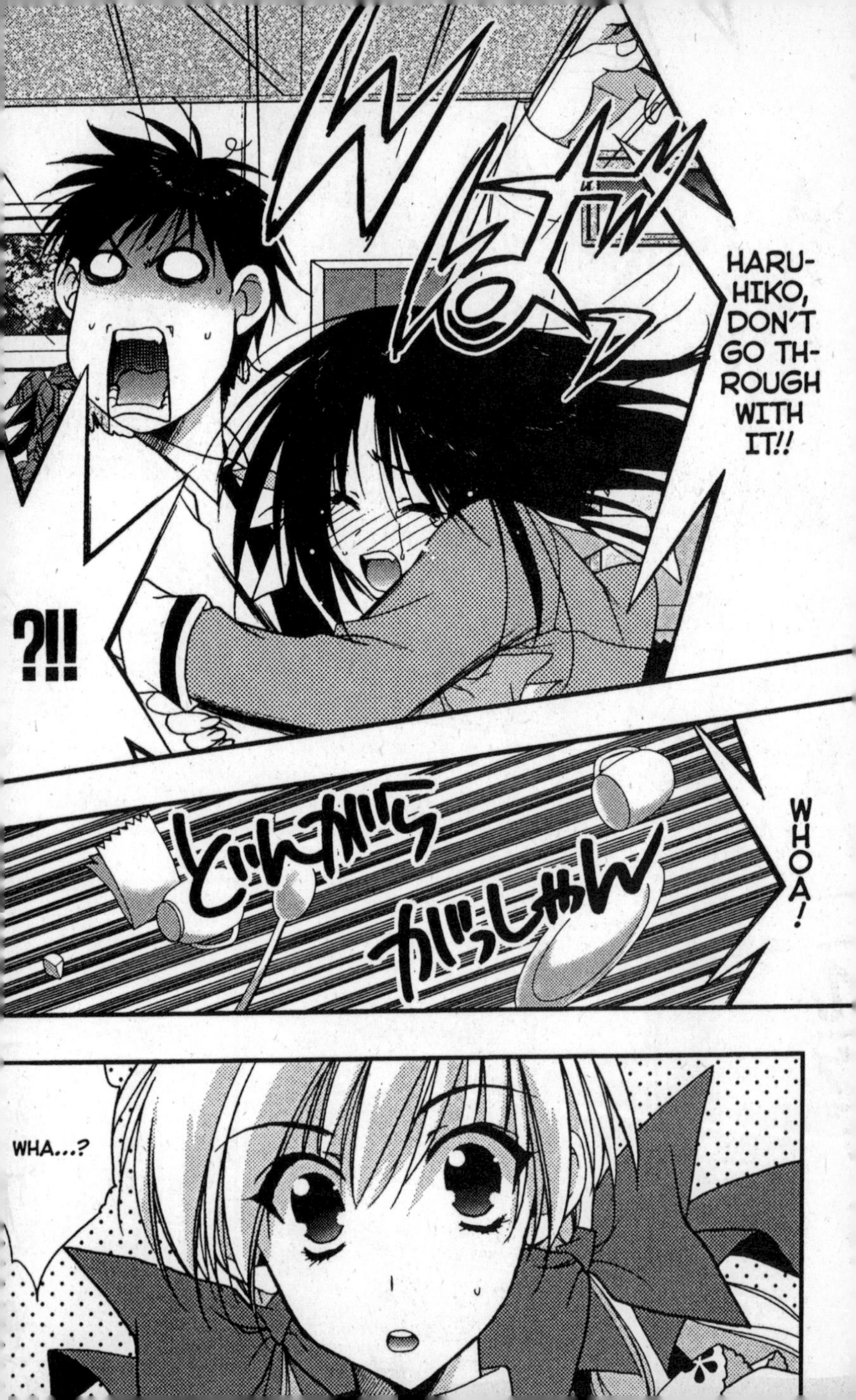
HARU-HIKO, DON'T GO TH-ROUGH WITH IT!!
?!!
WHOA!
WHA...?

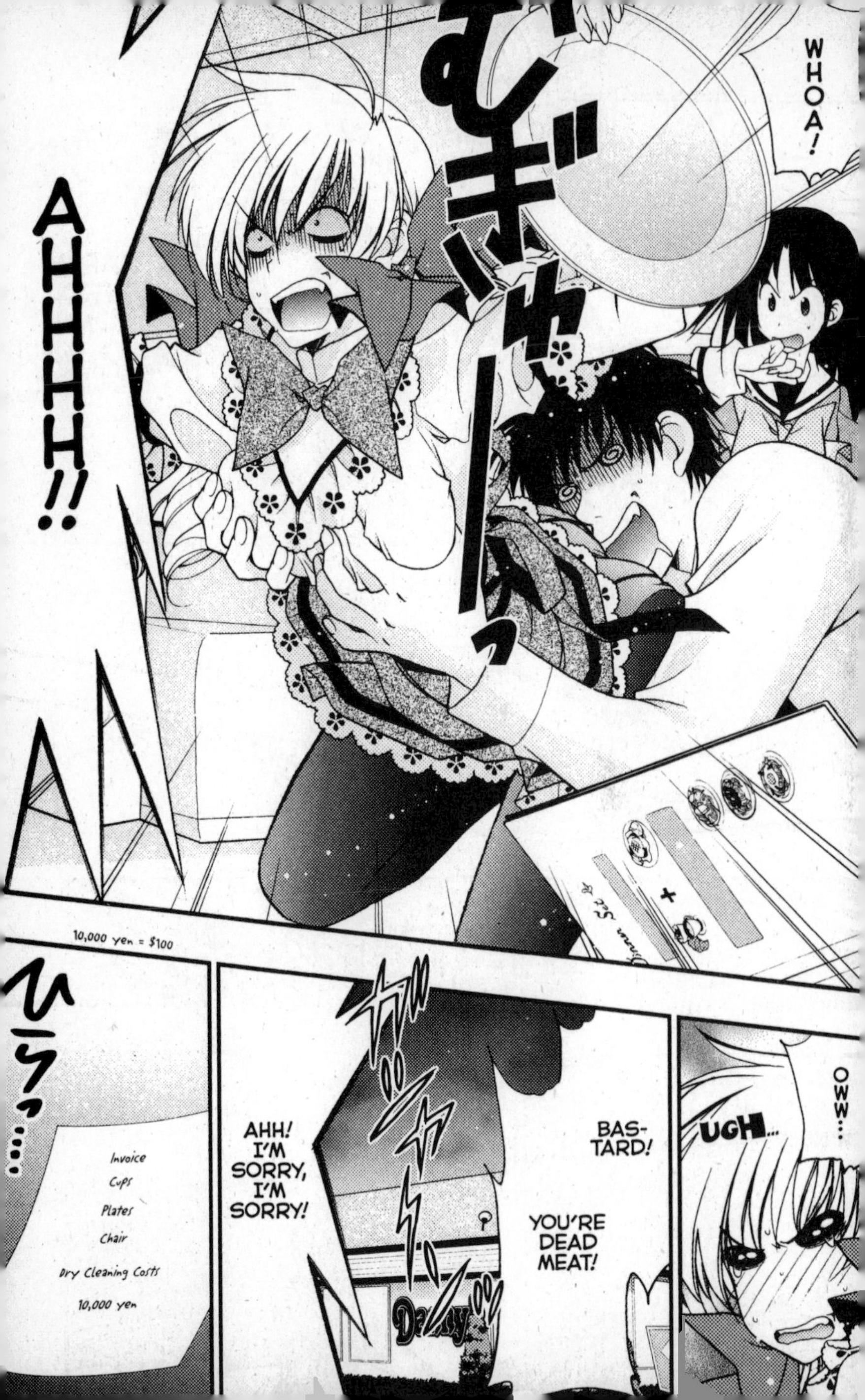
WHOA!
AHHHH!!
10,000 yen = $100
OWW...
UGH...
BAS-TARD!
YOU'RE DEAD MEAT!
AHH! I'M SORRY, I'M SORRY!
ひら〜…
Invoice
Cups
Plates
Chair
Dry Cleaning Costs
10,000 yen

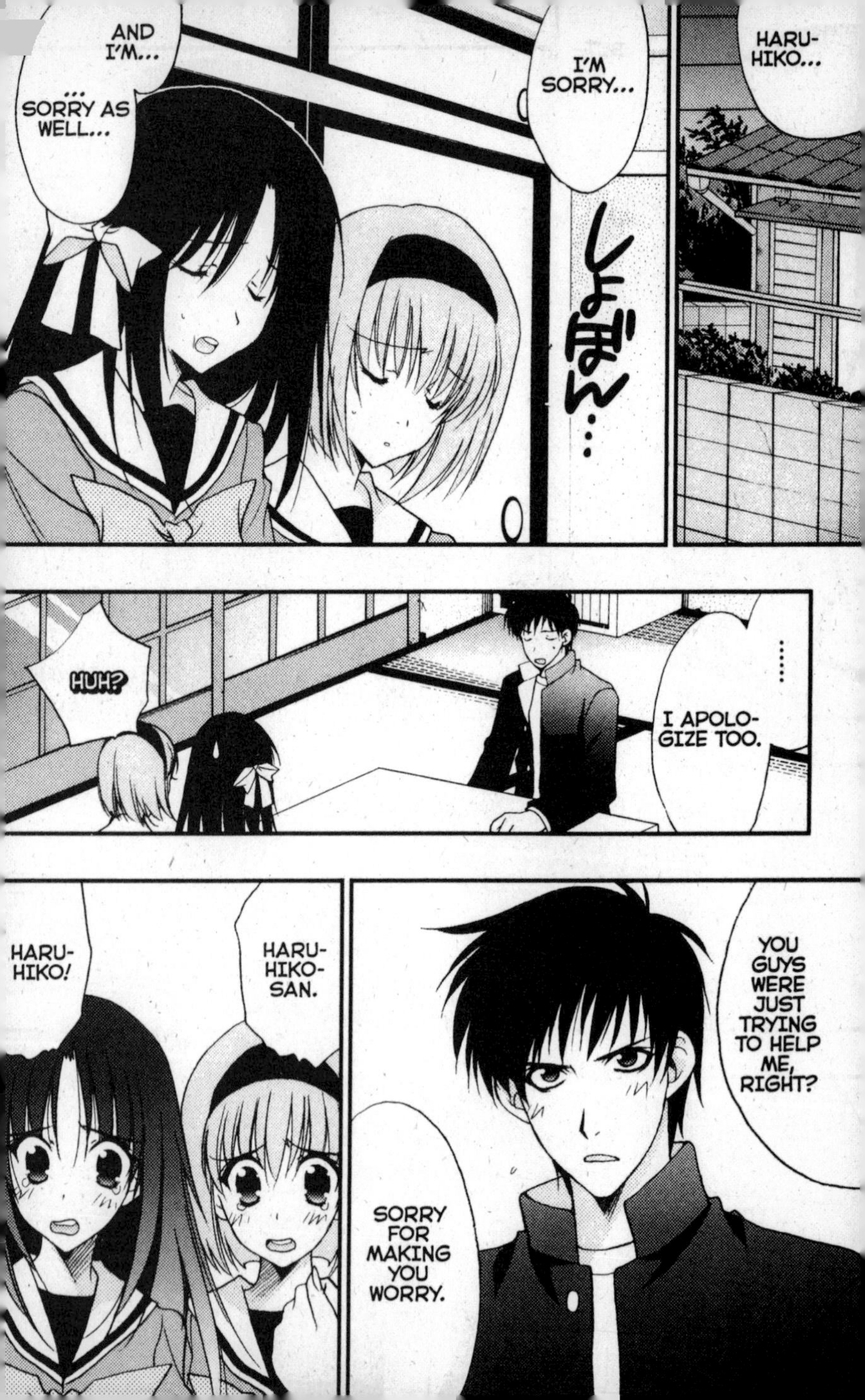
HARU-HIKO...
I'M SORRY...
しょぼん…
AND I'M...
... SORRY AS WELL...
......
I APOLO-GIZE TOO.
HUH?
YOU GUYS WERE JUST TRYING TO HELP ME, RIGHT?
SORRY FOR MAKING YOU WORRY.
HARU-HIKO-SAN.
HARU-HIKO!

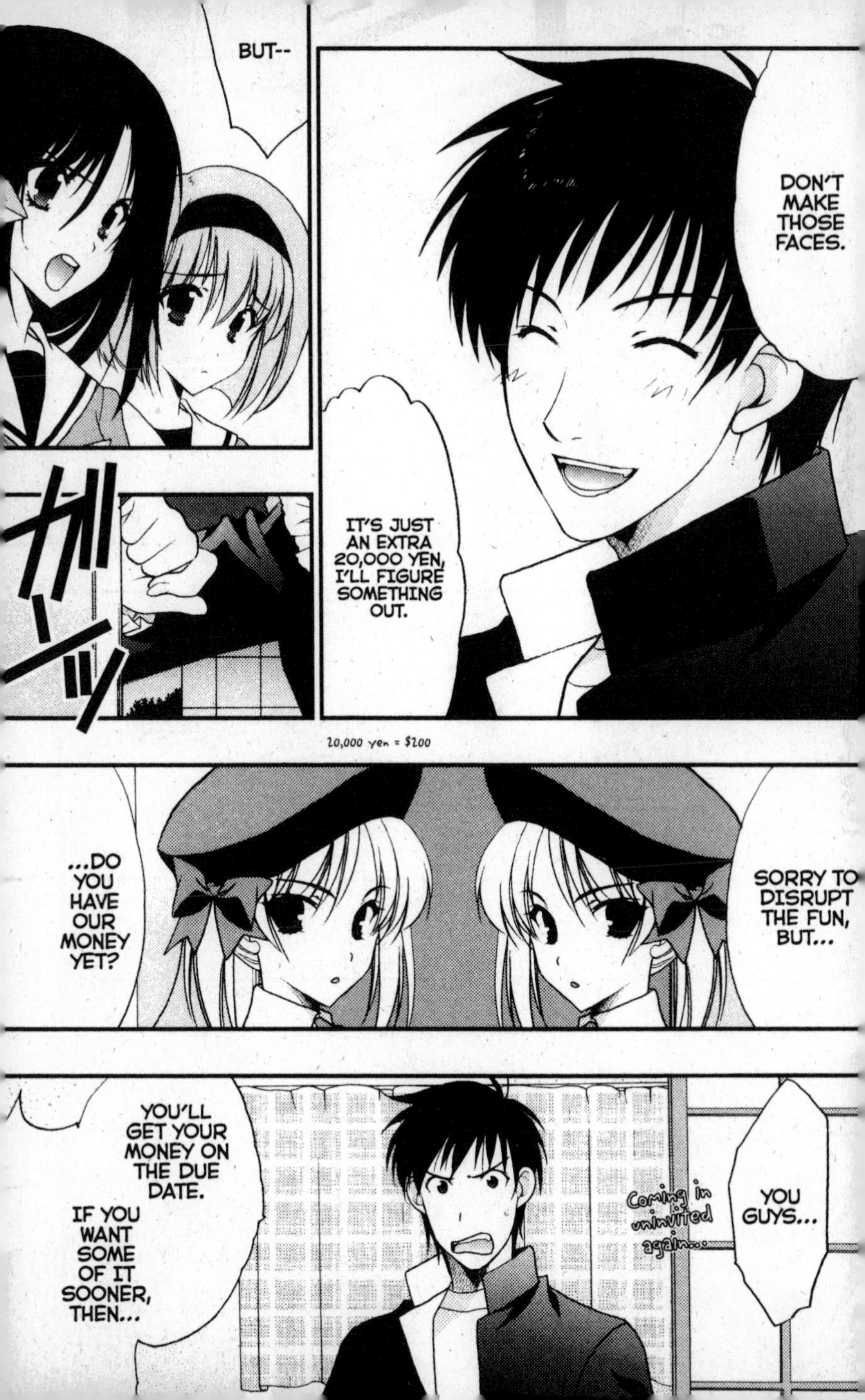
DON'T MAKE THOSE FACES.
IT'S JUST AN EXTRA 20,000 YEN, I'LL FIGURE SOMETHING OUT.
BUT--
20,000 yen = $200
SORRY TO DISRUPT THE FUN, BUT...
...DO YOU HAVE OUR MONEY YET?
YOU GUYS...
Coming in uninvited again...
YOU'LL GET YOUR MONEY ON THE DUE DATE.
IF YOU WANT SOME OF IT SOONER, THEN...

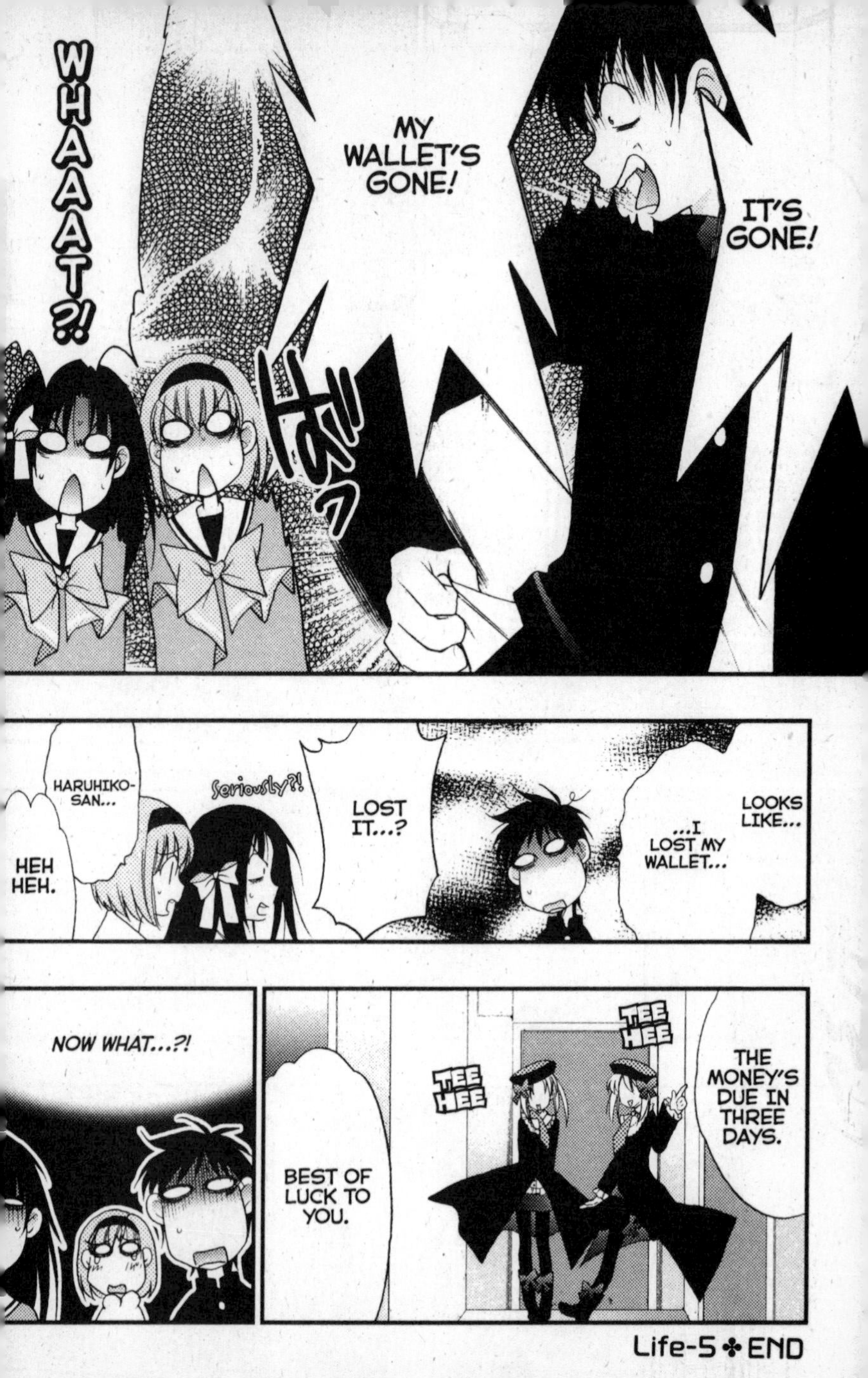
IT'S GONE!
MY WALLET'S GONE!
WHAAAAT?!
ハッ
LOOKS LIKE...
...I LOST MY WALLET...
LOST IT...?
Seriously?!
HARUHIKO-SAN...
HEH HEH.
THE MONEY'S DUE IN THREE DAYS.
TEE HEE
TEE HEE
BEST OF LUCK TO YOU.
NOW WHAT...?!

Life-5 ✤ END

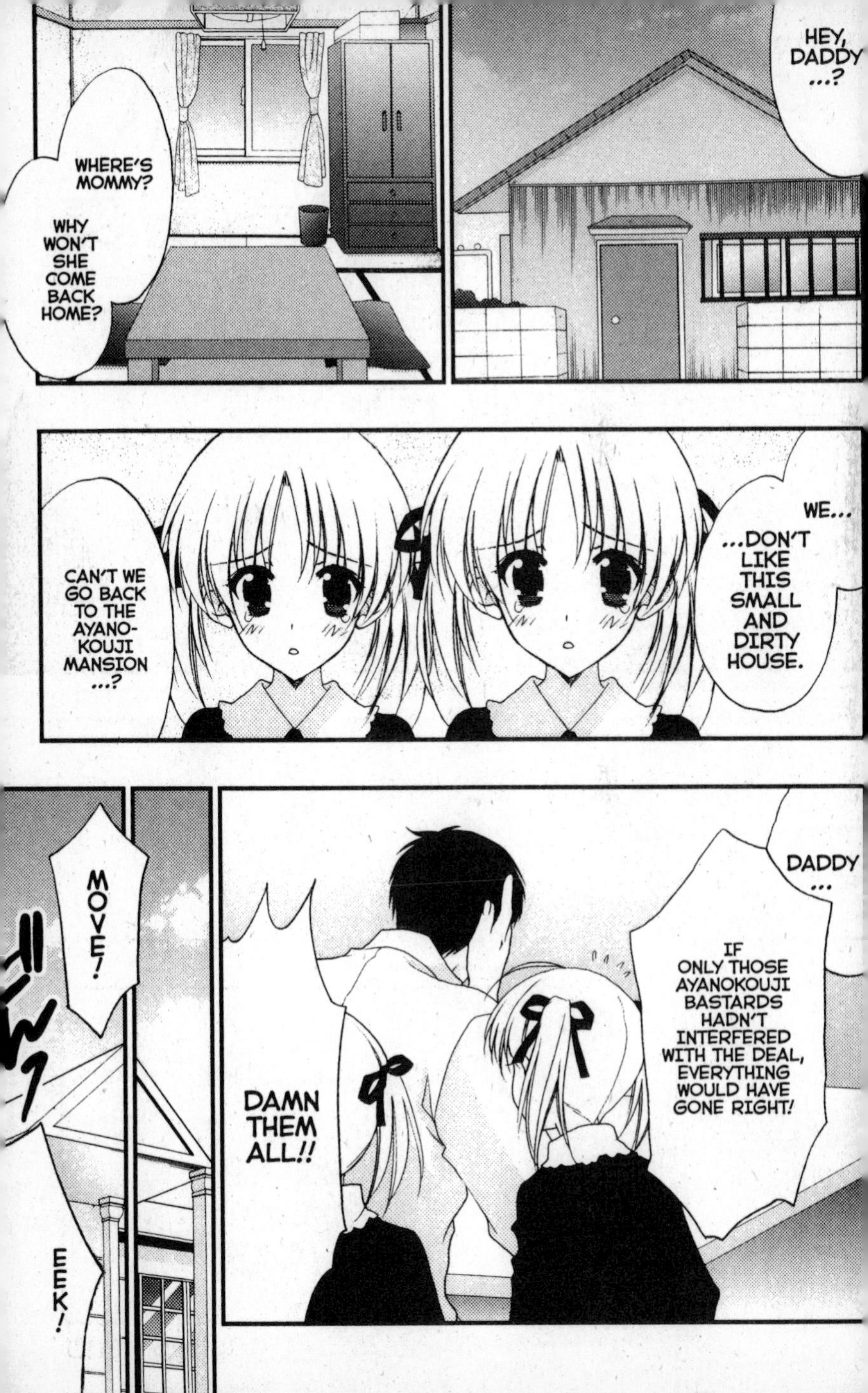
HEY, DADDY ...?
WHERE'S MOMMY?
WHY WON'T SHE COME BACK HOME?
WE...
...DON'T LIKE THIS SMALL AND DIRTY HOUSE.
CAN'T WE GO BACK TO THE AYANO-KOUJI MANSION ...?
DADDY ...
IF ONLY THOSE AYANOKOUJI BASTARDS HADN'T INTERFERED WITH THE DEAL, EVERYTHING WOULD HAVE GONE RIGHT!
DAMN THEM ALL!!
MOVE!
EEK!

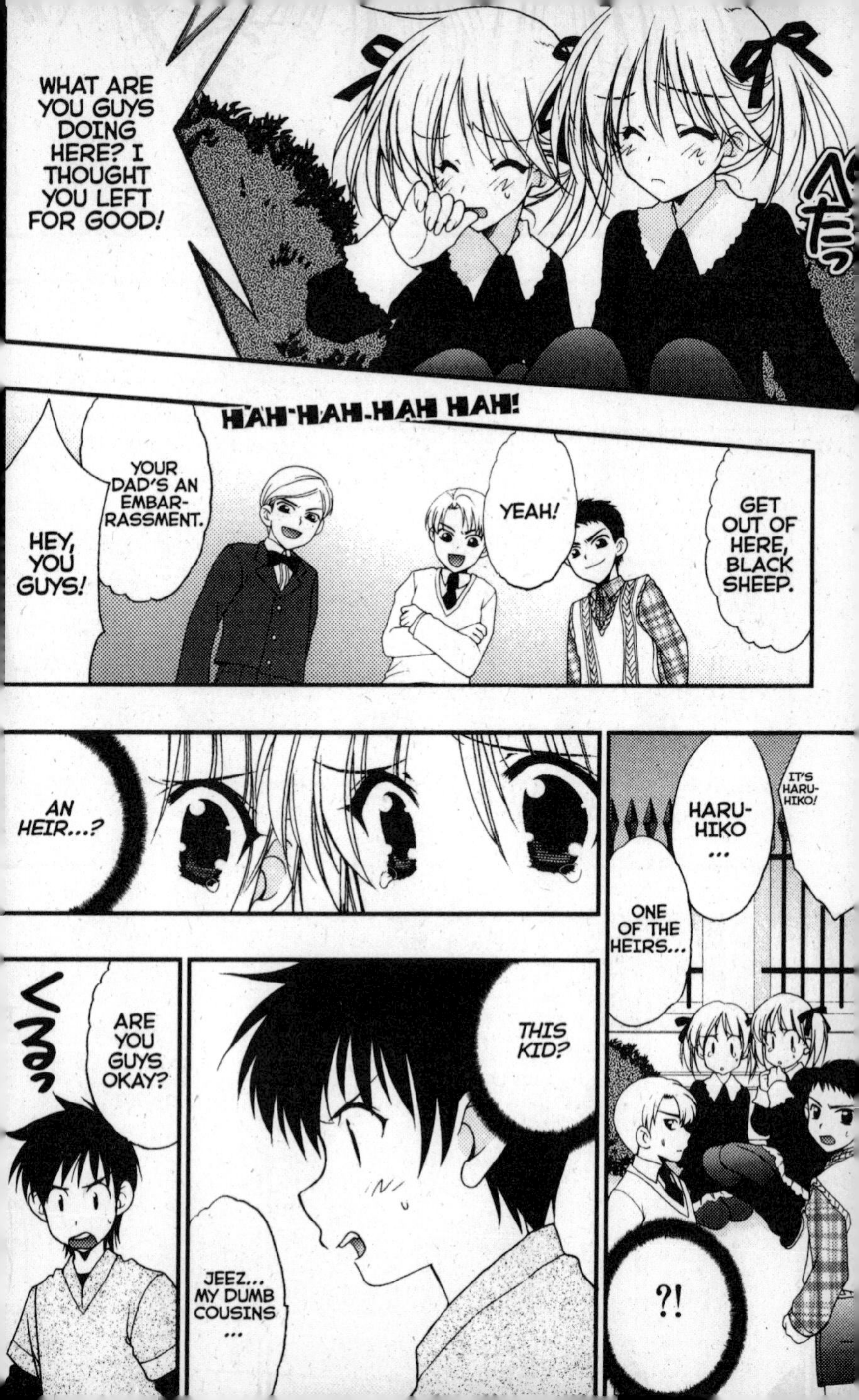
WHAT ARE YOU GUYS DOING HERE? I THOUGHT YOU LEFT FOR GOOD!
HAH-HAH-HAH HAH!
GET OUT OF HERE, BLACK SHEEP.
YEAH!
YOUR DAD'S AN EMBAR-RASSMENT.
HEY, YOU GUYS!
IT'S HARU-HIKO!
HARU-HIKO...
ONE OF THE HEIRS...
?!
AN HEIR...?
THIS KID?
JEEZ... MY DUMB COUSINS...
ARE YOU GUYS OKAY?

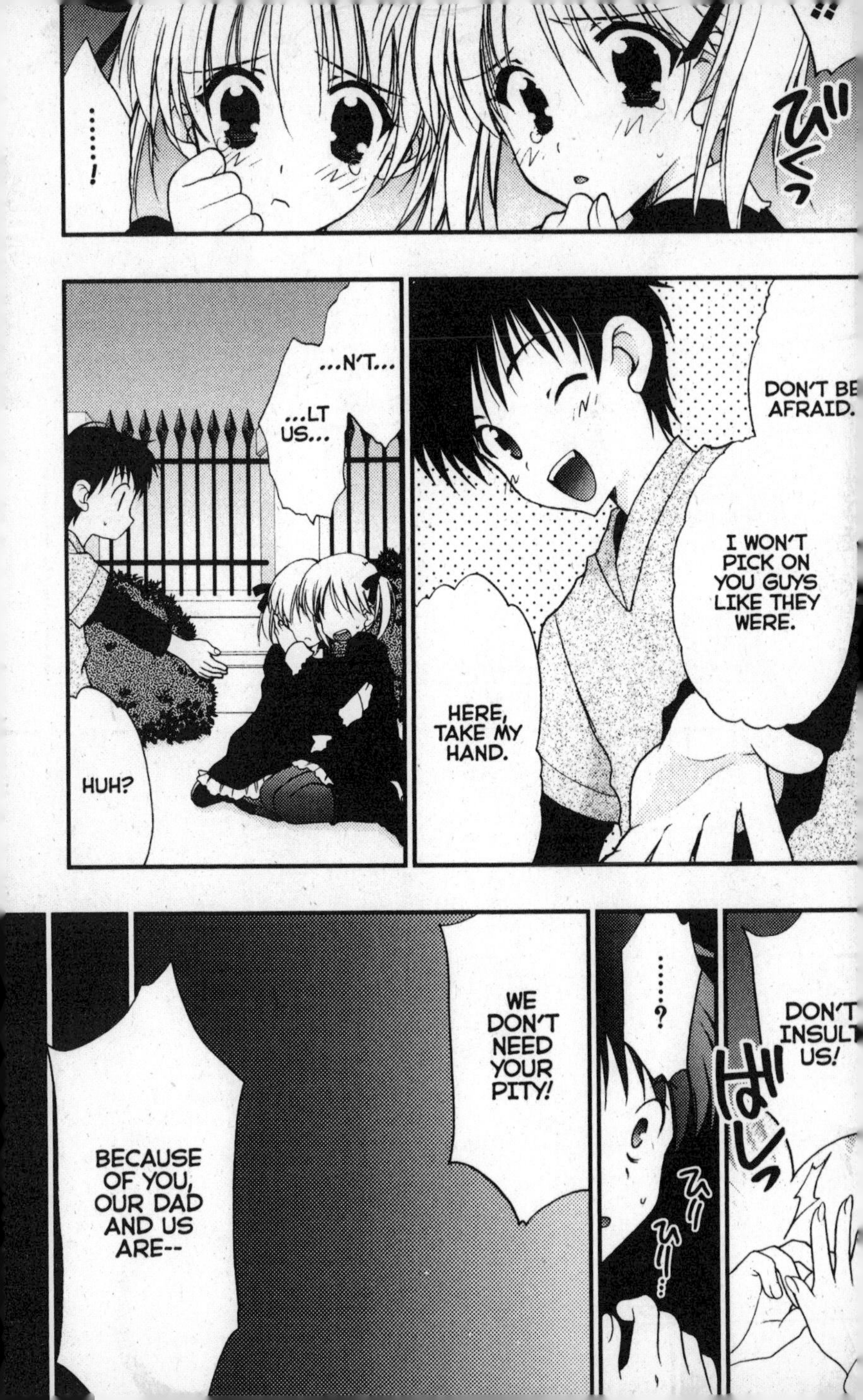
......!
びくっ
DON'T BE AFRAID.
I WON'T PICK ON YOU GUYS LIKE THEY WERE.
HERE, TAKE MY HAND.
...N'T...
...LT US...
HUH?
DON'T INSULT US!
ぱしっ
......?
WE DON'T NEED YOUR PITY!
BECAUSE OF YOU, OUR DAD AND US ARE--

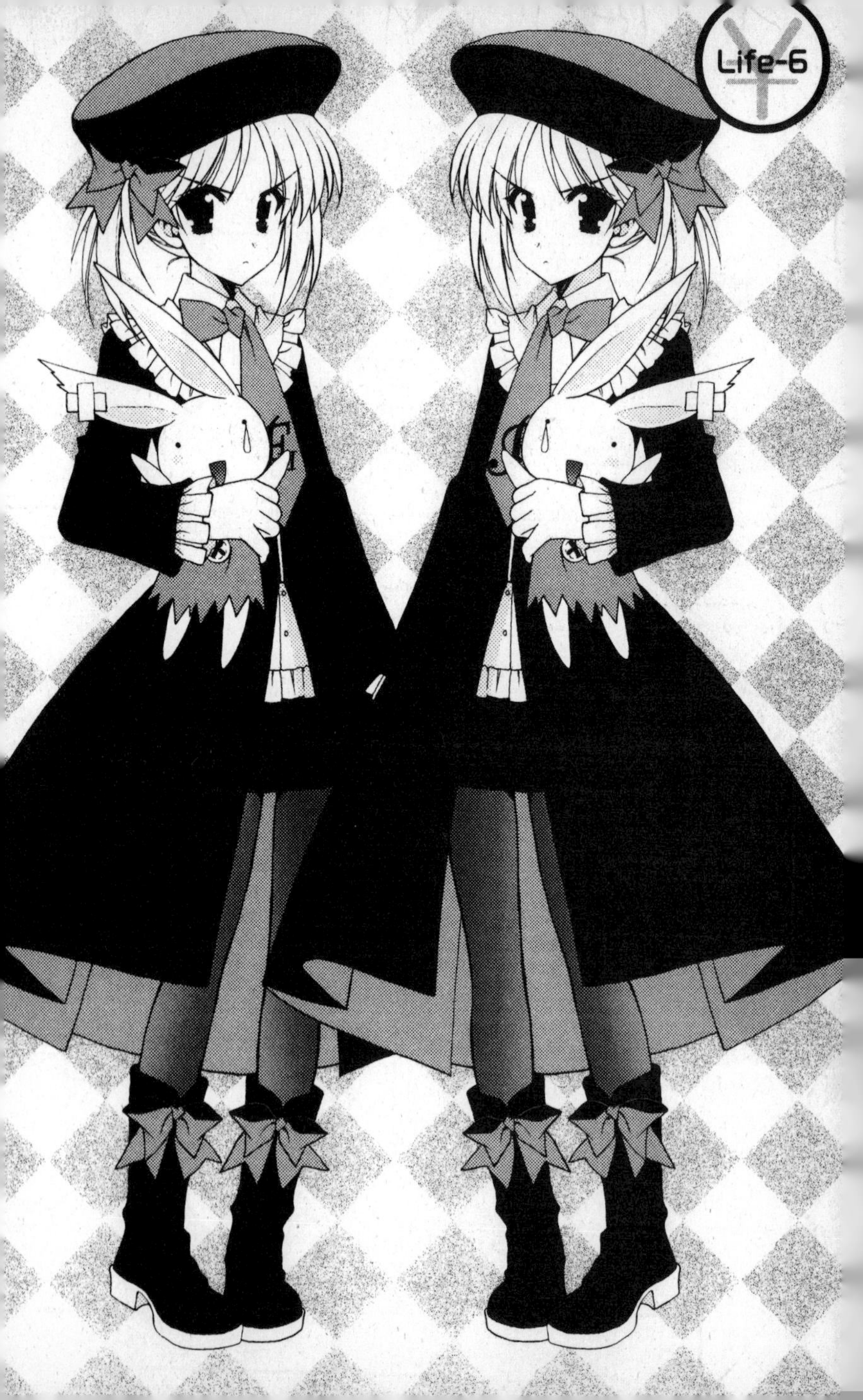
Life-6

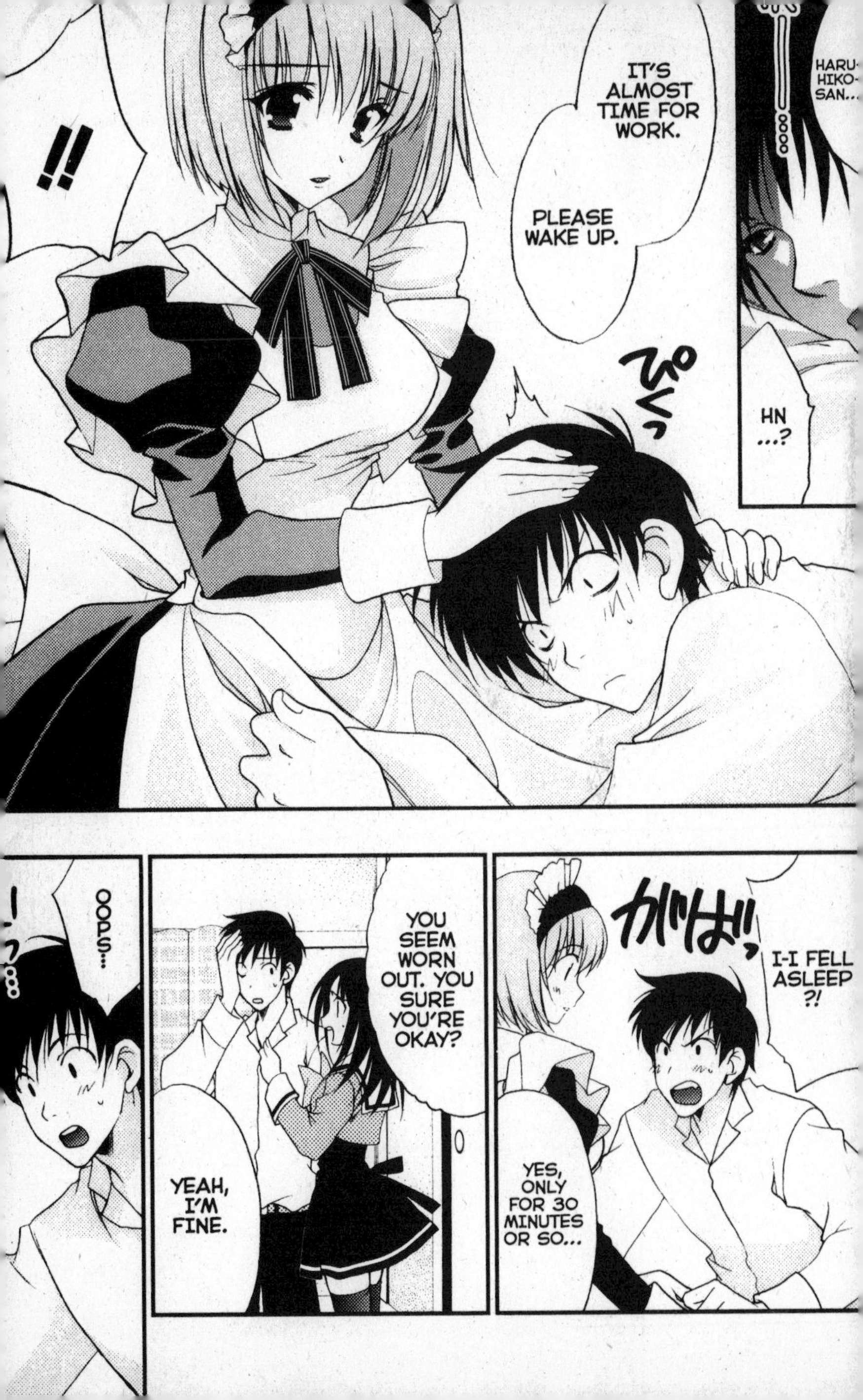
HARU-HIKO-SAN...
HN ...?
IT'S ALMOST TIME FOR WORK.
PLEASE WAKE UP.
ぴくっ
!!
がばっ!
I-I FELL ASLEEP ?!
YES, ONLY FOR 30 MINUTES OR SO...
YOU SEEM WORN OUT. YOU SURE YOU'RE OKAY?
YEAH, I'M FINE.
OOPS...

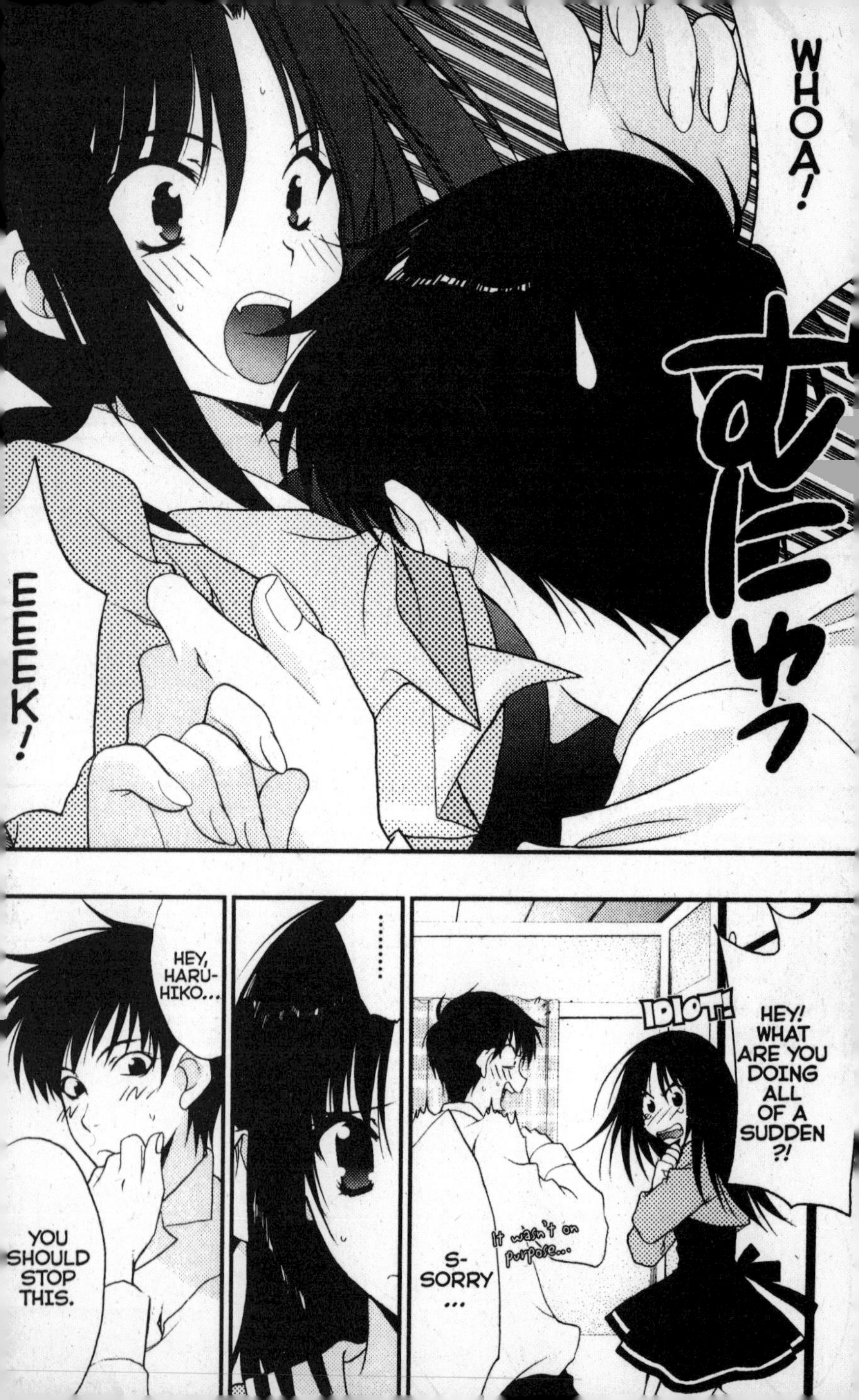

WHOA!
むにゅっ
EEEEK!
IDIOT!
HEY! WHAT ARE YOU DOING ALL OF A SUDDEN?!
It wasn't on purpose...
S-SORRY...
......
HEY, HARUHIKO...
YOU SHOULD STOP THIS.

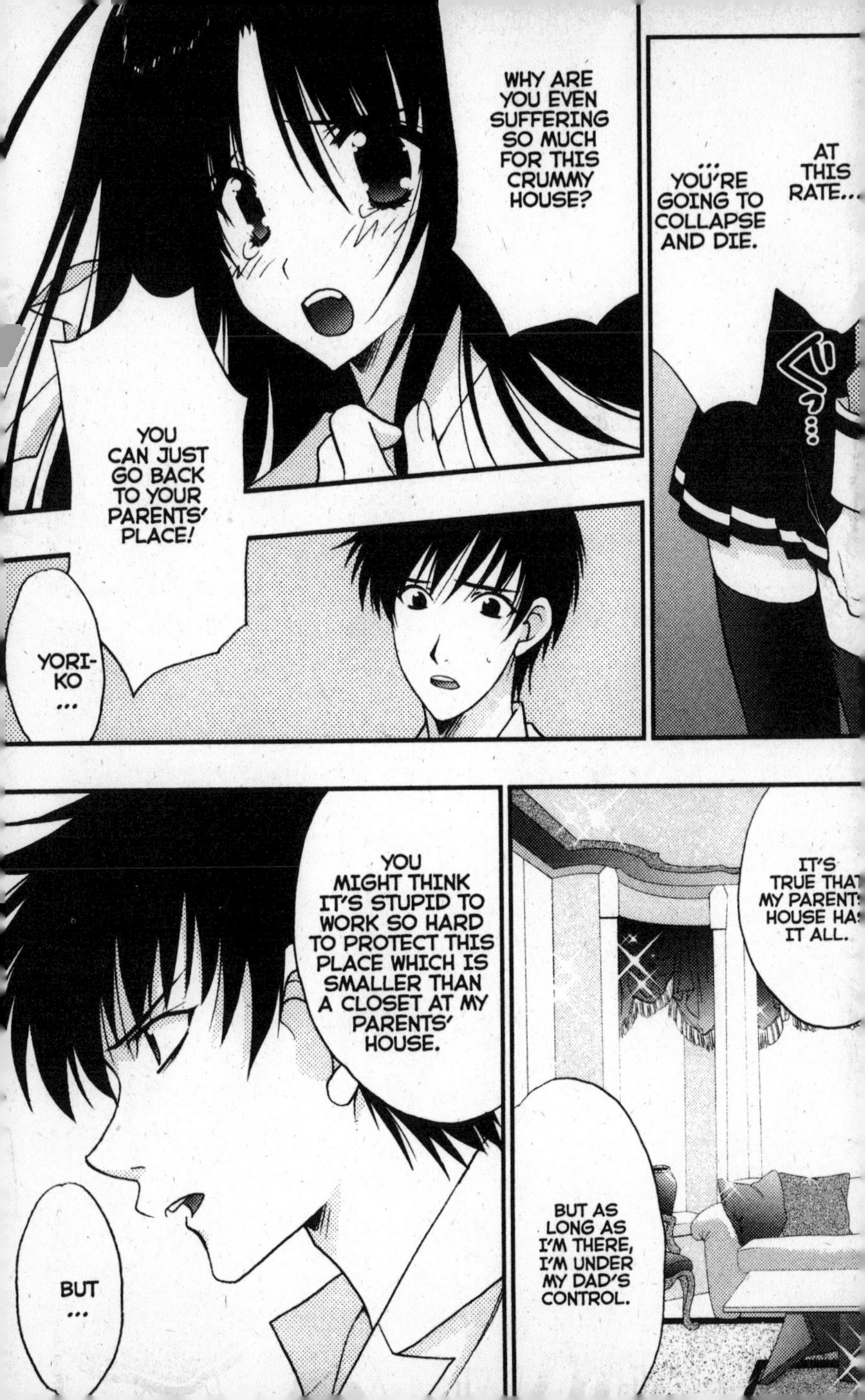
AT THIS RATE...
...YOU'RE GOING TO COLLAPSE AND DIE.
WHY ARE YOU EVEN SUFFERING SO MUCH FOR THIS CRUMMY HOUSE?
YOU CAN JUST GO BACK TO YOUR PARENTS' PLACE!
YORI-KO ...
IT'S TRUE THAT MY PARENTS HOUSE HAS IT ALL.
BUT AS LONG AS I'M THERE, I'M UNDER MY DAD'S CONTROL.
YOU MIGHT THINK IT'S STUPID TO WORK SO HARD TO PROTECT THIS PLACE WHICH IS SMALLER THAN A CLOSET AT MY PARENTS' HOUSE.
BUT ...

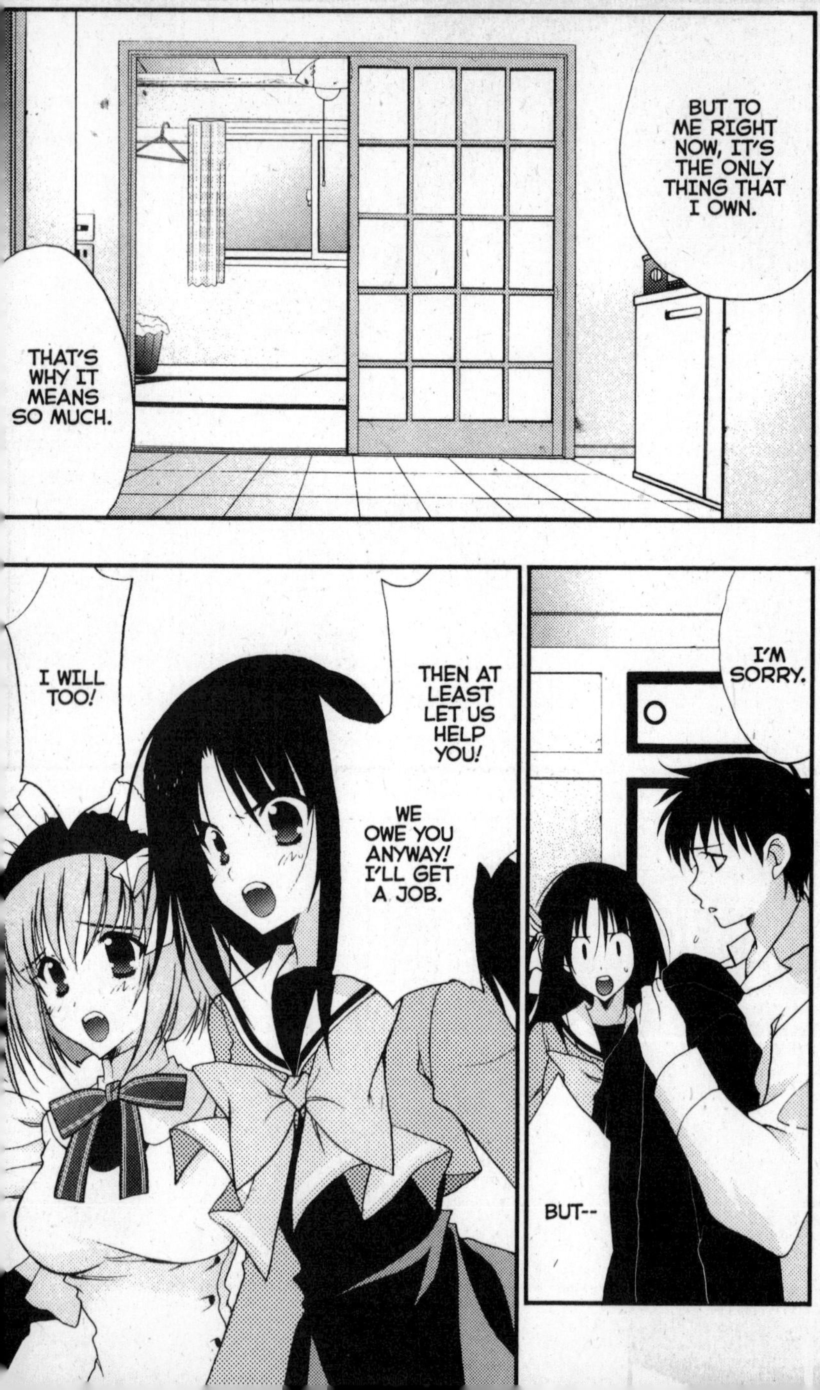
BUT TO ME RIGHT NOW, IT'S THE ONLY THING THAT I OWN.
THAT'S WHY IT MEANS SO MUCH.
I'M SORRY.
BUT--
THEN AT LEAST LET US HELP YOU!
WE OWE YOU ANYWAY! I'LL GET A JOB.
I WILL TOO!

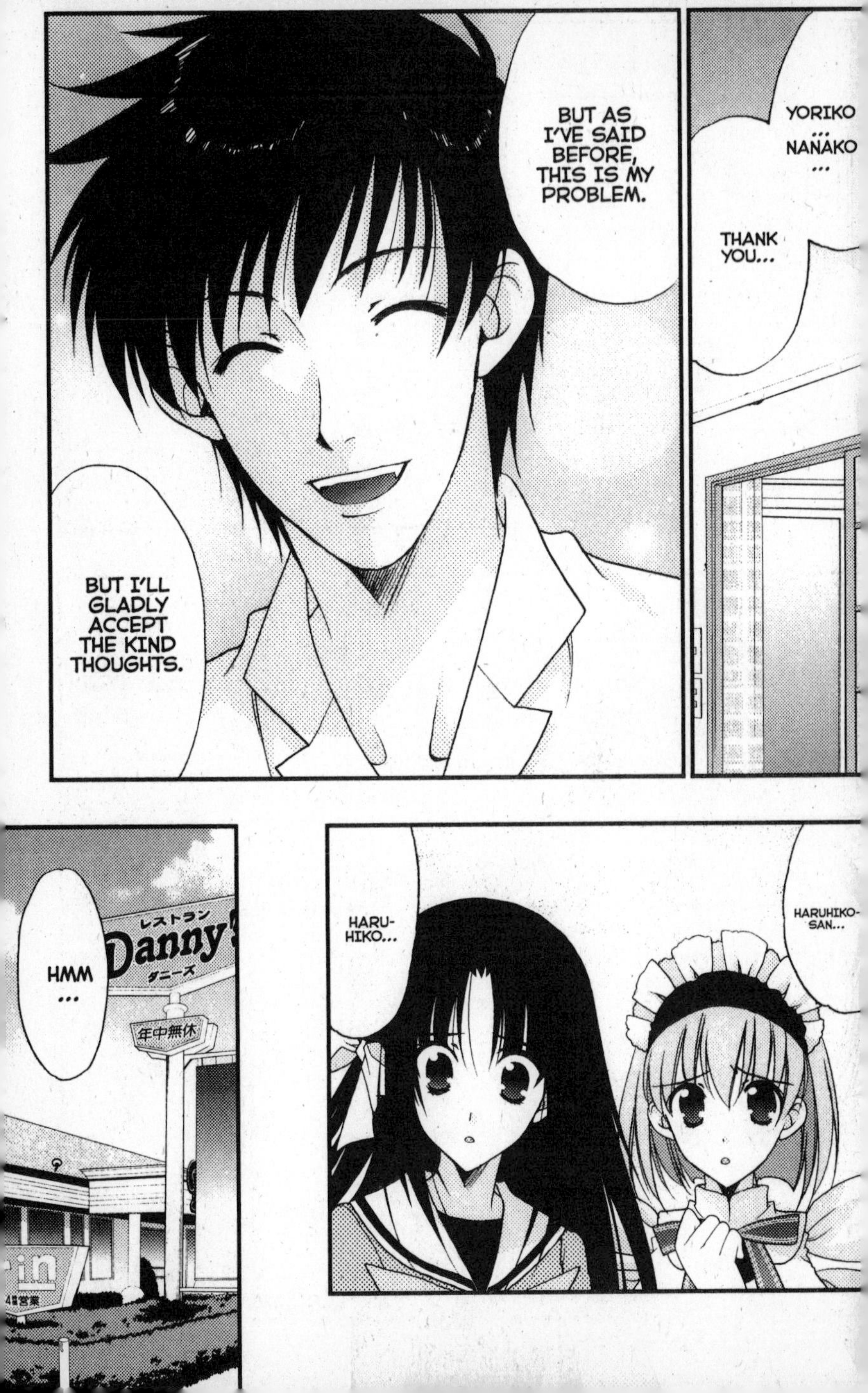
YORIKO ... NANAKO ...
THANK YOU...
BUT AS I'VE SAID BEFORE, THIS IS MY PROBLEM.
BUT I'LL GLADLY ACCEPT THE KIND THOUGHTS.
HARUHIKO-SAN...
HARU-HIKO...
HMM ...
レストラン
ダニーズ
年中無休

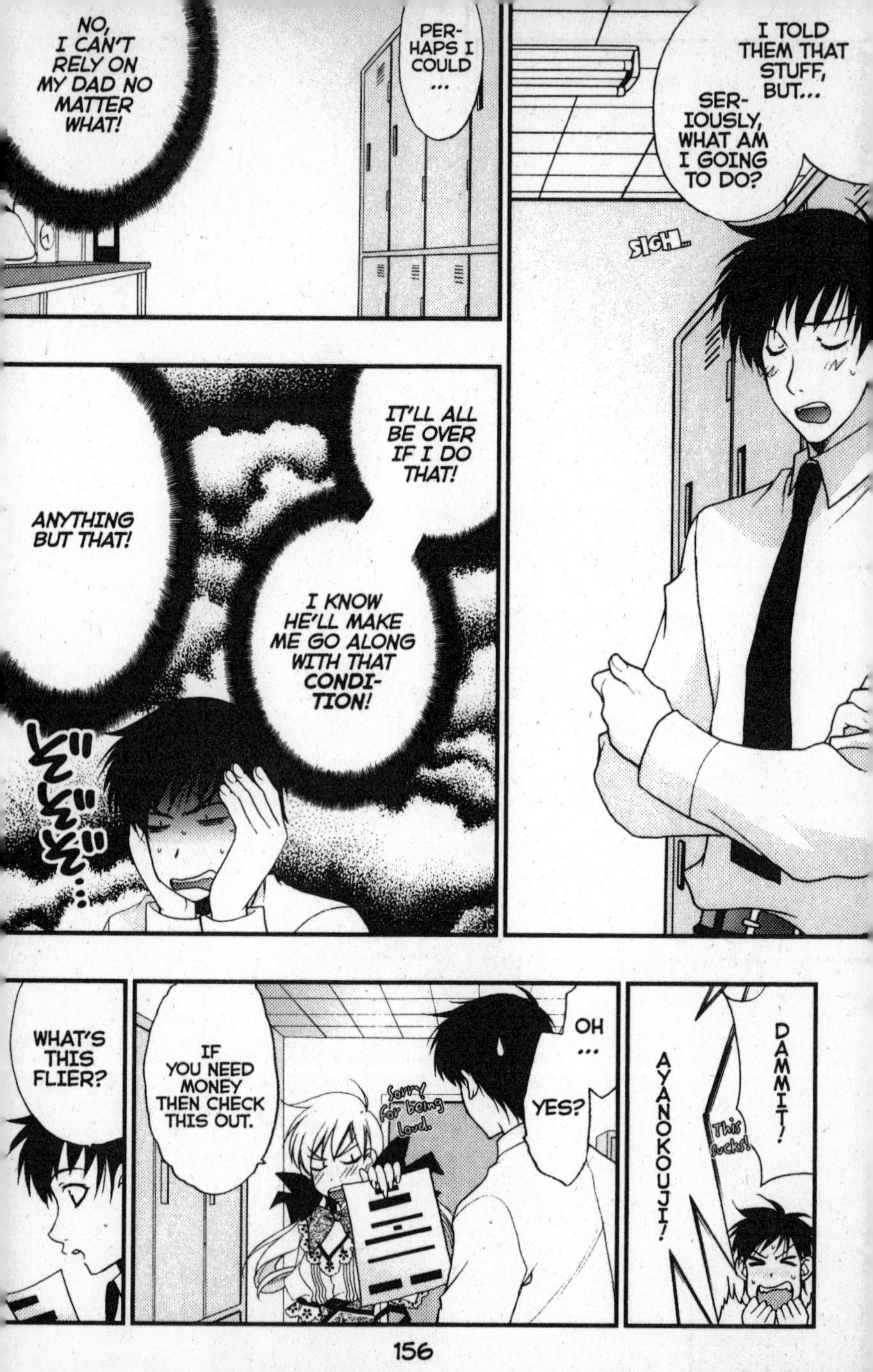
I TOLD THEM THAT STUFF, BUT...
SER-IOUSLY, WHAT AM I GOING TO DO?
SIGH...
PER-HAPS I COULD ...
NO, I CAN'T RELY ON MY DAD NO MATTER WHAT!
IT'LL ALL BE OVER IF I DO THAT!
I KNOW HE'LL MAKE ME GO ALONG WITH THAT CONDI-TION!
ANYTHING BUT THAT!
DAMMIT!
AYANOKOUJI!
This sucks!
OH ...
YES?
Sorry for being loud.
IF YOU NEED MONEY THEN CHECK THIS OUT.
WHAT'S THIS FLIER?

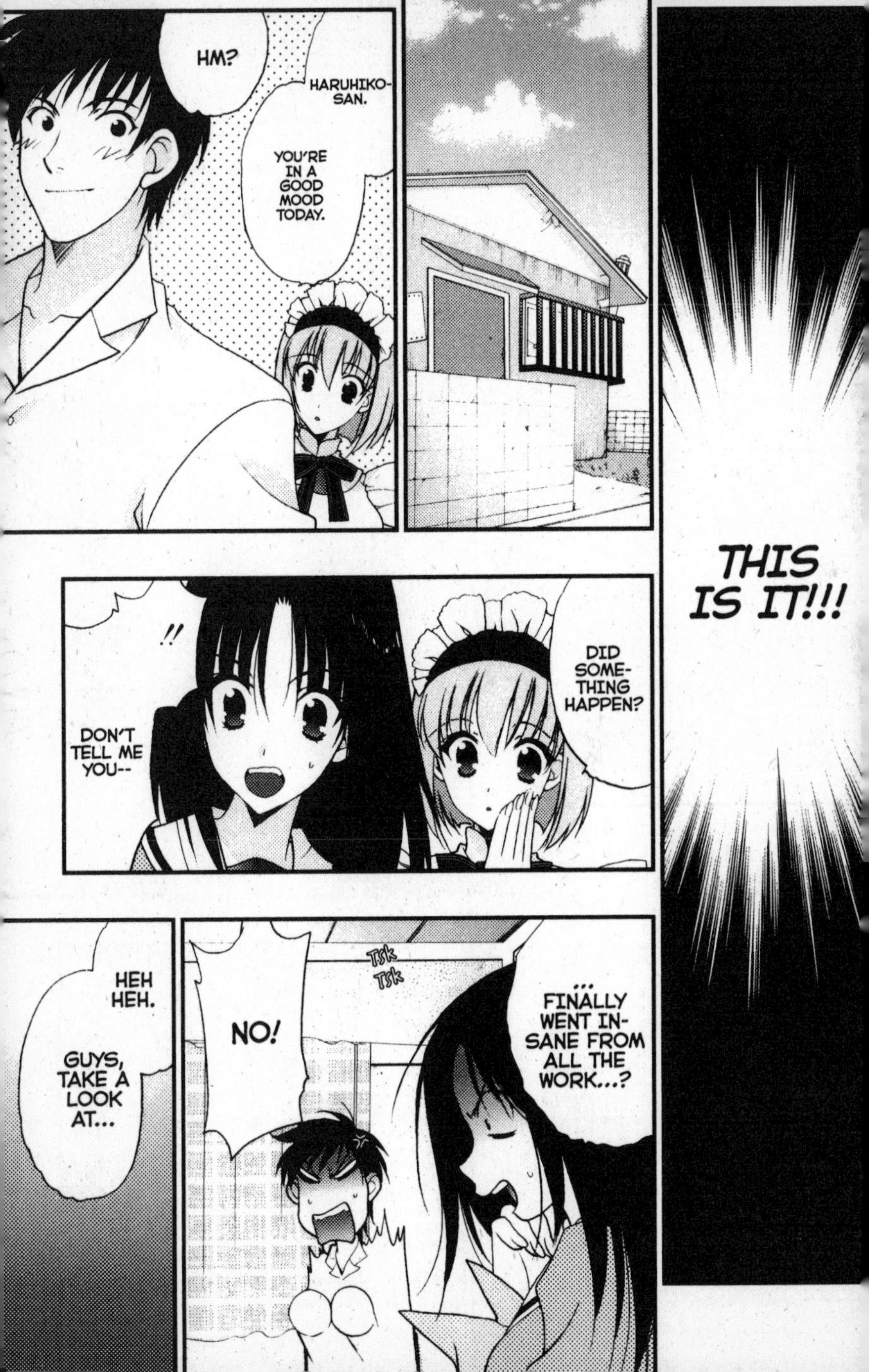
THIS IS IT!!!
HARUHIKO-SAN.
YOU'RE IN A GOOD MOOD TODAY.
HM?
DID SOMETHING HAPPEN?
!!
DON'T TELL ME YOU--
Tsk Tsk
...FINALLY WENT IN-SANE FROM ALL THE WORK...?
NO!
HEH HEH.
GUYS, TAKE A LOOK AT...

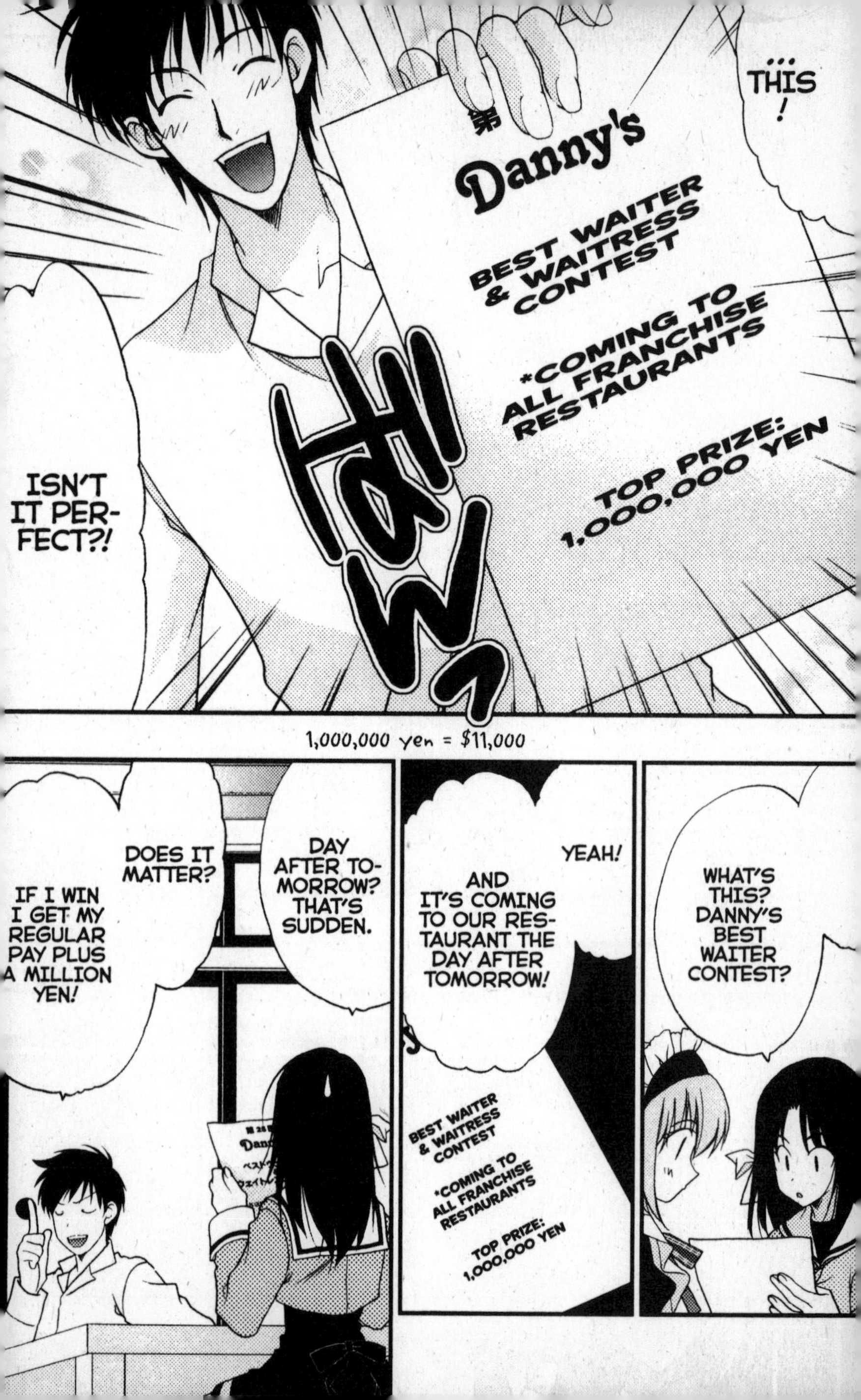
...THIS!
第
Danny's
BEST WAITER & WAITRESS CONTEST
*COMING TO ALL FRANCHISE RESTAURANTS
TOP PRIZE: 1,000,000 YEN
ISN'T IT PERFECT?!
1,000,000 yen = $11,000
WHAT'S THIS? DANNY'S BEST WAITER CONTEST?
YEAH!
AND IT'S COMING TO OUR RESTAURANT THE DAY AFTER TOMORROW!
BEST WAITER & WAITRESS CONTEST
*COMING TO ALL FRANCHISE RESTAURANTS
TOP PRIZE: 1,000,000 YEN
DAY AFTER TOMORROW? THAT'S SUDDEN.
DOES IT MATTER?
IF I WIN I GET MY REGULAR PAY PLUS A MILLION YEN!

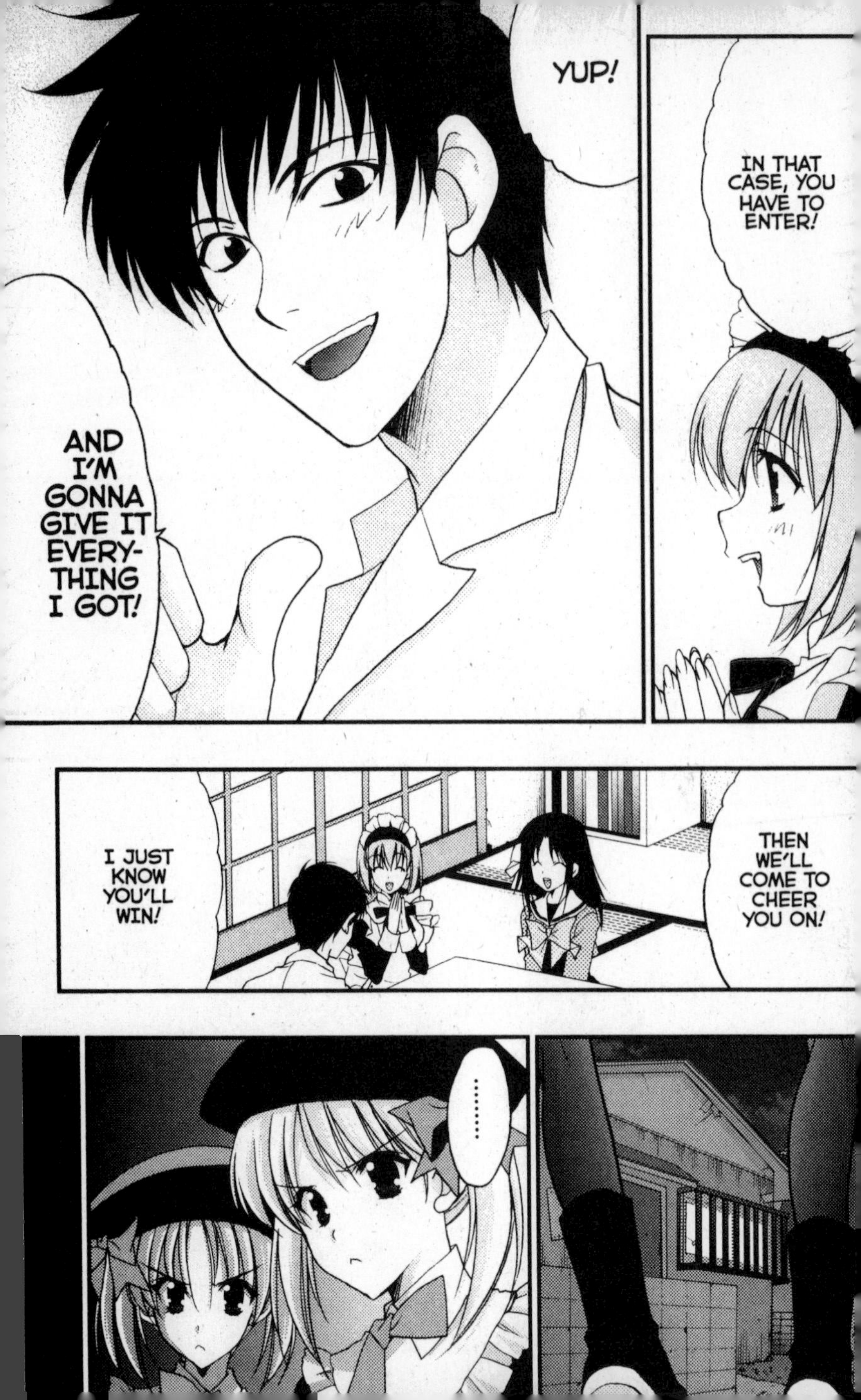
IN THAT CASE, YOU HAVE TO ENTER!
YUP!
AND I'M GONNA GIVE IT EVERYTHING I GOT!
THEN WE'LL COME TO CHEER YOU ON!
I JUST KNOW YOU'LL WIN!
……

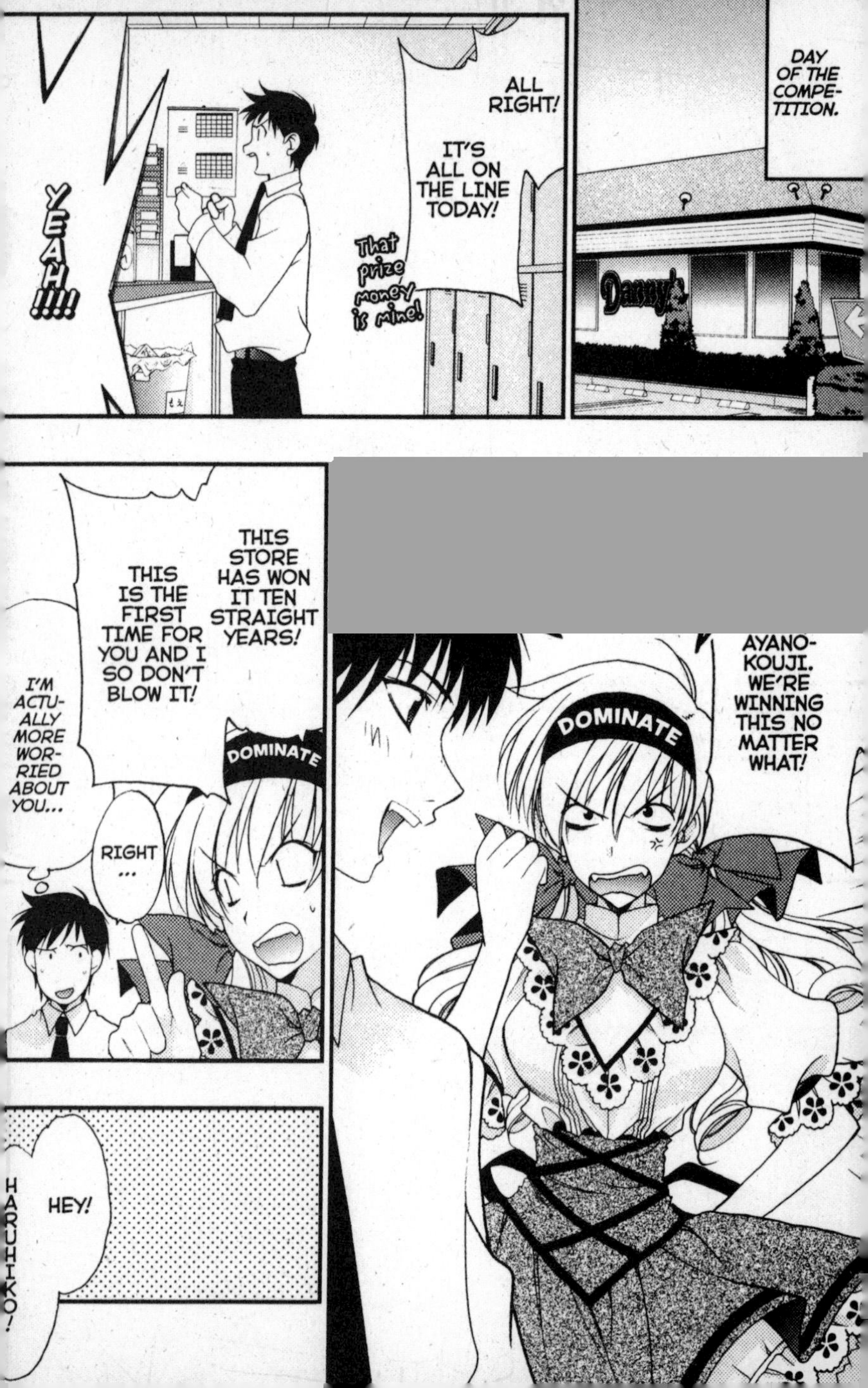
DAY OF THE COMPE-TITION.
Danny's
ALL RIGHT!
IT'S ALL ON THE LINE TODAY!
That prize money is mine!
YEAH!!!!
AYANO-KOUJI. WE'RE WINNING THIS NO MATTER WHAT!
DOMINATE
THIS STORE HAS WON IT TEN STRAIGHT YEARS!
THIS IS THE FIRST TIME FOR YOU AND I SO DON'T BLOW IT!
DOMINATE
RIGHT...
I'M ACTU-ALLY MORE WOR-RIED ABOUT YOU...
HEY!
HARUHIKO!

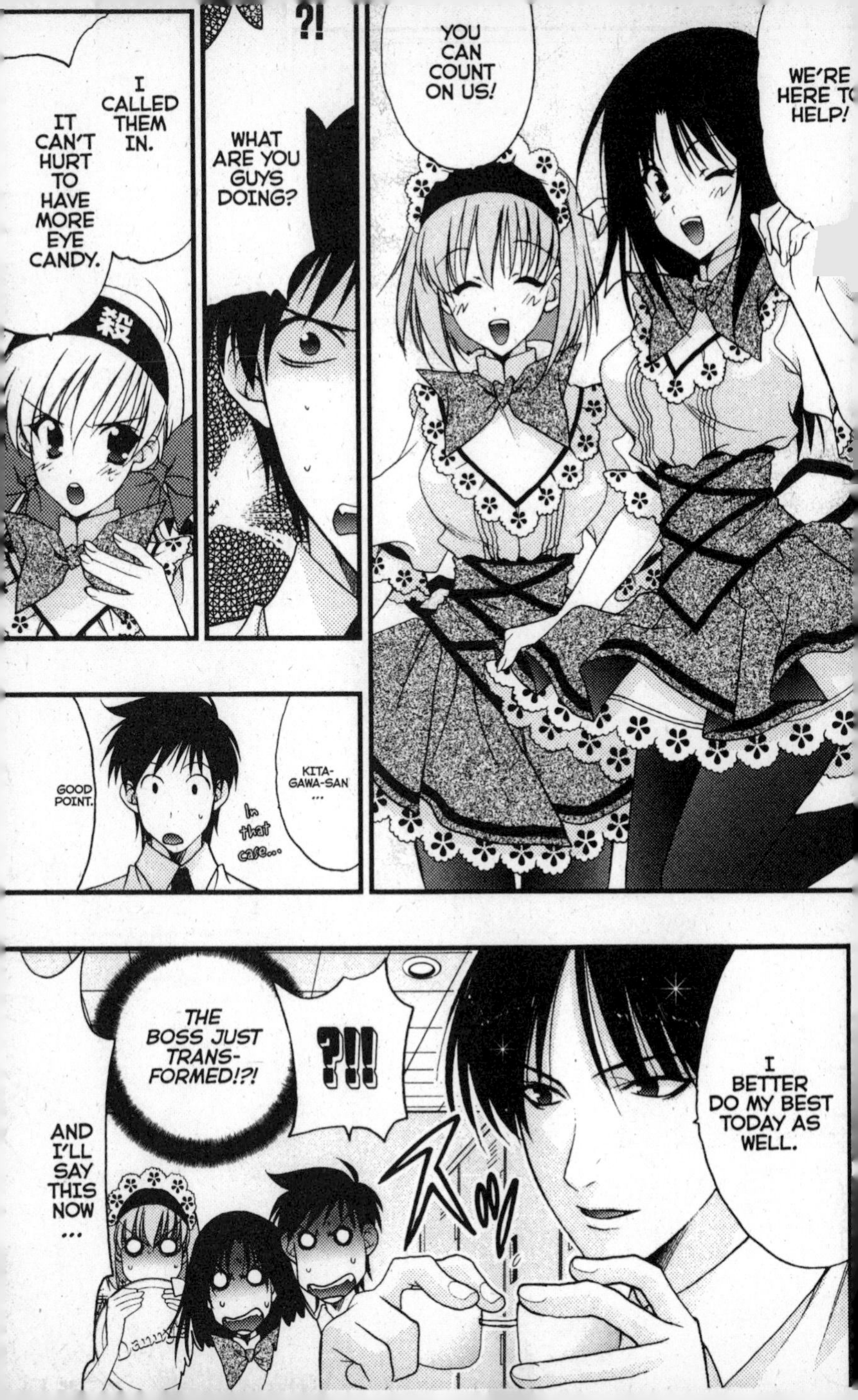
WE'RE HERE TO HELP!
YOU CAN COUNT ON US!
?!
WHAT ARE YOU GUYS DOING?
I CALLED THEM IN.
IT CAN'T HURT TO HAVE MORE EYE CANDY.
KITA-GAWA-SAN...
In that case...
GOOD POINT.
I BETTER DO MY BEST TODAY AS WELL.
?!!
THE BOSS JUST TRANS-FORMED!?!
AND I'LL SAY THIS NOW...

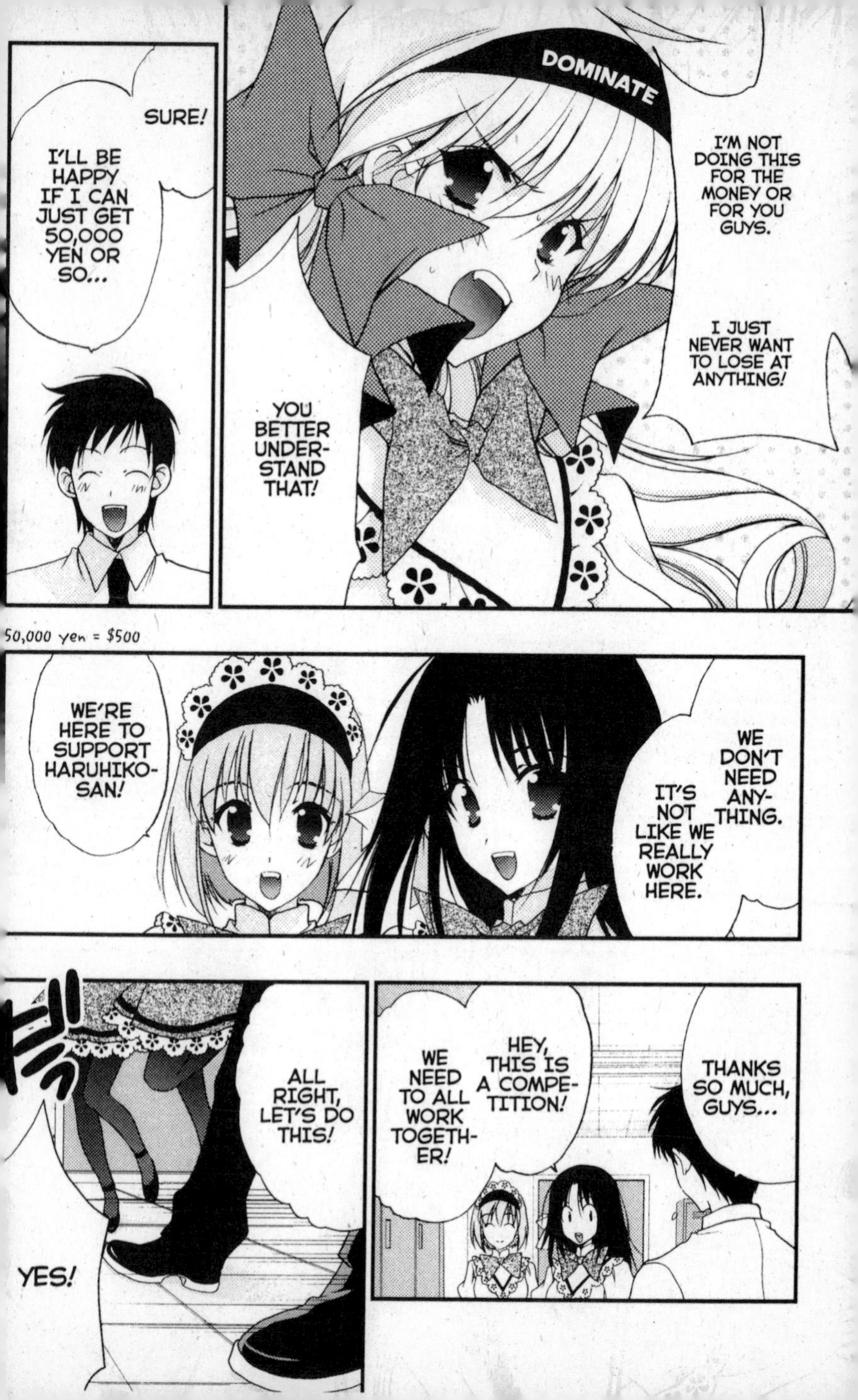
DOMINATE
I'M NOT DOING THIS FOR THE MONEY OR FOR YOU GUYS.
I JUST NEVER WANT TO LOSE AT ANYTHING!
YOU BETTER UNDERSTAND THAT!
SURE!
I'LL BE HAPPY IF I CAN JUST GET 50,000 YEN OR SO...
50,000 yen = $500
WE DON'T NEED ANYTHING.
IT'S NOT LIKE WE REALLY WORK HERE.
WE'RE HERE TO SUPPORT HARUHIKO-SAN!
THANKS SO MUCH, GUYS...
HEY, THIS IS A COMPETITION!
WE NEED TO ALL WORK TOGETHER!
ALL RIGHT, LET'S DO THIS!
YES!

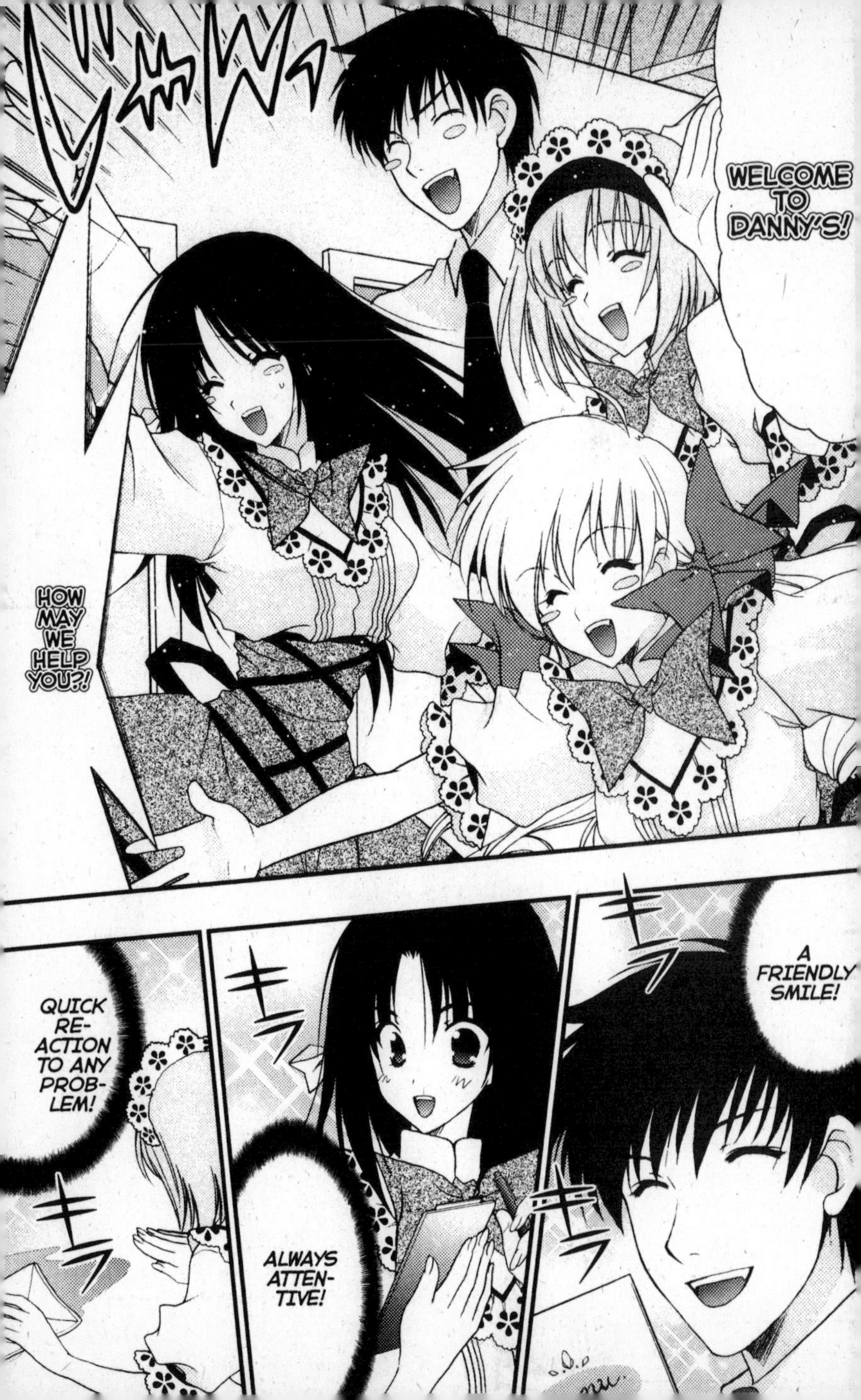
WELCOME TO DANNY'S!
HOW MAY WE HELP YOU?!
A FRIENDLY SMILE!
ALWAYS ATTEN-TIVE!
QUICK RE-ACTION TO ANY PROB-LEM!

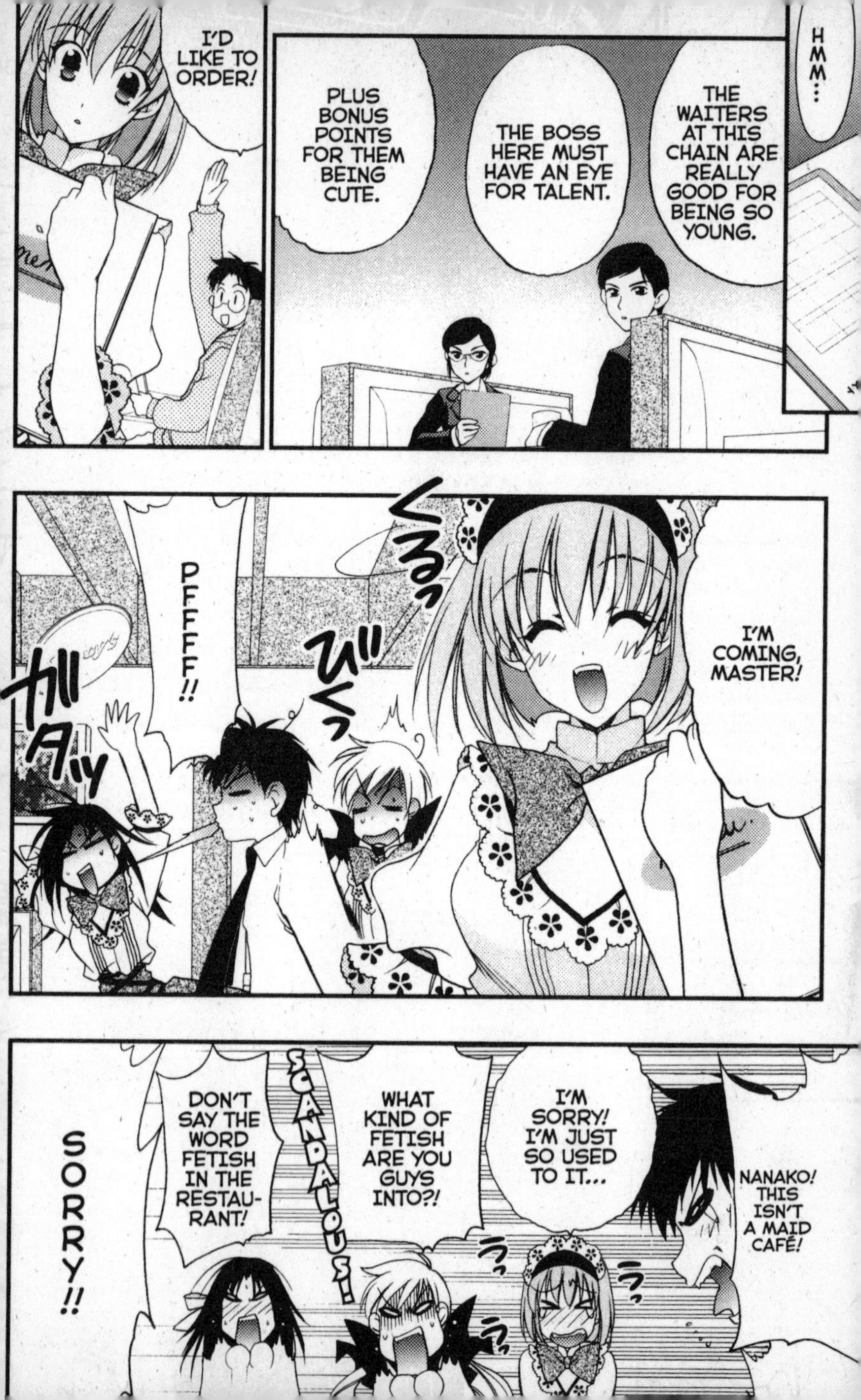
HMM...
THE WAITERS AT THIS CHAIN ARE REALLY GOOD FOR BEING SO YOUNG.
THE BOSS HERE MUST HAVE AN EYE FOR TALENT.
PLUS BONUS POINTS FOR THEM BEING CUTE.
I'D LIKE TO ORDER!
I'M COMING, MASTER!
くるっ
びくっ
PFFFFF!!
ガタッ
NANAKO! THIS ISN'T A MAID CAFÉ!
I'M SORRY! I'M JUST SO USED TO IT...
WHAT KIND OF FETISH ARE YOU GUYS INTO?!
SCANDALOUS!
DON'T SAY THE WORD FETISH IN THE RESTAU-RANT!
SORRY!!

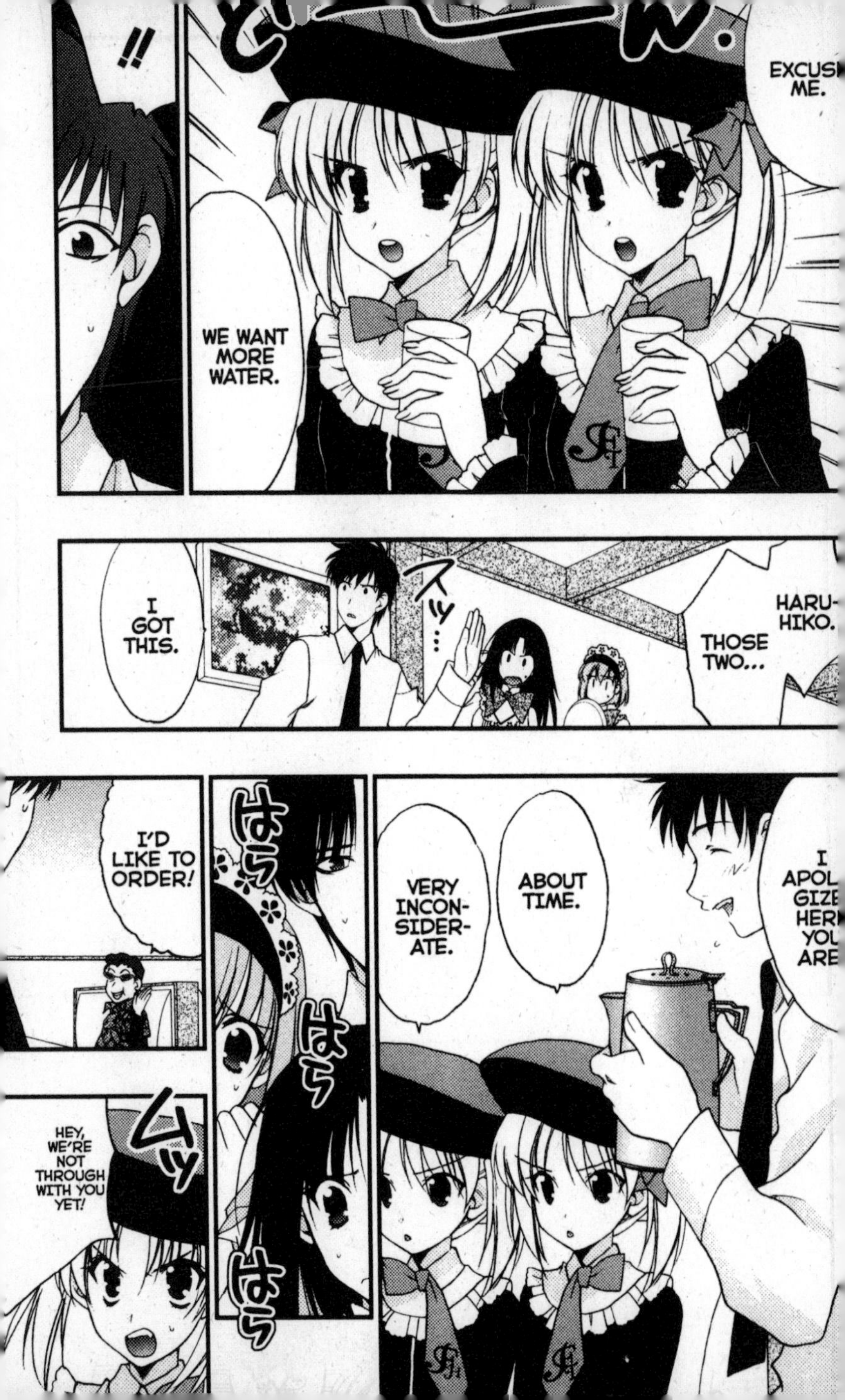

どーーーん.
EXCUS ME.
WE WANT MORE WATER.
!!
HARU-HIKO.
THOSE TWO...
スッ…
I GOT THIS.
I APOL GIZE HER YOU ARE
ABOUT TIME.
VERY INCON-SIDER-ATE.
はら
はら
はら
I'D LIKE TO ORDER!
ムッ
HEY, WE'RE NOT THROUGH WITH YOU YET!

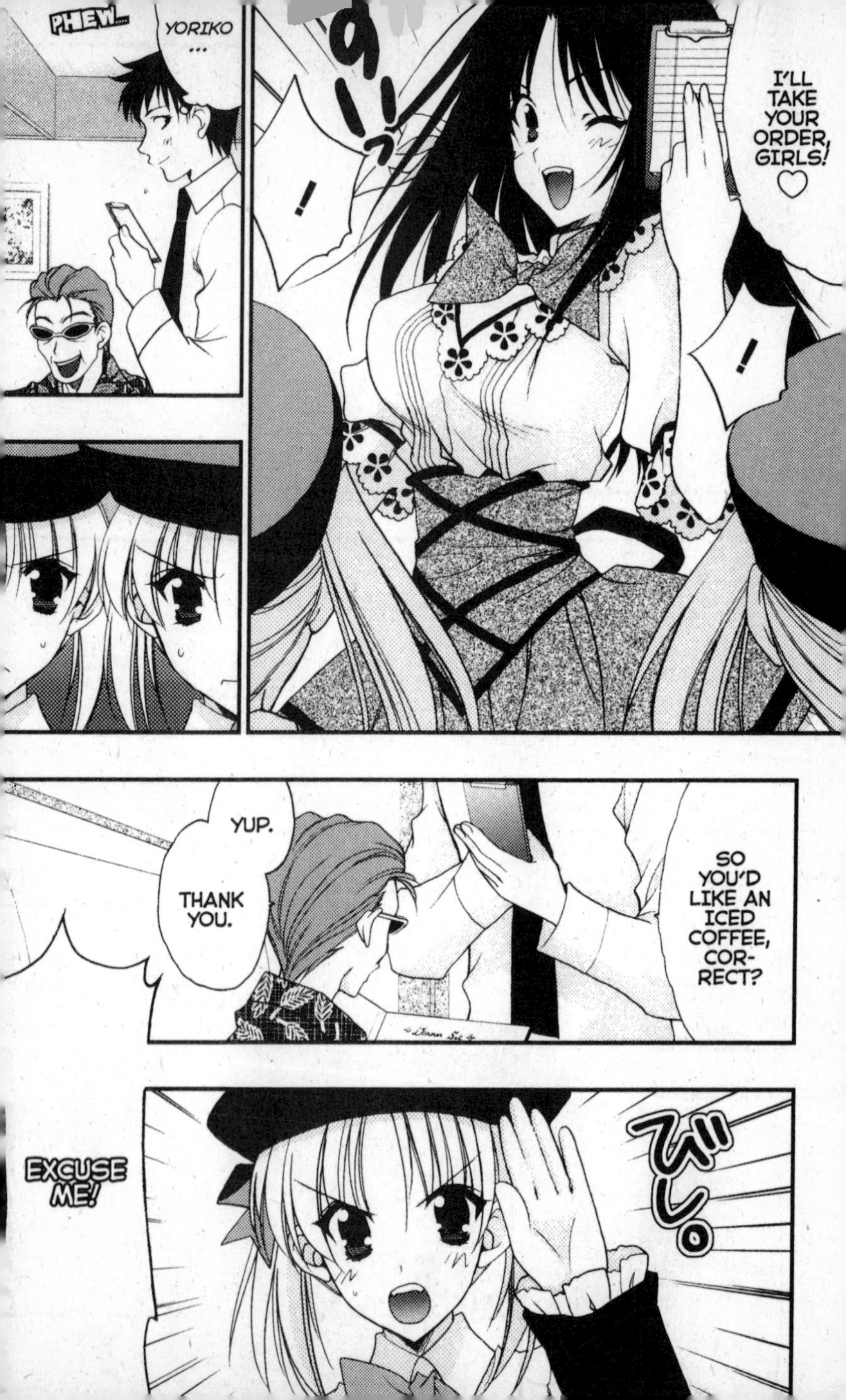
I'LL TAKE YOUR ORDER, GIRLS! ♡
!
!
PHEW...
YORIKO ...
SO YOU'D LIKE AN ICED COFFEE, COR-RECT?
YUP.
THANK YOU.
EXCUSE ME!

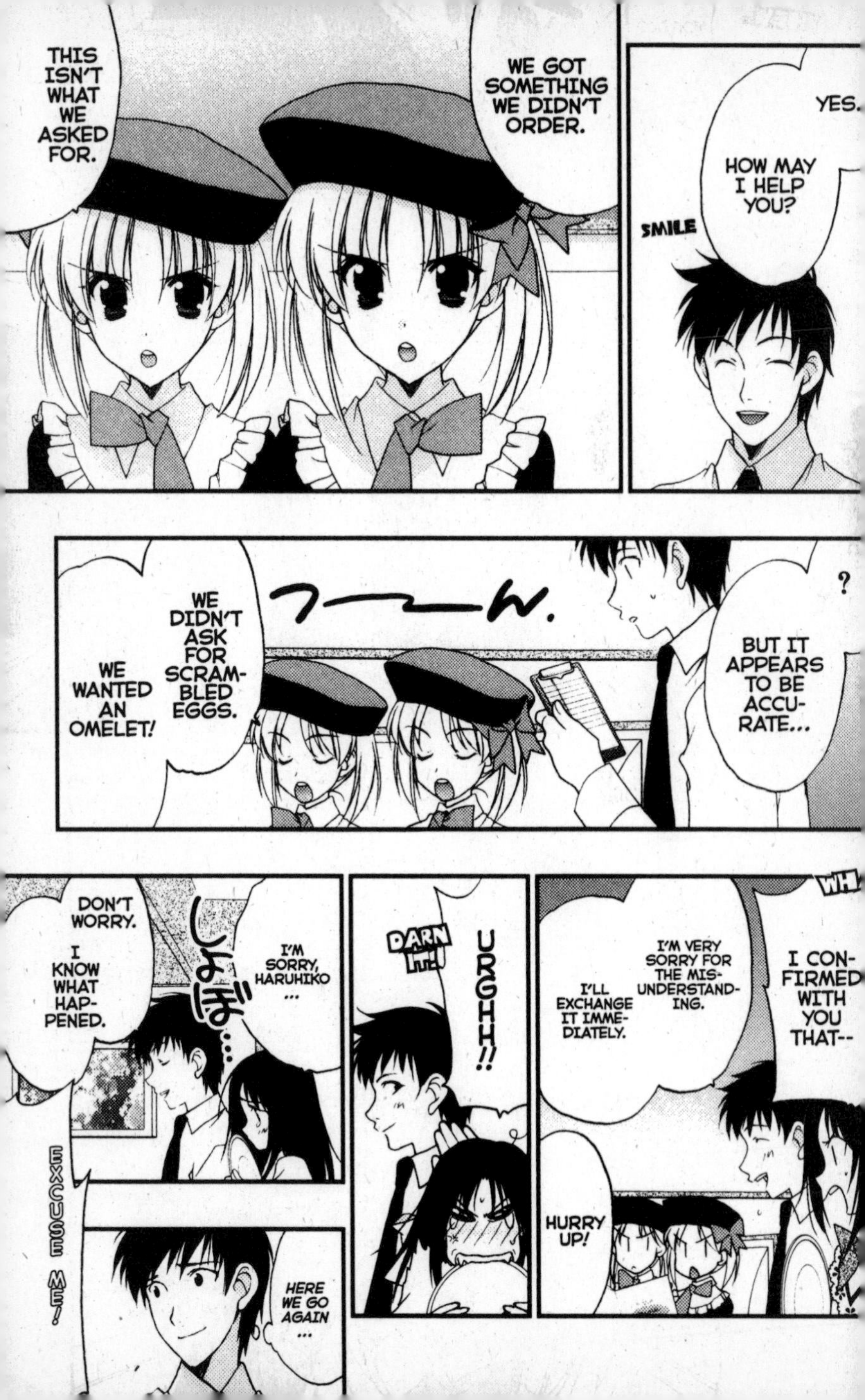
YES.
HOW MAY I HELP YOU?
SMILE
WE GOT SOMETHING WE DIDN'T ORDER.
THIS ISN'T WHAT WE ASKED FOR.
?
BUT IT APPEARS TO BE ACCURATE...
WE DIDN'T ASK FOR SCRAMBLED EGGS.
WE WANTED AN OMELET!
WH
I CONFIRMED WITH YOU THAT--
I'M VERY SORRY FOR THE MISUNDERSTANDING.
I'LL EXCHANGE IT IMMEDIATELY.
HURRY UP!
URGHH!!
DARN IT!
I'M SORRY, HARUHIKO ...
しょぼ...
DON'T WORRY.
I KNOW WHAT HAPPENED.
HERE WE GO AGAIN ...
EXCUSE ME!

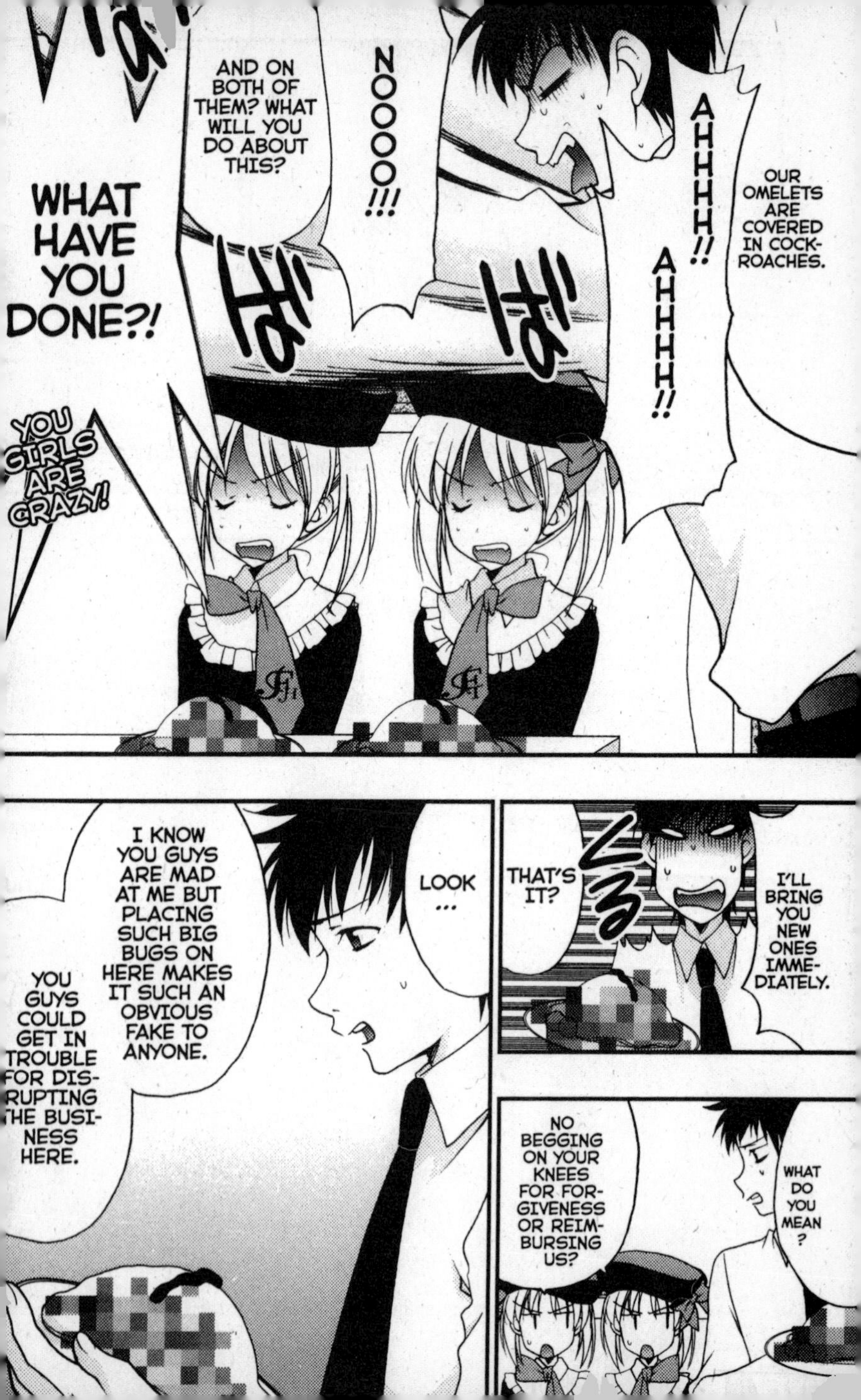
OUR OMELETS ARE COVERED IN COCK-ROACHES.
AHHHH!! AHHHHH!!
NOOOOO!!!
AND ON BOTH OF THEM? WHAT WILL YOU DO ABOUT THIS?
WHAT HAVE YOU DONE?!
YOU GIRLS ARE CRAZY!
I'LL BRING YOU NEW ONES IMME-DIATELY.
THAT'S IT?
WHAT DO YOU MEAN?
NO BEGGING ON YOUR KNEES FOR FOR-GIVENESS OR REIM-BURSING US?
LOOK ...
I KNOW YOU GUYS ARE MAD AT ME BUT PLACING SUCH BIG BUGS ON HERE MAKES IT SUCH AN OBVIOUS FAKE TO ANYONE.
YOU GUYS COULD GET IN TROUBLE FOR DIS-RUPTING THE BUSI-NESS HERE.

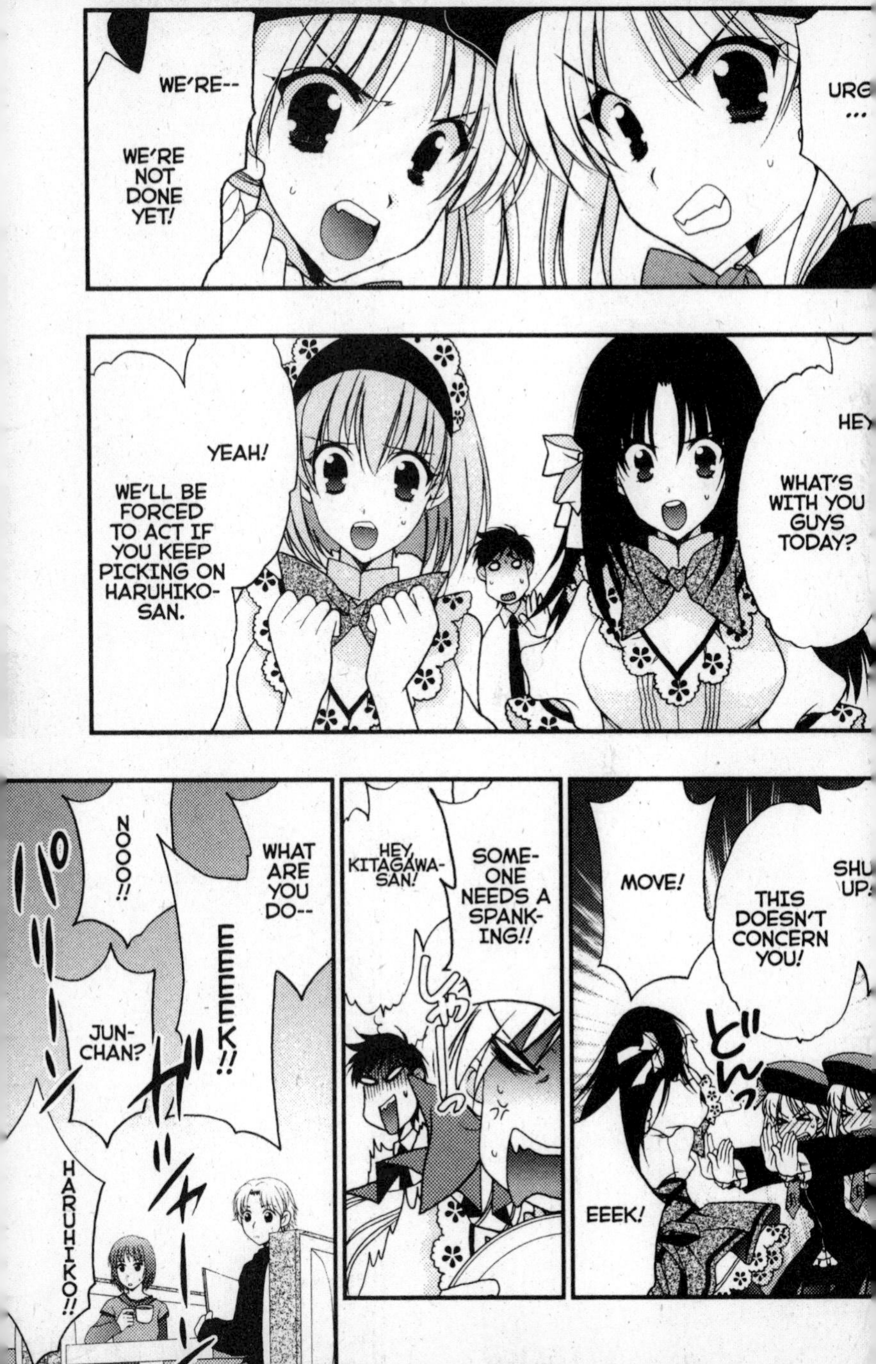
URG...
WE'RE--
WE'RE NOT DONE YET!
HEY
WHAT'S WITH YOU GUYS TODAY?
YEAH!
WE'LL BE FORCED TO ACT IF YOU KEEP PICKING ON HARUHIKO-SAN.
SHU UP.
THIS DOESN'T CONCERN YOU!
MOVE!
EEEK!
SOME-ONE NEEDS A SPANK-ING!!
HEY, KITAGAWA-SAN!
WHAT ARE YOU DO--
NOOOO!!
EEEEK!!
JUN-CHAN?
HARUHIKO!!

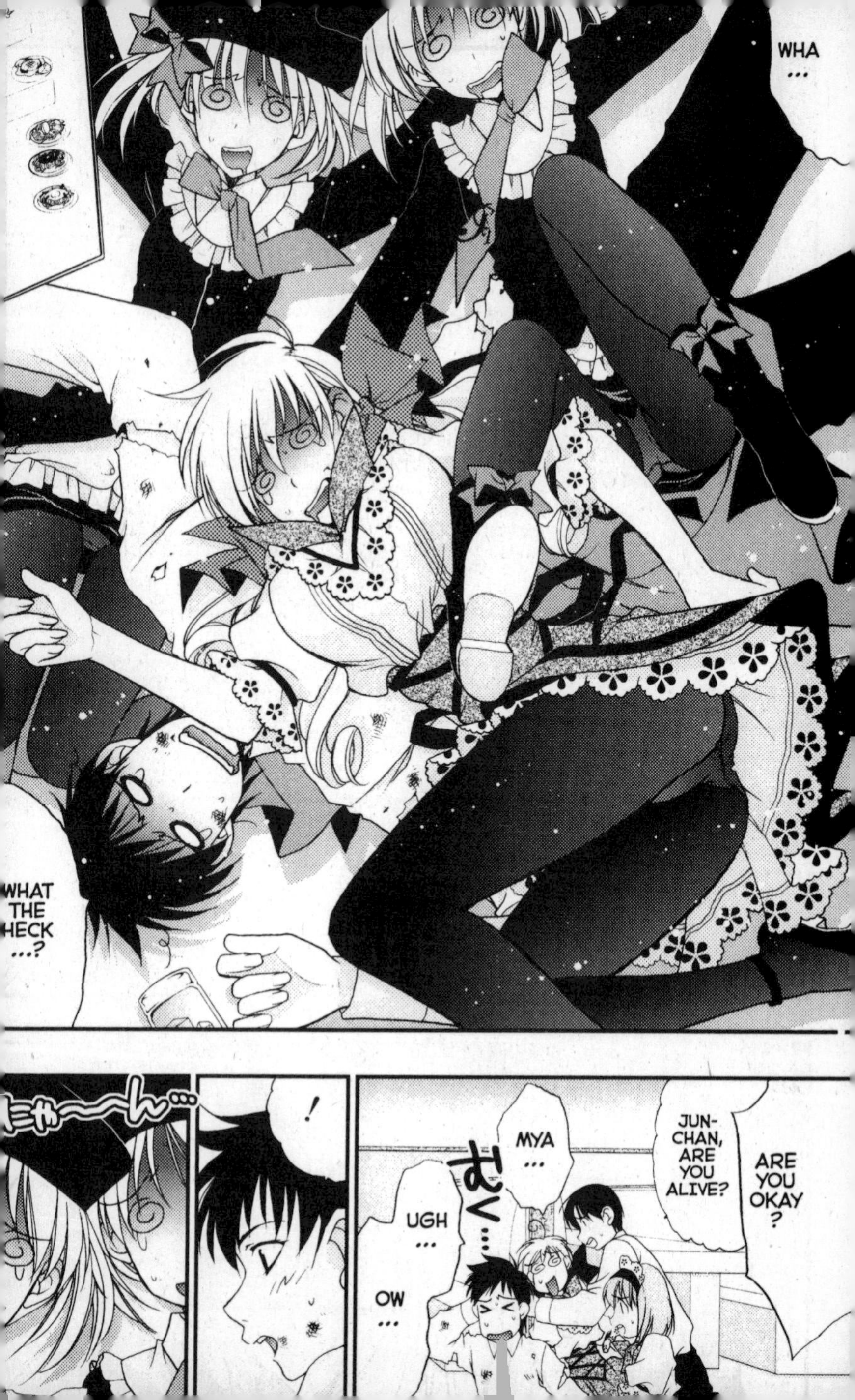
WHA ...
WHAT THE HECK ...?
ARE YOU OKAY?
JUN-CHAN, ARE YOU ALIVE?
MYA ...
むく…
UGH ...
OW ...
!
ゃ～～ん…

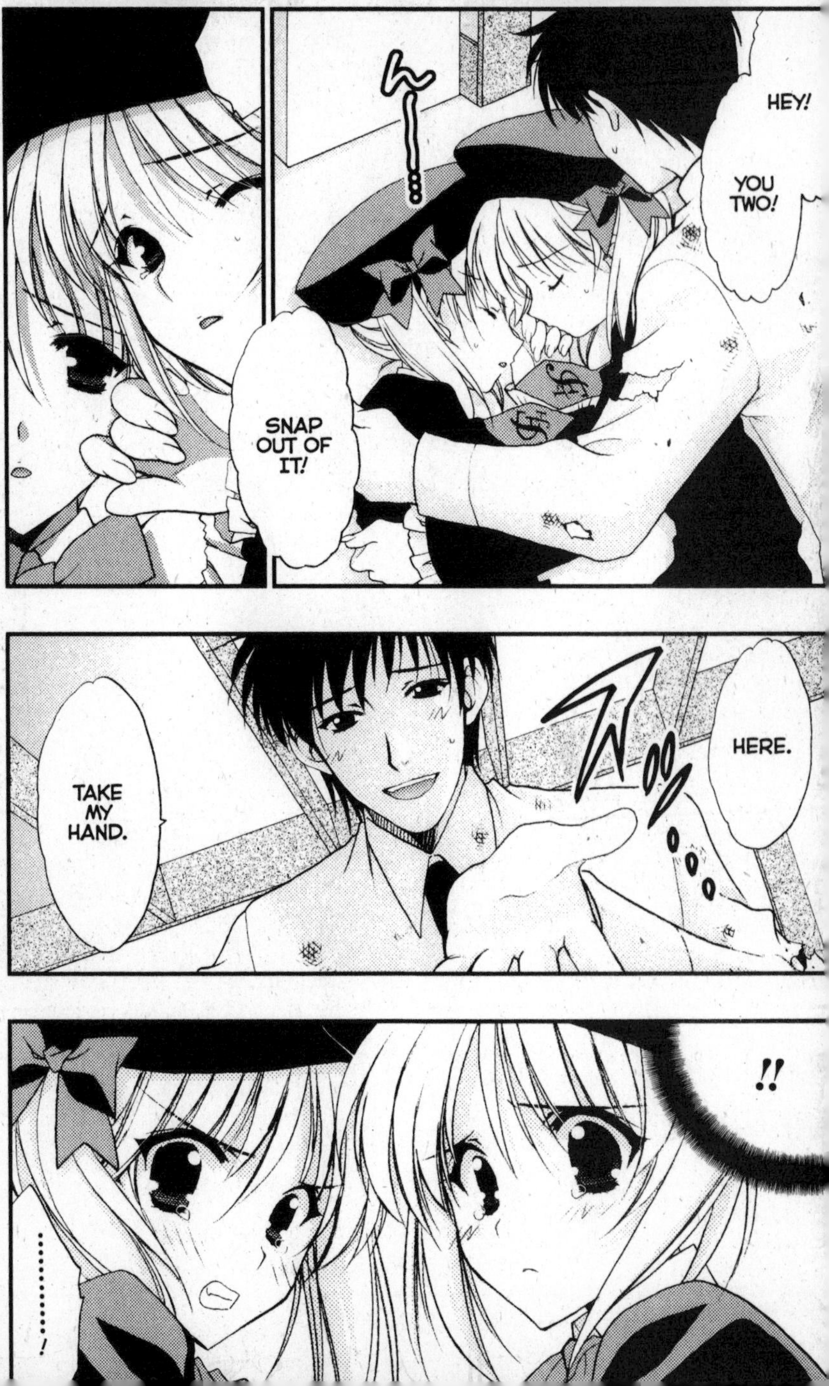
HEY!
YOU TWO!
ん…
SNAP OUT OF IT!
HERE.
TAKE MY HAND.
!!
……!

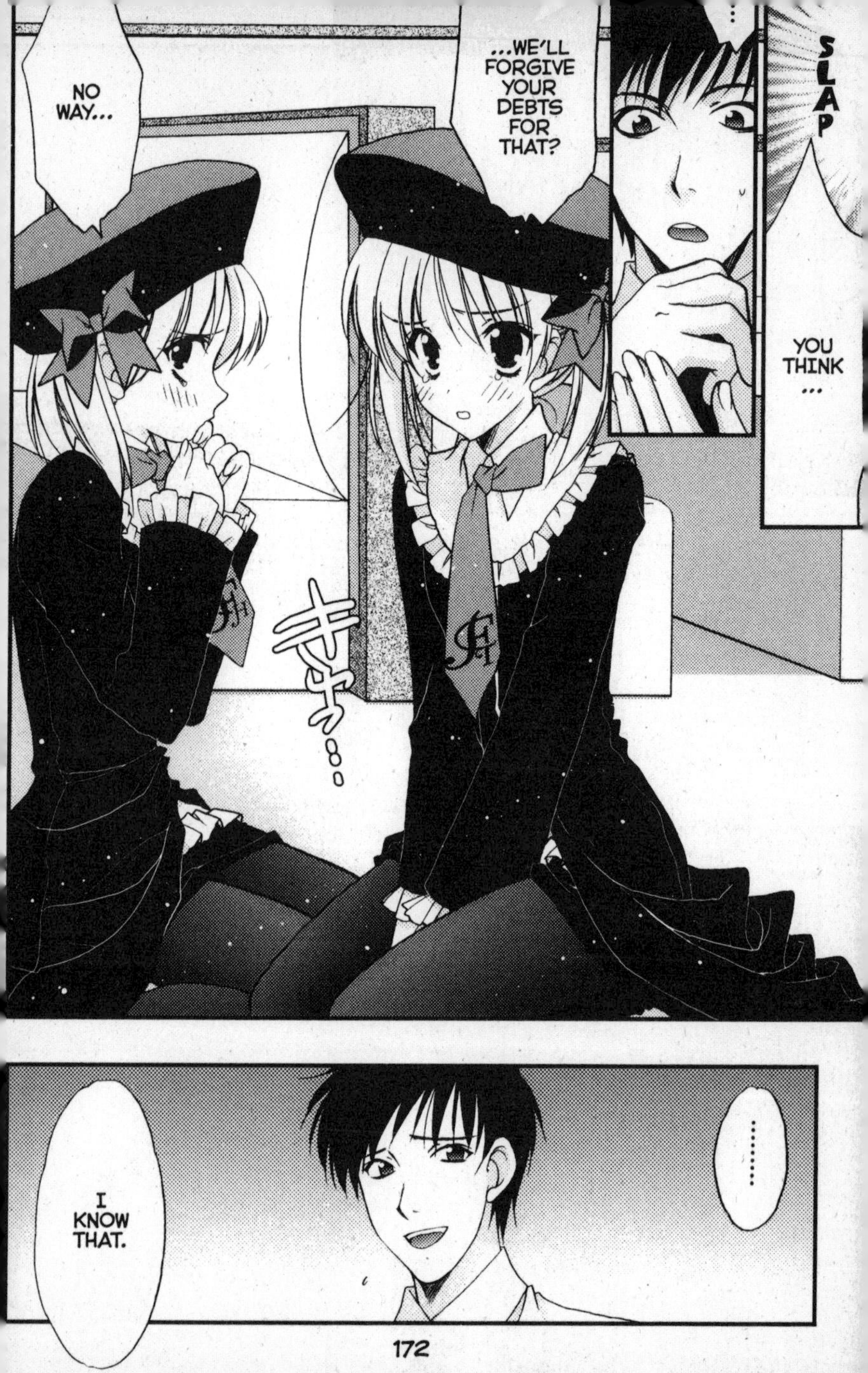
SLAP
YOU THINK...
...
...WE'LL FORGIVE YOUR DEBTS FOR THAT?
NO WAY...
......
I KNOW THAT.

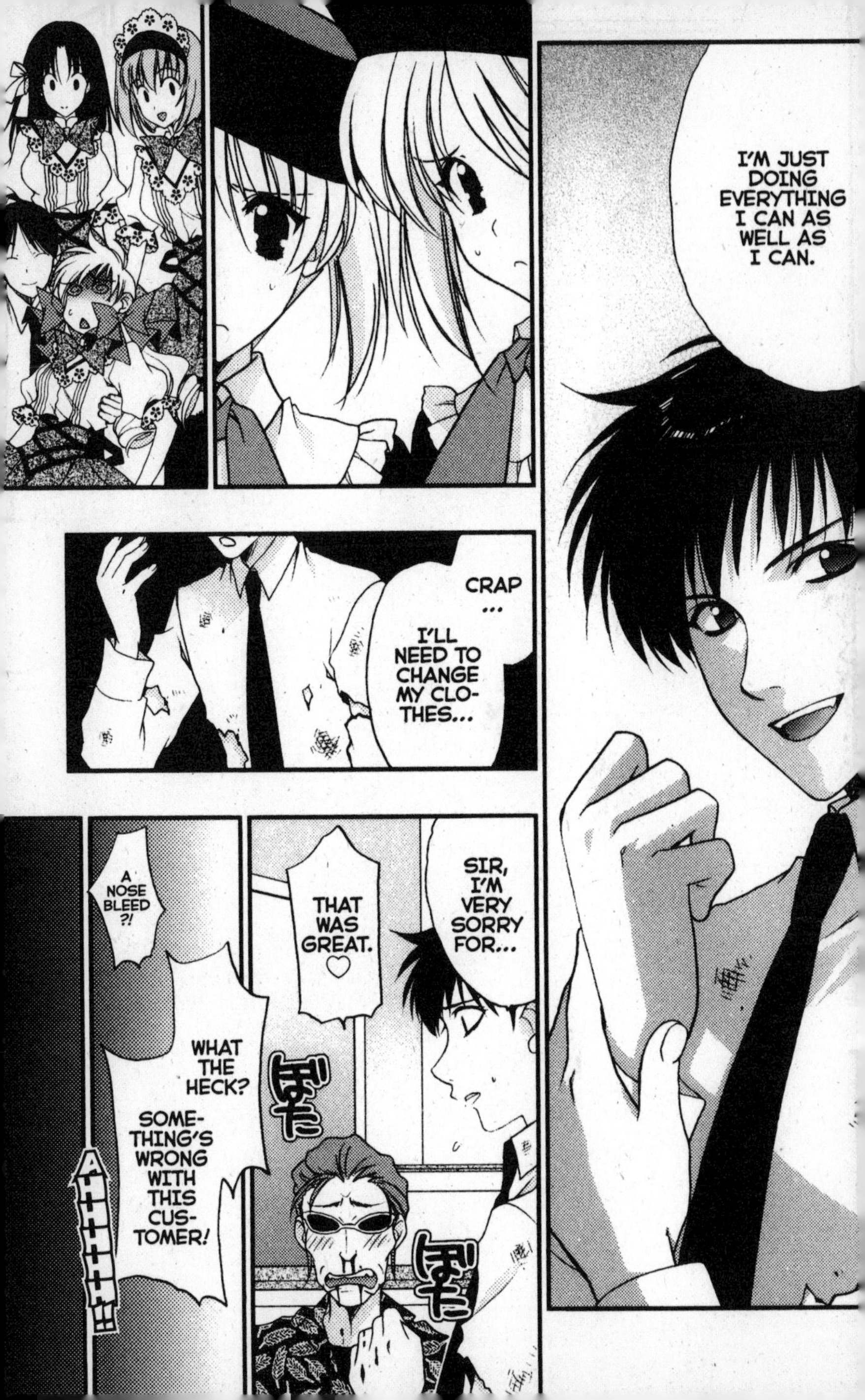
I'M JUST DOING EVERYTHING I CAN AS WELL AS I CAN.
CRAP ...
I'LL NEED TO CHANGE MY CLO-THES...
SIR, I'M VERY SORRY FOR...
THAT WAS GREAT. ♡
ぼた
ぼた
A NOSE BLEED ?!
WHAT THE HECK?
SOME-THING'S WRONG WITH THIS CUS-TOMER!
AHHHHH!!

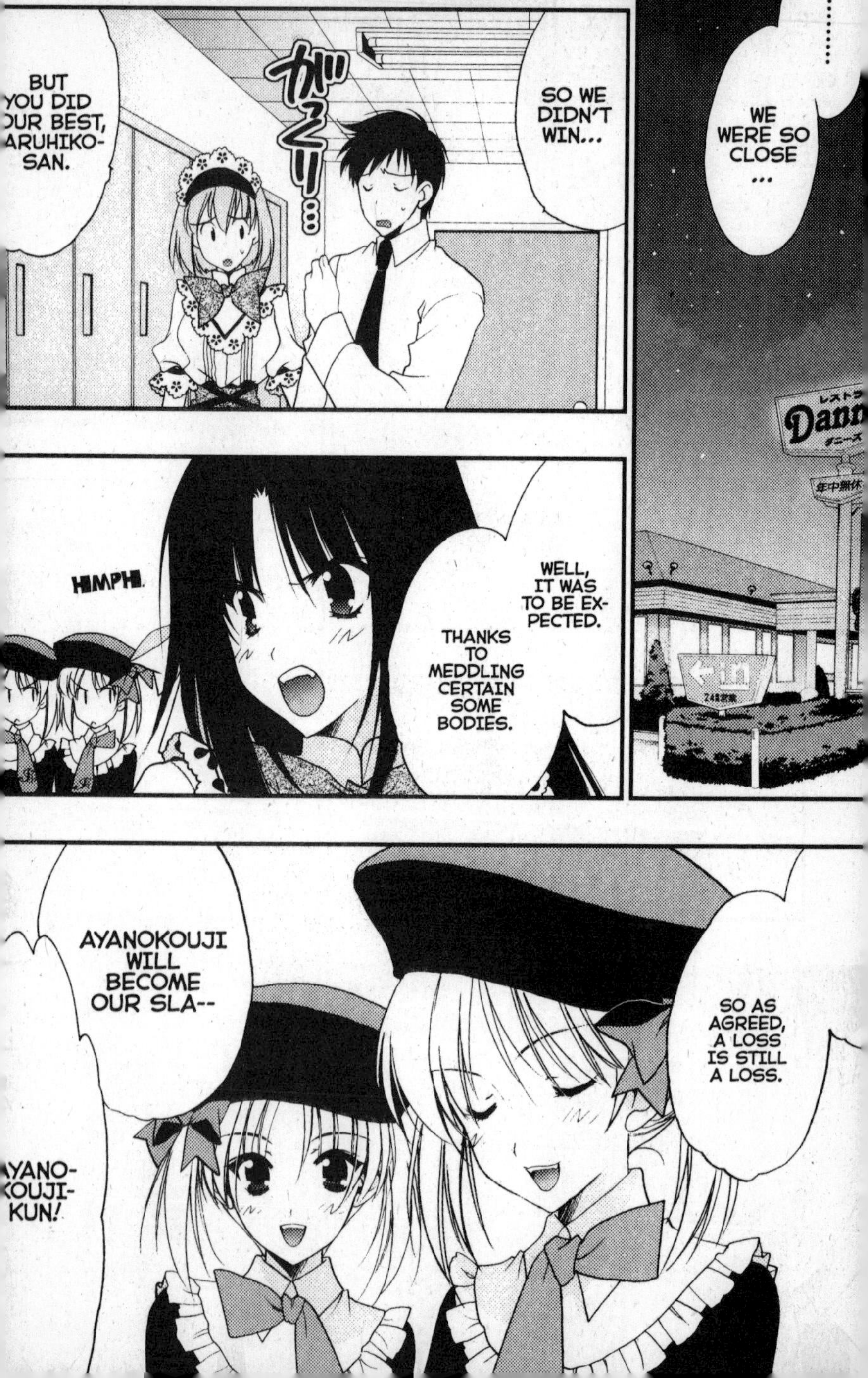

……
WE WERE SO CLOSE …
Dann
← in
SO WE DIDN'T WIN…
がっくり…
BUT YOU DID OUR BEST, ARUHIKO-SAN.
WELL, IT WAS TO BE EX-PECTED.
THANKS TO MEDDLING CERTAIN SOME BODIES.
HMPH.
SO AS AGREED, A LOSS IS STILL A LOSS.
AYANOKOUJI WILL BECOME OUR SLA--
AYANO-KOUJI-KUN!

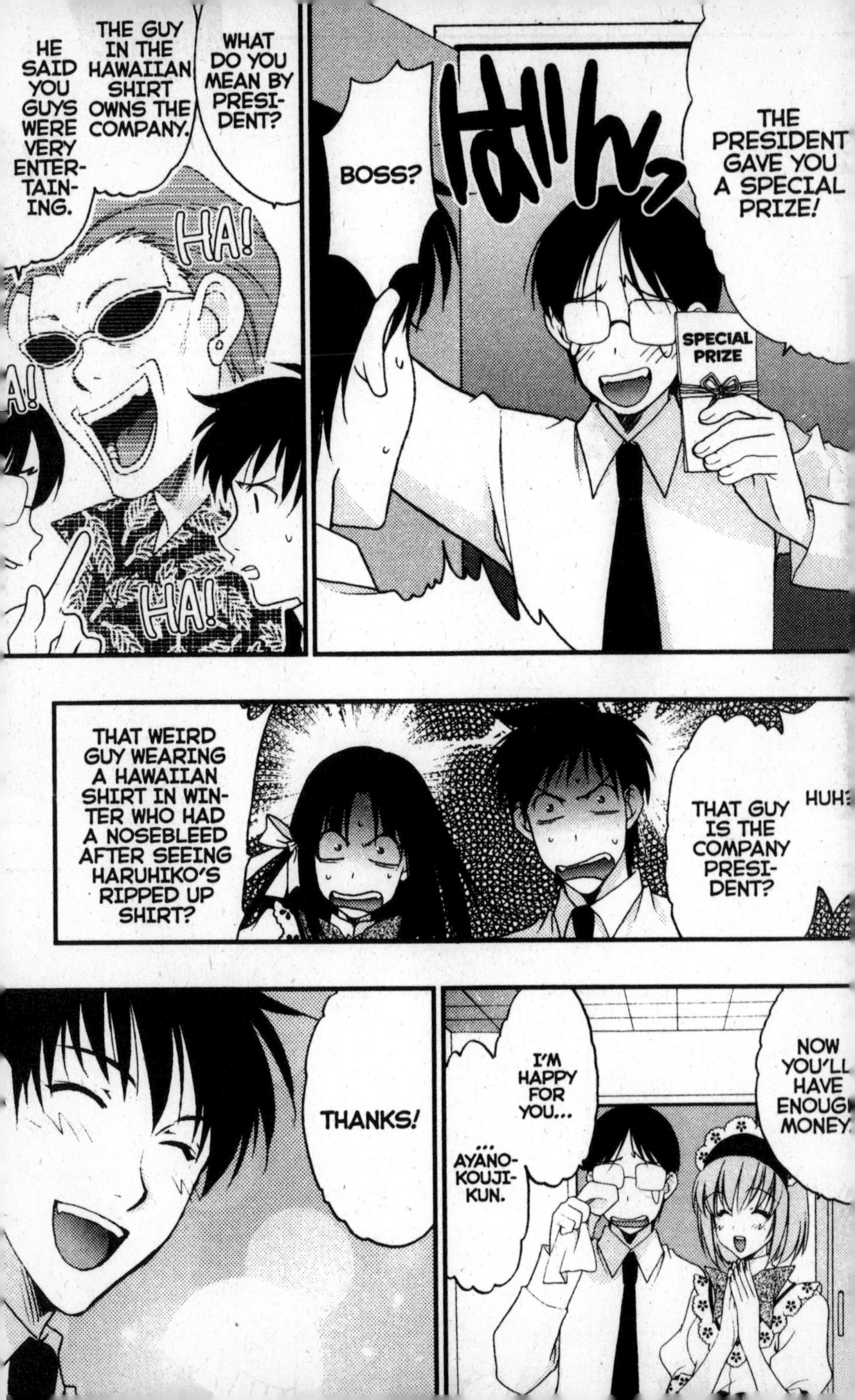

THE PRESIDENT GAVE YOU A SPECIAL PRIZE!
SPECIAL PRIZE
BOSS?
WHAT DO YOU MEAN BY PRESIDENT?
THE GUY IN THE HAWAIIAN SHIRT OWNS THE COMPANY.
HE SAID YOU GUYS WERE VERY ENTERTAINING.
HA!
HA!
HUH?
THAT GUY IS THE COMPANY PRESIDENT?
THAT WEIRD GUY WEARING A HAWAIIAN SHIRT IN WINTER WHO HAD A NOSEBLEED AFTER SEEING HARUHIKO'S RIPPED UP SHIRT?
NOW YOU'LL HAVE ENOUGH MONEY.
I'M HAPPY FOR YOU...
...AYANOKOUJI-KUN.
THANKS!

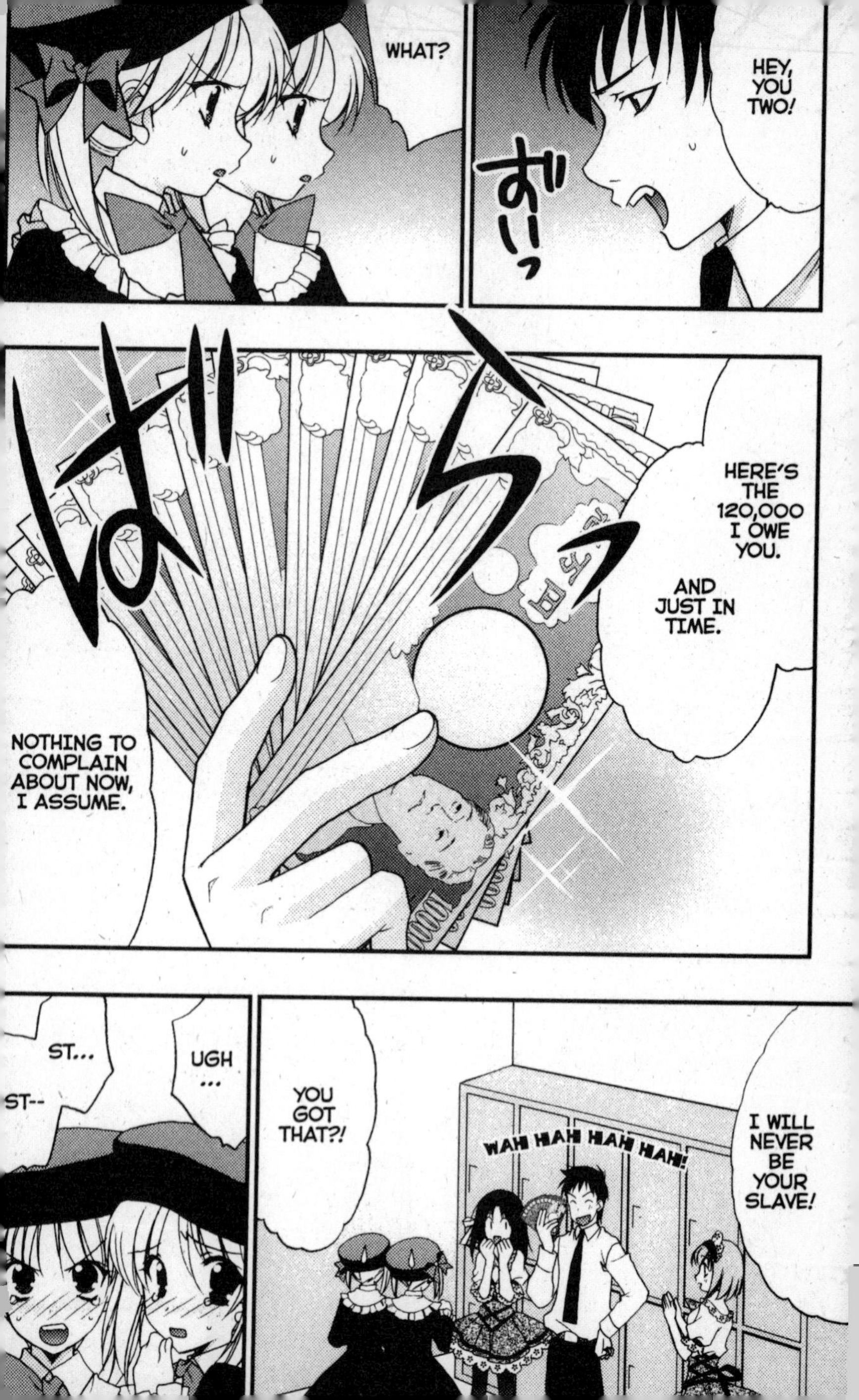
HEY, YOU TWO!
ずいっ
WHAT?
ばらっ
HERE'S THE 120,000 I OWE YOU.
AND JUST IN TIME.
NOTHING TO COMPLAIN ABOUT NOW, I ASSUME.
I WILL NEVER BE YOUR SLAVE!
WAH HAH HAH HAH!
YOU GOT THAT?!
UGH ...
ST... ST--

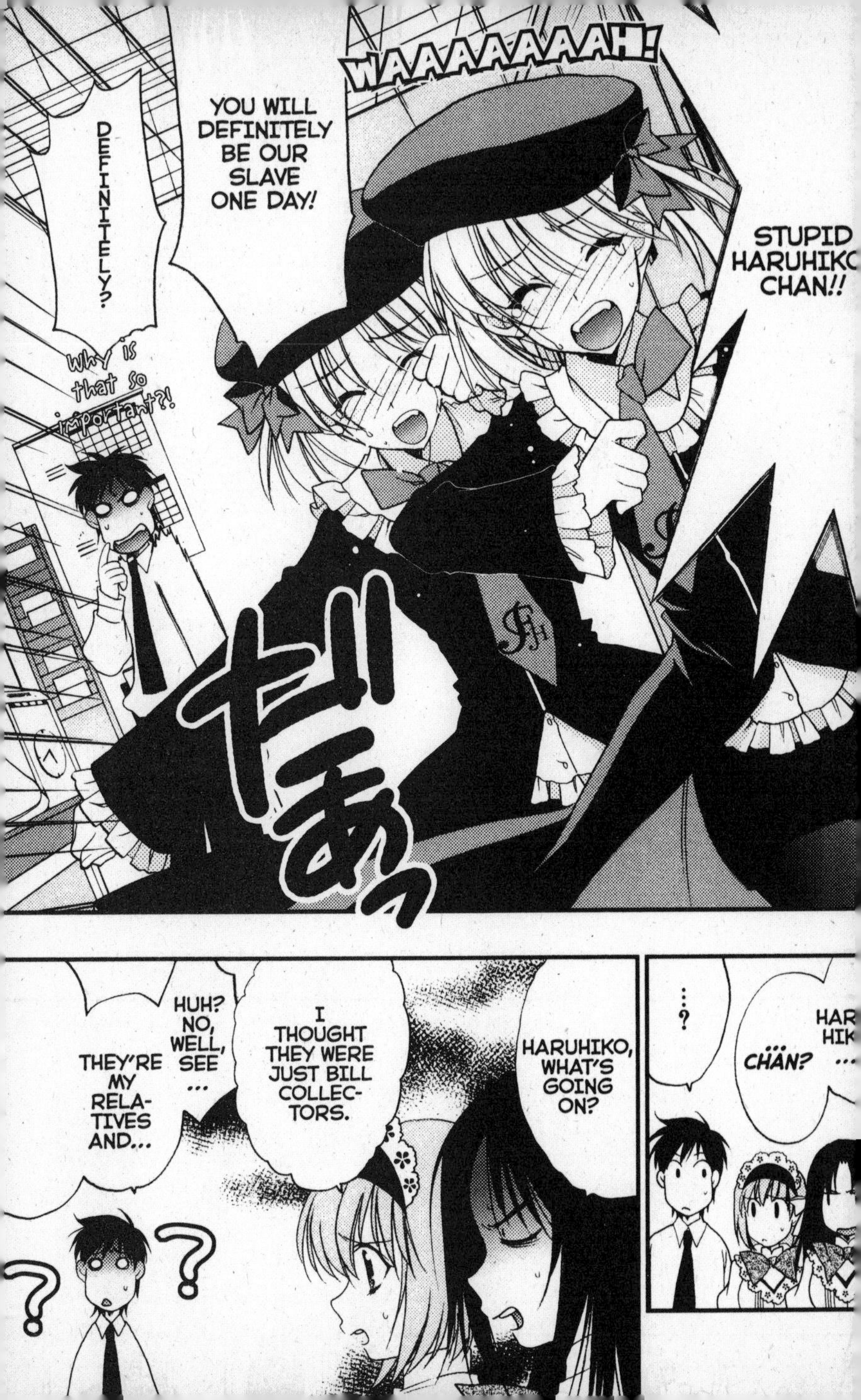
WAAAAAAAAH!
STUPID HARUHIKO CHAN!!
YOU WILL DEFINITELY BE OUR SLAVE ONE DAY!
DEFINITELY?
Why is that so important?!
HAR HIK CHÄN? ...
...?
HARUHIKO, WHAT'S GOING ON?
I THOUGHT THEY WERE JUST BILL COLLEC-TORS.
HUH? NO, WELL, SEE...
THEY'RE MY RELA-TIVES AND...

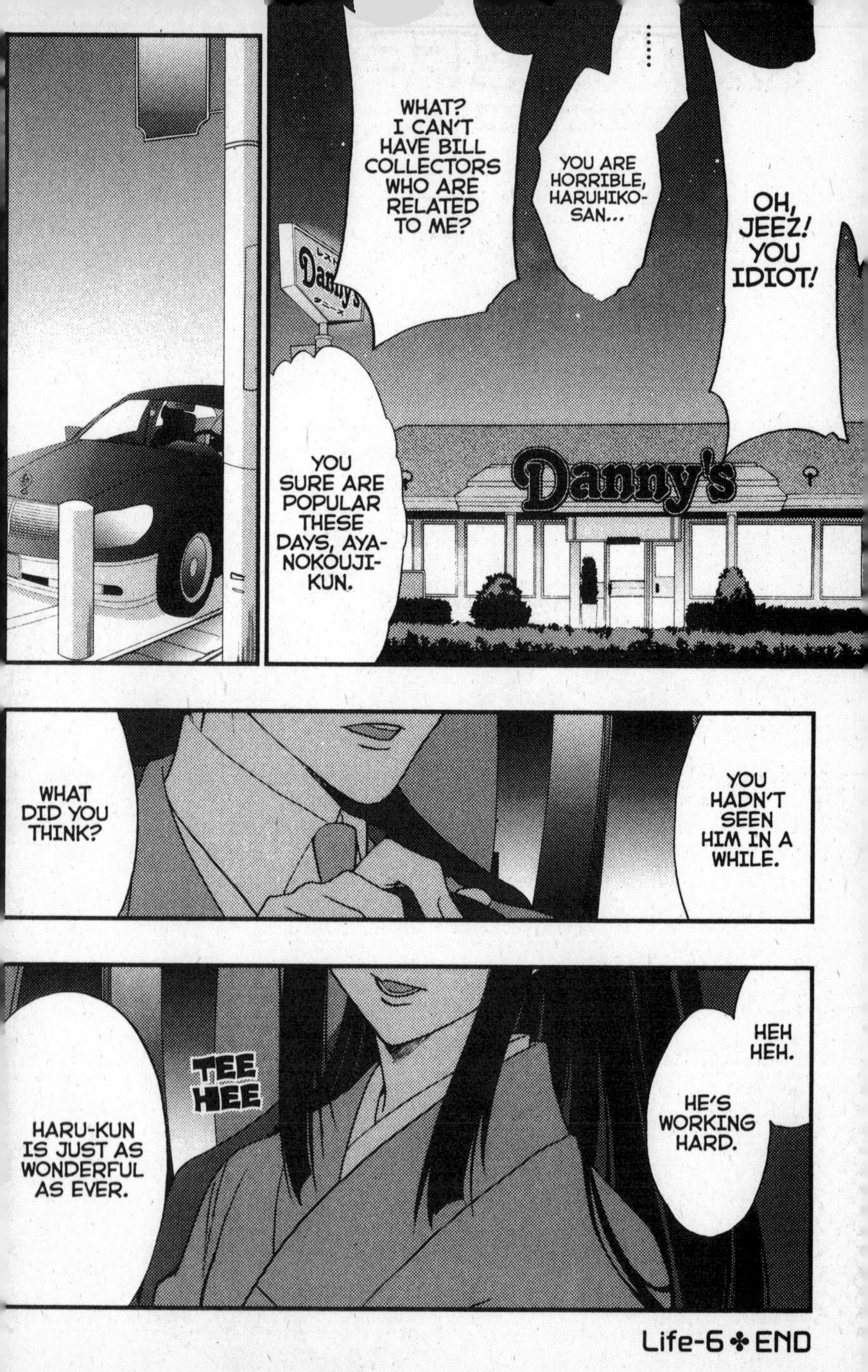
.....
OH, JEEZ! YOU IDIOT!
YOU ARE HORRIBLE, HARUHIKO-SAN...
WHAT? I CAN'T HAVE BILL COLLECTORS WHO ARE RELATED TO ME?
Danny's
YOU SURE ARE POPULAR THESE DAYS, AYA-NOKOUJI-KUN.
Danny's
YOU HADN'T SEEN HIM IN A WHILE.
WHAT DID YOU THINK?
HEH HEH.
HE'S WORKING HARD.
TEE HEE
HARU-KUN IS JUST AS WONDERFUL AS EVER.

Life-6 ✤ END

SAVING LIFE

NANAKO & YORIKO

NOW THAT I'VE PRETTY MUC
INTRODUCED THE ENTIRE
FEMALE CAST, IT'S TIME TO
START SHOWING THEM BEIN
CUTE. AND MAYBE SHOW
THE OTHER MEANING OF
"SAVING LIFE." IT'S A SIMPL
MANGA, BUT I'M WORKING
HARD IN HOPES YOU'LL
ENJOY IT. I HOPE TO SEE
YOU IN THE NEXT VOLUME!

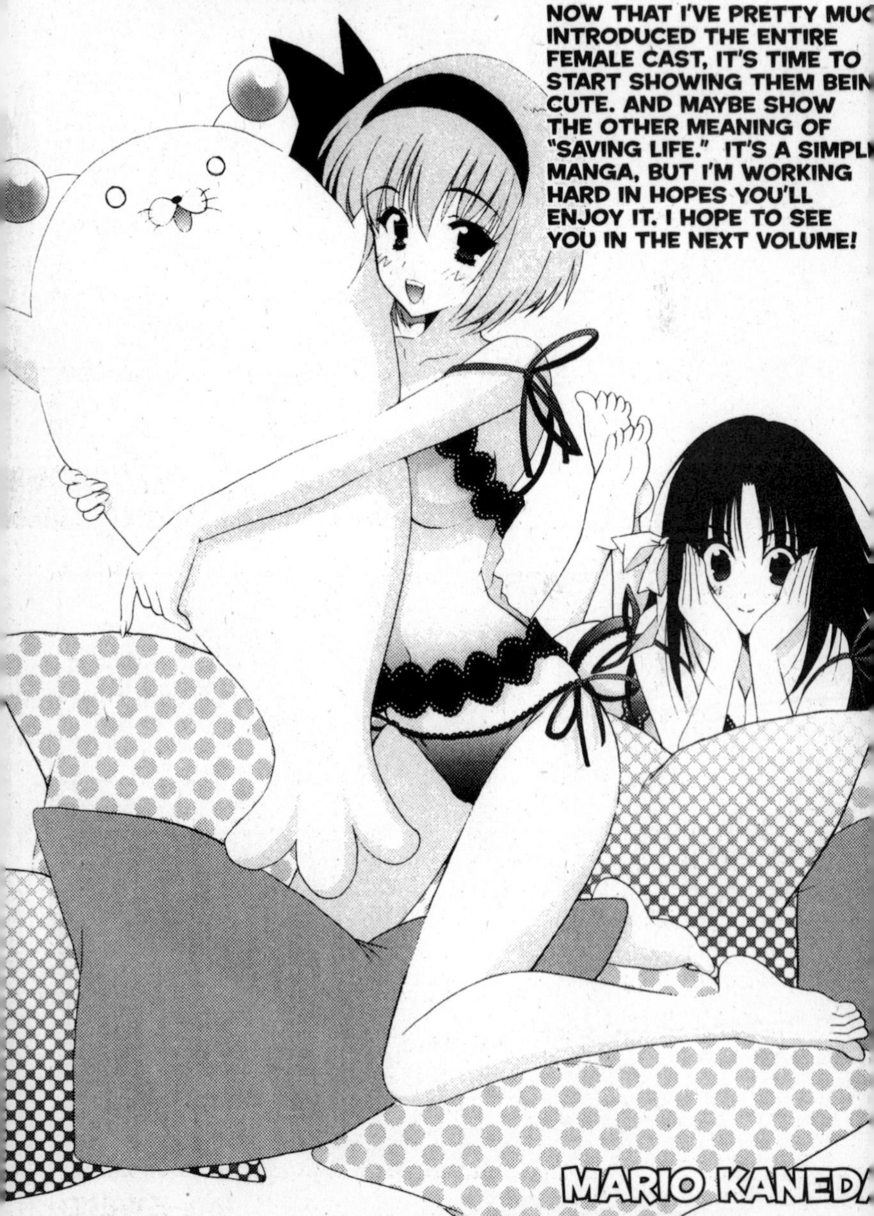

MARIO KANED

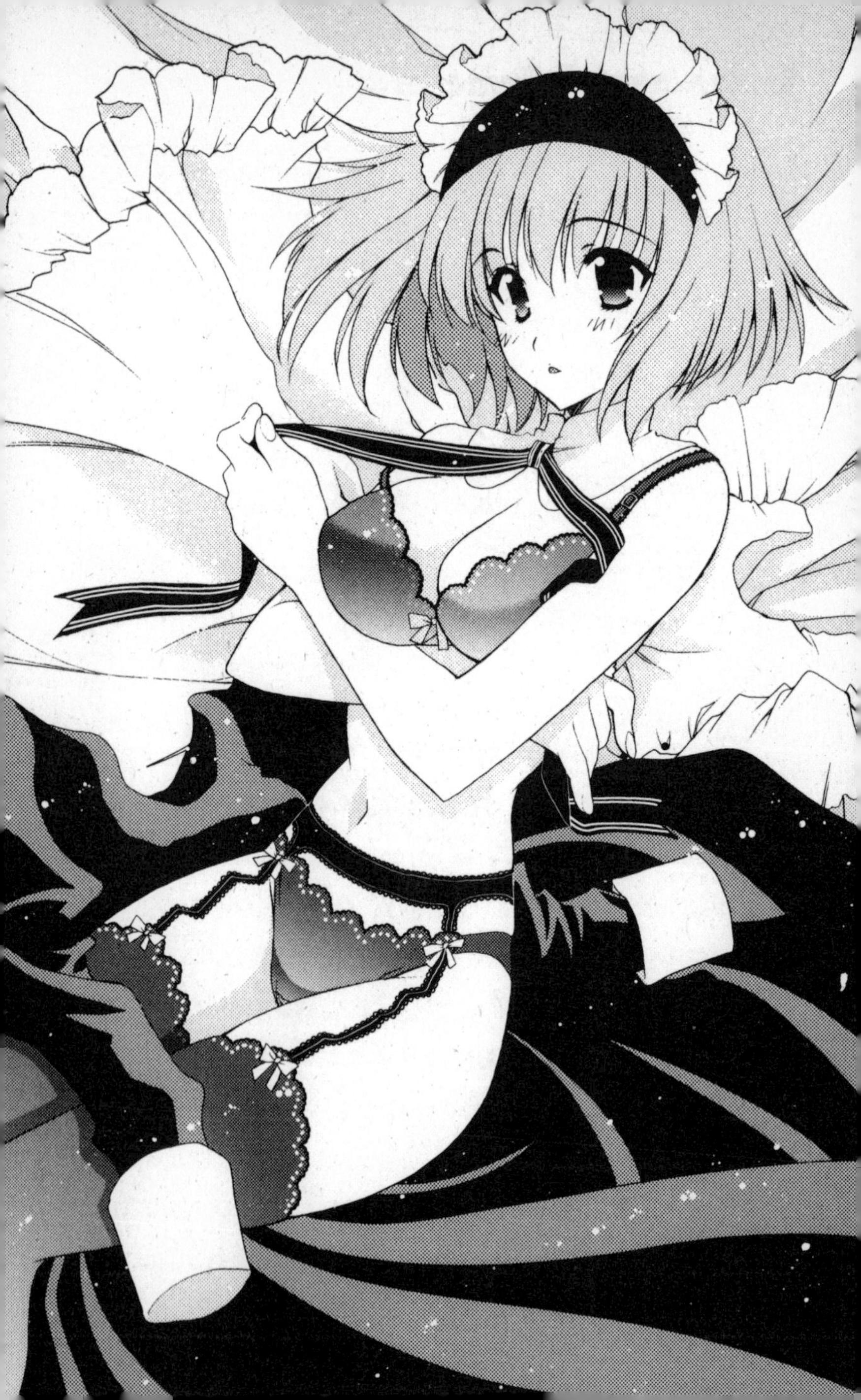

In the next volume of...

When Haruhiko returns home from his new job, he finds his apartment has gone through a major makeover -- a super rich one! And if his older brother's appearance wasn't bad enough for his frugal way of life, things just go from bad to worse when Haruhiko's supposed fiancée makes her debut. With so many girls and one tiny house (not to mention a tiny bathtub), how will Haruhiko ever live the simple life he desires?

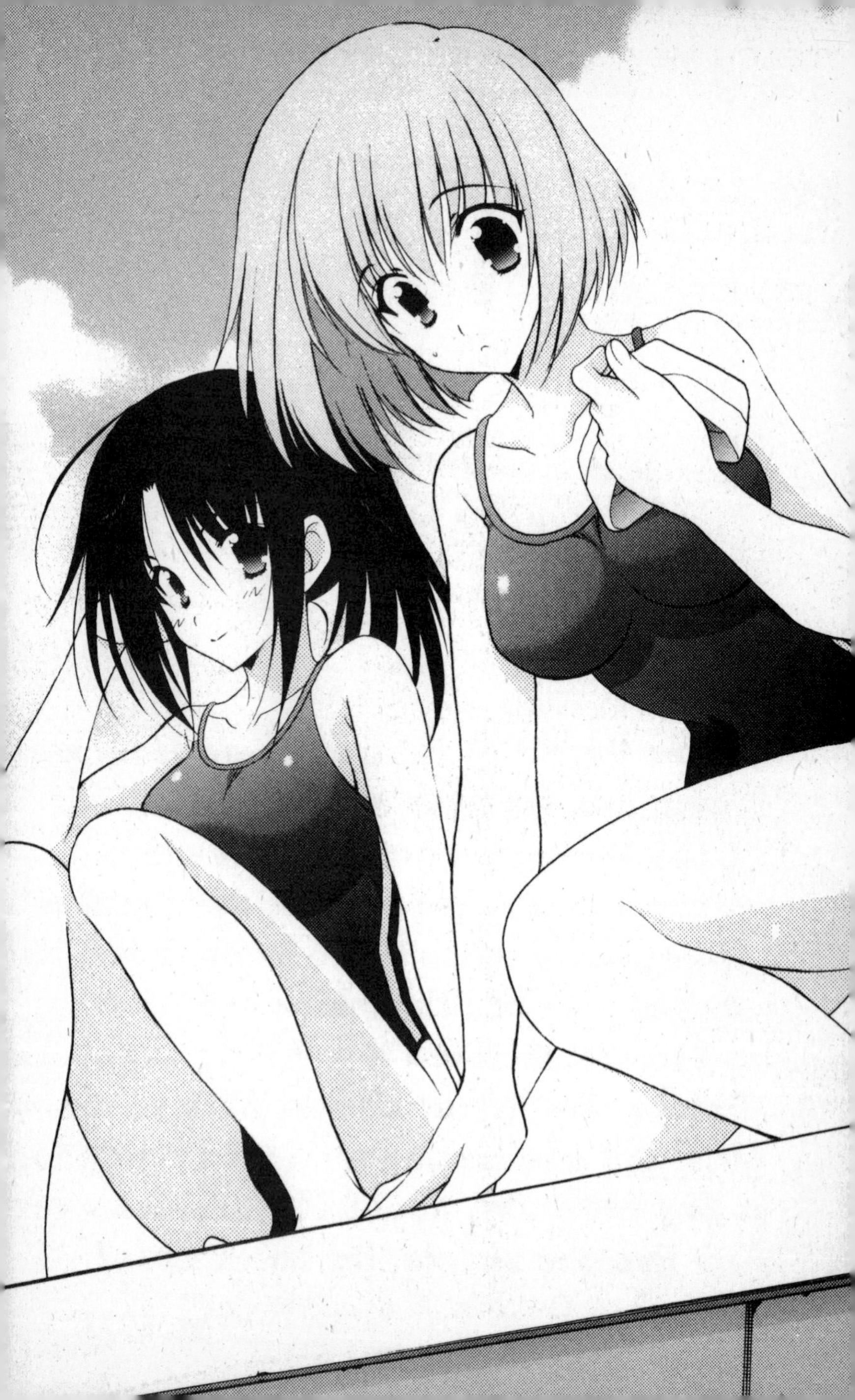

Collect Them All!

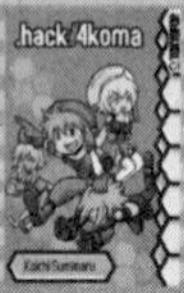
.hack//4koma
.hack//4Koma

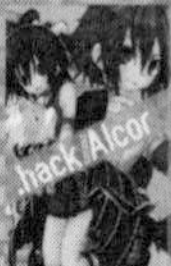
.hack//Alcor
.hack//Alcor

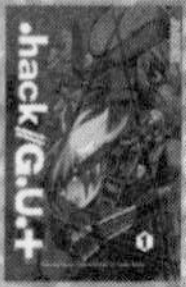
.hack//G.U.+
.hack//G.U.+
Volume 1

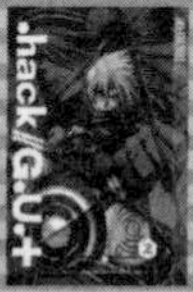
.hack//G.U.+
.hack//G.U.+
Volume 2

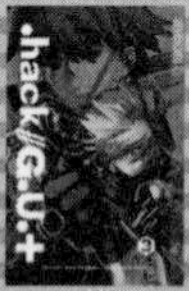
.hack//G.U.+
.hack//G.U.+
Volume 3

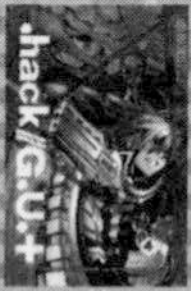
.hack//G.U.+
.hack//G.U.+
Volume 4

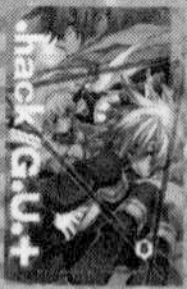
.hack//G.U.+
.hack//G.U.+
Volume 5

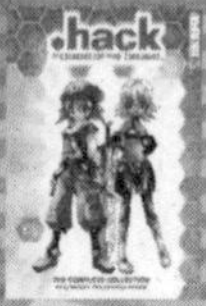
.hack
.hack//Legend of the Twilight:
The Complete Collection

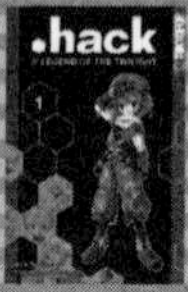
.hack
.hack//Legend of the Twilight
Volume 1

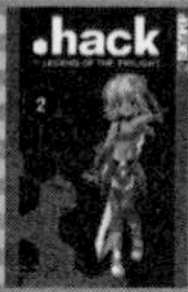
.hack
.hack//Legend of the Twilight
Volume 2

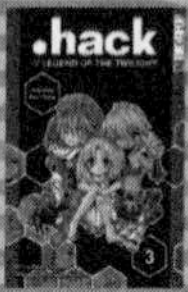
.hack
.hack//Legend of the Twilight
Volume 3

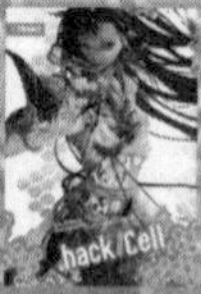
.hack//Cell
.hack//CELL
Volume 1

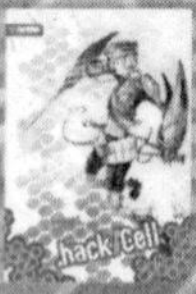
.hack//Cell
.hack//CELL
Volume 2

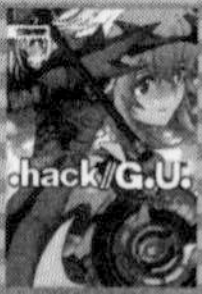
.hack//G.U.
.hack//G.U. Novel
Volume 1

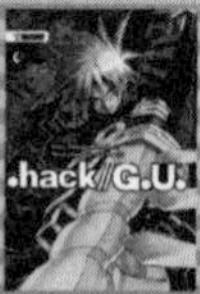
.hack//G.U.
.hack//G.U. Novel
Volume 2

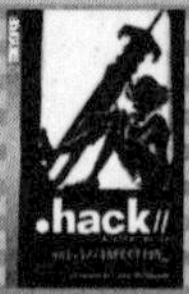
.hack//
.hack//Another Birth
Volume 1

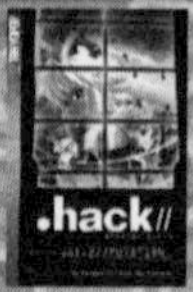
.hack//
.hack//Another Birth
Volume 2

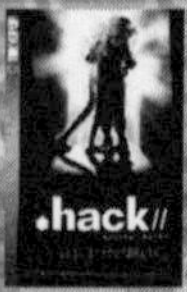
.hack//
.hack//Another Birth
Volume 3

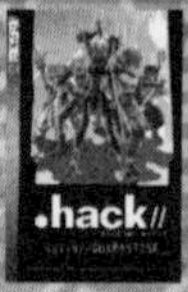
.hack//
.hack//Another Birth
Volume 4

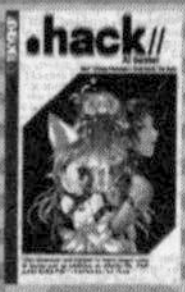
.hack//
.hack//AI buster
Volume 1

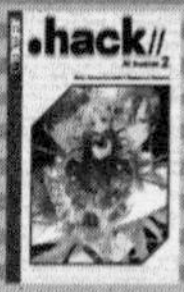
.hack//
.hack//AI buster
Volume 2

T TEEN AGE 13+

BUY THEM ALL AT WWW.TOKYOPOP.COM/SHOP

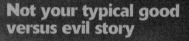

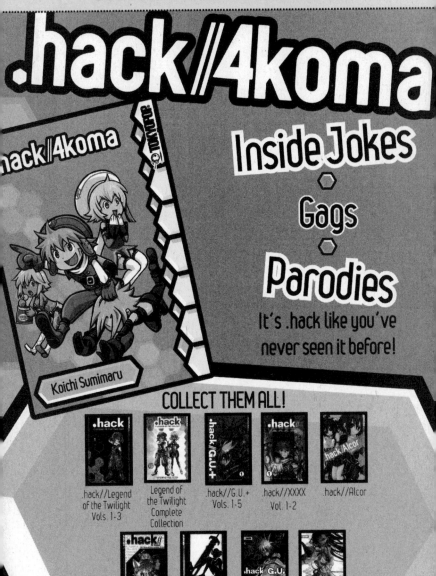

STOP!

This is the back of the book.
You wouldn't want to spoil a great ending!

This book is printed "manga-style," in the authentic Japanese right-to-left format. Since none of the artwork has been flipped or altered, readers get to experience the story just as the creator intended. You've been asking for it, so TOKYOPOP® delivered: authentic, hot-off-the-press, and far more fun!

DIRECTIONS

If this is your first time reading manga-style, here's a quick guide to help you understand how it works.

It's easy... just start in the top right panel and follow the numbers. Have fun, and look for more 100% authentic manga from TOKYOPOP®!